SCIENCE ANNUAL

A Modern Science Anthology for the Family

1986

Grolier Enterprises, Inc. offers a varied selection of both adult and children's book racks. For details on ordering, please write:

Grolier Enterprises, Inc.
Sherman Turnpike
Danbury, CT 06816
Attn: Premium Department

ACKNOWLEDGMENTS

Sources of articles appear below, including those reprinted with the kind permission of publications and organizations.

MASS EXTINCTIONS AND THE COSMOS, Page 15: Copyright © 1984 by The New York Times Company. Reprinted by permission.

MISSION TO JUPITER: PROJECT GALILEO, Page 20: Reprinted with permission from *Sky and Telescope.* © Sky Publishing Corporation.

A BOLD NEW THEORY OF THE MOON'S BIRTH, Page 28: Shannon Brownlee © *DISCOVER* Magazine 3/85, Time Inc.

MULTIPLE MURDERERS, Page 38: Copyright © 1984 by The New York Times Company. Reprinted by permission.

THE MYSTERY OF TEARS, Page 43: Reprinted with permission of the author; article first appeared in *Smithsonian,* June 1984.

CHILDREN'S WINNING WAYS, Page 50: Reprinted with permission of the author; article first appeared in *Psychology Today* magazine, December 1984.

REAL WORK FOR REAL PAY, Page 58: Reprinted with permission from *Psychology Today* magazine, © 1985 American Psychological Association.

ANT GARDENERS OF THE AMAZON, Page 70: Reprinted by permission of the publishers from *BIO-PHILIA* by Edward O. Wilson, Cambridge, Mass.: Harvard University Press, Copyright © 1984 by the President and Fellows of Harvard College.

AGING, Page 78: Gina Maranto © *DISCOVER* Magazine 12/84, Time Inc.

EAVESDROPPING ON TREES, Page 84: Reprinted by permission of Don Cogdon Associates, Inc. Copyright 1984 by Jeanne McDermott, article originally appeared in December 1984 issue of *Smithsonian* magazine.

ATTACK OF THE PHAGES, Page 92: Adapted by permission of *SCIENCE 85* Magazine, © the American Association for the Advancement of Science.

PAINTING BY COMPUTER, Page 104: From "Cybernetic Serendipity" by Dale Peterson in the November 1984 issue of *Popular Computing* magazine. Copyright © 1984 Byte Publications, Inc. Used with the permission of Byte Publications, Inc.

REINVENTING THE COMPUTER, Page 112: Reprinted with permission from *FORTUNE* Magazine. © 1984 Time Inc. All rights reserved.

INTEGRATED SOFTWARE, Page 120: Reprinted with permission from *TODAY'S OFFICE,* May 1984, Hearst Business Communications, Inc.

THE AGE-OLD REIGN OF THE ABACUS, Page 125: Martin Gardner © *DISCOVER* Magazine 5/85, Time Inc.

MOUNDS OF MYSTERY, Page 134: With permission from *Natural History,* Vol. 93, No. 6; Copyright the American Museum of Natural History, 1984.

THE SALT OF THE EARTH, Page 142: Reprinted with permission from *SCIENCE NEWS,* the weekly newsmagazine of science, copyright 1984 by Science Service, Inc.

DEEP-SEA STORMS, Page 149: Reprinted with permission from *TECHNOLOGY REVIEW,* M.I.T. Alumni Association, copyright 1985.

WHEN NORTH BECOMES SOUTH, Page 156: *The Sciences,* Nov./Dec. 1984 © by The New York Academy of Sciences.

THE REALITIES OF A FUSION FUTURE, Page 168: First appeared in *SCIENCE DIGEST,* © 1984 by The Hearst Corporation.

SAILING TO SAVE FUEL, Page 176: Reprinted with permission of the author; article first appeared in *Audubon,* March 1984.

THE LITTLE ENGINE THAT DOES, Page 188: Reprinted with permission from *TECHNOLOGY REVIEW,* M.I.T. Alumni Association, copyright 1984.

THE COMEBACK OF WESTERN WHITE PINE, Page 205: Reprinted from *AMERICAN FORESTS* Magazine, December 1984; the magazine of the American Forestry Association; 1319 18th Street, N.W.; Washington, D.C. 20036

HARD TIMES HIT THE BAY, Page 210: Copyright 1984 by the National Wildlife Federation. Reprinted from the April-May issue of *National Wildlife* Magazine.

STAFF

EDITORIAL

Editorial Director
Bernard S. Cayne

Executive Editor
Lynn Giroux Blum

Managing Editor
Doris E. Lechner

Art Director
Eric E. Akerman

Contributing Editor
Barbara Tchabovsky

Production Editor
Diane G. Buch

Editorial Assistant
Albert E. Raymond

Copy Editor
David M. Buskus

Chief Indexer
Jill Schuler

Proofreader
Stephen Romanoff

Indexer
Pauline Sholtys

Staff Assistant
Jennifer Drake

Manager, Picture Library
Jane H. Carruth

Chief, Photo Research
Ann Eriksen

Manuscript Typist
Joan M. Calley

Photo Researcher
Jane DiMenna

MANUFACTURING

Director of Manufacturing
Joseph J. Corlett

Production Manager
Teresa Kluk

Production Assistant
Patricia S. Jordan

CONTRIBUTORS

TOM ALEXANDER, Board of Editors, *Fortune*
REINVENTING THE COMPUTER

LAWRENCE K. ALTMAN, M.D., Medical reporter, *The New York Times*
REVIEW OF THE YEAR: HEALTH AND DISEASE

SUBIR K. BANERJEE, Professor of geology and geophysics at the University of Minnesota
WHEN NORTH BECOMES SOUTH

VIC BANKS, Free-lance writer and photographer specializing in science
THE PANTANAL: WONDROUS WILDLIFE REGION AT RISK

MARCIA BARTUSIAK, Free-lance science writer with a master's degree in physics
IN QUEST OF GRAVITY WAVES

ALISON B. BASS, Senior editor, *Technology Review*
ELECTRON MICROSCOPY IN LIVING DETAIL

JOSEPH BERGER, Staff reporter, *The New York Times*
MULTIPLE MURDERERS

CHARLES BERGMAN, Associate professor of English at Pacific Lutheran University
MOUNTAIN GOAT MONOPOLY

SHANNON BROWNLEE, Staff writer, *Discover* magazine
A BOLD NEW THEORY OF THE MOON'S BIRTH

GENE BYLINSKY, Associate editor, *Fortune* magazine
NEW TECHNOLOGY FOR TELEVISION

GEORGE W. COX, Professor of biology at San Diego State University
MOUNDS OF MYSTERY

DR. CRYPTON, Puzzles editor, *Science Digest;* former editor of *Scientific American*
THE GREAT MACHINE COMPETITION

TUI DE ROY, Author of *Galápagos: Islands Lost in Time*
THREE WAYS TO BE A BOOBY

BERNARD DIXON, Contributing editor, *Science 84*
ATTACK OF THE PHAGES

JAMES DODSON, Senior editor, *Yankee* magazine
TAPPING FUNDY'S THUNDERING TIDE

PAUL ERNSBERGER, Ph.D., Post-doctoral fellow at Cornell University whose doctoral thesis examined the effects of the "yo-yo syndrome" on blood pressure
THE DEATH OF DIETING

PATRICIA FORSYTH, Free-lance science writer; former research microbiologist at the University of Washington and Stanford University
THE GIFT OF SOUND

JOHN FREE, Senior editor, Technology, *Popular Science* magazine
BEAM "MAGIC"

MARTIN GARDNER, Former "Mathematical Games" columnist of *Scientific American* and one of America's best-known writers on mathematics
THE AGE-OLD REIGN OF THE ABACUS

KATHERINE HARAMUNDANIS, Research associate, Smithsonian Astrophysical Observatory; co-author of *An Introduction to Astronomy*
REVIEW OF THE YEAR: ASTRONOMY

T. A. HEPPENHEIMER, Ph.D., Author of *The Man-Made Sun, Toward Distant Suns,* and *Colonies in Space*
THE REALITIES OF A FUSION FUTURE

WRAY HERBERT, Senior editor, *Psychology Today*
REVIEW OF THE YEAR: BEHAVIORAL SCIENCES

GLADWIN HILL, Free-lance writer; former Environment editor of *The New York Times*
REVIEW OF THE YEAR: THE ENVIRONMENT

TORRENCE V. JOHNSON, Project scientist for Project Galileo at the Jet Propulsion Laboratory in Pasadena, California
co-author MISSION TO JUPITER: PROJECT GALILEO

VICTORIA KAHARL, Science writer at Woods Hole Oceanographic Institution and project coordinator of the High Energy Benthic Boundary Layer Experiment (HEBBLE)
DEEP-SEA STORMS

ALICE KAHN, Nurse-practitioner in Berkeley, California; free-lance writer
PREVENTING OSTEOPOROSIS

MIRIAM LEE KAPROW, Research associate at the Research Institute for the Study of Man; visiting assistant professor of anthropology at Syracuse University
GYPSIES

LOUISE KINGSBURY, Technical publications editor and history coordinator at the Intermountain Forest and Range Experiment Station, Ogden, Utah
THE COMEBACK OF WESTERN WHITE PINE

MARC KUSINITZ, Ph.D., Editor, *New Medical Science*
REVIEW OF THE YEAR: PHYSICAL SCIENCES

BENEDICT LEERBURGER, Free-lance science writer and editorial consultant
THE SPACE TELESCOPE
MYTHS AND TRUTHS ABOUT BALDNESS

GINA MARANTO, Staff writer, *Discover* magazine
AGING

WILLIAM MATTHEWS III, Regents' Professor and Head, Department of Geology, Lamar University, Texas; Director of Education, American Geological Institute
REVIEW OF THE YEAR: EARTH SCIENCES

WILLIAM McCLOSKEY, Senior staff member of the Applied Physics Laboratory at Johns Hopkins University in Maryland; board member of the Citizens Program for Chesapeake Bay
HARD TIMES HIT THE BAY

JEANNE McDERMOTT, Free-lance writer
EAVESDROPPING ON TREES

GARY McDONALD, Marine biologist with the University of California in Santa Cruz
THE INTRIGUING WAYS OF NUDIBRANCHS

KEVIN McKEAN, Staff writer, *Discover* magazine
NEW PARTS FOR DAMAGED BRAINS

MARTIN McLAUGHLIN, Free-lance consultant; former Vice President for Education, Overseas Development Council, Washington, D.C.
co-author REVIEW OF THE YEAR: PAST, PRESENT, AND FUTURE

BEVERLY McLEOD, Free-lance science writer
REAL WORK FOR REAL PAY

JULIE ANN MILLER, Life Sciences editor, *Science News*
SPECIES SURVIVAL: A ZOO VIEW

WILLIAM MILLS, Ph.D., Free-lance writer
WHITE LORDS OF THE ARCTIC

VIRGINIA MORELL, Free-lance writer specializing in science and natural history
JUNGLE MEDICINE

CAROL ANNE OGDIN, Technical director of Software Techniques, Incorporated, a consulting firm specializing in microcomputers and microprocessors
INTEGRATED SOFTWARE

BRIAN O'LEARY, Senior scientist at Science Applications International Corporation; former scientist-astronaut with the National Aeronautics and Space Administration (NASA); author of *The Fertile Stars, The Making of an Ex-Astronaut,* and *Project Space Station*
LUNAR BASE

ELAINE PASCOE, Free-lance writer
THE 1984 NOBEL PRIZES IN PHYSICS AND CHEMISTRY

DALE PETERSON, Author of *Genesis II: Creation and Recreation with Computers*
PAINTING BY COMPUTER

IVARS PETERSON, Technology/Policy editor, *Science News*
REVIEW OF THE YEAR: TECHNOLOGY

MAYA PINES, Contributing editor, *Psychology Today;* author of *The Brain Changers: Scientists and the New Mind Control*
CHILDREN'S WINNING WAYS

JANET RALOFF, Policy/Technology editor, *Science News*
REVIEW OF THE YEAR: ENERGY
THE SALT OF THE EARTH
BUILDING THE ULTIMATE WEAPONS

ANDREW C. REVKIN, Senior writer, *Science Digest*
NUCLEAR WINTER

JIM SCHEFTER, West Coast editor, *Popular Science* magazine
REVIEW OF THE YEAR: COMPUTERS AND MATHEMATICS

TOM SHEDD, Editorial director, *Modern Railroads* magazine
THE LITTLE ENGINE THAT DOES

ELLEN RUPPEL SHELL, Vannevar Bush fellow at the Massachusetts Institute of Technology; free-lance science writer
MEMORIES THAT LOSE THEIR COLOR

JOANNE SILBERNER, Biomedicine editor, *Science News*
REVIEW OF THE YEAR: BIOLOGY

BOB STROHM, Executive editor, *National Wildlife* magazine
REVIEW OF THE YEAR: WILDLIFE

CAROLYN SUMNERS, Director of astronomy and physics at the Houston Museum of Natural Science and co-principal investigator of the Informal Science Study at the University of Houston
THE PHYSICS OF FUN

CURT SUPLEE, Staff writer, the *Washington Post*
THE MYSTERY OF TEARS

BARBARA TCHABOVSKY, Free-lance science writer and editor
THE 1984 NOBEL PRIZE IN PHYSIOLOGY OR MEDICINE

STEPHEN M. VOYNICK, Free-lance writer
MINE-POISONED RIVERS

LESLIE WARE, Senior editor, *Audubon*
SAILING TO SAVE FUEL

PETER S. WELLS, Associate professor of anthropology, Harvard University; Associate curator of European archaeology at the Peabody Museum
co-author REVIEW OF THE YEAR: PAST, PRESENT, AND FUTURE

JOHN NOBLE WILFORD, Science writer, *The New York Times*
REVIEW OF THE YEAR: SPACE SCIENCE
MASS EXTINCTIONS AND THE COSMOS

EDWARD O. WILSON, Biologist at Harvard University and one of the originators of the science of sociobiology
ANT GARDENERS OF THE AMAZON

CLAYNE M. YEATES, Science manager for Project Galileo at the Jet Propulsion Laboratory in Pasadena, California
co-author MISSION TO JUPITER: PROJECT GALILEO

CONTENTS

ASTRONOMY AND

SPACE SCIENCE

REVIEW OF THE YEAR

ASTRONOMY AND SPACE SCIENCE

Astronomers continued to learn more about the solar system, our Milky Way galaxy, and the universe thanks to ground-based observations and observations and data gathered by space probes, orbiting satellites, and manned space vehicles. In space activities the United States shuttle program made notable achievements, amid some setbacks; the Soviet Union set a new record for human endurance in orbit and launched unmanned projects to investigate Halley's Comet; and the European Space Agency, Japan, and China stepped up their space endeavors.

THE SOLAR SYSTEM

A heated debate in astronomy is brewing. Does the Sun, the heart of our solar system, have a companion star? And is this companion, dubbed Nemesis, responsible for the mass extinctions of life forms that periodically occur on Earth?

According to the theory, Nemesis orbits the Sun in an elliptical orbit, and when it comes closest to the Sun, it perturbs a cloud of comets that orbit the Sun far beyond the planets. The hypothesis contends that each perturbation sends a shower of comets careening toward the inner solar system, many of which could collide with Earth and thus create Sun-obliterating dust clouds and temperature changes on the planet that could result in mass extinctions. One of the proponents of the theory, Richard Muller, and his colleagues at Lawrence Livermore Laboratory in Berkeley, California, are conducting a systematic search of the skies for a star with the required characteristics. (See "Mass Extinctions and the Cosmos" on page 15.)

Meanwhile, other scientists discount the possibility, saying that because of gravitational fields within the Milky Way galaxy, the orbit of any such companion star would be very unstable and not likely to be responsible for repeated and regular events such as the mass extinctions that have occurred on Earth at roughly 26-million-year intervals. Some of these scientists propose an alternative explanation of the periodic extinctions. They theorize that as the solar system passes through some of the denser parts of the galaxy, clouds of dust and gas cause comets to plunge toward Earth, where they could change Earth's atmospheric conditions and be responsible for large-scale extinctions.

Comets have been the subject of other studies as well. Astronomer Kenneth Brecher of Boston University and the National Aeronautics and Space Administration's (NASA's) Goddard Space Flight Center believes that icy cometary debris, dubbed the "Canterbury Swarm," may have caused the lunar impact observed by Gervase of Canterbury in 1178, the impact event in which a large object struck the Tunguska region of Siberia in 1908, and a major meteoroid storm on the moon in June 1975. ■ Some of the mysteries of comets may soon be solved—thanks to a unique controlled experiment in astronomy. The Active Magnetospheric Particle Tracer Explorer has generated an artificial comet of barium ions to study the effects on comets of the solar wind (the steady stream of charged particles emitted from the Sun) and the magnetosphere (a band of charged particles surrounding the Earth).

In addition to comets, meteorites also affect Earth. Two rock samples from the Yamata Mountains in Antarctica have been determined to be moon meteorites, and one rock sample from Antarctica may be a meteorite from Mars. Impacts on the surface of the Moon and Mars cause fragments of these bodies to be ejected out into the solar system, and some of the fragments ultimately fall to Earth. ■ And there may be more meteorites falling to Earth than previously thought. Analysis of data from several years of observations of fireballs falling to Earth made by a Canadian network called Meteorite Observation and Recovery Project (MORP) indicates that every year over 200 meteorites larger than 10 kilograms (18 pounds) should fall on land. This estimate comes as a surprise because very few meteorites are found.

The Earth's aurorae ("northern lights") have long intrigued both scientists and nonscientists. Now astronomers working with observations from the International Sun-Earth Explorer spacecraft have found that the Sun's magnetotail periodically throws off blobs of plasma, or ionized gas, that travel to Earth, helping to generate the aurorae.

Discoveries concerning other members of the solar system also continued during the year. Radar images transmitted from the Soviet Venera orbiters 15 and 16 have shown that many regions of Venus are uncratered. According to the analysis by researchers at the Vernadsky Institute in Moscow, there is much volcanism on Venus and the surface of the planet is less than 1 billion years old. Radio observations of the planet with the telescope facility at the Arecibo Observatory in Puerto Rico corroborate these findings.

A remarkable discovery about an asteroid has been made. C. T. Russell of the University of California at Los Angeles found that the asteroid

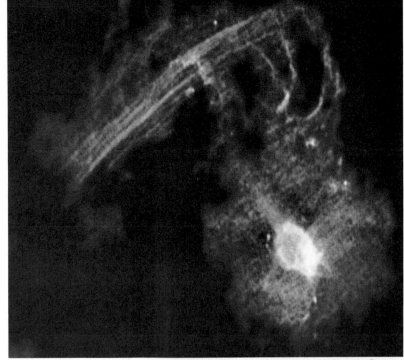

Radio observations of our Milky Way galaxy have revealed a huge, luminous arc of gas near the core formed of many parallel filaments. The multiple arc is unlike any known astronomical structure, and suggests the unsuspected presence of powerful magnetic fields.

The National Radio Astronomy Observatory

called 2201 Oljato is being trailed in its orbit by invisible matter that periodically outgasses and affects the magnetic field that exists between planets. The effect is particularly significant when Oljato passes near Venus.

When the U.S. Voyager 2 space probe passed by Jupiter, it provided astronomers with data to map the magnetic field around the planet. John Tranger of the California Institute of Technology has determined from these observations that Jupiter is surrounded by a magnetic nebula with three concentric, gaseous components. Closest to the planet lies a cool pancake-shaped disk. Surrounding that disk is a narrow hot ribbon that lies close inside the orbit of Io, one of Jupiter's moons. Outside both of these is a diffuse, hot, donut-shaped structure. The strongest magnetic field seems to be associated with the hot Io-driven ribbon of energy. ■ Io also causes a neutral sodium cloud that trails behind it in its orbit. Ground-based observations by B. A. Goldberg and his colleagues at the Jet Propulsion Laboratory (JPL) have made a remarkable series of photographs of the sodium cloud.

For the first time astronomers have observed the rotation of Neptune. Using the duPont telescope at Las Campanas Observatory in Chile, Bradford Smith of the University of Arizona and Richard Terrile of JPL report that Neptune rotates once every 17 hours 50 minutes.

MILKY WAY GALAXY

Astronomers have discovered what they think is the first planet to be detected outside the solar system. The discovery of the object orbiting the

star Van Biesbroeck 8 was made by Donald W. McCarthy Jr. and Frank Low of the University of Arizona and Ronald Probst of the National Optical Astronomy Observatories, using infrared telescopes. The object, called Van Biesbroeck 8B, appears to be large and gaseous. If, indeed, it is a planet, the discovery would be the first direct evidence of a planetary system other than our own. However, some astronomers think that the object might be too hot and too large to be a planet and that it is instead another kind of object—a type of failed star called a "brown dwarf." Whatever further analysis shows the object to be, it is a very important find that will provide insights into the formation and evolution of solar systems.

Indirect evidence hints that planetary systems may also be forming around other distant stars. Bradford Smith of the University of Arizona and Richard Terrile of JPL have found evidence that the star Beta Pictoris lies at the center of a large disk not unlike our solar system. And astronomers have found clouds of dust around two other stars—HL Tau and R. Mon.

Long shrouded in mystery, scientists think they are beginning to learn about the center of our galaxy. Radio observations of the core show spiral streams of ionized gas converging on the center. Astronomers conclude that there must be a black hole there that is 3 million times more massive than our Sun. Meanwhile other radio observations have revealed an enormous arc of ionized gas formed of many parallel filaments near the center of the galaxy. Scientists believe that the arc is made up of particles trapped by

Venturing away from the shuttle Challenger, Bruce McCandless takes the first untethered space walk.

strong magnetic force, which suggests the presence of powerful magnetic fields in the galaxy.

THE UNIVERSE

Galaxies may form around a cosmic string nucleus. P. J. E. Peebles of Princeton University suggests that galaxies and clusters of galaxies have a "frothy" distribution that may be a remnant of a network of protoclusters, or "pancakes," that produced the observable galaxies.

KATHERINE HARAMUNDANIS

U.S. SPACE ACTIVITIES

U.S. astronauts experienced successes and setbacks as they sought to expand the utility of reusable space shuttles during five missions in 1984—half as many as originally scheduled. The successes included the first repair of a satellite in orbit, the first retrieval and return to Earth of disabled satellites, the first space walk by a U.S. woman astronaut, and the first untethered space walk. The setbacks included rocket failures that sent two shuttle-deployed communications satellites into useless orbits, troubles with heat-shielding tiles, and a two-month delay after a last-minute abort of a shuttle launching.

On February 3, the space shuttle Challenger went into orbit on schedule, but the two satellites

it carried failed after deployment because of defective rockets. The disappointment was offset by the successful first test of backpacks with propulsion systems that allow astronauts to maneuver far away from a spacecraft without being tethered to it. Bruce McCandless and Robert L. Stewart, each wearing a backpack, used the jet-powered devices to venture 91 meters (300 feet) away from Challenger's cargo bay. Another accomplishment on this flight took place on February 11 with the first landing of a shuttle back at its launching base—the Kennedy Space Center in Florida.

On the next mission, launched April 6, the Challenger rendezvoused with Solar Max, an ailing scientific satellite. George D. Nelson and James van Hoften donned the jet-powered backpacks for a space walk to the disabled satellite, which they hauled into the cargo bay to replace its defective parts. The satellite was then released to resume investigations of the Sun. The crew returned to Earth April 13.

Discovery, the third shuttle added to the fleet, was set for its maiden flight on June 26. The main engines ignited, but when a fuel valve failed to open on first command, the computers automatically halted the launch just four seconds prior to the planned lift-off. The mission did not get underway until August 30. Before its return on September 5, Discovery deployed three satellites without trouble.

On October 5, Challenger carried the largest crew ever to fly in one spacecraft. One of the seven people aboard was Kathryn Sullivan, who became the first U.S. woman to walk in space. Another crew member was Marc Garneau, Canada's first space traveler. The mission ended October 13.

Discovery returned to orbit November 8 for an eight-day mission to release two new communications satellites and to salvage the two satellites that remained in useless orbits since the February mission. The stranded satellites were brought aboard the shuttle and flown back to Earth for refurbishment and relaunching.

In early 1985, mission events included the first classified U.S. Department of Defense launching from a shuttle and the flight of Senator Jack Garn, a Republican from Utah, as the first congressional observer.

OTHER U.S. SPACE ACTIVITIES

Other U.S. space activities in 1984 included the March 1 launching of Landsat 5, the final craft in the series of remote-sensing satellites used for Earth observations; the August 16 launching of the Active Magnetospheric Particle Tracer Explorer, a joint space-physics project with Great Britain and West Germany; and the continuing travels of Voyager 2, the instrument-carrying craft due to explore the vicinity of Uranus in January 1986.

Commercial use of space took a leap forward during the year when President Reagan announced a new policy to eliminate tax and regulatory provisions that discriminated against industries interested in doing business in orbit. Several corporations made initial investments in projects to produce materials as diverse as drugs, alloys, and crystals in the peculiar microgravity environment of space. Charles Walker, the first commercial engineer to work in orbit, operated a drug-processing unit aboard the August shuttle mission that was built by McDonnell Douglas Corporation in conjunction with Johnson & Johnson. ■ And microscopic latex particles, produced aboard a shuttle in 1983 for use in calibrating sensitive scientific instruments, became the first commercial made-in-space products offered for sale.

SOVIET SPACE ACTIVITIES

The Soviet Union continued operation of its Salyut 7 space station, breaking its own human endurance record in spaceflight. On February 8, a three-man crew—Leonid Kizim, Vladimir Solovyov, and Oleg Atkov—flew a Soyuz spacecraft to Salyut 7 where they lived and worked until October 2, setting a new record of 237 days in space. The previous record was 211 days, set in 1982 aboard Salyut 7. The Salyut crew had visitors in April, including the first astronaut from India—Rakesh Sharma—and again in July. At that time, cosmonaut Svetlana Savitskaya spent three hours outside the craft testing a welding device. She thus became the first woman ever to walk in space.

On December 19, the Soviet Union launched a scale model of what may become that country's first reusable shuttle. The craft orbited Earth once, glided back into the atmosphere, and splashed down in the Black Sea. The spaceplane, when fully developed and flown by pilots, could be used to deliver small payloads or to inspect or attack other satellites in low Earth orbit. A larger manned Soviet shuttle is also reported to be under development; it would resemble the U.S. version but would lack its own reusable engines.

Soviet spacecraft led the way in the international effort to greet and investigate Halley's Comet on its return to the inner solar system. In December, Vega 1 and Vega 2 were launched a week apart to reach the celebrated comet in March 1986. The two Vegas carried television cameras and an array of scientific sensors, one of which was designed by U.S. scientists. Other craft planning to make close-up observations of the comet are the European Space Agency's Giotto and Japan's Planet A.

OTHER SPACE ACTIVITIES

Other countries stepped up their space endeavors during the year. The 11-nation European Space Agency lofted four unmanned Ariane rockets, including two missions that placed twin communications satellites into orbit. The success of more powerful versions of the Ariane rockets increased Europe's competitive pressure on the U.S. shuttles in the lucrative market of launching communications satellites.

In 1984, Japan and China each launched two satellites. One of Japan's was the world's first operational high-power direct-broadcast satellite, which transmitted color television in March but failed in May.

JOHN NOBLE WILFORD

In 1984 cosmonauts Leonid Kizim, Vladimir Solovyov, and Oleg Atkov set a new record for human endurance in space.

Tass from Sovfoto

THE SPACE TELESCOPE

by Benedict Leerburger

Since Galileo first pointed a telescope toward the sky early in the 17th century, astronomers have tried to build better, more powerful instruments to study the mysteries of the universe. In 1986 their efforts will have a revolutionary impact on our understanding of the cosmos, when the Space Telescope is placed in orbit.

Unprecedented View of the Universe

The Space Telescope, a 12-ton scientific instrument about the size of a railroad boxcar, will be launched by the space shuttle. It will provide scientists with a clearer, sharper view of the universe than has been possible with any ground-based telescope ever developed. Because the orbiting observatory will be placed above the obscuring veil of Earth's atmosphere (which distorts the images of celestial objects when observed from Earth), it will be able to peer seven times farther into space than any telescope on Earth. It will also detect objects 50 times fainter than now possible, and its resolution (ability to see fine details of objects) will be 10 times greater. For example, the Space Telescope will be able to see Jupiter just as clearly as the U.S. space probe Voyager 1 did only five days before its closest approach to the planet. It will scan a volume of space that is 350 times larger than astronomers can now observe from Earth.

The Finest Mirror Ever Made

The telescope, officially called the NASA (National Aeronautics and Space Administration) Hubble Space Telescope, is named in honor of the renowned U.S. astronomer Edwin P. Hubble. The instrument is a conventional reflecting telescope, consisting of a pair of mirrors that were manufactured by the Perkin-Elmer Corporation of Wilton, Connecticut. The 240-centimeter (94-inch), concave, primary mirror is the most perfect of its size ever made. Donald V. Fordyce, director of Perkin-Elmer's Space Telescope program, says that deviations on the mirror's surface, which was polished and coated in a dust-free environment, amount to no more than 0.0000025 centimeter (0.000001 inch). The company claims that by comparison, if Earth's surface could be polished as perfectly, Mount Everest, nearly 10 kilometers (6 miles) high, would be reduced to 13 centimeters (5 inches).

A much smaller, convex, secondary mirror is mounted 5 meters (16 feet) in front of the primary mirror. As light strikes the primary mirror, it is reflected to the secondary, and is then reflected back through a hole in the primary mirror's center toward the back of the observatory. It is here that scientific instruments measure and make use of the incoming radiation.

Five Major Instruments

The telescope's supporting system was designed and built by the Lockheed Missiles and Space Company, which is also responsible for integrating the observatory's various components into a functioning spacecraft. Five major scientific instruments that complement the telescope are contained in a separate module. The module was cleverly constructed in that each instrument can be removed, replaced, or possibly repaired by astronauts working from the space shuttle. Should a major maintenance problem occur during the telescope's expected 15-year lifetime, the entire spacecraft can be picked up by the shuttle, repaired on Earth, and relaunched at a later date.

The Space Telescope's major instruments include the following:

• *The wide-field/planetary camera (WF/PC).* The WF/PC is probably the most advanced device of the five. The camera works in one of two ways to form images of celestial objects: the

Photos: Perkin-Elmer

Top: The primary mirror was polished to near perfection in a dust-free room. Topographic maps made before and after cleaning show how much its surface was changed.

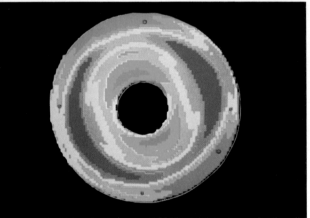

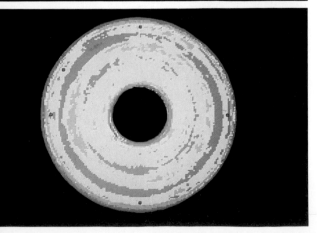

wide-field mode provides a vast view of space for studying large objects such as clusters of galaxies, and the planetary mode allows a much narrower field of view for observing fine details of the planets.

In either mode, incoming light is divided into four parts inside the camera, each of which is focused on an advanced silicon sensor known as a charge-coupled device (CCD). The CCD's are made up of an array of individual picture elements called pixels. When a photon (small particle of energy) of light strikes a pixel, it is converted into an electronic signal. The four CCD's together have more than 2.5 million pixels, and the signals they yield are eventually made into a mosaic image.

• *The faint-object camera (FOC).* The FOC is being supplied by the European Space Agency. This second camera is designed to complement the wide-field/planetary camera. The FOC will be able to detect the faintest objects that the telescope can see. It will require

After the Space Telescope relays data to a satellite, the data are sent to Earth for processing into images.

several hours of exposures to produce images of the objects it photographs.

• *The faint-object spectrograph.* A spectrograph is an optical device that splits incoming light according to its spectra (component wavelengths, or colors) much as a prism does, and measures their intensities. The faint-object spectrograph will observe faint stellar objects, examine quasars (the most distant, energetic objects known in the universe), and reveal more about the chemical nature of matter in the universe.

• *The high-resolution spectrograph.* This instrument is capable of accurately measuring fine spectral features that might not even be picked up with the faint-object spectrograph. It will be used to examine the interstellar medium, and the data it provides may be used to develop new models of stellar evolution.

Working in conjunction with each other, these spectrographs will be able to analyze wavelengths of light from the ultraviolet to the visible range of the electromagnetic spectrum (the entire range of wavelengths of electromagnetic radiation ranging from gamma rays to visible light to radio waves).

• *The high-speed photometer.* The high-speed photometer is the simplest instrument built for the Space Telescope—it contains no moving parts. The photometer is designed to detect the smallest objects observable with any of the other instruments. It has the ability to make precise measurements of the light intensity emitted by celestial sources over a wide range of wavelengths.

Along with these major instruments, one of the more remarkable technological advances in the design of the Space Telescope is the observatory's system of fine-guidance sensors. These sensors allow the Space Telescope to point precisely and lock on to distant objects for long periods of time. The sensors locate and track special guide stars at the outer edges of the telescope's field of view. They use the stars as reference points to keep the telescope in a stable plane. Perkin-Elmer claims that the system has a pointing stability that is equivalent to a beam of light locating a dime on the U.S. Capitol Building in Washington, District of Columbia, from atop the World Trade Center in New York City, and shining on that dime for 24 hours.

Looking Back in Time

There are many puzzling questions about the universe that have long plagued astronomers. The Space Telescope may eventually provide answers to many of these. For example, according to John N. Bahcall of the Institute for Advanced Study at Princeton University in New Jersey, the Space Telescope will be addressing such cosmic mysteries as: How big is the universe? How old is it? Did it have a beginning? Will it have an end? Will observations of black holes or quasars reveal new laws of physics? How are stars formed? What kinds of undiscovered things are there in outer space?

Since light transmitted from distant celestial objects takes so very long to reach us, the Space Telescope will allow scientists to look back in time some 14 billion years. The observatory is expected to see close to the edge of the observable universe. It may reveal the births of galaxies and quasars that occurred years ago.

Major Studies of Stars and Quasars Planned

With the vast capabilities of the wide-field/planetary camera, astronomers hope to discover if any of the 10 or more stars selected for initial study have planetary companions similar to those in our own solar system. At present, astronomers know of no other star with a planetary system comparable to ours, and question whether we are, indeed, unique. The Space Telescope may answer this age-old question. Since the exact motions of the stars under study are known, astronomers hope to detect any periodic ''wobbles'' in the paths of these stars. Such atypical movements would most likely be caused by the gravitational attraction of an unseen and unknown planet.

Another study using the WF/PC will involve the observation of quasars, which are brilliant and extremely compact sources of tremendous energy. Quasars emit about 100 times as much energy as a galaxy composed of 10 billion stars. Scientists have several theories about how such relatively dense objects are capable of generating such enormous amounts of energy. Some believe that quasars represent ''sick'' stages in the lives of galaxies. The WF/PC will be able to make such high-resolution images of

This photo shows how astronomers will use computers to create visual images from the incoming information.

NASA

The Space Telescope Institute will maintain an archive of the data obtained by the orbiting observatory.

quasars that astronomers should be able to determine whether a quasar is a young galaxy or an old one in a "diseased" state. This will resolve a previously unanswerable question.

The faint-object spectrograph will also examine distant quasars. By measuring their spectra, it should be possible to study the properties of matter as it existed more than 10 billion years ago during a very early stage in the evolution of the universe. Scientists who adhere to the "Big-Bang" theory of cosmology (which holds that a major explosion heralded the birth of the universe and that time had a specific beginning), believe that this age represents 85 percent of the way back to the beginning of time. According to Richard Harms, an astrophysicist with the University of California at San Diego who proposed the faint-object spectrograph, measuring the helium in quasars may yield clues to the amount of helium present very early in the universe. This information could have a profound impact on current theories of cosmology.

Analyzing Comets, Clouds, and Global Clusters

Many other major investigations will be made using the Space Telescope. For example, a detailed study of comets will be conducted by John Brandt, an astrophysicist at the Goddard Space Flight Center in Greenbelt, Maryland, and principal investigator for the high-resolution spectrograph. Unfortunately, problems in developing and testing the Space Telescope postponed its original 1985 launch date, thus missing the period when Halley's comet made its closest swing past the Sun. However, there are other comets for Brandt to study. He will use the high-resolution spectrograph to determine whether comets are formed outside or within our solar system. In measuring the amount of deuterium (heavy hydrogen) in comets, he will make comparisons with known values of deuterium in interstellar space. Says Brandt: "So by doing this magical stuff called spectroscopy, we—with a little luck—will tell you where comets are formed."

The study of interstellar clouds will also be undertaken with the high-resolution spectrograph. These large masses of celestial gases are believed to form stars when they come together and contract. How this occurs is one of the questions astronomers hope to answer by analyzing the ultraviolet-absorption features of each cloud.

The faint-object camera will help astronomers learn a great deal about stellar evolution. It will examine global clusters—giant swarms of close to a million stars that are visible from Earth with simple telescopes or binoculars. Astronomers believe the inner portions of these massive clusters are collapsing, but it is impossible to tell from Earthbound telescopes.

Current theory holds that the inner portion of each cluster contains between 10,000 and 100,000 stars in the last stage of their evolution. These aging stars, called white dwarfs, have burned up their gases, cooled, and collapsed. The faint-object camera is expected to detect these white dwarfs within their global clusters. Says Lyman Spitzer, a Princeton University astrophysicist: "To be able to resolve individual stars at the center of a cluster will be very nice. Then astronomers can calculate how old the stars are."

The high-speed photometer's ability to measure fluctuations in brightness will be used to study stars that are nearing the end of their lives, such as neutron stars and white dwarfs. According to Robert Bless of the University of Wisconsin, who is the developer of the high-speed photometer, "We should be able to measure the rate at which a white dwarf cools, and that's connected with its structure and composition. In a sense, we are stellar morticians." One of the first objects that Bless plans to study is the Crab pulsar, a neutron star that flashes 30 times a second.

The Space Telescope Science Institute

All of the Space Telescope's activities will be coordinated by the recently established Space Telescope Science Institute (STSI), which is located on the campus of Johns Hopkins University in Baltimore, Maryland. The institute is being operated for NASA by the Association of Universities for Research in Astronomy. Data obtained by the Space Telescope will be indexed, stored in an archive, and made available for study. "It's one of the most exciting new things about the space telescope," says Arthur D. Code of the University of Wisconsin and former director of the Space Telescope Science Institute. "People have been filing away photographic plates for years but rarely is there an efficient way for someone to get them again. Now we can store these data in a compact way."

One of the major problems facing the institute is deciding which scientists and what projects will be allowed time and access to the telescope. STSI director Riccardo Giaconni has attempted to solve the "access" problem by establishing several peer-review groups to evaluate the many proposals for telescope access submitted to the institute by astronomers from all over the world. In addition, Giaconni has reserved a small amount of time to be allotted at "the Director's discretion." Thus, the space telescope could be switched from a long-planned activity to an unscheduled study.

The institute has estimated that it will be able to accept only about one-third of the more than 2,000 observation proposals it expects to receive annually. Says Jeremiah Ostriker, a Princeton University astronomer and head of the institute's outside advisory committee on personnel: "It's going to require a change of style. Astronomers will have to change their mode of operation from that of 'one lone scientist' to that of working in large teams, like the physicists who work on the big [particle] accelerators." Among the first to use the observatory will be the seven teams that produced the Space Telescope's instruments. Each team is guaranteed 360 hours of observation time.

Old Puzzles Solved, New Mysteries Revealed

The Space Telescope will surely provide the world with incredibly detailed photographs of celestial objects never before seen. In addition, it may yield answers to many long-standing questions within a short time following its launching. Although the data gathered by the observatory will undoubtedly solve many puzzles, astronomers as a result will be forced to seek answers to new questions they never would have considered before □

SELECTED READINGS

"Exploring the universe." *Spinoff 1984*, a publication of the National Aeronautics and Space Administration.
"Glimpse of Infinity" by Mary Jo Boyd. *Science Digest*, July 1983.
"The space telescope" by John N. Bahcall and Lyman Spitzer, Jr. *Scientific American*, July 1982.

Morris Scott Dolens

MASS EXTINCTIONS and the COSMOS

by John Noble Wilford

With bounding curiosity and a theory to establish, astronomers are searching the skies for a star they call Nemesis, a small, dim companion of the Sun. Nemesis may or may not exist, but the quest goes on.

Other astronomers, similarly inspired, have revived interest in finding Planet X, the putative (assumed to exist) body that has long been sought beyond Neptune and Pluto. They are examining new data from a spacecraft for evidence of the planet's existence.

Heavens May Hold Clues to Mass Extinctions

Some of the best minds of science are thus at play these nights and days in a provocative and promising attempt to understand how the heavens may hold the answer to what happened to the dinosaurs. More important, the researchers are seeking clues to what caused all the mass extinctions that, according to new fossil evidence, seem to afflict the Earth every 26 million years or so. This effort may lead to a new view of mass extinctions and their possibly decisive role in evolution.

The informed imaginations of these scientists run to unseen heavenly forces, a star or planet yet to be discovered, that trigger a hail of comets through the solar system. Some of the comets collide with the Earth. The collisions fill the atmosphere with dust, blotting out sunlight

Arizona's Barringer Crater was created 25,000 years ago when an iron asteroid smashed into the Earth.

for months, and causing global death. This is a hypothesis in search of an activating mechanism—the source of the cosmic force.

The Nemesis Hypothesis

The possible mechanism that has stirred the greatest interest and debate recently is the one involving the Sun's theorized companion star called Nemesis, or the ''death star.''

Some skeptical scientists, checking the feasibility of such a star causing such periodic havoc, have questioned whether Nemesis could maintain an orbit sufficiently stable to make a close approach to our solar system precisely every 26 million years. But proponents, while modifying the hypothesis somewhat in an effort to satisfy these objections, insist that the Nemesis hypothesis could still hold the key to the mass extinctions that apparently occur in 26-million-year cycles.

Richard A. Muller, a professor of astronomy and physics at the University of California at Berkeley, says: ''It's been demonstrated beyond all doubt that the orbit of Nemesis is sufficiently stable to do what we said the star would do. I think the case in favor of Nemesis has become much stronger.''

Dr. Muller, with Marc Davis of Berkeley and Piet Hut of the Institute for Advanced Study at Princeton University in New Jersey, proposed the Nemesis hypothesis in 1983 in response to a stunning new paleontological study of mass extinctions. What happened is an arresting example of how science sometimes operates: one major hypothesis is followed by another related one and, together, they inspire a third hypothesis of even grander aspect.

Patterns to Extinctions Discovered

In the 1970's, Walter Alvarez, a Berkeley geologist, found a layer of clay in Italy that contained unusually large amounts of the rare element iridium, which is more usually found in extraterrestrial bodies such as asteroids. This led to the theory, advanced by him and his father, Luis Alvarez, a Nobel prizewinning physicist, that an asteroid struck the Earth 65 million years ago, creating months of darkness that wiped out the dinosaurs and countless other species.

In 1983, after an exhaustive study of the fossil record going back 250 million years, J. John Sepkoski and David M. Raup, paleontologists at the University of Chicago, reported a previously unrecognized pattern to mass extinctions: They may not be random events, as had been supposed, but appear to occur without fail every 26 million years.

This was inexplicable. No earthly phenomenon was known to occur in such lengthy cycles. But the Alvarez-asteroid hypothesis had conditioned scientists to consider extraterrestrial causes of earthly disasters, and so Dr. Sepkoski appealed to astrophysicists for suggestions.

At first, Luis Alvarez decided the Sepkoski-Raup hypothesis of periodic extinctions was wrong. However, to check himself, he asked Dr. Muller to play devil's advocate, in the course of which Dr. Muller recalled becoming persuaded that the Sepkoski-Raup hypothesis was right.

Dr. Muller and his associates then came up with a hypothetical situation that could account for such regular extinction patterns.

Is Star's Effect on Cometary Cloud to Blame?

Many stars, they knew, come in pairs—a smaller star orbiting the dominant one, or two relatively equal bodies orbiting a common center of gravity. In astronomy these are called binary systems. What if the Sun had such a companion? Such an object, if far away and very small (only 5 to 10 percent as massive as the Sun), could easily have escaped notice.

The companion star, they reasoned, could follow an eccentric orbit about 1.5 times as long as it is wide that would take it far out, as much as 3 light-years (1 light-year, the distance light travels in a year, equals approximately 9.5 trillion kilometers or 5.9 trillion miles) from the Sun, and bring it back to the vicinity of our solar system only once every 26 million years. It would make its closest approach out beyond the known planets in the midst of the cloud of comets believed to exist there.

Nemesis, a hypothetical star, may orbit around our solar system regularly every 26 million years.

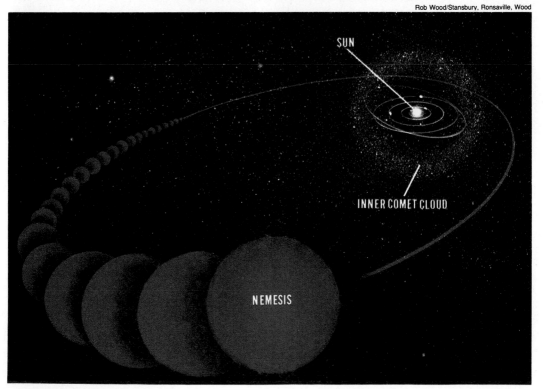

SUN

INNER COMET CLOUD

NEMESIS

No one has seen this cometary cloud, but astronomers assume from the trajectories (orbital paths) of known comets that they must come from that region, known as the Oort Cloud.

As the companion star passes in or close to the cloud, according to the hypothesis, its gravitational force would jostle hundreds of thousands of the comets and send many of them hurtling toward the Sun and the planets on possible collision courses.

The last time this must have happened, judging by the Sepkoski-Raup interpretation of the fossil record, was about 13 million years ago. Thus, Nemesis would now be at the farthest point in its orbit and not due back for another 13 million years.

Some Scientists Remain Doubtful

In articles and letters published recently in the British journal *Nature,* several scientists cast doubt on the hypothesis by pointing out that

No one really knows what caused mass extinctions on Earth. Did an unknown planet or star trigger a hail of comets (left) that caused global death (below)?

Left: Morris Scott Dolens; Below: Don Davis

such an elongated orbit reaching so far out from the Sun would be inherently unstable. The Sun's gravitational hold on Nemesis would be weak. Thousands of passing stars and clouds of interstellar matter could perturb Nemesis so that each time it returned, its orbit would be wider, taking it farther and farther from the Sun.

Marc Bailey, an astronomer at the University of Manchester in England, says the Nemesis proposal seems to be "quite incapable of producing the strictly periodic sequence of extinction events for which it was originally designed."

Dr. Muller complains that Dr. Bailey "totally mischaracterized" the report Dr. Hut wrote for *Nature*. Dr. Hut presented new calculations supporting the hypothesis, though he recognized that the orbit of Nemesis would vary by about 15 percent over the past 250 million years. Proponents of Nemesis note that such variation is not incompatible with the fossil record for extinctions, which paleontologists say could be off by 1 million years or more.

Taking into account the criticism, Dr. Muller and his associates have revised the hypothesis to postulate that when the companion star was formed 4.6 billion years ago, it must have traveled a tighter, more stable orbit closer to the Sun and only later moved outward to its present orbit.

Even so, Roman Smoluchowski, professor of astronomy and physics at the University of Texas at Austin, says the Nemesis hypothesis might apply to only one or two of the mass extinctions. "I have great difficulty conceiving of how the star could survive long enough to account for the 10 or 12 extinctions over the last 250 million years," he says.

This is all the more reason for Dr. Muller to be stepping up the search for Nemesis. Since April 1984, astronomers at the University of California's Leuschner Observatory have been focusing a 76-centimeter (30-inch) telescope in an attempt to detect any stellar object whose motions might betray its proximity, and hence its likelihood, as a solar companion. In March 1985, telescopes farther south began looking at other parts of the sky.

Dr. Hut says astronomers probably have a 50 percent chance of finding Nemesis by 1988, if it exists.

New Theory Points to Planet X

Daniel P. Whitmore, an astronomer at the University of Southwestern Louisiana at Lafayette,

came forward with a similar companion-star hypothesis at about the same time that Dr. Muller's group did. Recently he conceived of an alternative hypothesis.

Dr. Whitmore looks to Planet X as the possible heavenly force that perturbs the Oort Cloud every 26 million years. Such a distant planet has been predicted on the basis of the apparent wobbling orbital course of Uranus and Neptune, evidence of possible gravitational tugging from an unseen object.

According to the new hypothesis, developed with John Matese at Southwestern Louisiana, the planet would orbit the Sun once every 1,000 years in a region far beyond Pluto and in the inner fringe of the Oort Cloud. Being fairly close to the Sun, the orbit would be stable over the ages. The planet would have long ago cleared out a comet-free gap in the cloud.

But Dr. Whitmore thought of a way in which the planet could cross the comet disk twice every 52 million years. The planet's orbit could be tilted with respect to the plane of the other planets and the inner-comet disk. And because of perturbations from other planets, Planet X's orbit as a whole could precess, or slowly rotate, so that, even though it makes a close approach to the Sun once every 1,000 years, only twice in a 52-million-year rotation period would it actually cross through the cometary disk. Dr. Smoluchowski of Texas says the new hypothesis "is worth exploring."

Since Planet X, if it exists, must be quite dim, astronomers expect their best chance for proving its existence would come from heat emissions detected by infrared telescopes.

The infrared data for that region of the sky are now being processed, while astronomers look also for Nemesis—and perhaps for other possible explanations of the catastrophes that seemingly befall the Earth every 26 million years □

SELECTED READINGS

"Geological rhythms and cometary impacts" by Michael R. Rampino and Richard B. Stothers. *Science*, December 21, 1984.

"The cosmic dance of Siva" by Stephen Jay Gould. *Natural History*, August 1984.

"Cosmic winter" by Dennis Overbye. *Discover*, May 1984.

"Death star" by Cheryl Simon. *Science News*, April 21, 1984.

"Periodic impacts and extinctions reported" by Richard A. Kerr. *Science*, March 23, 1984.

Michael Carroll

Mission to Jupiter:
PROJECT GALILEO

by Torrence V. Johnson and Clayne M. Yeates

The outer solar system is the realm not of individual planets but of entire systems whose starlike central bodies are surrounded by intense magnetic fields, radiation belts, swarms of planet-size moons, and multiple rings. In recent years the twin U.S. Voyager spacecraft revealed to us the extraordinary complexity and interdependence of these elements in the Jupiter and Saturn systems.

But the Voyagers gave us only brief glimpses. Project Galileo will be our first chance to make an in-depth study of what amounts to a solar system in miniature. This is an important distinction. Early deep-space probes were considered ''Venus missions'' or ''Mars missions,'' but Galileo is not really planet-specific—it is a comprehensive survey of the Jovian system.

Mission Long in the Making

Project Galileo had its genesis during the mid-1970's when space scientists and National Aeronautics and Space Administration's (NASA's) mission planners were considering the next steps in outer-planet exploration. By that time U.S. space probes Pioneers 10 and 11 had flown past Jupiter, but the Voyager spacecraft were not yet launched. Choosing Jupiter as the obvious next target (it is the most readily accessible of the giant planets), they realized that an advanced mission should incorporate two vital elements: a probe to descend into the atmosphere, and a relatively long-lived orbiter to study the planet, its satellites, and the vast expanse of the Jovian magnetosphere (the region of space controlled by Jupiter's magnetic field). Such a mission was developed by NASA and approved by Congress in 1977. Although originally called Jupiter Orbiter-Probe, the program was soon renamed Project Galileo to honor the Italian astronomer who first viewed telescopically the four large satellites that now bear his name.

Galileo was designed to be the first American planetary mission to ride the space shuttle, a decision that subsequently proved troublesome. When development and schedule problems plagued the shuttle during 1979–82, Galileo underwent a number of frustrating and costly delays in its launch date. Now, with the shuttle operational and the development of a modified, more powerful Centaur upper-stage rocket, Galileo is scheduled for launch in 1986.

Precisely Timed Travels

The spacecraft will arrive in the vicinity of Jupiter after an interplanetary transit of a little more than two years. One hundred and fifty days from arrival, the probe will separate and head straight for the planet, while the orbiter backs off to fly in formation as both spacecraft drop into the Jovian gravity well.

Finally, sometime in December 1988, the pair reach their destination and begin a flurry of intense activity. (This arrival date was changed from August 1988 when NASA announced plans in December 1984 to incorporate an asteroid-flyby option to the mission, thereby revising Galileo's flight path. The final decision to investigate the asteroid, known as 29 Amphitrite, will be made after the spacecraft's launch. Amphitrite is one of the 30 largest known asteroids. The flyby would be the first close encounter with an asteroid ever made.) As the orbiter passes within 1,000 kilometers (620 miles) of the volcanic moon Io, the probe makes its plunge toward the swirling cloud tops girdling Jupiter's equator. A few hours later the orbiter reaches a point 230,000 kilometers (143,000 miles) from the planet and begins relaying to Earth the precious data being radioed by the probe as it descends by parachute into the atmosphere. About an hour after the probe completes its transmission, the orbiter's retro-rocket (an auxiliary rocket used to slow a spacecraft during its flight) burns for 46 minutes; this firing, in combination with the gravitational effect of the close Io flyby, eases the orbiter into a long, looping orbit with a period of 200 days.

As the spacecraft recedes from Jupiter along this path, scientists will have already begun to analyze the hour-long spurt of data gathered by the probe, and our thorough exploration of the Jovian system will be truly under way.

Harsh Atmospheric-Entry Conditions Defied

Galileo's probe is similar in concept to those on the 1977 Pioneer Venus mission, incorporating experiments to measure temperature and pressure along the descent path, locate major cloud decks, and analyze the chemistry of atmospheric gases. In addition, the probe will attempt to detect and study Jovian lightning both by looking for optical flashes and by listening for the radio "static" the flashes generate. The latter detector will also measure high-energy electrons close to Jupiter just prior to atmospheric entry.

Slowing the probe down as it "hits" the atmosphere presents a crucial engineering challenge. Unlike the Pioneers' relatively low entry speed at Venus—12 kilometers (7.4 miles) per second—the Galileo probe will be greatly accelerated by Jupiter's immense gravitational pull and will strike the atmosphere at about 50 kilometers (31 miles) per second, which is more than 160,000 kilometers (100,000 miles) per hour. Its deceleration will cause a tremendous buildup of heat in the probe's protective covering. These entry conditions, far more severe than those faced by returning Apollo astronauts, cannot be simulated in conventional wind tunnels. New facilities at NASA's Ames Research Center were required to test heat-shield materials, which make up approximately half the overall weight of the probe.

On the brighter side, once it survives its fiery entry, the probe will operate in a more benign environment than its Pioneer predecessors did. It won't have to cope with corrosive sulfuric-acid clouds or the furnacelike temperatures at Venus' surface. Jupiter's atmosphere is primarily hydrogen and helium, of little consequence to the spacecraft or its parachute, and for most of the descent the probe will be immersed in gases at or below room temperature. Eventually, however, it will sink below the visible clouds, where rising pressure and temperature will take their toll.

Innovative Design Accommodates Instruments

The orbiter, though largely derived from earlier spacecraft, has its share of new features. One important innovation is its "dual spin" design, with the antenna and certain instrument booms rotating about three times per minute while another instrumented platform and the spacecraft's aft (rearward) portion remain fixed in inertial space. This means the orbiter can easily accommodate both the four magnetospheric-physics experiments and the telescopic remote-sensing experiments, which require very accurate and stable pointing. Also, instead of utilizing a central computer as on previous spacecraft, Galileo uses dozens of microcomputers scattered among its subsystems and experiments to provide unprecedented operational flexibility.

On its spinning portion, the orbiter has instruments to measure Jupiter's magnetic field, the charged particles and plasmas trapped in the magnetosphere, and the electromagnetic and electrostatic waves propagating through this environment. One new instrument will examine the frequency and paths of micrometeoroids (extremely small particles in space) near Jupiter. Investigators will use the spacecraft's radio system to probe Jupiter's atmosphere and to search for atmospheres on the satellites.

The nonspinning portion carries four instruments on a pointable mounting boom (the "scan platform") that are all new in one way or another. A photopolarimeter-radiometer will measure the polarization of light scattered from Jupiter's clouds and the satellites' surfaces, and the instrument's infrared channels will sound the atmosphere and measure satellite temperatures. An ultraviolet spectrometer (an instrument that splits incoming light according to its component colors, or spectra) will identify gases in the Jovian atmosphere. The near-infrared mapping spectrometer, or NIMS, is a newly developed instrument designed to map the satellites in 200 spectral channels and

discern any compositional variation across their surfaces. The NIMS will also study cloud structure and gases in the Jovian atmosphere.

The most familiar scan-platform instrument—a television camera—is also included. Its optical portion is a Voyager spare, but the sensor electronics are entirely new. Instead of using a conventional camera tube, Galileo's camera has a charge-coupled device (CCD) at its focal plane. The CCD is a tiny silicon "chip" containing 640,000 individual sensors in an 800-by-800 array. It is over 100 times more sensitive than Voyager's optical device.

Gravity-Assist Trick Allows Satellite Flybys

While the probe's success is keyed to its ability to penetrate the Jovian atmosphere, the orbiter's success depends on its unique trajectory (the elliptical path that a body describes in space), which provides for unprecedented new measurements. Once captured by Jupiter's gravity, the orbiter would remain in its initial 200-day orbit if nothing were done; this would allow several Voyagerlike passes through the system before the spacecraft "died" from radiation effects or actually dropped at its low point into the atmosphere due to gravitational perturbations of the Sun. For Galileo to be utilized more effectively during its limited lifetime, the orbital period must be shortened and the spacecraft targeted to make very close flybys of the Galilean satellites.

If this had to be accomplished by rocket propulsion, the mission would be impossible—too much fuel (and weight) would be required to do the necessary maneuvers in Jupiter's strong gravitational field. Fortunately, NASA's mission designers have found a way to fly a very demanding, complicated mission using little fuel. They manage this trick by employing the gravity-assist technique that successfully redirected the Voyagers and other spacecraft as they swung by various planets along their routes.

In the case of Galileo, a celestial 11- or 12-cushion billiard shot will be set up, using the gravity of the massive Galilean moons to modify the orbiter's course during each pass. This simultaneously sends the craft on toward the next encounter and provides extremely close approaches to the satellites for scientific measurements. As a result, the entire "satellite tour" can be flown so that rockets need supply only about 100 meters (330 feet) per second of velocity change—60 times less than what would be needed without the satellites' help.

Mission Objectives

As all of the foregoing demonstrates, Galileo is definitely not just Voyager 3 with a probe. Its new systems and instruments have been matched with a computer-perfected flight plan that not only comes closer to all the Galilean satellites than either Voyager did, but also explores Jupiter's atmosphere and passes through uncharted regions of the magnetosphere. This will be a study of the entire Jovian system, with scientific objectives that fall into three broad categories: the structure and composition of Jupiter's atmosphere; the composition and physical state of the Galilean satellites; and the structure, composition, and dynamics of the Jovian magnetosphere. We can't anticipate Galileo's results, of course, but what follows gives some idea of the many interesting scientific questions that the mission will address.

Right: At Hughes Aircraft Company, the Galileo probe undergoes testing. Below: The probe will shed its red-hot nose cone as it penetrates the Jovian atmosphere.

Above: Hughes Aircraft Company; Below: JPL/NASA

Sampling the Jovian Atmosphere

Previous studies of Jupiter's atmosphere have been confined to observations from Earth-based telescopes or from flyby spacecraft. We have learned much this way, as we have about other planets. But remote-sensing techniques have intrinsic limitations: in particular, their inability to penetrate clouds and hazes (except at a few wavelengths) precludes investigations of deep-lying layers, and they can only indirectly detect the presence of many chemical constituents (such as helium, which apparently constitutes 10 percent of the Jovian atmosphere).

Our experience with Pioneer Venus and the Viking landers illustrates just how much *in situ* (Latin for "in place") measurements can tell us about the origin and evolution of planetary atmospheres, and the Galileo probe will give us a similar perspective for Jupiter.

After an hour's descent, the probe should reach a depth in the atmosphere corresponding to 10 to 20 times the sea-level pressure on Earth. This is still only the tiny outermost fraction of Jupiter's gaseous envelope, but it should be enough to penetrate all the major cloud decks. (The deepest one is expected to consist of liquid-water droplets.) As it drifts downward, the probe will get a chance to sample "average" Jupiter gas in addition to locating and characterizing each cloud layer in turn.

Careful examination of the probe data will aid our understanding of the Jovian atmosphere and those of planets in general. We even hope to learn something of the conditions in the solar nebula at the time of planetary formation. In many current theoretical models, the outer planets must have collected their huge gaseous envelopes by accretion (accumulation by gradual buildup) mechanisms that differ somewhat from those that led to the terrestrial planets. The

While drifting through Jupiter's upper atmosphere, the probe will characterize each cloud layer and sample gases.

James Hervat

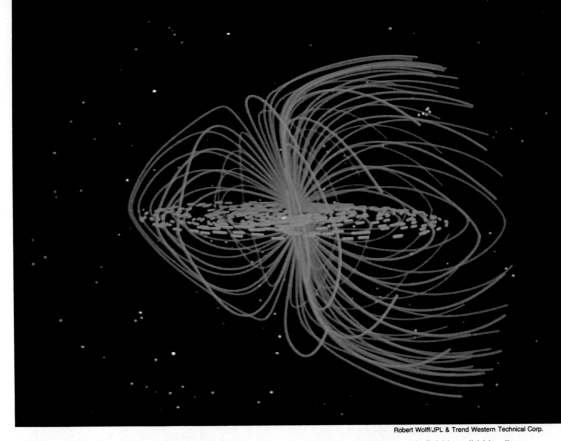

Robert Wolff/JPL & Trend Western Technical Corp.

A computer-based view of Jupiter's magnetosphere shows the planet's immense magnetic field in solid blue lines.

Jovian abundances of helium and rare gases such as xenon, neon, and argon are important indicators of conditions in the early solar system and of how the giant planets acquired and kept their atmospheres. Some cosmochemists believe, in fact, that in sampling Jupiter's atmosphere we will be studying the essentially unmodified aeons-old "star stuff" that formed the Sun, planets, and smaller objects.

We also want to know the current state of the Jovian atmosphere—where the clouds are and what they're made of, how solar energy is absorbed and how much energy is flowing out of Jupiter's still-cooling interior, how frequent lightning is, and whether small quantities of organic molecules are being created from methane and ammonia.

The Galileo orbiter also has a role to play here, for despite the great advantages of *in situ* sampling, the probe can observe atmospheric conditions at only one place and for a very limited time. Using its great remote-sensing power, the orbiter can place the probe's results in a global context—a perspective that will evolve over the orbiter's almost two-year mission.

Closer to Earth, the Space Telescope (ST) should also provide complementary Jovian observations during the mission. Although Galileo's camera is capable of much finer resolution than ST's, the orbiter won't be able to study Jovian cloud patterns while on the dark side of the planet. Therefore, atmospheric scientists hope the ST can be used to track Jupiter's weather during some of these periods and thus augment the Galileo data.

Analyzing the Dynamic Magnetosphere

Jupiter's magnetosphere is an immense structure—if visible to our eyes, it would appear from Earth several times larger than the full Moon. Teeming with energetic, charged particles (electrons and ions) from a variety of sources, the Jovian magnetosphere represents a huge obstacle to the outflowing solar wind.

To date, four spacecraft have penetrated this region for days to weeks at a time. Their results showed us that the Jovian magnetosphere is even more complex and dynamic than had been indicated from ground-based measurements and theoretical extrapolations from the

Earth's magnetosphere. Particularly remarkable are its outer regions, which move in and out by millions of kilometers in response to the solar wind and internal forces. The inner regions are greatly influenced by Jupiter's rapid spin and by the copious sulfur and oxygen ions spawned by Io. Jupiter also provides a relatively nearby electromagnetic "laboratory" for studying phenomena applicable to astrophysical objects and plasma processes in general.

Galileo will have several advantages over previous missions in exploring the magnetosphere. First, the orbiter carries improved instruments that should allow much better characterization of the sulfur, oxygen, sodium, and potassium coming from Io. Second, in contrast to the necessarily brief snapshots obtained before, Galileo will study this dynamic environment for nearly two years. Over this period we can determine, for example, how changes in Io's volcanic activity affect the populations of ions in the magnetosphere, or how fluctuations in the solar wind alter the magnetosphere's shape and character.

Third, the orbital tour will allow Galileo to visit uncharted regions of the outer magnetosphere and to periodically penetrate the energetic inner regions as well. In particular, the mission will include at least one long orbit in the "magnetotail," a distended, cone-shaped region formed as the solar wind sweeps the magnetic field back away from the planet. Voyager and Pioneer data only hint at what goes on there. Also, during the close satellite flybys, some orbiter experiments will observe these bodies' effects on the magnetosphere and even determine whether they have magnetic properties of their own.

Gathering Data on the Galilean Moons

Studies of the Galilean moons—Io, Europa, Ganymede, and Callisto—are an important part of the mission, and appropriately so. It is difficult to realize, in the wake of the Voyager discoveries, just how little we knew about satellites in the solar system only years ago. Prior to 1979 only our Moon and the two small objects circling Mars—Phobos and Deimos—had been explored in any detail. Then came Voyager's eye-opening glimpses of five Jovian satellites and over a dozen Saturnian ones. In fact, most of the solid bodies available for detailed study by planetary scientists are now satellites, not planets.

The Galileo orbiter passes by the south pole of Ganymede, one of Jupiter's moons that will be studied in detail.

Michael Carroll

Still, as with other facets of the Jovian system, the Voyager results have but scratched the surface of the complex scientific problems concerning these objects. Consider, for instance, that of the thousands of beautiful satellite images sent back by Voyager, only a handful are equal in resolution to an amateur's photograph of the Moon through a small telescope.

Galileo's photographic advantage stems mostly from the nature of its orbital tour. During each circuit, the orbiter will pass extremely close to one of the Galilean satellites. The altitude (or ''miss distance,'' really) of a typical encounter will be about 1,000 kilometers (620 miles) or less—that's 20 to 100 times closer than was the usual case with Voyager. Such proximity will allow Galileo's new CCD camera to record details only 20 meters (65 feet) or so across, comparable to much of the Viking orbiter's imagery of Mars. As a bonus, each time the spacecraft is tugged into a new orbit by a satellite's gravity, we will get a better value for the object's mass and, in turn, a better idea of its internal structure.

Ganymede and Callisto. The outer two Galilean moons, Ganymede (the solar system's largest satellite) and Callisto, are frequently considered together because of their similarities. Nearly the same size, and somewhat larger than Mercury, these ''ice giants'' have densities less than twice that of water; this suggests a roughly equal mix of ices and rocky materials in the makeup of each. However, their surfaces appear quite dissimilar in Voyager images, and Galileo will seek the reasons for these striking differences by studying the peculiar ''grooved terrain'' on Ganymede, determining whether the two have silicate cores, investigating the processes that have shaped their exteriors, and trying to deduce their surface composition.

Io. Innermost Io is perhaps the most interesting satellite in the solar system and also one of the most difficult to study. As was mentioned, Galileo will make one 1,000-kilometer approach to Io as the orbiter enters the Jovian system. During this initial pass we hope to obtain very high resolution views of Io's volcanic activity, determining both composition and temperature of the plumes and flows in the process. Gravity data, derived from the orbiter's motion, may also tell us whether Io has a completely molten interior, as is suggested by some theories.

But Io, situated deep within the Jovian radiation zone, is a dangerous target. For the rest of its mission, Galileo will remain beyond the immediate vicinity of Io to avoid accumulating too much radiation dosage. Each looping circuit will bring the spacecraft to about the orbit of Europa: from this vantage point it can still observe Io with more than sufficient resolution to monitor changes in volcanic activity and to make thermal maps of Io's ''hot spots.'' (Hot spots are places near the surface of a celestial body that are hotter than other places on that body due to the proximity of warm or molten rock beneath or at the body's surface.) In effect, for the many months of Galileo's basic mission, scientists will be treated to periodic reports from an ''Io Volcano Observatory.''

Europa. Europa, between Io and Ganymede, is the Galilean satellite seen most poorly by the Voyagers. As such it may well hold the greatest promise for surprise and discovery. For the most part, what we have now are tantalizing views of a bright, icy world that bears few impact craters and almost no surface relief but exhibits entire networks of mysterious, crisscrossed streaks or fractures.

The satellite's density (three times that of water) suggests that Europa is a silicate object covered with a moderately thick layer of ice. Surprisingly, very few craters were seen by the Voyagers, making it impossible to gauge how the surface age compares with those of the neighboring satellites. A very few images hint at the possibility that some kind of water-driven volcanism may be renewing the surface of Europa; this phenomenon could arise by internal-tidal forces similar to those heating Io's interior. The thickness of the icy crust is a key factor here, and observations by the orbiter should address this and many other questions about the intriguing body.

A New Era of Planetary Exploration

After years of planning and considerable political strife, Project Galileo is finally ready to head toward Jupiter and, perhaps, an asteroid along the way. It is the only mission to Jupiter currently under construction. However, there are several proposals involving Saturn, Uranus, and Neptune now under consideration both by NASA and by the European Space Agency. If approved, such a mission would benefit immensely from information gained by the two Galileo spacecraft. Their investigation of the Jovian system, along with other visits to Mars and Venus planned later this decade, will usher in a new era of planetary exploration□

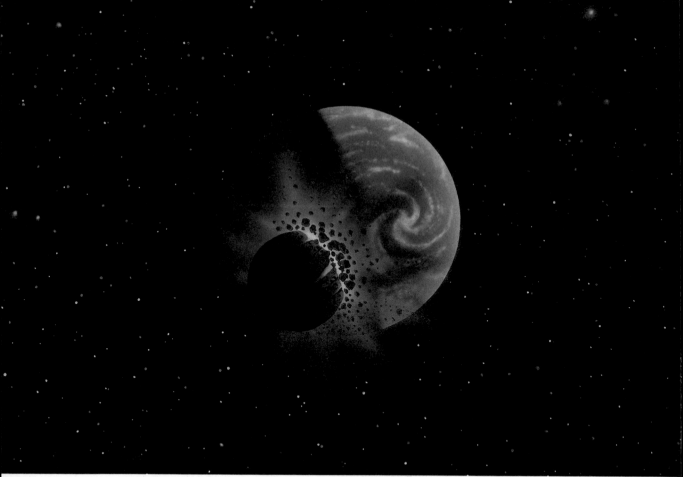

A BOLD NEW THEORY of the
MOON'S BIRTH

by Shannon Brownlee

I t was a tumultuous time. Throughout the solar system, giant spheroids, called plane- tesimals, caromed wildly about, crashing into each other or into the planets. One of the biggest of these errant objects—almost as big as Mars—came hurtling from the far reaches of the solar system toward the young Earth.

Impact Idea New Solution to Age-old Question

Barely 100 million years old, our lifeless planet still glowed hot under a blanket of poisonous gases, including carbon dioxide, methane, and sulfur. As the giant planetesimal struck, it plunged through the crust and deep into the mantle, vaporizing molten rock in its path. A huge plume of hot gases and debris spewed into space, rapidly forming a disk around the Earth.

Then came a reenactment of the steady process that formed the planets out of the origi- nal solar nebula. As the swirling cloud cooled, particles began clinging to each other to form larger and larger clumps. Clumps became rocks, rocks became boulders. After 1,000 years, the debris from the impact had coalesced into an entirely new celestial body: the Moon.

This cataclysmic scenario played out 4.6 billion years ago might have been written by that false prophet of cosmic catastrophe, the late Immanuel Velikovsky, author of *Worlds in Col-*

lision. In fact, it's the latest and apparently best answer to one of astronomy's fundamental questions: How was the Moon formed? Even as they look across the vast reaches of the universe, pondering exotic stars, galaxies, and the distant quasars, astronomers have yet to determine how the Earth came to acquire its Moon, an exceptional satellite among the more than three dozen moons known to orbit the planets of the solar system. Our Moon is one of the largest compared to its planet, one-quarter of the diameter of the Earth and one eighty-first its mass. By contrast, the two puny satellites of Mars, Phobos and Deimos, are each only about as big as the island of Manhattan in New York.

Mysterious Moon Has Vast Influence

The Moon exerts a profound influence on the Earth. Its gravity tugs at the oceans, helping create the tides—and the tidal marshlands from which the first primitive amphibians supposedly made their way out of the sea. Its reflected light stimulates the growth of plants, and signals the timing of reproductive cycles in many species of animals. Its luminescent presence is inextricably entangled in the web of human language and imagination. To the ancient Greeks, *menos* meant both moon and power. Selene, the moon goddess, was not only a giver but a destroyer of life, her celestial home a way station for the dead en route to the stars.

But for all the poetic imaginings kindled by the silvery orb, scientists have been hard pressed to account for it. They hoped that the Apollo landings would finally solve the mystery. Instead, the 380 kilograms (838 pounds) of rock and dust hauled back to Earth at great cost only presented a paradox: the lunar material turned out to be very much like terrestrial rock, yet different in significant ways. Scientists were forced to reconsider all earlier theories, both those that proposed that the Moon formed near the Earth and those that had it originating independently, possibly in a different part of the solar system.

Bizarre Theory Gains Acceptance

The first to suggest the impact theory (known irreverently as the Big Whack) was William Hartmann, a geochemist at the Planetary Science Institute in Tucson, Arizona, and a part-time painter of spacescapes. In 1976, a year after Hartmann and a colleague, Donald Davis (also a painter), unveiled their speculations, a more elaborate version of the theory was published by astrophysicists A. G. W. Cameron, of Harvard University, and William Ward, of California Institute of Technology's (Caltech's) Jet Propulsion Laboratory. Still, the Big Whack languished in obscurity as only one more explanation for the Moon's origin—and a bizarre one at that. Says Stephen Brush, a historian of astronomy at the University of Maryland: "This theory is so weird and cataclysmic, had it been proposed 20 years ago, it would've been laughed at."

What gave it respectability were some dramatic discoveries about the rate at which asteroids bombarded the young Earth—it was much greater than supposed—and about the chemical and physical consequences to the planet from such a fusillade. The Big Whack virtually eliminates the alternative theories—by accounting for the chemical similarities between lunar and terrestrial materials, and by providing an explanation of how the Moon got into its orbit.

The Fission Theory

Astronomers hadn't a clue to where the Moon came from until the 19th century, when improved telescopes and more accurate celestial measurements led to some remarkably sophisticated observations: that the day is getting longer by about one second every 50,000 years, and that the Moon is slowly spiraling away from the Earth at the rate of 2.54 centimeters (1 inch) each year. By the late 1800's, George Darwin (one of Charles' ten children) traced this process back, and found, erroneously, that 50 million years ago the Moon was only 9,700 kilometers (6,000 miles) from Earth (versus 386,000 kilometers [240,000 miles] now), and the day was just five hours long. As the molten young planet spun rapidly around the Sun, he said, the tug of solar gravity caused it to wobble violently, which grossly distended its shape. Eventually, a huge portion of the Earth broke off and was flung into orbit around it.

Subsequently, other proponents of this explanation of the Moon's beginnings, which came to be known as the fission theory, argued that the Pacific basin was the great scar left by the Moon's breakaway. (Geologists now ridicule the idea of such a primordial lunar birthmark, stating that the Earth's surface has been reshaped many times by movements of the crust.)

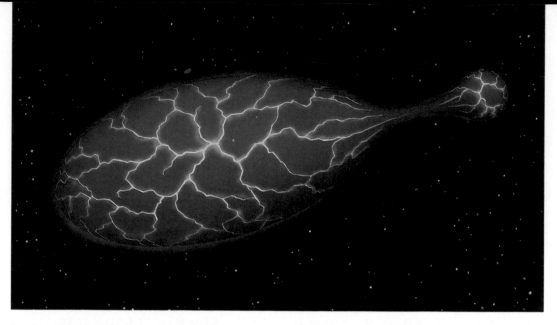

The fission theory holds that as the molten Earth spun around the Sun, a chunk broke off and became the Moon.

Two Other Views Vie for Favor

While astronomers debated Darwin's supposition, two rival theories emerged. One is called the capture hypothesis, because it postulates that the Moon formed at the outer reaches of the solar system and was trapped in the Earth's gravitational field as it passed by on a vast elliptical orbit around the Sun. The other theory arose out of French astronomer Pierre Simon de Laplace's nebular hypothesis of the birth of the solar system. According to this view, the Earth and Moon are sister planets, partners in a binary system in which the Moon condensed from a ring of gases swirling around the Earth, just as the Earth and other planets are assumed to have condensed from a similar ring around the newborn Sun.

The competing theories rose and fell on waves of scientific favor. There seemed to be no way to prove one or another until U.S. astronaut Neil A. Armstrong took the first step on the Moon in 1969. At the urging of Nobel-laureate chemist Harold Urey, a champion of the capture hypothesis, the National Aeronautics and Space Administration (NASA) agreed to have samples of the Moon brought back. "It was a terribly exciting time—there's never been anything like it," says John Wood, a geochemist at the Harvard College Observatory. "We all assumed the moon rocks would answer all our questions."

But the lunar samples were no Rosetta Stone (a giant stone bearing inscriptions whose discovery led to the decipherment of Egyptian writing). They didn't immediately reveal the secrets of the Moon's creation. Its original surface had been pounded by asteroids and carpeted with lava flows that all but destroyed it. The most ancient lunar sample was a mere 4.46 billion years old, at least 100 million years younger than the "genesis rocks" Urey had hoped for. Indeed, the rocks vastly complicated the picture. The discovery that their chemistry closely, but imperfectly, resembled that of the Earth's outer layers seemed at odds with all three prevailing theories of the Moon's origin. In the midst of this uncertainty, Hartmann and Davis published their impact hypothesis, but, Hartmann recalls, no one paid much attention. "It was hard to know just what to do with it."

Scientists Gather to Review Scenarios

In October 1984, nearly 100 scientists gathered at Kona, Hawaii, to reexamine the mystery of the Moon's birth. "Each of the theories had some highly convinced protagonists," says Wood, "but I figured that nobody would change anyone else's mind." Yet when the moon dust had settled, the Big Whack appeared to be slightly ahead.

A few diehards clung to a modern variation of Darwin's fission theory, despite the fact that they still couldn't explain how the proto-Earth came to spin so wildly that it tossed off a Moon-sized blob, then slowed to its present rate of rotation. Cameron scornfully described their efforts as "indistinguishable from magic."

The capture theory was already crumbling before the conference began. The lunar rocks had disclosed too much similarity between Earth and Moon for the Moon to have been formed in another part of the solar system. Proponents also found it difficult to show how the Earth's gravitational field could have captured a passing body without tearing it apart.

Serious Flaw Found in Binary Hypothesis

Even the binary hypothesis, the expected preconference favorite, went down in the frenetic calculating that accompanied the debate. Many scientists had always been disturbed by an essential requirement in such a scheme: that the Earth and Moon be composed of exactly the same material (which they aren't, despite their chemical kinship), since the two bodies would have formed side by side. But the theory's most serious shortcoming was the dread angular-momentum problem. Angular momentum is a measure of a body's spin, and depends upon its speed, direction of rotation, and how its mass is distributed. The classic demonstration of the relationship of these three properties is a twirling ice skater: when she extends her arms out and thus moves some of her mass away from the axis of rotation, she slows down; when she pulls them in, she spins faster.

Astronomers had believed that as the Earth and Moon were forming out of the ring of gases rotating around the Sun, they received their angular momentum from glancing blows of rocks and particles in the ring. According to laws of Newtonian physics (the principles put forth by Sir Isaac Newton), angular momentum is conserved; therefore, the binary theory held, any particles in orbit would be circling the Earth in the same direction in which the Earth was circling the Sun.

The thesis came crashing down when a handful of astrophysicists used mathematical simulations to prove that, in a case like this, angular momentum wouldn't govern the direction in which particles would circle the Earth. Particles approaching the planet wouldn't all fall into the same orbit; half would circle in one direction, while the other half would go the opposite way. Says Wood: "Most of us arrived agreeing with the binary-accretion theory in a halfhearted sort of way. That idea went right out the window."

Many Problems with Big-Whack Theory Overcome . . .

What was left was the impact theory, but it, too, needed a few more pieces before the puzzle could be put together. Nobody had been able to explain how a crashing planetesimal could loft enough material into orbit to form the Moon. "It would be great if you could just rip off a chunk of the Earth and put it into orbit, but it doesn't work that way," says Hartmann. "It's not like setting a rock down and hitting it with a golf club. The pieces would either fly into space or fall back to Earth."

Cameron and Ward overcame this obstacle, as well as a number of other difficulties, with some deft mathematical simulations of the Big Whack. The only way to keep the material

The obsolete capture theory contends that Earth's gravity slowed down a passing body and pulled it into orbit.

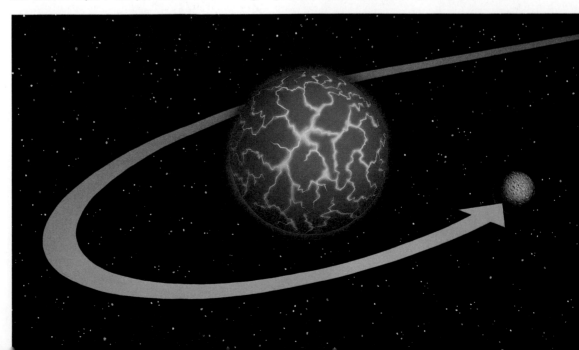

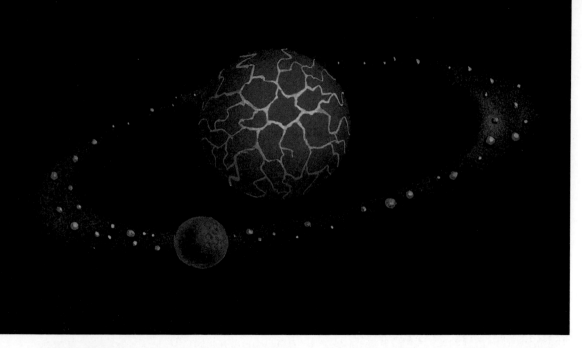

The discredited binary theory states that ancient dust particles circling the young Earth coalesced to form the Moon.

aloft was to turn it into gases. According to their calculations, the object that struck the Earth had to be enormous—at least half the diameter of the planet and about one-tenth its mass. It was racing along at a speed of at least 11 kilometers (7 miles) per second on an arcing path toward the Sun, and on the way struck the Earth a glancing blow. The force of the explosion tipped the Earth slightly on its side, and created such intense pressure and heat that much of the planetesimal's outermost layer as well as some of the Earth's were vaporized and turned to gas.

The searing gases exploded upward and outward, moving sideways around the Earth in the same direction in which the planetesimal had been traveling. More than twice as much material as was required to form the Moon was shot into space. Much of it fell back to Earth, while the rest continued into orbit. Geophysicists David Stevenson and A. C. Thompson of Caltech buttressed Cameron's simulations with calculations of their own, showing that the plume of gases would have completely girdled the globe within a few hours. After a century the disk would have expanded outward beyond the boundary where Earth's gravity could hinder the accretion of solid bodies out of the gases. A thousand years later, only a moment in the life of the solar system, bigger and bigger particles condensed from the cooling gas, and the Moon formed. This theory accounts for an important peculiarity in the chemical makeup of the moon rocks: the Moon is low in volatiles—easily vaporized chemicals—such as lead. These would have boiled away in the heat of the explosion.

. . . But Some Obstacles Remain

But two vexing problems remain. The first involves siderophiles (literally, iron-loving), elements that bind readily to iron. Compared to the Earth, the Moon has very few of these compounds, and in fact it has only one-quarter the iron expected in any rocky object in the solar system. Cameron has tried to explain this deficiency by saying the iron in the planetesimal and the Earth's crust and mantle weren't vaporized. Wood disagrees: "People forget that iron is actually quite volatile, and could have suffered much the same fate as the other volatiles, like sodium and water."

The second sticking point involves three isotopes (atoms of the same element that have the same atomic number but that differ in atomic weight) of oxygen, whose relative abundance indicates where in the solar system rocks were forged. As it turns out, moon rocks and earth rocks have identical oxygen-isotope fingerprints. This suggests that the object that struck the Earth (and contributed a great deal of its mass to the Moon) had to have formed nearby, as Hartmann and Davis speculated, rather than in some far-off place. Cameron has reconsidered this issue, and now says that a planetesimal originating near the Earth could just as easily have clobbered it as one zooming in from afar.

Recent discoveries about the nature of meteorite bombardment have made the impact theory easier to swallow. "Scientists seem to think something is more plausible if it's more boring," says Wood. In a sense he's right. It's only in the past two decades that geologists have found that the Earth is pocked with the evidence of collisions, making such catastrophic events seem commonplace. According to Hartmann's calculations, during the late stages of the planets' formation, the rate at which they were bombarded by small- to medium-sized asteroids was thousands of times higher than it is today. And there were enough big planetesimals rushing around the solar system çapable of delivering the blow required to make a moon. The low probability of such an event may explain the uniqueness of our satellite among moons in the solar system.

New Evidence May Enhance Theory's Credibility

Although the Big Whack captured the imagination of moongazers at Kona, will it ever be possible to prove it isn't empty talk? Hartmann thinks firm evidence may come from a better understanding of the chemical processes that formed the Moon. Says he: "If we could re-create the composition of the lunar rocks and establish that chemical changes in the Earth's crust and mantle would lead to such a composition, then I'd be convinced." But it's nearly impossible to simulate the incredibly high temperatures and pressures required to alter a rock's chemistry. Cameron takes a more theoretical approach. Using a supercomputer, he will model the behavior of the rocks and gases during and after an impact. Is there a test that would prove the theory? No, says Cameron: "It's not that no such test exists. It's just that our imaginations may not be good enough to conceive of it." At least not before we can travel beyond our own small corner of the universe to a place where we might be able to witness firsthand the genesis of another solar system, including a moon that shines down on some other earth □

SELECTED READING

"Whence came the moon?" by Alan E. Rubin. *Sky and Telescope,* November 1984.
"Nickel for your thoughts: Urey and the origin of the moon" by Stephen G. Brush. *Science,* September 3, 1982.
The Birth of the Moon by Lewis A. Manson. Dennis-Landman Publishers, 1978.

In another view of the new impact theory, vaporized rock that will eventually form the Moon orbits the Earth.

BEHAVIORAL
SCIENCES

REVIEW
OF THE
YEAR

BEHAVIORAL SCIENCES

During 1984 there was a comprehensive survey of mental illness in the United States, studies of hereditary links to depression and of the normal grief process, and research on child development and on childhood arson.

MENTAL ILLNESS

Nearly one in every five people in the United States—or approximately 29 million individuals—suffers some mental disorder, according to the U.S. National Institute of Mental Health (NIMH). Reporting the preliminary results of the most comprehensive survey of psychological problems ever conducted in the country, NIMH scientists noted that U.S. men and women had about equal rates of mental disability, contradicting the widely held belief that women are more prone to mental and emotional disturbances. The institute did find,

however, that men and women tend to have different problems: women are most often disabled by depression, anxiety, and phobias; men have higher rates of antisocial personality disorder—often involving crime and violence—and of alcohol and drug-abuse problems.

The most common psychological problem overall was found to be anxiety, including compulsiveness and panic attacks; more than 8 percent of the adult population—that is, an estimated 13 million people—experience some disability due to anxiety. An additional 10 million—or 6.4 percent—are debilitated by some form of substance abuse.

HEREDITY AND DEPRESSION

U.S. government scientists reported evidence that severe mood disorders may be linked to a biological vulnerability that is inherited—specifically, a hypersensitivity to a brain chemical called acetylcholine. Acetylcholine is a chemical messenger between nerve cells in the brain and elsewhere. Psychiatrist Elliot Gershon and his colleagues at NIMH studied a group of psychiatric patients suffering from manic-depression, a condition in which periods of severe melancholy alternate with periods of elevated or irritable moods. They also studied these patients' offsprings who were suffering from a variety of psychiatric disorders. In both groups they found an abnormally high density of chemical binding sites for acetylcholine, suggesting an uncommon sensitivity to the chemical. If the preliminary findings are confirmed, they hold out the possibility that a simple skin test might someday be used to detect vulnerability in relatives of depressed patients—since certain skin cells are good models of chemical activity in the brain.

GRIEF

A major government study of bereavement has challenged the long-standing view, set forth by psychiatrist Erich Lindemann in 1944, that following a tragic loss, everyone passes through predictable emotional stages: initial shock, intense sadness, withdrawal, protest, and finally, within a year, resolution. Patterns that deviated from the norm, Lindemann believed, were excessively morbid and pathological. The new report, from the Institute of Medicine, states that there is no normal bereavement process—no well-defined stages through which every mourner passes—and that the duration and intensity of the emotional reaction varies greatly from person to person, with some grieving as long as three years. Certain classes of survivors are at particularly high risk for illness, or even death, while grieving: children who have lost a parent or sibling, those who have lost someone to suicide, and those with a history of depression. For these mourners and some others who have difficulty coming to terms with their loss, therapy may help, but for many, the report concludes, outside intervention is neither desired nor needed.

CHILD DEVELOPMENT

A fundamental principle of most theories of child development is that early experiences—and in particular, those involving parents and children—play a crucial role in later psychological development; thus the emphasis in recent years on mother-infant bonding and early intellectual enrichment. Now a leading U.S. child psychologist is disputing that view. While not completely discounting the influence of parents and environment, Harvard University psychologist Jerome Kagan argues that biology—specifically, the normal development of the central nervous system—controls much of the child's intellectual, emotional, and even moral development during the first few years of life.

This challenge to the prevailing emphasis on nurturance in the centuries-old debate over nature versus nurture is particularly significant coming from Kagan, who throughout most of his career has attempted to demonstrate the dominant role of environment in child development. Kagan has been studying a group of children—ages 2 through 6—for four years, and as he reports in his book *The Nature of the Child,* children's basic temperaments appear to be inborn and quite stable. About one in 10 children is born with a strong inclination toward shyness and timidity, Kagan reports, while a similar number are born "bubbly" and sociable. While some of the bashful children have managed with their parents' guidance to become less fearful and more extroverted socially, they retain their root tendency toward hypervigilance—reacting to loud noises or social challenges with detectable changes in heartbeat and bodily tension. None of the naturally confident children has become fearful over the course of Kagan's study.

Kagan now believes that not even conscience can be taught but that it develops naturally as the brain becomes capable of emotions and empathy. It follows, too, that formal preschool education is a wasted effort; as long as the child is not in an utterly deprived environment, Kagan says, he or she will flourish according to a "pre-wired" developmental plan.

CHILDHOOD ARSON

The United States has the highest rate of arson in the world, costing an estimated $1 billion in property damage every year. It is also one of the nation's fastest-growing crimes, having quadrupled during the 1970's. While many arson fires are set for economic reasons, researchers now report that two out of every five arson fires are set by a child whose motivation is strictly psychological. Furthermore, the researchers say, childhood arson, unlike other childhood crimes, is a predominantly white, middle-class activity.

Sociologist Wayne Wooden and psychologist Martha Lou Berkey studied a group of juvenile arsonists who had been arrested over a four-year period in California, and they found distinct categories of fire-setting behavior. A very small percentage of young arsonists are severely emotionally disturbed, and for them arson is just one of many psychotic behaviors. But most young arsonists are not mentally ill, the researchers report. Some children, usually very young, are simply drawn to fire by its psychological magnetism and set accidental fires out of curiosity. For others, fire setting is a symbolic act, a way of expressing their stress and anxiety, and at the same time, calling for help. If such pleas are unanswered, the researchers note, fire-setting behavior is reinforced and often becomes habitual—a delinquent act of protest against authority.

WRAY HERBERT

Enrico Ferorelli/Dot

Henry Lee Lucas, who claims to have killed hundreds of people, calmly displays pictures of some of his victims.

MULTIPLE MURDERERS

by Joseph Berger

Before being convicted of murdering two women and a young girl in Florida and linked to the murders of 36 others, Theodore Bundy had helped the Seattle Crime Prevention Commission in Washington design a program for preventing rapes.

James Huberty, who shot 21 people to death at a McDonald's restaurant in San Ysidro, California, in July 1984, had previously been able to find work as a security guard.

Kenneth Bianchi, who confessed to five of the 10 "Hillside Strangler" murders in Los Angeles, California, in the late 1970's, was not only able to get a job as a security guard, but was also regarded by police officials in Bellingham, Washington, as a good prospect for law-enforcement work.

If these examples are any measure, American society is not very good at recognizing potential multiple murderers—neither mass murderers like Mr. Huberty who kill groups of people in a single outburst nor serial murderers who kill many victims over a long period.

Study Provides Broad Statistical Profile

Indeed, criminologists, psychiatrists, and law-enforcement officials say that research into the psychology and behavior of the multiple murderer is only in its infancy and that, in the words of one scholar, "the mass killer cannot be predicted."

Yet, more studies than ever before appear to be in progress, and they are confirming some preconceptions and confounding others.

Two Northeastern University professors— Dr. James Alan Fox, who teaches criminal justice, and Dr. Jack Levin, a sociologist—have written one of the few general studies of the topic, "Mass Murder: America's Growing Menace."

They studied data from the Federal Bureau of Investigation (FBI) on murders in the United States from 1976 to 1980 and found 156 episodes in which four or more people were slain. They also reviewed psychiatric reports and newspaper clippings, and interviewed principals in 42 serial or mass murders that occurred from 1974 to 1979.

Among their findings were these:

• New York State leads the country in the number of mass murders. From 1976 to 1980 the state had 30 multiple murders, while California had 21 and Texas 15.

• Multiple murderers are almost exclusively men. Only 10 of the 156 multiple murderers culled from FBI computer data were women.

• Multiple murders tend to be most often committed by white people. Although 50 percent of single-victim murders in the country are committed by blacks, Dr. Fox said, only 22 percent of the multiple murders were committed by blacks.

• Multiple murderers are older than the average murderer. While most people convicted of murder are in their teens or 20's, multiple murderers tend to be in their 30's.

• Like most killers, multiple murderers generally kill people they know, out of rage or frustration, or the misguided fit of jealousy that the police said characterized Christopher Thomas, the man charged with murdering 10 women and children in Brooklyn, New York, in April 1984. Murderers like Mr. Huberty or Charles J. Whitman, who shot 14 people at random from atop a tower at the University of Texas in Austin in 1966, are the exceptions.

• Some serial murderers roam from state to state searching for victims, but the majority find them near home.

• Multiple murderers are not, as a rule, insane, by most legal definitions. In the 42 cases Dr. Fox and Dr. Levin examined closely, 9 of the suspects pleaded innocent by reason of insanity and only 4 of those were found insane. "The typical mass murderer is extraordinarily ordinary," said Fox. "He doesn't stand out in the crowd. He's not a glassy-eyed lunatic."

We Can't "Rule People Out"

Yet, there is widespread disagreement about the psychology, character, and background of multiple murderers.

"We have some basic clinical knowledge of serial murderers that allows us to rule people out," said Dr. John Liebert, a psychiatrist at the University of Washington in Seattle. "What we don't have is how to rule them in." Dr. Liebert has been a consultant on three cases of multiple murder, including the "Green River" slayings in which more than 25 women, mostly prostitutes, have been killed in the Seattle area.

There is a peculiar public fascination with multiple murder. Abhorrent as a murder is, people can comprehend its typical rationales: a jealous rage, greed, or the need to eliminate a witness to a crime.

But the kind of murderer who kills again and again, sometimes choosing his victims at random and often driven by a seemingly unquenchable lust for blood, exercises a special grip on the public's imagination because his murders are so incomprehensible.

A Mass Murderer Explodes

Most experts feel the serial murderer and the single-outburst mass murderer are two distinct

Detective Frank Adamson is still seeking clues to the identity of Washington's "Green River" serial murderer.

Enrico Ferorelli/Dot

James Mayo/Chicago Tribune

Multiple murderer John Wayne Gacy showed no remorse for his crimes, a typical attitude of such killers.

types. The mass murderer is usually someone who explodes at a moment. While his frenzy at that moment can seem insatiable, it exhausts itself and he will probably never kill again.

"The type of a person who commits a mass murder," said Dr. Liebert, "is frequently more of a paranoid personality who just blows over his threshold."

That threshold is often crossed because of a tangible episode that follows a string of defeats and rejections. The threat of divorce drives an unstable man to murder not only his wife but their children and sometimes himself. The loss of his job as a security guard, Dr. Fox believes, may have driven Mr. Huberty to head toward the hamburger restaurant to even the score with the wider humanity that had so often frustrated him.

Psychotics and Sadists

Dr. Emanuel Tanay, a forensic psychiatrist at Wayne State University, feels that most mass murderers have lost contact with, or have a defective sense of, reality. He feels the number of such psychotic mass murders has risen in recent years because of a national policy of releasing large numbers of the mentally ill into their communities, particularly into communities where such firepower as the Uzi semiautomatic rifle used by Mr. Huberty is easily available.

A psychotic, Dr. Tanay said, has such a disorganized mind that he does not limit his need for aggression to a specific person. Had Mr. Huberty been rational, he might have contained his need for revenge to the man who fired him from his job.

Most serial killers are sexual sadists, the experts say. In his 1975 study, "Murder and Madness," Dr. Donald T. Lunde wrote that the sadistic murderer derives "sexual pleasure from the killing and mutilation or abuse of his victim."

Such killers, he wrote, "often have had no experience of normal sexual intercourse," yet the "act of killing itself produces very powerful sexual arousal in these individuals, some of whom will attempt sexual intercourse with the victim."

Dr. Tanay, however, notes that the serial killer—he prefers the terms compulsive murderer or lust murderer—does not give any visible signs of derangement, even under the most expert examination.

Dr. Tanay was called in as an expert witness by the judge in the Bundy case, and found Mr. Bundy, he said in an interview, "just as lucid and pleasant a person as you would want to meet."

"You don't find any overt psychopathology in examining him," Dr. Tanay said.

Indeed, Dr. Liebert says one of the personality types he rules out in cases of serial murder is characterized as a "very disorganized psychotic individual."

Killers Show No Remorse

Dr. Helen Morrison, a psychiatrist in Chicago, Illinois, thinks specialists cannot begin to detect the characteristics of the serial killer in routine interviews. That is why she has spent long periods with the multiple murderers she has interviewed, including 800 hours with John Wayne Gacy, a prosperous building contractor who was convicted in 1980 of murdering 33 young men and boys in the Chicago area. She believes the serial killer is a "new personality type."

First, she says, the serial killer does not distinguish between human beings and inanimate objects. Richard Macek, who gained notoriety as the ''Mad Biter'' for bite marks he left on the flesh of young women he tortured and murdered in Illinois and Wisconsin in the 1970's, once told her a dream in which he imagined attacking a person. ''Picked up the person, slammed them into wall, beating until death, lifeless, or unconscious,'' he wrote in describing the dream.

''He doesn't know the difference between those three states,'' Dr. Morrison observed in an interview. ''That's striking because to us death and lifeless are the same thing but to him it's not. He shows no awareness of the pain or feeling or the existence of another person.''

The serial murderers reveal absolutely no guilt, she said. Mr. Gacy, most of whose victims were found buried under his home, once said to her that all the police ''are going to get me for is running a funeral parlor without a license.''

Warped Views of Reality

Serial murderers have grandiose ideas about their power and also display peculiarly obsessive traits. Mr. Gacy, she said, kept notebooks that recorded what he did minute by minute,

Theodore Bundy helped design an antirape program before being convicted of murdering several females.

UPI/Bettmann

even logging such trivia as the precise moment he mailed a letter. ''This tremendous organization is about the only structure they have,'' Dr. Morrison said of the serial killers. ''In prisons they generally become trusties.''

She believes that ''the defect that occurs in these individuals occurs before they're 6 months old.'' For example, she said, as a newborn, Mr. Gacy was given daily enemas by his mother for no apparent reason. ''These early experiences tend to be expressed as a world that persecutes them,'' she said. ''They are very fearful. They have fears of death, of total helplessness, of total psychological fragmentation.''

Somehow, Dr. Morrison said, the childhood fear of psychological fragmentation translates itself into a confusion of roles. ''The victim becomes the persecutor and the persecutor becomes the victim,'' she said.

Once when she interviewed Mr. Macek in prison, he appeared before her with a terry cloth towel draped around his neck. Since Mr. Macek had been accused of killing his victims with a terry towel, Dr. Morrison was frightened and asked a prison guard to take away the towel. Mr. Macek, she recalled, was piqued, and said to her, ''You'd think I was going to kill you.''

Dr. Morrison said she believed that ''the killings seem to be a way'' for the murderers ''of integrating their psychological status.''

''Murder is a way for them to regain themselves from being fragmented,'' she said.

The ''curious question,'' she said, ''is what is it about the victims that they fulfill the mass murderer's psychological needs?'' While the murderers cannot explain why they chose particular victims, Dr. Morrison said she believed that the victims were symbolic of something or someone deeply significant in the murderers' lives. Some psychologists have specifically said the victims represent cruel parents on whom some murderers feel they cannot take revenge.

Dr. Liebert, while emphasizing that in-depth psychological research is sorely lacking, feels that perhaps in the first three years of the person's life, a flaw occurs in the bonding process between mother and infant so that they develop a sadistic, aggressive relationship with each other.

As a result, he suggests, these individuals either idealize the women they form relationships with or degrade them. They see women, Dr. Liebert said, ''as either angels or whores,'' and there seems to be no sensible middle ground.

The inadequacy of this theory, Dr. Liebert pointed out, is that "there have been lots of people like this and only a tiny, tiny percentage that ever killed."

Dr. Morrison suggests that psychology alone may not explain the aberration of compulsive murder. Since few multiple murderers are women, she speculates that possibly the mystery to the mass murderer may lie in the sex chromosomes. She also says the aberration "is not amenable to any intervention or treatment."

Are Multiple Murders on the Rise?

There is an argument over whether multiple murders are increasing or whether there has just been more attention to them in recent years. Certainly the victim counts have gone up. In 1973 it was thought that Dean Corll had set the record for serial homicides when 26 bodies were unearthed in three shallow graves in Houston, Texas.

But new levels of carnage were reached with Mr. Bundy and Mr. Gacy, and their acts were dwarfed by those of Henry Lee Lucas, who says he has killed 360 men, women, and children in several states.

Those who think the phenomenon is growing have several explanations. Dr. Liebert believes it has a lot to do with the age of television. "We have children in emotionally deprived families whose main nurturance is the TV set," he said. "By the time they're 15 years old, they've seen 10,000 murders on TV. The victims don't suffer. Murder is like going down to the store and getting a Popsicle."

Ann Rule, a writer who became a nationally recognized expert on serial murders, thinks the growth of sadistic pornography is partly to blame. Sadistic pornography, she cautions, does not create a murderous personality, but it can push potentially violent people over the edge.

Another underlying cause for the increase, Dr. Liebert said, is the rising incidence of family breakup, which can be crushing to the children involved. Mrs. Rule says that in a mobile society, children do not have aunts, uncles, and grandparents to fall back on when their parents fail them.

Pierce R. Brooks, a former police officer who is setting up a program at the FBI Academy at Quantico, Virginia, to coordinate information from local police agencies on serial killers, also thinks an increased mobility and dispersion of Americans is partly to blame for the rise in serial homicides.

"We are becoming more of a society of strangers," he said, and the stresses that result may be contributing to the growth of multiple murders □

SELECTED READINGS

"An American tragedy" by Brad Darrach and Dr. Joel Norris. *Life,* August 1984.
"Multiple murderers" by Glenn Garelik and Gina Maranto. *Discover,* July 1984.
Killer Clown: The John Wayne Gacy Murders by Peter T. Maiken and Terry Sullivan. The Putnam Publishing Group, 1983.

AP/Wide World

Kenneth Bianchi, one of two cousins who confessed to the "Hillside Strangler" murders in Los Angeles, California, was once regarded by police officials as being a good candidate for law-enforcement work.

Paul Schutzer/LIFE Magazine, Time Inc.

The MYSTERY of TEARS

by Curt Suplee

Alone among animals, we are the creatures that weep.

We weep in mourning. We weep for joy. When a person dies we weep. When a baby is born, we weep, too—some of us, perhaps in homage to the miracle, as if each new life were a brave defiance of fate, perhaps moved by the helplessness of a creature soon to face life's thousand dreads and murderous indifference. We are brought to tears as well for reasons multitudinous and trivial—the sight of a sunset, the sound of a national anthem, a flat tire, a broken washing machine.

Many Unknowns

Crying seems such a simple act. Instinctive as the beat of a pulse, spontaneous as a sigh. Yet in the moment of their coming, tears are a mystery. What do they mean? How and why do they come? Precisely what use do they serve? What, in fact, are these distillates of woe that, down

through the ages, have linked men and women in the common salt not only of suffering but of joy?

Modern science has no satisfactory answer. All tears have a certain amount of salt in them (about 0.9 percent). Women cry more than men. Everybody knows that, and the sciences, social and otherwise, confirm it, though not quite as universally as you would expect. But why do women cry more? Is it a matter of biology? Or sentimental conditioning? Or merely the difference in nose size, as one ingenious anthropologist contends (smaller nasal passages, less room for tears)?

Science can now distinguish physiologically between reflex tears (stirred, for example, by onions) and emotional tears (arising mainly from grief or joy). A Minnesota biochemist, William H. Frey II, who directs an ongoing study of tears, has established that emotional tears have a higher protein content than reflex tears. But neither Frey, nor anybody else, yet knows why, or of what use the protein-rich tears are to the weeper or to society in general.

Tears Have Varied Roles Across Cultures

One thing is clear: In myth and metaphor, in rites of mourning and rebirth, tears have always been deeply intermingled with the human heart and the history of mankind. In ancient Assyria, weeping seems to have accompanied agrarian (agricultural) fertility rites, perhaps symbolically replacing rain crucial to crop growth, a practice alluded to—or so some biblical students think—in Psalm 126: "They that sow in tears shall reap in joy."

Throughout the Old and New Testaments, the sacramental function of crying echoes steadily down from Job's "mine eye poureth out tears unto God," to Mary Magdalen's ritual washing of Jesus' feet with her tears in an act of humility and purification.

In Norse mythology, tears can be more directly utilitarian, in one instance being used to illustrate condensation. When the supreme god Odin's beloved son, Balder the Good, dies, the gods strike a bargain with the giantess of hell that Balder may be returned to the living if everything on Earth agrees to weep for him. "All things very willingly complied," says Bulfinch's translation, "both men and every other living being, as well as earths, and stones, and trees, and metals, just as we have all seen these things weep when they are brought from a cold place to a hot one."

Most tearful legends are unrelentingly grim. For example, the classic Greek legend of lachrymosity (tearfulness) is about Queen Niobe. Her tears, it is said, not only created a stream that runs to this day, but illustrated the dangers of being too proud of your children (and of boasting about them), thus tempting fate to take action. In Niobe's case, the gods killed all her children, and her grief-stricken husband took his own life.

The world has aptly been called "this vale of tears." Down through the ages, oceans of tears have been shed. Yet since time immemorial, people have had a hard time deciding (officially, at least) whether to be for tears or against them. The debate still rages. Tears are good, runs one currently fashionable argument. They are a sign of humanity, softening and refining our perceptions of the world. They make us feel better. Tears are bad, goes the other line of thought. They destroy the control

of reason. Shedding them in public makes us vulnerable, something few people can afford in this harsh world. Above all, though forgivable in women and children, they are highly suspect, not to say downright unworthy, when shed by men.

The Stigmas of Weeping

That view has been shifting. I recently heard of a young lawyer, well on her way to becoming a partner in her law firm, who suffered harsh criticism in her office. She wanted to cry but did not want to give her male colleagues the advantage of seeing her in tears. At lunchtime, still shaken, she rode down in the paneled elevator full of fellow lawyers, gritting her teeth and repeating to herself, "I will not cry in the elevator! I will not cry in the elevator!"

In view of such confusion of feeling and shortage of fact, it is not surprising that even a sage of Victorian sensibility like Alfred, Lord Tennyson, found lachrymosity perplexing: "Tears, idle tears, I know not what they mean, / Tears, from the depths of some divine despair / Rise in the heart, and gather in the eyes." Tennyson, of course, was talking about free-floating tearfulness, without evident cause (what Virgil called *lacrimae inanes,* "vain tears"). But the British poet laureate approved of tears. Being a late-19th-century romantic, he more or less had to. But approving of tears, idle or otherwise, for men at least, has been rare enough in England and the United States, as well as in many other places (and times) in world history. Two centuries earlier, Tennyson's countryman, lumpish philosopher Thomas Hobbes, put forth the perennial view of tears when he wrote sneeringly, "They are most subject to [weeping] that rely principally on helps external, such as are women, and children."

Worthless or Purposeful?

Early science was not a lot of help to the tearful, either. In the 17th century, for instance, William Harvey, the first man to understand the heart and the circulatory system, warned that yielding to strong emotion could disturb the heart rhythm, causing "vitiated nutrition and a want of native heat."

Somewhat later, Darwin speculated that when a baby cries, the blood vessels of the eye become engorged and the surrounding muscles contract to protect it, thus triggering the lachrymal glands. In time, he wrote, "it has come to pass that suffering readily causes the secretion of tears,'' but he regarded the tears themselves as a purposeless by-product, not linked to evolutionary survival.

Anthropologist Ashley Montagu disagrees. He sees human tears as having arisen precisely because the process of natural selection helped those who could produce tears to survive. ''Even a short session of tearless crying in a young infant,'' he notes, ''is likely to dry out the mucous membranes of the nose and throat, rendering the child vulnerable to the invasion of harmful bacteria and even viruses.'' Unless, that is, the membrane is soaked by lysozyme, an enzyme that is secreted by tears. Whether they sobbed or not, ''dry-eyed babies,'' Montagu concludes, would have ''less chance of surviving than those who cried with tears.'' In time, as humans evolved, ''their responses to the weeping child increasingly sensitized them to the emotional behavior of their fellow humans.''

Dry weeping? Oh, yes. In fact, says Alan Savitz, chairman of psychiatry at Washington, District of Columbia's, Greater Southeast Community Hospital, ''we don't even understand why children begin to have tears.'' Your average weepy human being, it turns out, is born without the ability to weep emotional tears at all. The skill doesn't develop until somewhere between the second and twelfth week of life (well before laughter, however, which does not arrive until about five months). Many scientists now suspect that weeping may be crucial to well-being. Studies show that infants with an illness that prevents them from producing tears with crying are unable to handle much emotional stress. Besides their extra protein, emotional tears are different from reflex tearing in other ways. They can appear, for example, even after the cranial nerve that controls reflex weeping is severed.

Crying Behavior Examined in Depth

William Frey is the only scientist, so far, to concentrate heavily on the chemistry of emotional tears and the biochemical changes related to emotional states. For five years Frey and his colleagues have been collecting the emotional outpouring of hundreds of volunteers from Minneapolis and St. Paul, Minnesota, who are sub-

The social acceptability of men shedding tears has changed with the times, except in circumstances of tragedy.

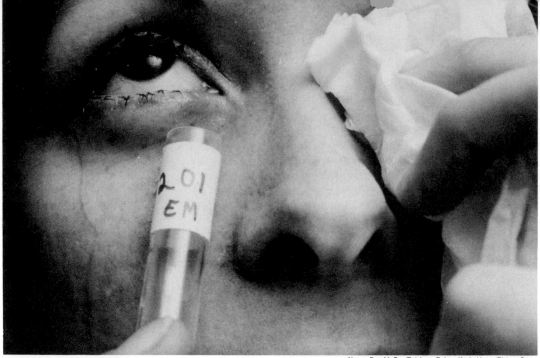

Above: Dan McCoy/Rainbow; Below: Kevin Horan/Picture Group

jected to "four-handkerchief" movies to make them start weeping. (*Brian's Song*, a film about a young football player's death from cancer, was the most effective for many months, but lately it has been replaced as champion tear-jerker by Jon Voight in *The Champ*, in which a boxer dies while his little boy looks on.) At first each subject was given special eyeglasses with little cups to catch the runoff. But, Frey notes, "they didn't fit everybody." Now he uses small test tubes.

Such samples permitted Frey to establish the high-protein content of emotional tears. They also led him to a theory he has yet to prove, which is simply that tears, "like other excretory functions, remove from the body toxic substances that build up as a result of stress." Just exactly what substances, however, Frey doesn't yet know.

Inevitably Frey's studies have also moved off into human behavior. In 1982 he conducted the first study ever of adult crying behavior, a project that involved 331 people (45 men and 286 women). He found that the average duration of a crying session in both sexes was six minutes. Also, for women the number of crying episodes almost doubled during the heavy evening rush hour of television drama (between 7 and 10 P.M.). It wasn't necessarily television tragedy that did it, though. The women were at home at that time and likely to have emotional encounters.

Forty percent of female crying was over

Above: In a Minnesota research laboratory, a volunteer's tears are collected for chemical analysis by Dr. William Frey (below). The volunteers may be asked to watch sad movies or sniff onions to induce crying.

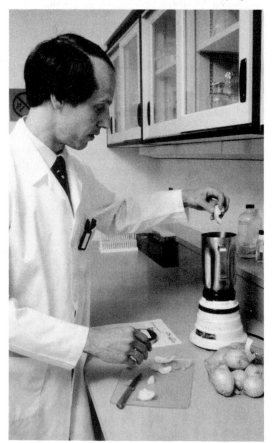

arguments, weddings, and love affairs, all lumped under a broad heading Frey called "interpersonal relations." (Men cried over "interpersonal relations" only 36 percent of the time.) But a greater percentage of men (36 percent versus 27 percent of women) cried over movies, television, and books. And, curiously enough, male crying was 3 percent greater in an ambiguous causal category labeled "sad thoughts."

The standard psychological view of tears today is that they help relieve emotional stress (a good thing). The corollary, which Frey puts rather modestly, is that "if crying relieves emotional stress," suppressing tears "may increase our susceptibility to a variety of physical and psychological problems." California sociologist and grief specialist Thomas Scheff, author of *Catharsis in Healing, Ritual and Drama,* is briefer—as well as reassuringly concise. Says he: "Crying is a necessary condition for removing sadness" and tears are "a necessary biological component." The late stress expert Hans Selye said that failure to cope with emotional tension exacerbates such things as high blood pressure, gastric and duodenal ulcers, and certain types of rheumatic, allergic, cardiovascular, and kidney diseases.

Men's Weeping Goes In and Out of Vogue

If the current crop of experts who now point out that crying is not only a psychological comfort, but probably necessary to health and happiness, are right, the result of another of Frey's findings, though not surprising, seems to be gloomy news for men. For in Frey's study, women wept four times as often as men: 5.3 times per month, in fact. And during any given month, only 6 percent of females reported no crying at all, versus 45 percent of males.

According to Gordon Clanton, a sociologist at San Diego State University in California, emotional fashions in crying change over time, just like fashions in everything else. Periods of economic depression, Clanton feels, tend to cause emotional repression. Affluence, on the other hand, makes us more emotionally expressive, experimental, and tolerant—as if, indeed, showing emotion were a luxury in which a society can rarely afford to indulge. As Clanton puts it: "Relative prosperity was the social precondition for emotional innovation and for outpourings of fashionable feelings among the classical Greeks of the fourth century B.C., the courtly lovers of Medieval France, the early 19-century Romantics in England, and the hedonistic [he-

People start pollution.
People can stop it.
Keep America Beautiful

Keep America Beautiful Inc.

A famous antipollution poster plays on the Indian's stoic reputation to drive home its point.

donism is the doctrine that pleasure or happiness is the major good in life] young Americans of the 1920's and late 1960's. And such innovation in the rules which shape emotional feeling and display often makes tears more acceptable."

In the United States, at least, passionate displays—tears included—were not totally tolerable, even in women, until the first rock-and-roll splash of the late 1950's. The postwar baby boom was entering its teens. A vast hormonal stew of sweet pain, young lust, and heartache inundated pop music with hot-eyed lamentation.

For one reason or another, the United States embarked not merely on a cultural revolution, Clanton says, but on a decade "much more expressive of a whole range of emotions from anger to delight." And if the nation has since retreated to a "cautious reassessment of that decade," there was, he says "one lasting effect—men can show feelings." With the feminist movement demanding male "sensitivity" (of which tears are regarded as unimpeachable proof), men are actively encouraged to do so.

However, there are signs that public acceptance of tears, in men at least, is in decline again. It is probably significant that for the first time since the 1950's, the word "wimp" is back in currency. A resurgent patriotism is reviving public regard for stoic military bearing. As

Frey's sampling shows, these days men don't appear to be pulling their lachrymal weight anymore. And to make matters worse, some of their tears may not even be genuine. Says Suzanne Braun Levine, managing editor of *Ms.* magazine: "There are some fake-sensitive men out there," who use crying as a means of attracting liberated women. "But they're crocodile tears."

Despite bad word of mouth about crying, it was always more or less permissible for tears to be wrung from men by great grief—though anything that could properly "make strong men weep," as the traditional phrase goes, was supposed to be pretty overwhelming.

When the Greek hero and friend of Achilles, Patroclus, was slain before the walls of Troy, the great Achilles' very horses wept. As for their master, as arrogant and coldhearted a sacker of cities as history or mythology provides, he not only wept, but picked up the dark dust in both his hands and poured it on his head, and "cast himself down on the earth." Shakespeare's Laertes is deeply ashamed, but he, too, weeps over his drowned sister in Hamlet, opin-

ing: "Nature her custom holds, / Let shame say what it will. When these [tears] are gone, / The woman will be out."

Tears Associated with Being Weak

The special conventions controlling what tears are acceptable and what tears are not have been inconsistent. Even before the latest campaign to make crying "safe" for American males, nobody seemed to think the worse of a famous football player who wept openly after his team lost the Super Bowl. Yet what has never been officially approved of in men is tears shed in response to transient frustrations or mere adversity, and as late as 1972, tearfulness in the wrong circumstances could ruin a male political career. Senator Edmund Muskie lost his bid for the presidential nomination at least in part because the spectacle of the manly candidate apparently weeping, over harsh words from a right-wing newspaper attacking his wife, was too much for the voters.

By associating tears with "weakness," and weakness with women, men like Laertes and the antitear forces have, in an odd, back-

Senator Edmund Muskie's tearful response to public criticism of his wife hurt his political career in the 1970's.

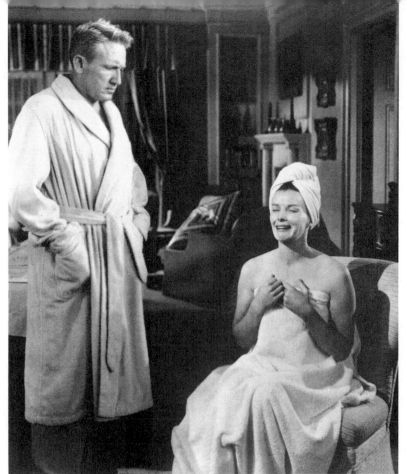

When Katharine Hepburn weeps in the movie *Adam's Rib*, Spencer Tracy refers to her tears as "the old juice."

handed way, encouraged tearfulness in the human female. (It was no coincidence that witches, regarded as unwomanly daughters of beguiled Eve, collaborators with the devil, were considered incapable of weeping.) In *Malleas Maleficarum,* the famous antiwitchcraft handbook from 1490, the ability to shed tears is regarded as a test for women accused of being witches. Judges are urged to try to make these women cry, adjuring them to do so by the "tears shed on the Cross by our Saviour, the Lord Jesus Christ."

According to some men, at least, women have license to cry at virtually any contingency, not only as an emotive birthright of the "weaker sex," but also as a compensatory mode of aggression. In the long skirmish between the sexes, tears have been represented as a mighty female weapon. A disaffected John Donne (one of the world's greatest love poets, as well as a Protestant minister) warned 400 years ago that "hearts do not in eyes shine, / Nor can you more judge womans thoughts by teares, / Than by her shadow, what she wears." Yet in life as in fic-

tion, the manliest specimens have regularly been reduced to gibbering helplessness at the sight of a loved woman weeping.

Until quite recently, that kind of emotional leverage was nowhere more frequently or blatantly invoked than in the movies. Even the strongest female characters, like Katharine Hepburn in *Adam's Rib* (in which she plays a successful lawyer), are often accused of possibly unscrupulous use of what in the film Spencer Tracy calls "the old juice."

One thing is clear: Until researchers like William Frey learn what tears do, and what use that extra protein in emotional tears serves, as well as where it comes from—or until women are quite unsexed and men are made of stone—nothing will be certain but death, tears, and taxes. As the famed English poet Lord Byron wrote: "Away! we know that tears are vain, / That Death nor heeds nor hears distress: / Will this unteach us to complain? / Or make one mourner weep the less? / And thou, who tell'st me to forget, / Thy looks are wan, thine eyes are wet" □

Photos: J. Guichard/Sygma

Children's Winning Ways

by Maya Pines

When Hubert Montagner, a French ethologist (scientist who studies animal behavior) noted for his studies of wasp communication, moved in 1970 to the University of Besançon, near the border of Switzerland, psychologists at the university's Institute for School Psychology threw him a challenge he couldn't refuse: "They thought that existing psychological tests and psychoanalytic theory were not sufficient to understand children's behavioral disorders," Montagner recalls. "So they asked me to begin a systematic observation of children in school and to establish behavioral scales which could predict certain difficulties," he says. "They told me they'd be very interested in getting some new tools with which they could better understand why children behaved as they did in school."

A Revolutionary Study

This was an unusual request to make of an expert in social-insect behavior, but Montagner was interested in the research, and devoted most of his time in the ensuing years to studying humans. The fruits of his labors, after 15 years and 320 kilometers (200 miles) of film, are new ways to interpret the social behavior of young children, particularly the individual nonverbal-communication styles that affect long-term social roles in groups, such as who will be attractive to others or who will become a leader.

Working in the tradition of Nicholas Blurton Jones, William MacGrew, and Iranëus Eibl-Eibesfeldt, who began to apply the methods of ethology to humans in the 1960's, Montagner has developed a system for observing and classifying the gestural language of children. He has

Opposite: Behavioral expert Hubert Montagner developed a way of interpreting children's gestural language.

also tracked down some of its origins. In addition, his long-term observations of children have given him a sense of the normal- and abnormal-developmental timetable for the emergence of specific types of gestures and body language. He can calculate how many of a young child's gestures belong to certain categories of behavior, and can then derive a series of significant ratios, such as the ratio of pacifying to aggressive behavior, that appear to predict some behavioral problems.

Montagner's other contributions include careful studies of how biological factors, particularly stress hormones, are related to behavioral characteristics. In his search for the roots of children's behavioral patterns, he has gone back to the earliest moments of interaction between mothers and newborns, and has explored the role of scents in their communications.

A child exhibits classic gestures of fear and retreat when another youngster tries to take away her doll.

In sum, this European researcher, whose work is not yet well known in the United States, has provided new insights into critical aspects of social interaction and communication. And he has done it by studying children in their natural settings—not in a laboratory—just as his fellow ethologists study birds, apes, or wasps.

Physical Interactions Observed

When Montagner began his study of children, he chose to observe two- and three-year-olds at a local day-care center. "I thought I could use an ethological approach to study their nonverbal interaction," he says. "They do speak at that age, but only a few words. And later on I found out that even when children use language, they continue to show the same sequences of behavior as before, in the same contexts, with the same functions."

Coming from outside the psychological tradition, Montagner paid no attention to how much these children understood about objects, a prime concern of the famed and influential Swiss psychologist Jean Piaget. Nor did he try to analyze the underlying emotions revealed by children as they played with dolls, worked on puzzles, or engaged in make-believe play. Instead, hidden behind a screen, he and his team focused exclusively on how these children interacted with one another. The researchers recorded and classified with great precision all the children's gestures toward others. They observed the interactions of 1,500 children between the ages of 6 months and 6 years, including 100 children whose behavior was studied very intensively for a period of three years, and some youngsters whom they followed all the way up to their teens.

Five Distinct Types of Behavior

The observations yielded five general categories of social behavior, which are distinguished as follows:

• *Actions that pacify others or produce attachment:* offering another child toys or candy, lightly touching or caressing the other child, jumping in place, clapping one's hands, smiling, extending one's hand as if begging, taking the other child's chin in one's hand, cocking one's head over one shoulder, leaning sideways, rocking from left to right, pirouetting, or vocalizing in a nonthreatening way.

• *Threatening actions that generally produce fear, flight, or tears in the target child:* loud vocalization, frowning, showing clenched teeth, opening one's mouth wide, pointing one's index finger toward the other child, clenching one's fist, raising one's arm, leaning one's head forward, leaning one's whole trunk forward, or shadow boxing.

• *Aggressive actions:* hitting with hands or feet, scratching, pinching, biting, pulling the other child's hair or clothes, shaking the other child, knocking the other child down, grabbing something that belongs to the other child, or throwing something at the other child.

• *Gestures of fear and retreat:* widening one's eyes, blinking, protecting one's face with bent arms, moving one's head backward, moving one's trunk or one's whole body backward, running away, or crying after an encounter with another child.

• *Actions that produce isolation:* thumb-sucking, tugging at one's hair or ear, sucking on a toy or a blanket, standing or sitting somewhat apart from other children, lying down, lying curled into the fetal position, or crying alone.

Gestural Language Universal

Montagner's observations also yielded the realization that certain children used gestures from some categories more than from others. Even as early as age 2, some children regularly used more gestures from the aggressive category than from the pacifying-or-attaching category. Other children used pacifying-or-attaching gestures four times as frequently as aggressive gestures.

Those unwitting choices became increasingly consistent as the children grew up, and resulted, for many, in relatively stable ways of relating to others. Thus, each child spoke a gestural language that other children could understand clearly, even if adults could not necessarily decode it, and it affected how others treated the child. Surprisingly, tiny gestures seemed to spell the difference between success and failure in getting along with others, winning friends, and becoming a "leader" whom others would willingly follow.

The building blocks of the gestural language Montagner has identified emerge early, "between the ages of 9 and 12 months," he says. And they appear to be universal. He notes that the very same gestural repertoire has been observed among children in other parts of France and in Africa; most of them also have been described among American and English children by such researchers as Blurton Jones, MacGrew, and David Lewis. All children de-velop the ability to perform the full range of gestures, but the combinations they "choose" and how frequently they choose them differ widely from child to child.

Specific Sequence Triggers Positive Response

According to Montagner, the secret of success with others—at least in the preschool set, though possibly beyond—is to use many gestures from the pacifying-or-attaching category. Perhaps the most "magical" sequence within this category is a tilt of the head over one shoulder combined with a smile. Sometimes it includes extending one hand toward the other child, as if to shake hands. Either way, the sequence triggers a friendly response or an offering of some kind in 80 percent of the cases Montagner has observed. Children on the receiving end seem to melt. They will often calm down and show affection, he says, and some will even give up cherished objects of their own free will.

The power of this sequence is evident in many of the films Montagner's team shot at local day-care centers. In one film, a two-year-old girl approaches two boys and tilts her head sideways while smiling at one. The boy immediately smiles back at her. Meanwhile, the second boy gets up, reaches for his toy car—his only one, according to Montagner—and offers it to her.

Children often use this sequence to get the things they want. However, its primary effect is to trigger warm feelings, Montagner says. Especially among younger children (ages 18 months to 2½ years), this sequence produces signs of affection or love.

Adults can use it, too, Montagner points out. In fact, some parents do so instinctively. "It is one of the most efficient ways to appease a crying child," he notes. He has repeatedly observed that when young children see this tilt of the head and a smile on someone they like, they will reach toward this person, stroke him or her, or rush into the person's arms.

Montagner is aware that advertising agencies exploit this sequence very effectively. Just look at the pictures of young women with their heads tilted ingratiatingly in television commercials or fashion magazines, he notes.

Despite its power, this sequence is not used by all children, according to Montagner. Some hardly ever use pacifying-or-attaching gestures, and therefore never receive similarly affectionate or friendly gestures in return. This failure may spoil their relationships with others for the rest of their lives, Montagner believes.

Leaders Behave Differently Than Other Kids

By now, Montagner can read the behavior of two-year-olds well enough to know pretty well what these children will be like, socially, at age

10. By age 2, certain children are already on their way to being extremely "attractive" to others, Montagner says, meaning that their behavior "provoke[s] approaches to the child by two or more children."

According to Montagner, the children who become real "leaders" (meaning that they engage in acts that provoke others to follow and/or imitate them) emerge from the group of "attractive" children, rather than from the more aggressive ones. Adults often make the mistake of thinking that children who rely on overt aggression, such as biting or hair-pulling, and who push others around to get what they want, are the leaders. But these "dominant-aggressive" children, as Montagner calls them, cannot make lasting coalitions. They are generally disliked by others, and any groups that form around them disintegrate rapidly in a chaos of aggressive acts.

The real leaders—the ones whom other children seek out and follow—are quite different, Montagner says. They use pacifying-or-attaching sequences as frequently as children who are merely attractive. But in addition, they participate in many competitions for desirable toys or preferred space, and they generally succeed. Their signals are clear: They do not seek

Left and below: A friendly pat or an offering of a toy to another are actions that solicit warm responses.

A little girl reacts to a playmate's aggressive attempts to grab her toy tractor by threatening to hit him.

or start fights but will fight and stand their ground if attacked. "These are the children who start new activities for the whole group more than 75 percent of the time," Montagner says. "We call them 'leaders,' even in French."

He emphasizes that children who are leaders never mix gestures from different categories. "When a child offers a toy with one hand and pulls hair with the other hand, his whole behavior is decoded as aggressive," he says. Children who mix their signals in this way are highly unpopular with others, according to Montagner. "When they approach other children, the others tend to run away or cry," he observes.

Other children who are highly attractive seldom take any leadership role (except in groups of two or three children) because, for some reason, they hardly ever participate in competitions. They don't even try to get the goodies that others seek.

Montagner has also identified another group of children who do not get involved in competition but alternate between periods of self-isolation and sudden, apparently pointless, acts of aggression. "They will bite another child without provocation and without trying to take any object away," says Montagner, who is still puzzled by this sort of strange and unpredictable behavior.

Kids' Behavior Affected by Parents

What produces these different patterns? Montagner does not believe that genetic factors play a very important role. But he does see a correlation between the children's behavioral profiles at age 2 or 3 and "the kind of behavior usually expressed by their parents, especially their mothers, towards them.

"We have observed that the parents of children who become leaders communicate with them a great deal, using mimicry, gestures, words, and squatting down at their level to talk to them," he says. "They often ask the child what he wants to do. Does he want to climb on their back? Does he want to play a particular game? They listen to what the child says and pay close attention to his spontaneous behavior. They don't threaten, except in potentially dangerous situations, and they are neither aggressive towards him nor overprotective. Their behavior is very stable."

On the other hand, "When we looked at how parents of dominant-aggressive children treated them, we observed that the mother was either rather aggressive or totally permissive, paying no attention to what her child was doing," Montagner says. "Let me give you a typical case: At the end of the day, when his mother comes to get Nicolas, she opens the door of the playroom and calls for him. But when he comes running towards her, she doesn't interact with him. Instead, she turns toward the day-care worker and asks, 'Well, was he naughty today? You see, I have so many difficulties with him. He hits his little sister, [and so on].' So as the child approaches but gets no attention from his mother, he turns away and runs to another part of the room. Then the mother begins to shout at him, 'Come on, Nicolas, I'm in a hurry!' But by then the child is in the distance, smiling. So she becomes impassioned and aggressive, first in words, then in her behavior. It's not rare to observe overt aggression when she finally succeeds in catching her child, not rare at all!"

Montagner has not found any differences between the parents of the attractive children who become leaders and those who don't, however. "So we don't know why some children rarely participate in competitions."

As to the most fearful children, "we found that usually the mothers were overprotective," he says. "They appeared constantly anxious about their children's health, behavior, or the possibility of accidents, and very rarely let them go outside to play with the other children."

Behavior Most Alterable at Early Age

The youngest children's patterns sometimes changed when their home situations changed, Montagner says. For example, one little boy who had been a nonaggressive leader suddenly became highly aggressive when his baby brother fell ill and his anxious mother no longer had any time or patience for him. When the baby got well and the mother returned to normal, however, the boy's aggressiveness waned and he became a leader once again. In one or two cases in which parents became more attentive to their children after talking to Montagner's team, the children began to use many more pacifying-or-attaching sequences.

"But in children older than 5, we did not observe any major changes," says Montagner, who notes that unless the feedback mechanism between parent and child is altered early, the behavior of both becomes reinforced.

"The children who had been most aggressive at age 2 or 3 were still very aggressive when we looked at them at age 10 or 11," he says. "And the most attractive ones remained among the most attractive. Only the fearful ones seemed changed: Some of them appeared to have overcome their fears—perhaps their parents stopped being overprotective. Yet some of the most fearful appeared to be still fearful."

Olfactory Signals Linked to Behavior

Throughout his work, Montagner has tried to combine physiological measurements with his observations of behavior. For example, he monitored some of the children's stress hormones regularly (as measured in their urine) and found that the daily curves of the leaders' hormone levels were most stable over time while those of the most aggressive children varied greatly.

Even his studies of mother-child interaction have a biological side, for he has focused on how children and their mothers communicate through odors. Since Montagner is an expert on communication among insects, which is often accomplished through chemical messages, this choice of subject matter is not surprising.

In 1974 Montagner showed that two- and three-year-olds can generally recognize the smell of a T-shirt worn by their mother, and that when they are given such a T-shirt, their behavior changes. "They may stop whatever they were doing and rub this shirt on their face, put it in their mouth, or lick it," he wrote. "They become less aggressive than on other days and have fewer interactions with other children."

This clue led him to track down the origins of some of the feedback mechanisms between parent and child. So he went back to the very first days of life, studying mother-infant communication through smells, which had been demonstrated in the pioneering work of Mac-Grew and Aidan Macfarlane.

Infants react differently to pieces of gauze that their own mothers have worn against their necks and breasts than to gauze worn by other mothers, Montagner's team showed in a series of experiments with newborns that began in 1978. The researchers calculated that as the infants turned towards these pieces of gauze, the area swept by their noses and arms was narrowed and their behavior more peaceful than when they were confronted with alien smells. This difference appeared on the third day of life, the team found, just when the blindfolded mothers began to recognize the odor of T-shirts worn

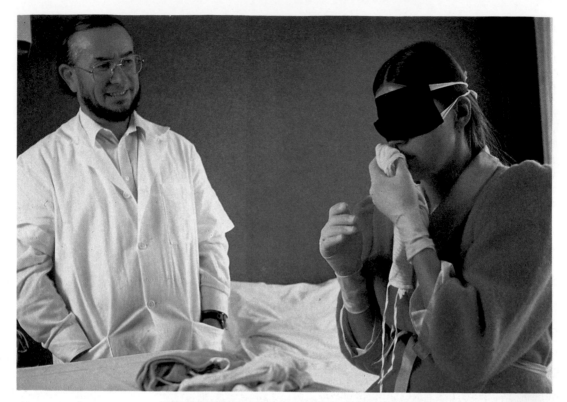

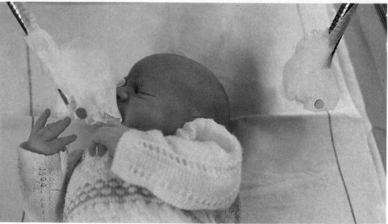

Above: Hubert Montagner tests a mother's ability to distinguish the scent of her own baby from those of other newborns by sniffing an item of clothing. Right: An infant immediately turns toward a piece of gauze that was worn by his mother and ignores the strange-smelling sample.

by their own infants and to distinguish such shirts from those worn by other newborns. Olfactory signals of this sort can play a role in the attachment between mother and child, Montagner suggests.

Recognizing Developmental Failures

Now Montagner and his colleagues are looking for early signs of trouble in the mother-child relationship, as well as in children's behavior toward other children. With Albert Restoin and

Danilo Rodriguez, he has roughed out a timetable for the normal development of communication behavior.

They know, for instance, that it is normal for 12-month-old children to isolate themselves from others occasionally and to lie down flat on their stomachs. But the researchers also know that this particular posture usually disappears around 18 months of age, and that older children normally lie down on their sides.

Along the same lines, they have found that

at 12 months, a child who seeks comfort in an adult's lap will generally sit facing the adult directly; by 15 months, this child will sit sideways. A certain kind of rocking that is normal for one-year-olds also disappears before their second birthday. "When a child of 2 or 3 often lies down flat on his tummy, away from others, rocks himself, or offers toys to a child who is facing in another direction, it is a sign of serious trouble," Montagner warns. Such children tend to become extremely isolated from the others as they grow up or to alternate between isolation and bouts of aggression.

The researchers also check whether young children know how to threaten others effectively, a very important skill, according to Montagner. When children begin to walk, they encounter more conflicts and competitions, and must develop a system to participate in these with a minimum of aggression. "Threats can prevent aggressions," Montagner explains. "We have looked at many instances of conflict and calculated that children between the ages of 7 and 18 months who don't use threatening behavior such as loud vocalization when it is appropriate are the targets of other children's aggression 59 percent of the time. Those who do use threats receive aggression only 41 percent of the time."

Peer Interaction Best Indicator of Well-being

In this way, Montagner's group is beginning to build a list of possible danger signals that, if heeded, might prevent many of the difficulties children encounter both in school and later in life. Their work fits in very nicely with that of other researchers who have studied the development of social competence in monkeys.

"In our animals, the first danger signals come from peer interaction. If a young monkey who had pretty smooth relationships with peers becomes very aggressive or stops participating in play, usually it's a sign of some disturbance in the mother-child relationship," says Stephen J. Suomi, an ethologist who conducts primate-behavior research for the National Institute of Child Health and Human Development and the National Institute of Mental Health. Suomi observed hundreds of monkeys while collaborating with Harry Harlow at the University of Wisconsin.

Though monkeys normally try to play with whomever they can, "play behavior is very fragile," according to Suomi, and in case of trouble or stress, it is the first behavior to disappear. Thus, peer interaction is "a nice barometer of overall psychological well-being," he believes. It can serve to diagnose problems and also to predict future adjustment. "A young monkey who's hyper-aggressive towards others, or else unusually shy and reluctant to participate in peer interactions, will generally show more serious difficulties later in life," Suomi says.

Similarly, careful monitoring of children's gestural language and relationships with others could serve as a barometer of their mental health and a possible predictor of how they will function in the future. □

A child's lack of interest in playing with his peers may be a danger signal of psychological trouble or stress.

Photos: Richard Buettner

REAL WORK for REAL PAY

by Beverly McLeod

O ne of the unspoken fears of expectant parents is the possibility that their child will have mental retardation. For most, such worries are unfounded. Yet a small but significant percentage must face the fact that their child, indeed, will never develop as normal children do.

Improved Outlook Reflects Major Change

When a child has an intelligence quotient (IQ) of 70 or below—the point at which people are considered mentally retarded—parents must abandon many dreams and adjust to their child's severely limited prospects. But how limited

Above: A retarded man learns how to assemble circuit boards in a special employment-training program.

must such a life be? Must their child live forever in an institution or, if at home, be permanently dependent on the family or the state?

Until quite recently, the answer seemed to be "yes." As Lou Brown, a special educator at the University of Wisconsin, has observed, people with mental retardation "have been devalued, undertaught, their life spaces have been tragically constricted, and many negative generalizations have become embedded in the minds and hearts of millions."

Consider, for example, the case of David Nettleman (all names of people with mental handicaps are pseudonyms), a teenager with mental retardation. His parents, like many others, were told that he would "always be a child," and he was treated accordingly. Even as a tall, powerful young man at a special school, he was never asked to do more than string beads. But today he is receiving on-the-job training at a bowling alley, and he has learned to do home chores that may help him get the janitorial job he wants.

Or consider the story of Michael Ortega, a young man with moderate retardation who had spent more than 20 years in an institution. His typical occupation was rubbing his face and staring at his hands. Not a likely prospect to be working steadily for more than six years and earning $6 an hour training dishwashers, as he now does.

These accomplishments have happened in part because during the past decade attitudes toward the abilities of people with mental retardation have changed—quietly but profoundly. In fact, the Association for Retarded Citizens now estimates that, given appropriate training, 75 percent of children with mental retardation could be completely self-supporting as adults, and another 10 to 15 percent could be partially self-supporting.

The appropriate training, many experts now say, involves enhancing real-world coping skills through meticulous behavioral analysis and modification. The techniques are relatively old, but the determination to apply them to provide greater opportunities for people with mental retardation to become self-supporting is rather new.

Oregon Training Program Paves the Way

Many factors underlie this change, including greater advocacy and recognition of the rights and dignity of all handicapped people. But for those with mental retardation, one key factor has been the widespread influence of a successful employment-training model developed by G. Thomas Bellamy at the University of Oregon about a decade ago. The Oregon program showed that people with severe mental retardation could acquire the skills needed for productive work. That experiment and others that followed raised expectations, first among a few researchers, then throughout the mental-retardation field. As Robert W. Flexer of Kent State University in Ohio and Andrew S. Martin of United Marketing Services in Lubbock, Texas, describe the change, ''. . . instead of saying, 'These people . . . cannot learn and cannot be trained,' we are now saying, 'We have not been competent enough to teach.' The failing is not with the severely handicapped, but with us.''

The Oregon experiment sparked the development of many similar training programs across the country. One of the newest is Electronics Assembly Services (EAS) in Virginia, which exemplifies the new approach.

Shortly after 9 A.M., Donna Hodges wheels herself into EAS to begin her job of assembling and bagging circuit boards. She cannot count, so as she finishes each board, she places it next to one of the five black circles on her desk. When all five boards are filled, she puts them in a bag and starts over again. She earns a quarter for every 30 completed boards, and is saving her money to buy a blouse held on layaway in the shop downstairs.

A Success Story

Soon the other 11 EAS employees walk in and begin their various tasks. When greeted by Anne O'Bryan, general manager of EAS, they

A trainee at Electronics Assembly Services performs simple tasks for which she earns a nominal wage. A timer helps to regulate her productivity.

look in her direction but say nothing; most cannot talk. She and her two assistants circulate constantly among the employees, praising and paying them for completed tasks, guiding and helping them if necessary.

O'Bryan takes Ali Mehrabian to a corner of the room and guides his hands during a training session in cutting, stripping, and soldering wires. Another staff member accompanies William Jackson to the rest room for a training session in its use. He evaluates Jackson's progress on a chart listing several dozen minute steps to be followed.

Meanwhile, Robert Antonelli begins to growl. One of the staff members immediately makes him stand facing a corner of the room, sets a kitchen timer for one minute, and makes a note on his chart. After a minute of silence, Antonelli is returned to his seat. Twenty minutes later, when he begins growling again, the procedure is repeated.

Antonelli, who had lived in an institution for most of his life, had spent the better part of his waking hours growling. During his first month at EAS, he growled an average of 450 times a day. By giving Antonelli a sip of his favorite coffee whenever he was silent for a few minutes and by standing him in the corner whenever he growled, O'Bryan limited him to 300 growls on the first treatment day, 150 on the second, and 100 on the third. By the second week's end, his growling had practically ceased. But during a recent hospital stay, his usual good behavior had slipped a little.

At noon some employees eat bag lunches or buy food from a vending machine; others order lunch at a nearby fast-food restaurant by holding up picture cards showing hamburgers, french fries, and soft drinks. Hodges collects her quarters and pays another installment on her blouse.

The city of Alexandria hired O'Bryan to set up an employment program for its severely retarded adults. "We don't have a minimum IQ requirement here," she says. "We have a maximum. None of the employees has an IQ above 35, and many of them had lived in institutions for years."

A retarded woman proudly purchases a blouse with savings she earned in an employment-training program.

At first it was chaotic, she recalls. The staff members kept popcorn in their work aprons, ready to pop into anyone's mouth who was quiet for even a few seconds. But within only four months, most of the employees had become quiet and productive, and a few months later, they began doing increasingly complex tasks.

Two Primary Training Approaches

EAS represents one of two new approaches to providing job training and employment to adults with severe mental retardation. Like other "supported-employment" programs, it provides whatever ongoing support is necessary to enable people with mental retardation to find and keep jobs. Some programs, like EAS, employ a small group of people with mental retardation who do subcontract work for larger companies. In other programs, a group of separately supervised employees works together at a larger company. "Competitive-employment" programs provide transitional training and short-term support to prepare people for independent employment, then place them in regular jobs that pay a minimum wage or better.

Many competitive-employment programs dispense with standardized tests to determine skill levels for specific tasks. Because such tests, designed for the physically handicapped, do not accurately predict job success for people with mental retardation, clients are often placed directly in the actual job situation, then assessed as the training proceeds. "This is a significant departure from traditional placement approaches which require the client to be quite 'job ready,' " says Paul Wehman, director of the Virginia Commonwealth University Rehabilitation Research and Training Center. "And it has been crucial to making our track record successful with clients traditionally excluded from services."

Behavioral Techniques Vital to Many Programs

Many of the new employment-training programs rely heavily on the techniques of behavior analysis and modification. Trainers analyze in detail how nonhandicapped people perform a job, then teach their trainees to follow the same procedures.

When Susan Jameson went to work in a beauty salon, her trainer broke down the job of collecting and washing towels into 85 steps, drying them into another 32, and folding and putting them away into another 100. Training was initially very intense, but Jameson now works on her own with only an occasional visit from her trainer.

Like many other people with mental retardation, Jameson also needed to learn social skills, such as smiling and greeting her co-workers. People who have lived in institutions often do not learn how to interact with others or to care for themselves in socially acceptable ways.

Developing these skills was an important part of a University of Washington program that trained people with moderate to severe mental retardation to work in three on-campus restaurants. Most of the trainees could not read, write, tell time, use money, or ride the city bus, and many had poor grooming habits. Special educator JoAnn Sowers and her colleagues at the university devised a set of picture cards showing clean hands, combed hair, neat clothing, and brushed teeth to teach proper grooming habits. Another set of cards showed two clocks and a lunch box. One clock showed trainees when to go to lunch, and the other showed when to return to work. By matching the cards to a wall clock, trainees were able to keep to the work schedule even though they couldn't tell time.

Similar "shortcuts" are used at EAS. Hodges, for example, uses the five black circles on her desk to help her "count," and employees can buy food with their picture cards even if they can't say the words. Instead of spending hours painfully trying to write, clients can use a name stamp to cash their paychecks.

New Training Setups Better than Older Ones

How successful are these employment-training programs? Though many are new, they promise greater success than traditional sheltered workshops or activity centers in placing people in the conventional work force—and at higher earning levels.

Federally funded in the 1950's, sheltered workshops were intended as transitional training centers to help trainees move into the job market. But only about 10 percent of sheltered-workshop clients are placed in competitive jobs each year, and few have severe retardation.

Other programs, called "activity centers," usually serve people with IQ's below 50—traditionally seen as too severely disabled for competitive work and ineligible for vocational training.

Such day programs were expanded by 600 percent between 1972 and 1979, partly due to

Above: Laurie Joe McCarthy, an Electronics Assembly Services' (EAS) rehabilitation coordinator, sets up a daily schedule of tasks for the trainees. Left: EAS staff member Mike Vrable shows a new trainee how to sort parts using a series of circles as a counting aid.

deinstitutionalization, and now they are serving more than 100,000 people. Not surprisingly, very few clients move on to higher-level vocational programs.

In contrast, competitive-employment programs, which serve a similar clientele, have done much better. In three projects supervised by R. Timm Vogelsberg, a special educator at the University of Vermont, clients had been classified as "mentally retarded, severely disabled, and unemployable" by traditional vocational-rehabilitation services. Despite these dire labels, in a five-year period, 70 percent of those placed were still on the job.

In a similar time span, Wehman and his colleagues have placed 145 people in competitive employment, which Wehman defines as "working for at least a minimum wage with

EAS trainees learn proper grooming habits and social skills that are essential for employment in the "real" world.

nonhandicapped workers and with no subsidized wage in any way." These people, with a median IQ of 48, were also considered unemployable by traditional-rehabilitative services. But they are now working in hospital laundry rooms, medical-equipment manufacturing facilities, and food-service settings. They have been on the job for an average of 15½ months, compared to less than five months for their nonhandicapped counterparts.

Earnings a Significant Issue

The earnings of trainees in the newer programs are equally impressive and have potentially profound economic consequences. Sheltered-workshop employees earn an average of only 80 cents an hour, or little more than $400 per year. Activity centers, licensed to serve only "inconsequential producers," by law cannot pay their clients more than 25 percent of the minimum wage. Some states do not allow activity-center clients to earn any money, and even in those that do, "work for pay is viewed as primarily therapeutic, rather than as a means of support," according to Kent State's Flexer and United Marketing Services' Martin. The U.S. Department of Labor estimates that clients in such centers earn an average of 33 cents an hour, or $160 per year.

The employees of the Olympus program in Seattle, Washington, all of whom have severe mental retardation, earn more than $100 monthly. Started in 1977 as a community replication of the University of Oregon's Specialized Training Program (the model for EAS as well), Olympus does electronics-assembly work for several firms. Because of employees' earnings, the state was able to reduce their support from a daily average of $22.50 per person to less than $10.

Money is a big issue for these employment programs. Federal and state governments will spend more than $14 billion this year on services to people with mental retardation, primarily in institutions. A substantial amount of Supplemental Social Security Income (SSI) payments goes specifically to unemployed workers who are mentally retarded. In all, 8 percent of our gross national product is spent on disability programs. Many experts in the mental-retardation field believe that these enormous costs are likely to skyrocket unless policies affecting the employment of people with mental retardation change significantly.

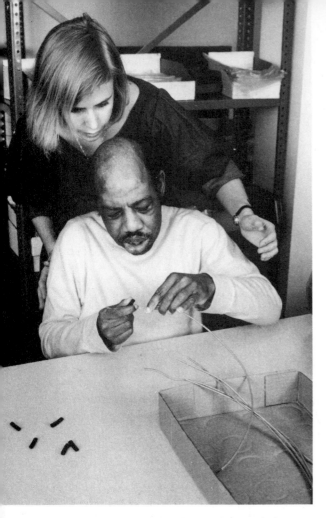

An EAS supervisor assists a retarded man as he learns to assemble electronic cables one step at a time.

Benefits of Training Substantial

Mental retardation is a problem that will not go away soon. One in 10 Americans has a mentally retarded family member, and the rate in the United States—3 percent of the population (6 million Americans)—is rising.

As the public burden of supporting adults with mental retardation grows, so do the economic benefits of the new programs. Intensive, individualized, and ongoing training tends to be expensive. But advocates contend that it is less expensive in the long run than total public support. A review of six supported-employment programs in Oregon and Washington found that they cost 20 percent less than traditional day-activity programs.

Training costs in the newer employment programs range from $2,500 to $7,500, but that is a one-time cost, after which most trainees become at least partially self-supporting. The 145 clients of Wehman's competitive-employment program have earned more than $900,000 during a recent five-year period and have paid $126,634 in taxes. The average employee earned $4,500 per year—almost equaling the public cost of maintaining a person in an activity center.

The cost of training is recouped in four years, and during a lifetime a worker will earn more than $10 for every dollar spent in training. That person will also contribute $530 yearly in taxes.

Reforming Federal and State Policies

Despite the many arguments favoring widespread adoption of the newer employment-training programs, there are many obstacles, not the least of which is the welfare system. Many Social Security–eligibility rules actually prohibit work and thus discourage recipients from taking a chance on employment training. Such disincentives force people who should have partial support to be either completely self-supporting or completely dependent.

Recent changes in federal law now allow severely disabled people to do paid work without fear of losing their SSI payments and Medicaid eligibility. But even with these changes, many more are needed. Reforming the welfare system is such an overwhelming task that some experts prefer working around it. Special educator Brown even advocates the controversial step of allowing people with mental retardation to work for nonmonetary payment—or even for free—when in danger of being trapped by the Catch-22 of federal-eligibility rules. He believes that for employees, the unfairness of this approach is outweighed by the benefits of participating in a normal working life. The public at large benefits, too, by knowing that disability payment recipients "are at least trying to give something in return."

Some researchers and activists are focusing their efforts on state-level reform. Because a pioneering program at the University of Washington showed that adults with moderate retardation could succeed in competitive employment, the state of Washington has now made it public policy to support employment programs for people with mental retardation. State-funding policies were changed in 1982 to allow community colleges and other agencies to compete for training funds previously restricted to conventional centers, which had little interest in moving people out. "That one change in state law has had more impact on adults with mental retardation than anything else we could have done," says James Moss, employment-training program director at the University of Washington. "It broke a monopoly that profited more from keeping people on the welfare rolls than in getting them off. If this were to happen nationwide, the impact would be phenomenal."

School Programs Complement Other Efforts

Efforts to provide better job training and work placement for adults with mental retardation have a counterpart in the sphere of public education. Since 1975 children with handicaps have been entitled to free public education. The first wave, nearly 100,000 strong, is now finishing school at age 21 to face an adult-service system that provides few options. But some school districts are beginning to develop programs to ready such students for the workplace.

In Madison, Wisconsin, a transition teacher and several vocational teachers work closely with community agencies to provide training, placement, and follow-up services for students with mental retardation. Before the program started, only 1 of the district's 53 graduates with severe handicaps worked in a nonsheltered environment. Since it began in 1979, 47 of 61 graduates have found jobs in the community. The program saves taxpayers more than $3,000 yearly for every person working in a regular job.

But this program is still an exception. Most school programs concentrate on teaching the alphabet, rote learning, and working on puzzles instead of on developing good work habits and attitudes, according to Paul Bates, special educator at Southern Illinois University at Carbondale.

Three schools in Montgomery County, Maryland, are providing the kinds of functional training essential for independence. Students with mental retardation spend about half of each school day learning how to ride public buses, shop for food, and cook lunch at classmates' houses. They also attend school with nonhandicapped students their own age. One student, Joyce O'Malley, while living in a private residential school with autistic and mentally retarded children, had hardly spoken a word. Now she sings in the school choir, gossips with her friends, and works in a movie theater after school.

The "behavior problems" seen in young-sters with mental retardation in segregated schools often improve dramatically when they are surrounded by models of normal behavior. Jack Hanson's parents and teachers had tried unsuccessfully for 17 years to get him to stop drooling. But when his boss at a fast-food restaurant told him that he would have to shape up or be fired, Hanson stopped drooling in no time.

In the future, good school programs such as these may supplant intensive job training for many adults with mental retardation. They will also help nonhandicapped youngsters learn more about people with mental retardation. Special educator Brown says, "The best way for [all kinds of people to learn] to function effectively with people with severe handicaps is to grow up and attend school with them."

Such experience is even more crucial for those nonhandicapped students who will one day have children with mental retardation, says Brown. In his view, they may be better prepared than many parents today who are "30 to 35 years old and have never seen a person with a severe handicap except on a poster or a telethon."

Special educator Frank Rusch, of the University of Illinois, is counting on today's parents to push for adequate programs for their children with handicaps. "Parents have always been the greatest reformers in this country," he says. "They should find out what kind of vocational program their schools plan for their children, and make sure that . . . the education process results in meaningful employment upon graduation."

Job Training for Retarded a Societal Must

The innovative training programs described here, both for adults and for youth, make up only a tiny fraction of those available. But they provide a powerful demonstration that, with help, even people with severe handicaps can move from the welfare rolls to the employment rolls. The next step, in the view of advocates for this "last minority," is to see that in the future, such programs are in the majority. Both humane and economic considerations argue in their favor.

"Before the introduction of substantial welfare [benefits], it was questionable whether this society could afford to train its mentally retarded people for employment," says educator Sowers. "Today it is clear that society cannot afford not to provide such training." □

BIOLOGY

REVIEW
OF THE
YEAR

BIOLOGY

In 1984 biologists continued their war on pests, engineered births of babies conceived in places other than the wombs from which they were delivered, discovered new species, and learned more about the behavior of others.

BIOBATTLES

The war on bugs and bacteria continued at a good clip in 1984. A neurologist at the Harvard Medical School, suspecting that the reason some plants produce caffeine is to ward off insects, found powdered tea leaves and coffee beans kill tobacco hornworm larvae (immature forms of insects). The direct application of a chemical in the same class as caffeine kills mosquito larvae. The chemicals are thought to block the action of an enzyme vital to the transmission of nerve impulses in the bugs. ■ Meanwhile, Yale University chemists found a new way to kill the American cockroach that involves duplicating its natural sex attractant. Several quadrillionths of a gram of the synthetic aphrodisiac is enough to send half a dozen male cockroaches into sexual frenzies that ultimately result in death.

And in the plant world, University of Illinois biologists developed an herbicide that causes weeds to self-destruct in sunshine. The scientists exploited a biodegradable chemical, found in both plants and animals, that plants use to make light-catching chlorophyll. When the herbicide is applied, the weeds are overwhelmed by sunlight, and they wither and die. Many crop plants are able to deactivate the process and so are not destroyed.

Humans and their crops are not the only organisms faced with pests. During 1984 honeybees in the United States, in New England, the Northern Plains area, and the South were beset by parasitic mites, and a quarantine was put into effect in states with infected bees. Mother mites lay eggs in bees' windpipes, and the hatchlings suck the bees' body fluids, which weakens the bees. Scientists as yet know of no way to kill the mite without killing the bee.

Diseases also took their toll. A mysterious

Top: Dan Sheehan/Black Star; Above: The Press Association Ltd.

Top: A technician in Florida torches diseased citrus seedlings infected with a bacteria-caused canker. Left: This strange-looking cross between a goat and a sheep was created by researchers via embryo fusion.

illness hit sea urchins in the Caribbean, causing a mass die-off. Scientists from various institutions reported the near extinction of black sea urchins.

Of more direct import to humans, the $2.5 billion Florida citrus crop was threatened by citrus canker, a bacteria-caused disease that can wreak havoc on all citrus crops. The bacteria infect the leaves, twigs, and fruit of citrus plants. There is no known cure, and the diseased trees must be burned. Of interest to scientists is the fact that the bacteria responsible for the new outbreak appear unlike the bacteria pegged in recent citrus attacks in Mexico and South America.

ENGINEERED BIRTHS

Research—and success—in engineering births continued in 1984. Improved techniques in transferring and implanting embryos coupled with advances in genetics led to several novel births.

The first embryo transfer in humans was achieved. Doctors at the University of California at Los Angeles successfully washed an embryo out of one woman and implanted it in another. The baby boy may prove to be the first of many children born to women who are unable to produce their own eggs or who have genetic disorders they fear passing on to their offspring. ■ In Australia a frozen embryo was successfully thawed and implanted. With the technique of embryo freezing, a number of eggs can be collected from a female for storage and eventual use if "fresh" embryos don't make it. ■ And, in England, *in vitro* (test-tube) fertilization was used to counter male infertility. A London obstetrician collected sperm surgically removed from a man whose ejaculate contained no sperm and used them to fertilize an egg from the man's wife.

Several novel births were achieved in other mammals. Following embryo transfers, a quarter horse gave birth to a zebra, an African antelope bore a rare bongo in the first successful embryo transfer between animals from two different genera, and an infertile animal—a mule—bore a thoroughbred colt. ■ Researchers in Cambridge, England, created a goat in "sheep's clothing" by fusing cells from four- and eight-celled embryos of goats and sheep. This odd-looking crossbreed has been dubbed a geep.

Engineering at the gene level was conducted in laboratory tests by U.S. Department of Agriculture researchers, who now want to insert human growth hormone in sheep and pigs to grow bigger livestock. The work may, however, be blocked by the Foundation on Economic Trends, a group critical of genetic-engineering efforts. Through court actions, the federation delayed plans to field-test genetically engineered organisms.

Does extinct mean extinct? At the University of California at Berkeley, genes from a quagga—a relative of the horse and zebra that has been extinct for more than a century—were obtained from an old hide. The feat is believed to be the first successful cloning of genes from an extinct animal.

FASCINATING FINDS

New species—some quite exotic—were discovered during the year. Atop an 1,800-meter (6,000-foot)-high mesa in Venezuela, explorers found an isolated ecosystem sporting such bizarre creatures as caterpillars that look like cotton candy, pointy-nosed frogs, and 8-centimeter (3-inch)-long moth larvae covered with bright pink hair. Scientists claim that much of the strange flora and fauna exist nowhere else on Earth, and that the area is a laboratory of evolution. ■ Smithsonian Institution botanists discovered a previously unknown species of marine algae growing deeper and in less light than was ever believed possible. The finding has a major impact on scientists' understanding of the role plants play in marine food chains.

Smithsonian Institution scientists were also responsible for finding a "Garden of Eden" of echinoderms (the phylum of marine animals including starfishes and sea urchins) in the Bahamas. Of 120 species collected, 5 or 10 may be new to science.

And, a new species of midge (a flightless relative of the mosquito) was found in a less hospitable locale—on a glacier. With temperatures dipping as low as $-16°$ C ($3°$ F), it is not known how the tiny insect is able to survive. The midge is believed to eat bacteria and algae.

In a laboratory at Indiana University a bacterium with a peculiar method of photosynthesis was found after a student "ruined" an experiment. A flask slated for discard was noted to have a green film growing on the bottom. Close examination showed that the film was bacteria of a previously unidentified form, and possibly the descendants of the earliest photosynthesizing organisms on Earth. Photosynthesis in the newly found bacteria employs a much more primitive form of chlorophyll than that used by most photosynthetic organisms today. The bacteria lack the internal structure found in most other photosynthetic bacteria, and they cannot perform photosynthesis in the presence of oxygen. Study of these "primitive" bacteria may shed light on the development of early life-forms.

And, finally, a University of Georgia biologist has some good news regarding the giant bee, last seen more than 100 years ago: the bee, about 4 centimeters (1.5 inches) long, is buzzing around Indonesian islands. Adam Messer reports having found seven bee nests and says that despite the bee's size, its bite isn't too bad.

JOANNE SILBERNER

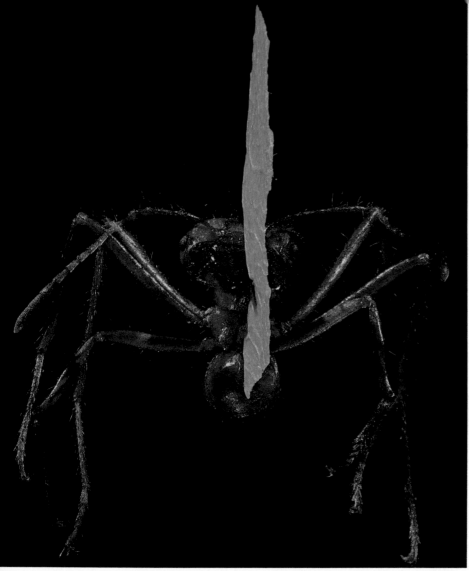

A leafcutter ant worker, shown here 25 times larger than its actual size, grasps a sliver of leaf in its jaws.

Darwin Dale

ANT GARDENERS of the AMAZON

by Edward O. Wilson

Looking for a particular species of tropical ant in the teeming diversity of the Amazonian rain forest might seem to present a problem, but this was no ordinary ant. I had arrived in Brazil, at a field station of the World Wildlife Fund, to study the leafcutter ant. The *saúva,* as it is called locally, is one of the most abundant and visually striking animals of the New World tropics. I had devoted years of research to the species in the laboratory, but had never studied it in the field.

Voracious Foragers

Part of the special fascination of the leafcutters comes from the fact that with the possible exception of a few tropical termites, they alone have evolved the ability to turn fresh vegetation into mushrooms. The evolutionary event occurred only once, millions of years ago, somewhere in South America. It gave the ants an enormous advantage: they could now send out specialized workers to collect the vegetation while keeping the bulk of their population safe in subterranean retreats. As a result, the 38 different species of leafcutters together dominate a large part of the American tropics. They consume more vegetation than any other comparable group of animals, including the more abundant forms of caterpillars, grasshoppers, birds, and mammals.

Leafcutters are also the leading agricultural pests of large portions of Central and South America. A single colony can strip an orange tree or bean patch overnight, and the combined populations inflict more than a billion dollars' worth of damage yearly. It was with good reason that the early Portuguese settlers called Brazil the Kingdom of the Ants.

Rain Forest Study Prompts Ant Observation

The field team of the World Wildlife Fund was concerned not with agricultural pests but with the ravages of agriculture on the rain forest. When a piece of primeval forest is set aside and the surrounding forest cleared, it becomes an island in an agricultural sea. The question is, How extensive must the island be to sustain permanently most or all of the kinds of plants and animals protected within its boundaries? As my hosts drove me to a campsite where I could study the leafcutters, they were in the midst of monitoring a series of experimental islands of varying sizes that would be left standing near the edge of the rain forest. It is an experiment that is expected to run into the next century.

The tropical rain forest north of Manaus, like that in many other parts of the Amazon basin, is being clear-cut from the edge inward. It is being removed from the ground like a carpet rolled from a bare floor, leaving behind vast stretches of cattle range and cropland that need artificial fertilization to sustain even marginal productivity for more than two or three years.

Although I knew of this in advance, I was still shaken by the sight of newly cleared land around Manaus. The pans (natural depressions in the land) and hillocks were littered with blackened tree stumps, and had the aspect of a freshly deserted battlefield. Spherical termite mounds sprouted from the fallen wood in an ill-fated population explosion, while vultures and swifts wheeled overhead, a few remaining representatives of bird fauna that have mostly vanished. Bony white cattle clustered in small groups around the scattered watersheds. Near midday the heat of the sun bounced up from the bare patches of soil to hit with an almost tactile force. It was another world altogether from the

Bert Hölldobler

Workers use their sharp-toothed mandibles to rapidly shear off fragments of foliage from tropical plants.

shadowed tunnels of the nearby forest, and a constant reminder of what had happened: tens of thousands of species had been scraped away as by a giant hand and will not be seen in that place for generations, if ever. The action can be defended (with difficulty) on economic grounds, but it is like burning Renaissance paintings to cook dinner.

Passing through this desolate zone, we rode in a Wildlife Fund truck to a camp just inside the forest border at Fazenda Esteio, where the biologists were conducting one of the initial surveys. I savored the cathedral feeling expressed by naturalist Charles Darwin when he first encountered tropical forest near Rio de Janeiro ("wonder, astonishment & sublime devotion, fill & elevate the mind"). I could hold still for long intervals to study tiny sections of tree trunk or ground, finding some new organism at each shift of focus.

Most of the time I worked with a restless energy to get ahead on several research projects I had in mind. I opened logs and twigs like presents on a Christmas morning, entranced by the endless variety of insects and other small creatures that scuttled away to safety. In the tropical forest, with thousands of mostly unknown species all around, the number of discoveries per investigator per day is probably greater than anywhere else in the world.

Insects Guided by Special Substance

As if to dramatize the point, the insect I most needed to find, the leafcutter ant, made its appearance soon after my arrival at Fazenda Esteio, with no effort of my own and literally at my feet. At dusk on the first day in camp, as the light failed to the point where we found it difficult to make out small objects on the ground, the first worker ants came scurrying purposefully out of the surrounding forest. They were brick red in color, about 0.6 centimeter (0.25 inch) in length, and bristling with short, needle-sharp spines. Within minutes several hundred had arrived and formed two irregular files that passed on either side of our hammock shelter. They ran in a nearly straight line across the clearing, their paired antennae scanning right and left, as though drawn by some directional beam from the other side. Within an hour the trickle expanded to twin rivers of tens of thousands of ants running ten or more abreast. The columns could be traced easily with the aid of a flashlight.

They came up from a huge earthen nest 90 meters (100 yards) from the camp on a descend-ing slope, crossed the clearing, and disappeared again into the forest. By climbing through tangled undergrowth, we were able to locate one of their main targets, a tall tree bearing white flowers high in its crown. The ants streamed up the trunk, scissored out pieces of leaves and petals with their sharp-toothed mandibles (jaws), and headed home, carrying the fragments over their heads like little parasols. Some dropped the pieces, which floated to the ground, where most were picked up and carried away by newly arriving nestmates. At maximum activity, shortly before midnight, the trails were a tumult of ants bobbing and weaving past each other like miniature mechanical toys.

For many visitors to the forest, even experienced naturalists, the foraging expeditions are the whole of the matter, and individual leafcutter ants seem to be inconsequential ruddy specks on a pointless mission. But a closer look transforms them into beings of another order. If we magnify the scene to human scale, the forager runs along the trail for a distance of about 16 kilometers (10 miles) at a velocity of 26 kilometers (16 miles) an hour. It picks up a burden of

Above: Edward S. Ross; Right: Bert Hölldobler

Antennae Serve as Sensory Centers

One millimeter (0.04 inch) above the ground, where ants exist, things are radically different from what they seem to the gigantic creatures who peer down from a thousand times that distance. The ants do not follow the trail substance as a liquid trace on the soil, as we tend to think. It comes up to them as a cloud of molecules diffusing through still air at the ground surface. They sweep their paired antennae back and forth in advance of the head to catch the odorant molecules. The antennae are the primary sensory centers of the ant. Their surfaces are furred with thousands of nearly invisible hairs and pegs, among which are scattered diminutive plates and bottleneck pits. Each of these sense organs

Left: An army of leafcutters scurry along, carting small pieces of leaves to their nest and hurrying back to their source for more. Below: Lured by the odor of a newly cut plant, two ants quickly saw through its stem.

340 kilograms (750 pounds) and speeds back toward the nest at 24 kilometers (15 miles) an hour. This marathon is repeated many times during the night, and in many localities on through the day as well.

From research conducted jointly by biologists and chemists, it is known that the ants are guided by a secretion paid (released) onto the soil through the sting, in the manner of ink being drawn out of a pen. The pure substance has an innocuous odor judged by various people to be faintly grassy, sulfurous, or fruitlike with a hint of naptha (I am not sure I can smell it at all). But whatever the impact on human beings, it is a fluid of extraordinary power for the ants. One milligram (.00004 ounce), if dispensed with theoretical maximum efficiency, is enough to excite billions of workers into activity or to lead a short column of them three times around the world. The vast difference between us and them has nothing to do with the trail substance itself, which is a biochemical material of unexceptional structure. It lies entirely in the unique sensitivity of the sensory organs and brains of the insects as opposed to those of human beings.

is serviced by cells that carry electrical impulses into the cable-like central nerve of the antenna. Then relay cells take over and transmit the messages to the integrating regions of the brain. Some of the antennal organs reach to touch, while others are sensitive to slight movements of air, so that the ant responds almost instantaneously whenever the nest is breached by intruders. But most of the sensors monitor the chemicals that swirl around the ant in combinations that change through each second of its life. Human beings live in a world of sight and sound, but social insects exist primarily by smell and taste. In a word, we are audiovisual where they are chemical.

The oddness of the insect sensory world is illustrated by the swift sequence of events that occurs along the odor trail. When a forager takes a wrong turn to the left and starts to run away from the track, its left antenna breaks out of the odor space first and is no longer stimulated by the guiding substance. In a few thousandths of a second, the ant perceives the change and pulls back to the right. Twisting right and left in response to the vanishing molecules, it follows a tightly undulating course between the nest and tree.

During the navigation it must also dodge moment by moment through a tumult of other runners. If you watch a foraging worker from a few centimeters away with the unaided eye, it seems to touch each passerby with its antennae, a kind of tactile probe. Slow-motion photography reveals that the forager is actually sweeping the tips of its antennae over parts of the other ant's body to smell it. If the surface does not present exactly the right combination of chemicals—the colony's unique odor signature—the ant attacks at once. It may simultaneously spray an alarm chemical from special glands that are located in the head capsule, causing other ants in the vicinity to rush to the site with their mandibles gaping, ready to assist.

An ant colony is organized by no more than 10 or 20 such signals, most of which are chemical secretions leaked or sprayed from glands. The workers move with swiftness and precision through a life that human beings have come to understand, as far as we do understand it, only with the aid of mathematical diagrams and molecular formulas.

Colony Organized by Size

At the end of the trail, the burdened foragers rush down the nest hole, into throngs of nest-mates and along winding channels that end near the water table 5 meters (15 feet) or more below. The ants drop the leaf sections onto the floor of a chamber, to be picked up by workers of a slightly smaller size, who clip them into fragments about 1 millimeter (0.04 inch) across. Within minutes, still smaller ants take over, crush and mold the fragments into moist pellets, and carefully insert them into a mass of similar material. This mass ranges in size from a clenched fist to a human head, is riddled with channels, and resembles a gray cleaning sponge. It is the garden of the ants: on its surface grows a symbiotic fungus that, along with the leaf sap, forms the ants' sole nourishment. (Symbiosis is the living together of two different organisms in a mutually beneficial relationship.) The fungus spreads like a white frost, sinking its hyphae (a mass of threadlike appendages) into the leaf paste to digest the abundant cellulose and proteins held there in partial solution.

The remainder of the gardening cycle proceeds. Worker ants even smaller than those just described pluck loose strands of the fungus from places of dense growth and plant them onto the newly constructed surfaces. Finally, the very smallest—and most abundant—workers patrol the beds of fungal strands, delicately probing them with their antennae, licking their surfaces clean, and plucking out the spores and hyphae of alien species of mold. These colony dwarfs are able to travel through the narrowest channels deep within the garden masses. From time to time they pull loose tufts of fungal strands resembling miniature stalked cabbage heads, and then carry them out to feed their larger nest-mates.

Virtually the entire leafcutter economy is organized around this division of labor based on size. The foraging workers, about as big as houseflies, can slice leaves but are too bulky to cultivate the almost microscopic fungal strands. The tiny gardener workers, somewhat smaller than this printed letter *i*, can grow the fungus but are too weak to cut the leaves. So the ants form an assembly line, each successive step being performed by correspondingly smaller workers, from the collection of pieces of leaves out-of-doors to the manufacture of leaf paste to the cultivation of dietary fungi deep within the nest.

The defense of the colony is also organized according to size. Among the scurrying workers can be seen a few soldier ants, 300 times heavier than the gardener workers. Their sharp mandibles are powered by massive abductor muscles that fill their swollen head capsules. Working like miniature wire clippers, they chop enemy insects into pieces and easily slice through human skin. The behemoths are especially adept at repelling large invaders. When entomologists digging into a nest grow careless, their hands become nicked all over as if pulled through a thorn bush. I have occasionally had to pause to stanch the flow of blood from a single bite, impressed by the fact that a creature one-millionth my size could stop me with nothing but its jaws.

The Making of a Queen

At full size a colony contains 3 million to 4 million workers and occupies 3,000 or more underground chambers. The earth it excavates forms a pile 6 meters (20 feet) across. Deep inside the nest sits the mother queen, a giant insect the size of a newborn mouse. She can live at least 10 years and perhaps as long as 20. In her lifetime an individual can produce more than 20 million offspring, which translates into the following: a mere 300 queen ants, a small fraction of the number emerging from a single colony in a year, can give birth to more ants than there are human beings on Earth.

Photos: Edward S. Ross

Right: A group of busy workers excavate a nest chamber by removing soil one grain at a time. Below: A procession of ants file into a nest entrance.

Above: Small workers snip new leaves into bits, which are then molded into moist pellets by other ants and added to the fungus garden. Right: A virgin queen emerges from a nest for the first time to seek a mate. After being fertilized, she will break off her wings and start a garden and colony of her own.

Top: Bert Hölldobler; Above: Edward S. Ross

The queen is born as an almost invisibly small egg among thousands laid daily by the old mother queen. The egg hatches as a grublike larva, which is fed and washed incessantly by the adult worker nurses throughout its month-long existence. Through some as yet unknown treatment, perhaps a special diet controlled by the workers, the larva grows to a relatively huge size. She then transforms into a pupa, whose waxy casement is shaped like an adult queen in fetal position, with legs, wings, and antennae folded tightly against the body. After several weeks the full complement of adult organs develops within this cuticle, and the new queen emerges. From the beginning she is fully adult and grows no more in size. She also possesses the same genes as her sisters, the colony work-

ers. Their smaller size and indistinguishable behavior is not due to heredity but to the different treatment they received as larvae.

Following a heavy rain, the virgin queen comes to the surface of the nest and flies up into the air to join other queens and the darkly pigmented, big-eyed males. Four or five males seize and inseminate her in quick succession, while she is still flying through the air. Their sole function having now been completed, they die within hours without returning to the home nest. The queen stores their sperm in her spermatheca, a tough little muscular bag located just above and behind her ovaries. These reproductive cells live like independent microorganisms for years, passively waiting until they are released into the oviduct to meet an egg and create a new female ant. If the egg passes through the oviduct and to the outside without receiving a sperm, it produces a male. The queen can control the sex of her offspring, as well as the number of new workers and queens she produces, by opening or shutting the passage leading from her sperm-storage organ to the oviduct.

The newly inseminated queen descends to the ground. Raking her legs forward, she breaks off her wings, painlessly because they are composed of dead membranous tissue. She wanders in a random pattern until she finds a patch of soft, bare soil, then commences to excavate a narrow tunnel straight down. Several hours later, when the shaft has been sunk to a depth of about 25 centimeters (10 inches), the queen widens its bottom into a small room. She is now set to start a garden and a colony of her own.

The Cycle Completed

But there is a problem in this life-cycle strategy. The queen has completely separated herself from the mother colony. Where can she obtain a culture of the vital symbiotic fungus to start the garden? Answer: she has been carrying it all along in her mouth. Just before leaving home, the young queen gathered a wad of fungus and inserted it into a little pocket in the floor of her oral cavity, just back of the tongue. Now she passes the pellet out onto the floor of the nest and fertilizes it with droplets of feces.

As the fungus proliferates in the form of a whitish mat, the queen lays eggs on and around its surface. When the young larvae hatch, they are fed with other eggs given to them by the queen. At the end of their development six weeks later, they transform into small workers. These new adults quickly take over the ordinary tasks of the colony. When still only a few days old, they proceed to enlarge the nest, work the garden, and feed the queen and larvae with tufts of the increasingly abundant fungus. In a year the little band has expanded into a force of a thousand workers, and the queen has ceased almost all activity to become a passive eating and egg-laying machine. She retains that exclusive role for the rest of her life. The measure of her success is whether some of her daughters born five or ten years down the line grow into queens, leave on nuptial flights, and—rarest of all achievements—found new colonies of their own. In the world of the social insects, by the canons of biological organizations, colonies beget colonies; individuals do not directly beget individuals.

An Intricate, Precise System

People often ask me whether I see any human qualities in an ant colony, any form of behavior that even remotely mimics human thought and feeling. Insects and human beings are separated by more than 600 million years of evolution, but a common ancestor did exist in the form of one of the earliest multicellular organisms. Does some remnant of psychological continuity exist across that immense evolutionary gulf? The answer is that I open an ant colony as I would the back of a Swiss watch. I am enchanted by the intricacy of its parts and the clean, thrumming precision with which it operates. But I never see the colony as anything more than an organic machine.

Let me qualify that diagnosis. The leafcutter colony is a superorganism. The queen sits deep in the central chambers, the vibrant growing tip from which all the workers and new queens originate. But she is not in any sense the leader or the repository of an organizational blueprint. No command center directs the colony. The social master plan is partitioned into the brains of the all-female workers, whose separate programs fit together to form a balanced whole. Each ant automatically performs certain tasks and avoids others according to its size and age. The superorganism's brain is the entire society; the workers are the crude analog of its nerve cells. Seen from above and at a distance, the leafcutter colony resembles a gigantic amoeba. Its foraging columns snake out like pseudopods (false feet) to engulf and shred plants, while their stems pull the green pieces down holes into the fungus gardens. Through a unique step in evolution taken millions of years ago, the ants captured a fungus, incorporated it into the superorganism, and so gained the power to digest leaves. Or perhaps the relation is the other way around: perhaps the fungus captured the ants and used them as a mobile extension to take leaves into the underground chambers.

In either case the two now own each other and will never pull apart. The ant-fungus combination is one of evolution's master clockworks—tireless, repetitive and precise, more complicated than any human invention, and almost unimaginably old. To find a colony in the South American forest is like coming upon some device left in place ages ago by an extraterrestrial visitor for a still-undisclosed purpose. Biologists have only begun to puzzle out its many parts, to reflect on its history and ultimate meaning ☐

Aging

by Gina Maranto

Carl Mydans/Black Star

Roy Walford is getting thin, but his diet will probably never make the best-seller lists. Since 1981 he has eaten low-calorie, high-quality foods, and has taken vitamins to provide extra nutrients. As if this restricted regime were not enough, he jogs 16 to 24 kilometers (10 to 15 miles) every week along the boardwalk in Venice, California, dodging between the skateboarders, street dancers, jugglers, and magicians.

Walford's habits are more than some California fad. One of the country's leading researchers on aging, he is performing an ongoing experiment, with his own 60-odd-year-old body as its subject. Having explored ways of prolong-ing the lives of animals in the laboratory, Walford is testing a theory that a substantial reduction of food intake can actually stave off what Ralph Waldo Emerson deemed "the only disease," the one into which "all others run": old age.

Research Enthusiasm Abounds

A burgeoning elderly population—there are now 23 million people over the age of 65 in the United States, and that figure is expected to reach 55 million by the year 2030—has prompted Walford and a growing number of other scientists to step up their studies of one of the most intractable puzzles in biology: how and why organisms inexorably slide into feebleness and, finally, death. The federal government joined this search by forming the National Institute on Aging (NIA) in 1974 to pursue biomedical research aimed at easing the plight of the elderly in coming decades. Although still an immature field, gerontology, the study of the aging process, has gained respectability among senior researchers as well as among many young scientists just embarking on investigative careers. "The establishment of the NIA has confirmed that there are questions to be asked, and that they are good ones," says Richard Greulich, the NIA's scientific director.

At three major conferences held recently on various aspects of aging, enthusiasm ran high. Lewis Thomas, the eminent physician and writer, underlined this new mood at a meeting on the cellular basis of aging held at the Brookhaven National Laboratory on Long Island in October 1984. "There is the most surprising optimism, amounting to something almost like exhilaration, in the community of basic biological researchers," he said. The excitement comes not so much from a new understanding of how to prevent the diseases to which aging bodies fall prey—including dementia, cancer, arthritis, heart disease, and pneumonia—nor even of how to minimize many of the aches and sensory failures that accompany the normal aging process. Instead, it comes from a suspicion among researchers that they are finally finding out just how cells work. This knowledge of fundamentals may eventually enable scientists to ease the infirmities of aging, even if they cannot eliminate them.

The Undernutrition Connection

The roots of current aging research—in particular, on undernutrition—go back at least 40 years, to experiments by Clive McCay of Cornell University in New York. McCay drastically underfed young rats and found that he was able to extend their customary life span of about three years by a third or more. At the University of California at Los Angeles in the early 1970's, Walford achieved similar results with fish, merely by lowering their body temperatures. Combining the two techniques on mice, Walford and his colleague Richard Weindruch have found that these methods can lengthen life even when they are begun with adult animals.

Although not terribly germane (appropriate and relevant) to human beings, these experiments served to spark further investigation. Re-

Zimberoff/Gamma Liaison

By significantly underfeeding mice, aging expert Roy Walford was able to extend their usual life spans.

searchers reasoned that near-starvation, or the kind of active hibernation Walford induced in fish, may have retarded degeneration by blocking the biochemical processes that usually bring it on. For example, Walford has observed that many of the immune-system deficiencies that accompany aging can be avoided by undernutrition.

Accounting for Cellular Failures

Research done in the past several years has revealed that many alterations in cells accompany the more evident effects of aging. The cells of older creatures are able to carry out only haltingly the tasks that keep the body going, such as utilizing nutrients, removing wastes, repairing gene damage, and manufacturing vital protein molecules. In short, elderly cells, like the organism they form, have lost the ability to function efficiently.

Nearly every gerontologist has put forward, or at least mulled over, his own pet explanation of how these cellular failures occur. But because no biochemical tools for studying cell function within the body yet exist, scientists are still at the stage of constructing theories. In recent years their hypotheses have tended to fall into two broad groupings: wear-and-tear theories, based on the assumption that the inescapable ravages of the environment do cells in; and genetic-clock theories, which assume that the genetic makeup of the body dictates its demise. Much current research, then, attempts to determine whether human beings are biologically fated to the biblical threescore and ten (70 years), or whether certain practices might enable them to live well past that age, "zipping," as Lewis Thomas put it, "from tennis court to deathbed at age, say, a hundred and twenty."

DNA-Mutation Theory Now Doubted

One of the earliest wear-and-tear theories, now generally discredited, held that aging was merely the result of a buildup of mutations in a cell's governing mechanism—its long chains of DNA (deoxyribonucleic acid). Millions of these little errors occur over the course of an organism's life. DNA, which controls the production of proteins by cells, is easily damaged. When exposed to such things as changes in body chemistry, ultraviolet radiation, or toxins (poisonous substances), the long double strands of DNA may break or shear, sometimes losing in the process some of the bases, or nucleotides, that make up the rungs of its spiral-staircase structure. The substitution or loss of even a single base in a gene can foul up the production line. According to this view, as more mutations occur along the DNA chains, the cell becomes less able to craft protein properly, and consequently less able to function. The organism is gradually crippled.

Neat as this theory is, it fails to take into account the cells' prodigious ability to repair themselves. In young, healthy cells, DNA is constantly being reconstructed by enzymes that cut out incorrect or faulty nucleotides and patch in new ones. Takatoshi Ishikawa of the Cancer Institute in Tokyo, Japan, estimates that during a human lifetime of 70 years, the cell's indomitable enzymes—proteins themselves—may perform nearly 128 billion repair jobs. Since DNA is so well maintained, most researchers now think it unlikely that mutations could accumulate to a point that would overwhelm the entire organism. Bernard Strehler of the University of Southern California (USC) insists, "Such mutations are not responsible for age changes."

Harmful Proteins or Other Chemical Culprits?

Instead, says Strehler, one of the foremost molecular biologists in the field, "aging may be the loss of very, very few key genes." A single error in a crucial gene—say, in one responsible for manufacturing an enzyme that carries out DNA repair—could lead to the demise of an entire cell line after several generations. Researchers have put this type of wear and tear under the "error catastrophe" theory, and it would seem to cover any number of age-related protein changes. Robert Gracy of North Texas State University has noticed at least three such changes in enzymes: they become less stable, less efficient, and less plentiful.

But these alterations may not in fact be the product of conventional mutations, of breaks in DNA, or the deletion or mixing up of bases. Instead, some researchers suggest, mothballed genes may somehow be revved up after a certain amount of time, and begin cranking out proteins harmful to the cell. James Smith of the virology and epidemiology department at Baylor College of Medicine in Houston, Texas, suspects that one such protein might prevent cell division. He fused old cells with young ones, and found that the hybrids were unable to make copies of their DNA, a necessary step in cellular reproduction. He theorizes that "the old cells produced a protein, probably on their surface, that blocked DNA reproduction in the young cells. But we haven't yet isolated it."

Other researchers pinpoint other chemical culprits disruptive to cells, including the metabolic products lipofuscin (a fatty, brown pigment) and glucose (a sugar). Lipofuscin, created when the body breaks down fats, is found within cells and collects with age. Scientists agree that cells choked with the pigment cannot work correctly. But some contend that lipofuscin accumulation does not bring on aging; it merely indicates that it is occurring.

Glucose, on the other hand, may actually be a prime cause of aging. Researchers led by biochemist Richard Bucala at Rockefeller University in New York have discovered that glucose damages proteins, including collagen, the main component of the connective tissue that supports and enmeshes cells. In a test tube, glucose binds collagen fibers together, and such linking has been observed in the tissues of elderly people as well. It also occurs in cooking (for instance, in the skin of a broiling chicken). "In a sense," says Bucala, "we may all be baking at 98.6 degrees [F, or 37° C]."

Bucala and his colleagues have further found that glucose can accrete (become attached) along the DNA helix itself. With time, the protein-making genetic machinery could be jammed by the glucose-derived deposits.

DISCOVER Magazine, Time Inc.

Evelyn and Bill in 1944

Wayne Sorce

Evelyn and Bill in 1984

Free Radicals Considered Major Factor by Some

Cell workings could also be gummed up by free radicals, which are unstable molecules containing only a single electron in their outer shells. Any molecule can be transformed into a free radical by natural means, including the body's processing of oxygen, or by contact with such substances as smog or cigarette smoke. Some free radicals are especially menacing in cells because they steal electrons from the atoms of otherwise stable biological molecules, which creates more free radicals and thus a series of biological chain reactions. Says Denham Harman, a physician and biochemist at the University of Nebraska: "They're produced in small quantities continuously. Some are normal and necessary for sustaining life, but others are a constant source of damage." Older cells are packed with them. Harman is convinced that free-radical reactions are the major factor in aging. "There is accumulating evidence," he says, "that the sum of these reactions constitutes the aging process or is a major contributor to it."

Other investigators do not accept the free-radical theory, yet they support the contention that cells are damaged primarily by the mutability of molecular fortune. They believe that organisms do not run down as some master genetic clock slows, but fail here and there, as a spring pops out or a gear jams.

Gerald Davis/Contact

Leonard Hayflick, a proponent of the genetic-clock theory of aging, believes that cells are programmed to die.

Is Prolonged Life Possible . . . ?

If wear and tear at the molecular level is in fact the prime cause of aging, couldn't researchers find ways to guard cells against attacks, and so prolong life? Some scientists are convinced that the answer is yes, and they are hunting for ways to do it. Free radicals are a main target. A class of chemicals known as antioxidants may thwart the toxic effects of free radicals by making them more stable chemically, and thus less likely to react with passing molecules. Vitamin E is an antioxidant, as is carotene, a substance found in vegetables that the body converts to vitamin A. In mice, says Harman, "antioxidants increase the average life expectancy by 20 percent or more, and decrease the incidence of diseases associated with aging." Skeptics, however, doubt that antioxidants will prove to be elixirs of eternal youth. "In experiments done years ago," says Smith, "we found that antioxidants didn't extend the life of cells in culture."

Another possible retardant might be limiting food intake. Harman proposes that reduced feeding may cut down on free radicals in cells and lengthen maximum life span. Walford reports that mice receiving 30 to 40 percent fewer calories than normal live 20 to 50 percent longer than control mice on normal diets. These findings are confirmed by Edward Masoro, chairman of the physiology department at the University of Texas health science center in San Antonio, who has found that any limited healthy diet can extend the life of laboratory animals.

Neither Walford nor Masoro knows why cutting down the amount eaten yields such striking results, although Masoro has ruled out some explanations. For example, food restriction does not appear to work through the hormones that trigger growth and development; nor does it slow the rate of metabolism as hibernation does. In addition to experimenting on himself, Walford is also exploring what happens when food restriction is begun early in a laboratory animal's life, and is looking for ways to monitor the cellular effects.

Masoro remains dubious. "People dig up a lot of anecdotal evidence to say that there is a connection between rat and human data," he says. ". . . I don't think there's any logic in saying we're going to get past 105 or 110 years for humans."

. . . Or Is Time to Die Preprogrammed?

In that respect, Masoro is in agreement with proponents of genetic-clock theories, who argue that death is programmed. At a certain point in an animal's life, they think, something is triggered, either within individual cells or by the brain, or both, that tells the cells it is time to die. Leonard Hayflick, head of the Center for Gerontological Studies at the University of Florida, observed in 1961 that a population of normal cells from human embryonic tissue will double only about 50 times in the laboratory before dying. Still, Hayflick is quick to point out that his observation is merely an example of aging at the cellular level rather than its cause. "Cell division is only one cell process," he explains. "I don't believe cells or human beings die because cells stop dividing, but from functional changes that occur before cell division stops."

W. Donner Denckla, formerly a biochemist at Harvard University in Cambridge, Massachusetts, thinks that the key change may be the secretion by the pituitary gland of a "death hormone," released over the course of an animal's life, beginning at puberty. Denckla left research in 1980 after his funding was cut amid considerable controversy over his theories. But before doing so, he had managed to produce some signs of aging in young rats by giving them a crudely isolated form of this hormone. In other rats, he reported having delayed signs of aging by removing their pituitaries and dosing the rats with other hormones. Denckla may be the only researcher to have succeeded in making the clock run backward.

No one really knows why some people suffer illnesses that result in early deaths while others, such as these Russian centenarians, exceed average human life spans robustly.

John Launois/Black Star

Interacting Centers in Body May Lead to Demise

Complex as it is, aging may not be entirely genetic or entirely environmental. Caleb Finch, a neurologist at USC, suggests that the events leading to cellular demise form an "interacting cascade." In his view, no one master clock exists; cells in different parts of the body age at different rates. At the same time, he points out, there is no reason to assume that any cell is exempt from interaction. Finch's experiments have shown that the pituitary gland and the ovaries are linked; when the pituitary of a mouse is removed, the ovaries age more slowly. Finch likens the body to the economy, contending that several centers control aging. "There is no single pacemaker, but there are changes in many locations at many levels. What controls the economy? The Federal Reserve? The banks? The import-export ratio? They all interact at different levels."

Aiming for Life-Quality Improvement

Despite the many discoveries that have been made in recent years about how cells age, scientists still do not know why some people live to be 80 or 85, robust, able to see and hear only slightly less well than in their youth; and why others must traverse a painful path on their way to a miserable death.

Before scientists can produce answers to these questions, more basic research must be done, and more long-term studies, like the Bal-timore Longitudinal Study of Aging, which has been tracking more than 700 men for over 25 years, must be launched. Richard Greulich expects the study to continue for at least another 25 years, investigating, among other things, why women, who were added to the project in 1978, live longer than men.

At present, science can offer no antidotes to aging, no magic potion, no fountain of youth—only some tantalizing clues about what may be governing this inevitable process. The NIA's goal is to improve life, rather than to extend it, director Greulich emphasizes: "We're interested in the quality, not the quantity, of life." Research into the causes of aging will probably continue to take a secondary role to inquiries into its effects. Says Greulich: "Most old people don't give a [darn] how they got that way." Indeed, many researchers argue that the proper role of gerontology is not to search for the key to immortality but to find ways of improving the lot of the swelling number of old people □

SELECTED READINGS

"Biomarkers: beating body burnout" by Ruth Winter and Judith Groch. *American Health,* May 1984.

"Life spans" by Mary Batten. *Science Digest,* February 1984.

"Seeking clues to the mystery of aging" by Barbara Ford. *National Wildlife,* December 1983–January 1984.

The Dynamics of Aging by Forrest J. Berghorn et al. West-view Press, 1981.

Illustrations by Cameron Gerlach

Eavesdropping on Trees

by Jeanne McDermott

A drive through the countryside of eastern Pennsylvania offers a welcome respite from the hustle of the city, especially in the spring. Sunlight showers through an oak forest whose leaves are still curled tight as a fist, ready to open as winter relinquishes its grip. In the orchards, apple trees stand in neat rows, arranged in splendid isolation, pink blossoms fluttering in the wind. The pastel landscape breathes a bucolic peace, wooded tranquillity. Or so it seems. "I look at trees in a different way now," says Ian Baldwin, doctoral student in biology at Cornell University in New York.

Tree "Talk" No Longer a Myth

Baldwin, along with David Rhoades, a zoologist at the University of Washington, and Jack Schultz, an entomologist at Pennsylvania State University, have been eavesdropping on leaves since 1981, and much to everyone's surprise, including their own, they have evidence that trees "talk." Not to you and me but to each other. While these scientists are far from identifying the nuances of a dialect or the rules of a grammar, they suggest that there is a chemical language of the forest and that it functions as an early-warning system to protect trees from insect attack. The hypothesis is not yet out of the woods, but it marks a marvelous turning point in our view of trees.

The idea that trees talk seems, at first, worthy of Dr. Dolittle or Grimm's fairy tales. Who would believe that trees truly have more bark than bite? Who would imagine that if a tree falls in the woods and no one is around, its fellow trees might hear the crash? The concept of a tree—as an abiding fixture of the landscape, long-lasting pillar of the plant kingdom, alive only in a vegetable way—is deep-rooted. Noah did not load the Ark, two by two, with saplings and seedlings. You might say that trees have been taken for granted and underestimated ever since.

Plant-Defense Study Leads to Discovery

Davey Rhoades, who has a doctorate in both chemistry and zoology, was the first to suggest that trees can communicate. Rhoades combines an adventurous streak with a naturalist's quiet desire to understand the broad picture. His office, with its working clutter of paper stacks and half-shut drawers, overlooks droopy evergreen treetops. "I wasn't looking for plant communication," he says. "I stumbled on it. It was serendipitous. I was looking at how plants defend themselves from insect attack."

In the spring of 1979, Rhoades worked at a field site outside Seattle, Washington, studying what happens to willow trees when tent caterpillars attack. Rhoades paired the trees into two groups, one for the experiment and one nearby for the control. He infested the experimental trees with caterpillars and left the control trees alone. Fourteen days later he plucked leaves off the experimental trees, fed them to caterpillar larvae (immature insects) in the laboratory, and found that these caterpillars grew quite slowly. What surprised Rhoades was that a diet of leaves from the unattacked control trees made the laboratory caterpillars grow slowly, too. Both trees had apparently flooded their leaves with an unsavory chemical that discouraged the insects' growth.

What made the unattacked trees produce a nasty-tasting chemical? Presumably, they had

Scientists now suggest that plants can communicate (opposite) to warn each other of insect infestations (below).

no reason to arm themselves since they had not been attacked. Did the experimental trees slip the control trees a signal? Rhoades wondered. He made sure that there wasn't any connection between the roots of the plants and concluded, at a talk he gave in 1982, that the trees did communicate by releasing a chemical into the air.

"Communication was the most parsimonious [stingy] explanation of the data," says Gordon Orians, professor of zoology at the University of Washington and Rhoades' colleague. It was also a radical and unprecedented explanation that raised more than a few eyebrows. While Orians is quick to declare that Rhoades is a careful experimenter, he suspects that this initial work on tree communication will look "quaint and fuzzy" 10 years from now when more far-ranging studies have been done.

Plants Are Not Passive or Helpless

"I should caution you," says Tom Eisner, Cornell biologist and a founder of the field of chemical ecology. "I don't feel that the evidence for tree communication is quite compelling yet. For any unusual idea, that evidence has to be ironclad. But the theoretical basis—that it pays to eavesdrop on the troubles of one's neighbors—is compelling." In fact, the essence of the research so excites Eisner that he proposed to teach a course on plant behavior, the first one ever offered at Cornell.

Rhoades seems comfortable with the fact that he has gone out on a scientific limb, yet is at a loss to explain why he noticed something that other researchers missed. "The plant-communication experiment could have been done 100 years ago," he says, adding that it did not involve any fancy, high-technology equipment. He admits that his own thinking was shaped by the knowledge that insects frequently communicate using airborne chemicals called pheromones. But at the base of Rhoades' search lies a keen and profound dissatisfaction with the traditional view of plants.

That view maintained that plants are passive, helpless bystanders, acted upon rather than acting upon their environment. What changed that belief was the observation that plants carry and release an impressive, ever-changing array of thousands of chemical compounds whose functions have still not been fully cataloged, inspected, or analyzed. For years, botanists ignored these often exotic compounds, assuming them to be waste products without any crucial role in the plant's life. But eventually a few

voices argued that plants are too thrifty to waste their energy manufacturing useless substances.

Meanwhile, scientists had discovered that plants possess uncanny ways to disarm their enemies, actively and on the spur of the moment rather than passively. Not only do plants hide behind their woody armor, they also fight back when provoked. In the early 1970's, Peter Albersheim, a biochemist at the University of Colorado, launched a study on how fungi can trigger plants to produce antifungal substances known as phytoalexins. At the same time, biochemist Clarence Ryan at Washington State University discovered how potato plants produce a powerful inhibitory protein within hours of being munched by beetles.

Weapons and Tactics to Deter and Destroy

"Like any other organism, plants have one common goal in life—to grow up and reproduce," says Baldwin. "In order to do that, they have to live long enough, they have to defend themselves." Suddenly, the mysterious compounds were seen to have a purpose. At least some researchers came to view plants more as if they were slow animals, forced by their immobility to develop in subtler ways. A plant cannot run away, bare its teeth, or spray a foul odor. It can fold up its leaves or expose its thorns, but the most spectacular and unexplored defenses operate on a molecular level.

Trees excel at chemical defense. They have no choice. Trees may live for centuries, and thus longevity distinguishes them from other plants. Unlike weeds, trees stand and combat their enemies year in and year out from the same spot. A hundred different species of insects and nematodes (parasitic worms), not to mention untold numbers of bacteria and fungi, chomp and devour, nibble and munch. "There's always something chewing on a tree. At the end of the season, every leaf has some damage," says Rhoades. Pests mutate easily and seemingly overnight concoct more virulent ways to attack a tree or more cunning tricks to avoid its countermeasures.

This "arms race" is a no-win situation even though trees spend more of their budget on defense than anything else. "What stops any arms race from spiraling out of control is the cost," says Rhoades. "Up to 50 percent of a tree may be composed of things that are defensive. These chemical compounds are costly to synthesize because they are often present in large quantities."

Trees concentrate their chemical weapons at the most vulnerable sites—the leaves—and employ a staggering variety of tactics to deter and destroy their insect enemies. Trees produce tannins; the same type of compound that gives the skin of the unripe apple its bitter taste also gives the insect a bad case of indigestion. They make alkaloids that wreak havoc with the insect's nervous system. They concoct dummy amino acids that the insect mistakes for the real thing and uses to produce defective proteins. Not only do the trees possess most of these unsavory chemicals from birth to death, but they can synthesize them on the spot, in hours or days.

Seeking the Chemical of Communication

Of all the defensive tactics that trees muster, communication may be the most sophisticated and the most baffling. Are all trees equally fluent? Can oak trees talk only to oak trees? Do weeping willows understand Sitka willows? Have insects learned how to jam a tree's message—for example, by attaching a counteracting chemical to the message molecules even as the insects are eating the leaves? No one knows.

It seems likely that trees communicate about more than defense. Rhoades thinks some topics are more likely than others. Communication may help synchronize flowering to facilitate cross-pollination and foil insects that eventually eat the fruit of the flower. For example, if the fruit on apple trees all ripens simultaneously, the apple maggots will not have as much time to reproduce—and, more importantly, to devastate the crop.

No one will really decipher what trees are saying until the chemical involved in communication is isolated. Rhoades is now in hot pursuit. He collects the gases emitted by leaves in a specially sealed, brightly lit laboratory. Clamping a petri dish over a torn leaf, he suctions the gases off, collects them in ampules, and then analyzes the contents in the gas chromatograph—an instrument used for identifying unknown compounds. Rhoades flips through readouts from the gas chromatograph, long ribbons of paper covered with thousands of jerky spikes, each of which represent a unique molecule. It is next to impossible to pinpoint which peaks and troughs carry the meaningful signal without a lucky hunch or a lot of testing. To some scientists, the search would seem overwhelming, but Rhoades is optimistic. "The phenomenon of tree communication won't be established until we have our hands on an active plant product with which we can affect the plant's behavior," he says.

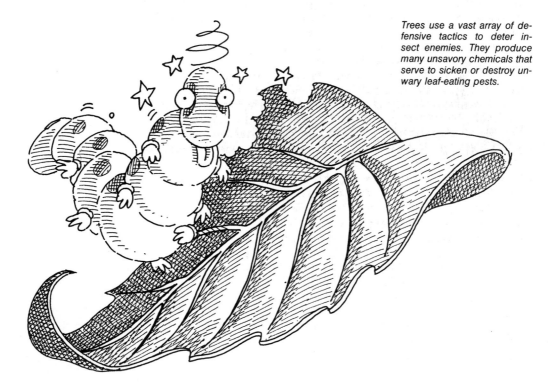

Trees use a vast array of defensive tactics to deter insect enemies. They produce many unsavory chemicals that serve to sicken or destroy unwary leaf-eating pests.

Besides coordinating strategies to ward off insects, trees may facilitate cross-pollination via chemical communication.

Plant Experiment Prompts Public Awareness

Rhoades is not the only one to hear trees talk. When Jack Schultz, who knew Rhoades from their days as graduate students at the University of Washington, heard about the communication experiments, he could not resist trying some of his own. At the time, Schultz was teaching at Dartmouth College in Hanover, New Hampshire, and was taking a census of the local insect populations, a project for which he had hired Ian Baldwin, then an undergraduate, to climb trees. After Baldwin took an intellectual interest in the tree-communication possibility, Schultz commandeered a few shelves in a crowded campus greenhouse for experiments.

Instead of working outdoors, Baldwin and Schultz potted 45 poplar plants. They placed 30 of them in a chamber together, and the remaining 15 in a faraway chamber. Then, rather than subject the trees in the first chamber to insect attack, they mechanically ripped the leaves of

15 of them, leaving the other 15 untouched. After 52 hours had passed, they analyzed the leaves, looking for specific noxious compounds that insects disdain, called phenolics. They found that the leaves from both the ripped and the unripped trees in the first chamber showed significant increases of phenolics. Leaves from unharmed poplars in the faraway chamber showed no such change.

"I was home when Ian got the first results," says Schultz. "He said, 'Hey, poplars talk!'" Baldwin and Schultz published their findings in the journal *Science,* and immediately received a worldwide blitz of attention. The odd but pleasing possibility that trees talk delighted the public imagination.

Trees May Play Major Role in Insect Outbreaks

Now a professor at Pennsylvania State University in State College, Schultz continues to investigate tree communication, but now he emphasizes its influence on insect outbreaks. Like epidemics, insect outbreaks trigger panic, especially among paper and lumber companies, who hate to see their profits literally eaten up. A few cyclical insects, like the 17-year cicada, appear punctually and at regular intervals; but many important pests, like the spruce budworm, forest tent caterpillar, or the gypsy moth, arrive at irregular intervals that defy prediction. The blame has been laid on everything from climate changes to bird populations, but scientists still fail to predict exactly what triggers the outbreaks. Although Schultz doubts that there is a single trip-wire event, he believes that the plant is the pivot, the point on which all other variables turn. "What roles does the tree play in reducing an outbreak?" That is the question that Schultz wants to answer.

Outbreaks occur frequently in monocultures (populations of a single kind of plant), where communication may be most likely to occur. "In the case of the gypsy-moth caterpillar, the caterpillar drops on his silk if he does not like a tree," Schultz says. "It might be advantageous for a tree to appear less appetizing when organisms are swinging from tree to tree."

But Schultz also suggests that communication between two trees may not be as important as communication between leaves on the same tree. He sees a tree as a mosaic of leaves, each of which adopts a different defense strategy. "The tree keeps the insect guessing and thus at a disadvantage," says Schultz. "It is a shell game." Like the pebble concealed under one of three shells, the tasty leaves are hidden among

Unattacked trees growing near caterpillar-infested ones will also produce bitter chemicals to repel the pests.

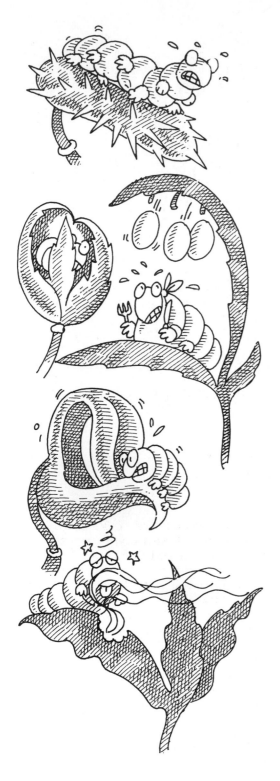

the poisonous ones, forcing the insect to sample and scavenge for its meal. The tree and the insect have evolved a workable peace in which the tree slows the evolution of the insect (which would change the terms of the conflict) by satisfying its enemy some of the time, and yet the tree avoids destruction by destroying its enemy some of the time, too. Although the evidence is slim, Schultz argues that intratree communication would allow the leaves to coordinate a defense strategy when faced with an onslaught.

Oak Study May Pay Off in Better Pest Control

Schultz will be entertaining these ideas as he conducts a three-year study on the changing defense patterns of red oak trees at a field site near the university. By hand, he and his crew are defoliating 70 percent of the leaf area on one set of trees, 30 percent on another set, and leaving one set untampered. Then they will place gypsy-moth caterpillars on the leaves, monitor how well they grow, and analyze how the compounds in the leaves change over time. At the end of the summer, they will collect the larvae and place them back on the same trees in the spring. They will repeat the experiments for two more years to see if and how defensive changes induced by caterpillars persist.

It would be to the tree's advantage to learn from the past. Rhoades speculates that trees may be able to acquire immunity from insect enemies, just as we acquire immunity from chicken pox after we develop it once as children. In order to develop immunity, the tree would have to first recognize the insect as a dangerous one, itself a quirky and poorly understood process. If trees do acquire immunity, it probably wears off after a few years and, in fact, its loss may be involved in triggering cyclical pest outbreaks.

The research on tree communication may pay off with better pest management, with an approach that succeeds where the wholesale spraying of pesticides has largely failed. If evergreens do develop an immunity to the spruce budworm, then it might be counterproductive to kill the insect off immediately. It might be better to wait and not spray at the first sign of infestation but let the plant marshal its own defenses. Another possibility is equally intriguing. If tree communication has evolved, plant breeders might be able to select for new species that "speak" in particularly loud and robust tones. Forget the whispering pines. Bring out the hollering poplars.

Researcher Jack Schultz believes that communication between leaves on a single tree allows each leaf to adopt a different method of foiling hungry insects.

Scientists may someday be able to breed species for their "vocality," resulting in better pest control.

Intentional or Incidental?

Still, a conflict arises over how tree communication might have evolved. In the conventional view, there appears to be no evolutionary reason, no selective advantage, for one tree to send messages to another. In simplified terms, if two trees are genetically different—that is, if they are not clones—then they are in competition for resources and the attacked tree does not in any way gain or benefit from communication. On the other hand, there is an evolutionary advantage for one tree to receive messages from its ailing neighbors. It is unclear at this point whether tree communication is active (that is, initiated by the attacked tree) or passive (that is, perceived by the neighboring tree). "I would like to think that it is active, that there is an organized behavior of plants," says Rhoades. "But that is really a fond hope."

Although the hypothesis that trees communicate remains unproved, it is attractive enough to draw other researchers. Thomas Kimmerer at the University of Kentucky is investigating the phenomenon in cottonwoods. In 1983 Dave Perry and Gary Pitman at Oregon State University began investigating the possibility that it occurs between Douglas firs. They had been monitoring the chemical defenses used by Douglas firs against the Western spruce budworm when an epidemic broke out near their test site. Suddenly, the chemical-defense system of their test trees changed in an unexpected way. Had a warning message been released? Perry hopes to know soon.

In the meantime, scientists will never contemplate trees in quite the same way. "There is a large unseen behavioral repertoire of plants that has not yet been explored because we haven't known where to look. It is the unseen that fascinates me," says Ian Baldwin. And it is the unseen that has shaken our knowledge of trees to the very roots □

"Do you mean to say you think you've discovered an infectious disease of bacteria, and you haven't told me about it?" the chief asks young Martin Arrowsmith in Sinclair Lewis' novel of the same name. "My dear boy, I don't believe you quite realize that you may have hit on the supreme way to kill pathogenic [disease-causing] bacteria."

Long-Forgotten Notion Gains New Favor

The very idea that bacteria could be demolished by even tinier parasites sounds suspiciously like a diversion into fantasy by this fine American novelist. But it was nothing of the sort. When *Arrowsmith* came out in 1925, hopes were very much alive for combating infection in exactly this fashion. Sinclair Lewis, in writing this book, had help from Paul de Kruif, a bacteriologist and author of a popular book called *Microbe Hunters*. The golden age of antibiotics was still far in the future, and physicians were desperate for tools to fight well-understood but frequently fatal diseases such as pneumonia, tuberculosis, cholera, and diphtheria.

But the ingenious notion of attacking large germs with smaller germs didn't prove practicable in the world of fact or fiction. So it was discarded and became a mere footnote in accounts of the history of microbiology—until very recently. In one of medical science's startling twists, two British bacteriologists have demonstrated that bacteria responsible for maladies such as meningitis and enteritis can be dealt with in this way. Experiments so far have all been on animals. But H. Williams Smith, head of the department of microbiology at Houghton Poultry Research Station, in Huntingdon, England, and his colleague Michael Huggins already have set infectious-disease specialists pondering a radically new strategy for tackling diarrheal diseases that cause human misery and mortality throughout the Third World.

The First Discovery of Phages

The story began nearly three-quarters of a century ago. In 1915 Frederick Twort, working at the Brown Institution in London, England, reported a "transparent dissolving material" that

ATTACK of the PHAGES

by Bernard Dixon

seemed to attack bacteria. Two years later Felix d'Herelle, a Canadian on the staff of the Pasteur Institute in Paris, France, described an "invisible microbe" that destroyed the bacterial strain responsible for dysentery. Twort and d'Herelle soon realized they had stumbled upon a previously unknown group of viruses, similar to those that infect animals and plants. D'Herelle called these parasites "bacteriophages"—which means, literally, bacteria eaters.

D'Herelle and Twort's theory that phages could combat bacterial diseases quickly became fashionable, but experimental results were mediocre. While phages destroyed bacteria with great ease in the laboratory, they often failed to perform as well when patients swallowed tumblerfuls. The whole idea was eventually abandoned after Twort and d'Herelle died.

Better Knowledge of Virology Prompts Reinvestigation of Phage Therapy

Today, however, the stage is set for what might be the far-reaching culmination of the saga. Working with farm animals, Williams Smith

and Michael Huggins have found that phages work extremely well against bacteria inside the body—a finding that will give veterinarians a new, probably better method of treating rapidly spreading intestinal diseases in livestock. More important, phage therapy could prove equally effective for humans. Diseases such as cholera are caused by related bacteria, and while antibiotics are now used for such diseases, more and more frequently the drugs are ineffective because the bacteria involved are resistant.

Smith began his studies in 1981 after puzzling over the disappointing results of earlier investigators who used phages to treat cholera and dysentery in humans. As viruses are now understood, Smith knew this tactic ought to work.

Bacteriophages contain genetic material, either DNA (deoxyribonucleic acid) or RNA (ribonucleic acid), and they multiply dramatically when conditions are right. Phage invasion begins when the virus attaches itself to a vulnerable spot on the surface of the bacterium. The phage then injects its DNA or RNA, which co-

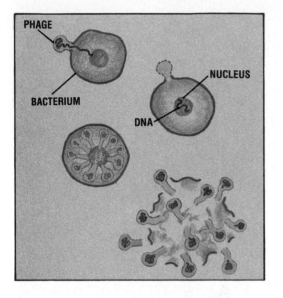

After attaching itself to a bacterium, a bacteriophage injects its genetic material (DNA or RNA), which orders the bacterium to make hundreds of new phages. Eventually the bacterial cell bursts, releasing the viral army.

opts (takes over) the bacterium's own genetic material to clone crops of new phage particles. In about an hour, an army of phages fills the bacterial cell, smashes it open, and moves on to others.

Intensive study of this genetic process, in fact, provided much of the evidence upon which noted biochemist Max Delbrück and his collaborators laid the foundations for molecular biology in the 1940's. Moreover, virologists now recognize countless different phages, each with a specific relationship to a type of sensitive bacteria. Surely such carefully selected microparasites should demolish invading bacteria.

Successful Results in First Tests with Mice

Smith and Huggins' first efforts at Houghton centered on a type of *Escherichia coli*—bacteria that normally live harmlessly in the intestines of humans as well as other animals but occasionally appear in virulent form (a form capable of overcoming the body's defenses). The strain they chose had caused meningitis in a human infant. After growing the bacterium in their laboratory, the scientists went ''fishing'' for a phage to attack it. They screened samples of sewage—a bacterial environment that supports great numbers of phage types—and isolated one that was particularly devastating against the *Escherichia coli* strain. They injected it into mice with infections induced from the same microbe.

Smith and Huggins found that the phage not only cured the infections but was more effective than four out of five of the antibiotics that they compared it with. Unlike those dismal failures in the past, the phage's performance in an infected body reflected its activity in a test tube. There was more good news as well. Although a few *Escherichia coli* mutants, resistant to the phage, did emerge during treatment, they had little virulence. The resistant mutants lacked the surface attack point necessary for phage entry, the same spot that carries enzymes associated with virulence. Antibiotics employ different strategies for assaulting bacteria, and resistant bacteria tend to be as virulent as the parent strains, or more so.

Phages Overcome Livestock Infections

The Houghton scientists next decided to attack bacteria responsible for diarrheal infections. Again they chose strains of *Escherichia coli*, this time those that cause considerable losses to farmers because of their rapid spread in calves, piglets, and lambs. And again they used sewage to find phages capable of destroying the bacteria when cultured artificially.

In one series of tests, Smith and his colleagues gave calves lethal doses, by mouth, of an infectious *Escherichia coli* strain. They then fed them a mixture of two phages and found that it protected the animals against this otherwise fatal infection if given before diarrhea had started, though not if given afterward. The phages were combined to help combat naturally occurring resistant mutants, and worked by preventing the bacteria from becoming established in great numbers. The scientists also found that, contrary to what Twort and d'Herelle had found, one of the phages seemed to be much more effective in sick animals than in laboratory cultures. When they tried replacing the weaker of the two phage types with a third, the new mixture worked well even if infection was well established and the calves had diarrhea.

Smith and Huggins then launched phages against another variety of *Escherichia coli* in piglets and found that only one phage type was needed to cure diarrhea. In contrast to the studies with calves, resistant mutants were not a problem, and it wasn't necessary to use a second phage to achieve a cure. When lambs were tested, the outcome was less dramatic, though here again a single phage ameliorated the course of infection.

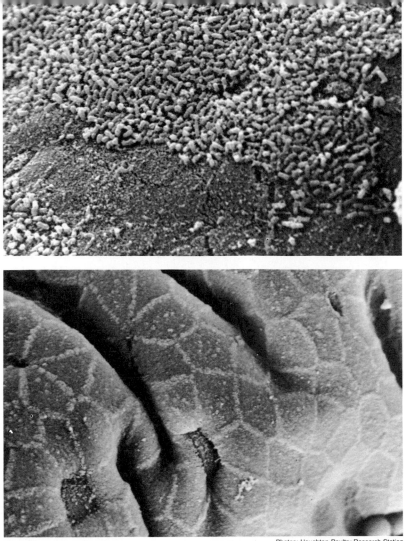

These micrographs compare the small intestine of an infected calf before and after treatment with phages. At top, the calf's intestine is coated with Escherichia coli *bacteria.* Below, no bacteria remain after phages were applied.

Photos: Houghton Poultry Research Station

Phages Far Superior to Antibiotics

So history, it seems, is being revisited and revised. These investigations point to future offensives against bacterial disease, in animals and in humans, that are superior in several respects to antibiotics. First, phages need to be given in just a single dose. Unlike antibiotics, which become diluted by blood and other body fluids and soon disappear altogether, phages multiply inside their host bacteria and increase dramatically in concentration. This "amplification" occurs precisely where the attack is wanted—at the site of infection. And the assault continues until the bacteria are vanquished.

Second, all phage-resistant mutants that have emerged are much less virulent than their parent bacteria. Third, there isn't the worrisome problem of cross-infection when livestock are exposed to the feces of sick animals. Because phages also are eliminated via the intestinal tract, calves, piglets, and lambs can actually acquire them along with the bacteria.

Now that they know phage therapy can work, bacteriologists are baffled by the earlier failures. Several explanations are likely. The early tests were not properly controlled, leading to perplexing contradictions and confusion of claims. Methods of preparing phages in pure, concentrated form were crude. Investigators had no decent animal "models" in which to develop optimal methods before treating human patients. And they seem to have been much less discriminating than Smith in selecting phages that are particularly effective against the target bacteria.

Promising Future for Use in Humans

The success of this rediscovered technique in animals has illuminated its potential in the war against human disease. Virtually every species of bacteria investigated is attacked by one or more types of phage (which are already used to identify disease-causing organisms during epidemics). But this probably does not mean that phage therapy could be applied to the entire spectrum of human infections. It is unlikely, for example, that phages would be effective against conditions caused by bacteria that flourish inside the victim's cells, such as gonorrhea, for the simple reason that phages cannot get at them. Prospects for phage therapy are excellent, however, against bacterial invaders that proliferate freely in the intestine and are thus vulnerable to counterattack. Cholera is one of the best-known human infections of this sort. A major threat over huge tracts of the globe, cholera has caused alarm during recent years by turning up in places as diverse as Naples, Italy, the south of England, and the Texas Gulf Coast.

Further studies are necessary, but already Stefan Slopek and colleagues at the Polish Academy of Sciences in the province of Wroclaw have tested phages on humans and found them valuable in controlling drug-resistant bacteria in blood infections. The immediate need is to look for phages that, like some antibiotics, can attack a wide range of infectious bacteria. Their discovery could be as significant as the successive developments of sulfa drugs, penicillin, and streptomycin earlier this century. What could be more welcome than disease weapons that reproduce themselves? □

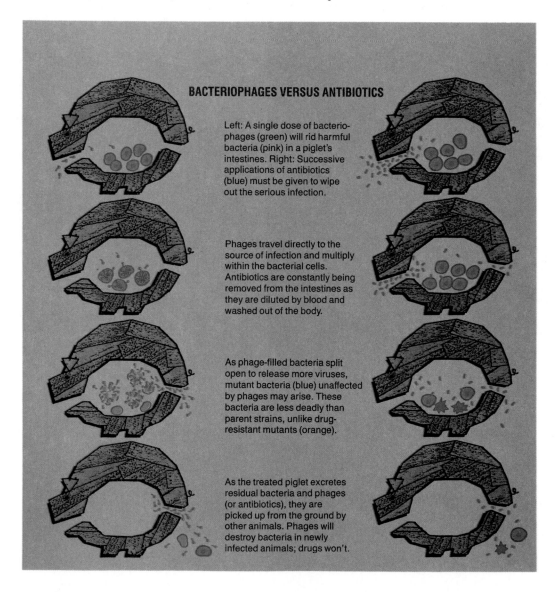

BACTERIOPHAGES VERSUS ANTIBIOTICS

Left: A single dose of bacteriophages (green) will rid harmful bacteria (pink) in a piglet's intestines. Right: Successive applications of antibiotics (blue) must be given to wipe out the serious infection.

Phages travel directly to the source of infection and multiply within the bacterial cells. Antibiotics are constantly being removed from the intestines as they are diluted by blood and washed out of the body.

As phage-filled bacteria split open to release more viruses, mutant bacteria (blue) unaffected by phages may arise. These bacteria are less deadly than parent strains, unlike drug-resistant mutants (orange).

As the treated piglet excretes residual bacteria and phages (or antibiotics), they are picked up from the ground by other animals. Phages will destroy bacteria in newly infected animals; drugs won't.

THE 1984 NOBEL PRIZE
Physiology or Medicine

by Barbara Tchabovsky

The 1984 Nobel Prize in Physiology or Medicine was awarded to three men for their pioneering work in immunology. The recipients of the prize—the most prestigious award in medicine—were César Milstein of the British Medical Research Council's laboratory in Cambridge, England; Georges J. F. Köhler of the Basel Institute of Immunology in Switzerland; and Niels K. Jerne, professor emeritus of the Basel Institute. Their work has provided basic keys to understanding how the body naturally defends itself from disease.

In announcing the award the Karolinska Institute of Stockholm, Sweden, called Dr. Jerne "the leading theoretician in immunology during the last 30 years." Dr. Milstein and Dr. Köhler were cited for their discovery of a technique for producing antibodies in the laboratory—a finding the Karolinska Institute called "one of the most important methodical advances in biomedicine during the 1970's."

Antibodies are natural proteins that the body produces to attack antigens, or foreign substances, such as bacteria or viruses, that enter the body. The antibodies produced by the technique that Milstein and Köhler developed are called monoclonal antibodies. They are already widely used as research and diagnostic tools in laboratories throughout the world, are bring put to use for the treatment of a wide range of diseases, and are the basis of an entire biotechnology industry.

Immunology Theoretician

Dr. Jerne's greatest talent in immunology is as a theoretician. As John H. Humphrey, an immunologist at the National Institute for Medical Research in London, England, put it, Jerne is noteworthy for "his preoccupation with the philosophical problems of immunology, his grasp of what observations are the most pertinent to those problems, and his capacity to put forward bold but conceptually clear hypotheses—and his tendency to be proved right!" His theories, based on his own research findings and those of others, have provided a coherent picture of how the immune system works and at the same time stimulated further research.

In announcing the award, the Nobel committee cited Jerne for three "visionary" theories in particular. In the first Jerne explained how antibodies are produced in the body to match any invader—be it a bacterium, fungus, or virus—that attacks the body. Antibodies are highly specific; they are structured to attack one and only one particular attacker, much as a key fits into a particular lock. A second theory explained how the immune system develops and matures.

The third theory, called the network theory, has been called Jerne's "most significant and fruitful" contribution to science. Developed in 1974, the theory describes the processes by which the body's immune system wakes up to respond to an attack, coordinates and regulates the numerous complex mechanisms involved in combating the disease-causing invader, and then becomes inactive when no longer needed.

The award announcement appeared to summarize Jerne's contributions in stating that his "view on the nature of the immune system constitutes the basis for modern immunology."

Producing Antibodies

In 1975, Georges Köhler was a postdoctorate fellow working at the Laboratory of Molecular Biology at Cambridge University with senior scientist César Milstein. The two were seeking to produce long-lived laboratory cell lines that would make a known and easily identifiable antibody that they could use in their research. The researchers were unable to find such a line. They had cells from the spleen of a mouse that produced such an identifiable antibody, but these cells did not live for a long time in the laboratory. They also had cells of a cancer (a

Right: César Milstein and his wife share a toast to celebrate his Nobel Prize award. Below: Georges Köhler, who collaborated with Milstein in the discovery of a technique for producing monoclonal antibodies, also won a Nobel Prize.

Above: UP/Bettmann Archive; Left: AP/Wide World

Through modifications of this basic technique scientists can now produce unlimited amounts of pure cloned antibody against almost any known antigen. As practiced now, the technique involves several basic steps. A mouse is injected with a specific antigen and allowed to begin producing antibodies against that antigen. The antibody-producing mouse cells are then fused with malignant tumor cells from another mouse. The resulting fused cell—called a hybridoma—in turn produces the desired antibody. The hybridoma is, so to speak, a "cell factory."

Monoclonal antibodies are uniform, pure, and exquisitely sensitive—capable of distinguishing molecules with only tiny chemical differences. Their availability has, according to the Nobel committee, "opened completely new possibilities for basic as well as applied biomedical medical research," and their practical applications have already had a major impact on medicine. As diagnostic aids, monoclonal antibodies have been used in developing improved tests for hepatitis B and some streptococcal infections and in recognizing cases of acquired immune deficiency disease (AIDS). They are also being used in studies of autoimmune diseases such as rheumatoid arthritis, of normal and abnormal brain function, and of hormonal action and certain hormonal diseases such as thyroid disorders and juvenile diabetes. Certain

myeloma) that would grow indefinitely but that did not produce a specific, easily characterized antibody they could work with.

Köhler and Milstein then came up with the idea of fusing the cells they had in the hope of producing the two characteristics they needed in the hybrids—long life in laboratory culture (to come from the myeloma cells) and production of a known and distinguishable antibody (to come from the mouse cells). The fused cells solved the problem. The scientists had, in the words of the Nobel citation, "immortalized antibody-producing cells by fusing them with tumor cells."

monoclonal antibodies have also been used in preparing bone marrow for transplant and in treating leukemia. Their greatest value in the area of medical treatment may be as a step closer to the long-sought "magic bullet" that would destroy a disease agent or diseased part while not harming other areas of the body. This avenue of research is being explored in cancer therapy. Doctors are trying to link potent anti-cancer drugs with monoclonal antibodies, hoping that the antibodies will zero in like "guided missiles" only on the cells affected by cancer (or other disease) and leave other healthy cells unaffected by the toxic drug.

Niels Jerne was born December 23, 1911, in London, England, of Danish parents. He grew up in Denmark and worked for many years as a researcher at the Danish State Serum Institute before receiving his doctorate in medicine from the University of Copenhagen in 1951.

Jerne held numerous teaching and research positions in Switzerland, West Germany, and the United States, including work as a research fellow at the California Institute of Technology during the 1950's and as professor of microbiology at the University of Pittsburgh in the 1960's. He helped establish the Basel Institute of Immunology in Switzerland and served as its director from 1969 to 1980.

Now retired and living in France, Jerne remarked after winning the prize, "I will enjoy the prize and enjoy life."

César Milstein was born October 8, 1927, in Bahia Blanca, Argentina. He studied at the University of Buenos Aires and later at Cambridge University, receiving his Ph.D. there in 1960. After two years at the National Institute for Microbiology in Buenos Aires, he began his association with Cambridge University. He now heads the University's division of protein and nucleic-acid chemistry.

Milstein at first did research on enzymes but in the mid-1960's switched his attention to immunology. In addition to his work with Köhler on the production of monoclonal antibodies, Milstein had studied the genetic control and structure of antibodies.

Before the Nobel award, Milstein received many other honors, including the Louisa Gross Horwitz Prize from Columbia University and the Wolf Prize in Medicine from the Wolf Foundation of Israel.

Georges Köhler was born April 17, 1946, in Munich, Germany. He received his doctorate in biology from the University of Freiburg in 1974. Then he spent two years as a postdoctoral fellow at the Laboratory of Molecular Biology in Cambridge, England, where he worked with César Milstein; it was there that the two men collaborated in the discovery of monoclonal antibodies.

From 1976 to 1985, Köhler was on the staff of the Basel Institute of Immunology in Switzerland. In 1985 he became one of three directors of the Max Planck Institute for Immune Biology in Freiburg, West Germany.

Little known outside the world of immunology, the young, casual Köhler trembled on hearing of his Nobel honor. Later he remarked, "It will be a terrible burden for me because it will not always be easy to prove that I can still do better in my work" □

Niels Jerne, an immunology theoretician, also shared the 1984 Nobel Prize in Physiology or Medicine.

AP/Wide World

COMPUTERS AND

MATHEMATICS

REVIEW
OF THE
YEAR

COMPUTERS AND MATHEMATICS

The trend toward smaller, more capable, and less expensive computers accelerated in 1984, triggering sales of more than 3 million new machines for homes and offices in the United States. High-performance computers at bargain prices marked the year as several companies introduced new machines. At the same time, the software that makes the machines work opened vast new horizons for users. In mathematics there were several major breakthroughs.

NEW AND BETTER MACHINES HEAT UP COMPUTER WARS

After soaring to industry dominance in the microcomputer field, International Business Machines Corporation (IBM) and its best-selling personal computer, the IBM PC, felt the jolt of strong competition in January 1984 when Apple Computer, Incorporated, announced an innovative high-performance machine—called Macintosh—so easy to use that its routine functions can be

learned without an instruction book. Apple followed that announcement with the new Apple IIc, a miniature version of its popular IIe machine. The new $1,300 computer with a built-in disk drive won numerous awards for its simple and beautiful design.

The Macintosh integrated and simplified the mouse-and-window operating concept introduced one year earlier in the Lisa computer. But competition drove down its price from an initial $2,500 to $2,000 or less by year's end. A key Macintosh feature—extremely high-quality on-screen graphics—opened the door for new ways to use a computer. Apple Software designers created a program called "MacPaint" that allows users to draw freehand on the screen with the mouse device, enables Macintosh to draw precise geometric shapes to order, and allows users to call up disk libraries of designs by professional artists. The concept behind the program was quickly adapted throughout the industry, making painting by computer a popular and easy feature.

Another unique Macintosh feature is how it stores information. The screen serves as a replica of a desktop, and each separate file, after being named, is shown as a small drawing called an icon. Another icon on the desktop looks like a file folder, which can be duplicated and given various names. At that point, it is easy to use the computer's ability to move items around the screen to place data-file icons inside file-folder icons. One file folder might be named

"Correspondence," for instance, and contain dozens of other icons, each of which are individual letters that can be retrieved from a disk. The system keeps the screen (or desktop) uncluttered because only a few file folders might be visible until one is "opened" by using the mouse.

Within weeks of Apple's announcement, IBM began shipping its new PCjr, a smaller and cheaper version of the PC. But the machine was initially a disaster: it couldn't run many of the business programs that had helped make the PC a success, and its rubberized keyboard made typing and data entry difficult. By mid-1984, IBM replaced the keyboard, increased the machine's memory to let it use more software, and lowered its price.

At the high-priced end ($5,000-plus) of the personal-computer market, IBM revealed an advanced version of its PC with connections for two remote terminals that allow three operators—running different programs—to use the computer simultaneously. Called the AT (for advanced technology), it performs operations nearly three times as fast as the original PC and stores four times more information on a single disk. ∎ Competition came from a similar high-speed computer introduced by American Telephone & Telegraph Company.

INNOVATIVE

Software is the programs, or sets of internal instructions, that tell a computer how to do specific tasks. Now software experts are finding ways to write programs that let computers perform functions that previously required hardware (physical-component) changes or additions. Digital Research, Incorporated, of California released software in 1984 that turns any computer compatible with an IBM PC into a multiuser system. Up to four remote terminals can be connected to a PC, and each terminal screen can be divided into up to five windows, with each window running a separate program.

Other software unveiled or improved during 1984 included Microsoft's "Flight Simulator II," which puts you in the pilot seat of a single-engine plane; Waveform's "Color Tone Keyboard," which lets you compose or play music at the keyboard; and The Learning Company's "Robot Odyssey," which uses a game format to teach children how computer circuits work.

SOLVING THE "UNSOLVABLE"

Three important puzzles in pure mathematics, long thought to be all but unsolvable, were solved in 1984. First came the factoring of a 69-digit number. Factoring is the process of dividing a number into smaller numbers, each greater than 1, that can be multiplied together to yield the original number. Until recently, mathematicians, even using large computers, could not factor numbers with more than 50 digits. But now a group at Sandia National Laboratories in New Mexico has developed a breakthrough program for a high-speed Cray supercomputer. The computer, performing several hundred million calculations per second, took 32 hours to factor a 69-digit number taken from a 300-year-old list created by a French mathematician. Three factors were found—with 21, 23, and 26 digits themselves. An intellectual exercise? No. The best security codes are based on factoring, and cracking the factoring puzzle could pave the way for more secure codes.

Linear programming is a laborious way for computers to keep track of large numbers of variables, but until late 1984 it was the only way. Airlines use it to come up with complex schedules of flights, crew assignments, equipment, costs, and revenues; some truck companies use it to find the most efficient routes for deliveries. But the method can be slow and bogs down when there are 20,000 or so variables. Now Bell Laboratories mathematician Narendra Karmarkar has puzzled out an intricate formula that makes linear programming faster and more effective. Instead of sampling every possible combination among the variables, the formula quickly eliminates useless combinations and finally centers on the best of all solutions.

The Bieberbach conjecture is a puzzle in pure mathematics with no known practical use. Still, it has intrigued mathematicians for 70 years. The conjecture involves coefficients of power in a series representing certain analytic functions. The German mathematician Ludwig Bieberbach guessed that each coefficient in the series must fall within a range equal to plus or minus the number of elements in the series—or, in other words, that a three-element series could not have a coefficient more than 3 or less than −3. Until Purdue University mathematician Louis de Branges proved Bieberbach correct, some mathematicians had devoted their careers to solving the puzzle. The solution may open new approaches to math research.

DECLINE IN MATH RESEARCH

A panel of scientists from the National Research Council reported a 15-year decline in research funding and doctoral graduates in mathematics, and cited increases in computer sciences as a factor in drawing researchers away from pure math.

JIM SCHEFTER

Painting by Computer

by Dale Peterson

It's December 1951. Edward R. Murrow interviews Massachusetts Institute of Technology (MIT) professor Jay Forrester on the television show "See It Now." Professor Forrester demonstrates something new and exciting—an "electronic digital computer" called Whirlwind that is attached to a television set. In addition to playing "Jingle Bells," the computer displays two interesting images: the graph of a rocket trajectory based on the computer's manipulation of raw data, and the visual simulation of a bouncing ball.

This was the first significant public demonstration of a computer producing visual images on a screen. That new concept—computer as image producer—led quite directly to the rapidly expanding use of computers in scientific, technical, and business applications. What professor Forrester very likely did not foresee, however, was that within a few decades, large numbers of professional artists would use computer-generated images in almost every aspect of their art.

Computer-generated Works Come of Age

Artists and aesthetically minded scientists began displaying computer-generated work in small exhibits as early as the mid-1960's. In 1968 a major exhibition of computer-based art—including music, poetry, prose, sculpture, and visual art—opened at the Institute of Contemporary Arts in London, England. Called *Cybernetic Serendipity,* the exhibition demonstrated what its name suggested—that certain cybernetic (automatically controlled) machines, rigid and mechanical though they may seem, could become intimate elements in the lucky accidents and deliberate events we call art. Of course, computers were different then. Most of the early works produced in collaboration with the ma-

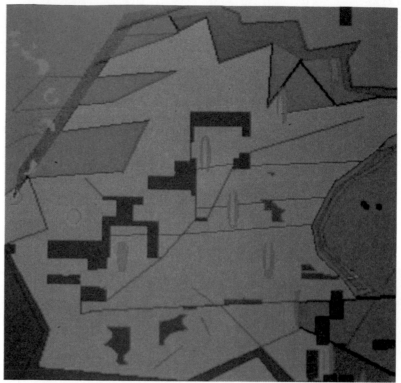

Darcy Gerbarg

chines promised more than they proved. It was art more cybernetic than serendipitous, more interesting than delightful.

But today's computer is becoming an ever more viable medium for producing visual art, and today's art establishment has granted legitimacy to computer-generated works. In fact, computer-generated animation for television advertising and special effects in films has become a $25 million-a-year industry almost overnight, spawning incredibly powerful (and incredibly expensive) image-generating systems.

Vast Capabilities

More important, today's inexpensive computers afford even ordinary (impoverished) artists a chance to experiment and create. These powerful machines produce very precise and well-defined images with astounding choices of color and hue, while increasingly refined software (the programs, or instructions, that tell a computer what to do) techniques now let artists carry out tremendously useful manipulations of images on the screen. Cybernetic serendipity has arrived.

Computers are such flexible tools that the number of particular ways in which artists use

them remains limited more by the artist's imagination than by the particular capabilities of the machines. In addition, the development of new imaging techniques and more sophisticated hardware (the physical components of a computer system) makes the potential even vaster.

Despite this diversity, though, there are four general, or basic, ways in which visual artists work with computers. Some rely on standard hardware/software tools, while others employ custom tools often developed for nonartistic tasks; still others manipulate images on the programming level, and a few even program creativity into the machines themselves.

Standard Computer Tools

The work of New York artist Darcy Gerbarg superbly illustrates how standard computer tools can be used to create original works of art. Gerbarg frequently uses a ''paint system'' to produce highly abstract, asymmetrical visions on the computer's display screen. She typically transforms these screen images into large, museum-quality reproductions through standard photography.

Much like a word-processing system, the paint system does not require sophisticated tech-

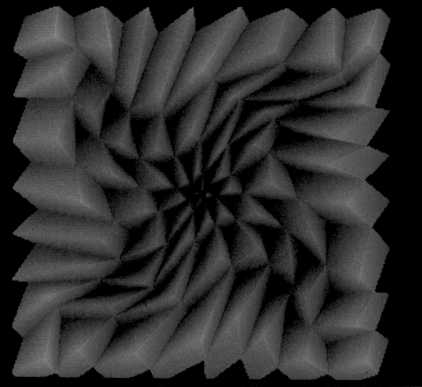

Artist Ruth Leavitt created this colorful geometric image with a custom software program.

nical knowledge from its user. The artist still makes all aesthetic decisions—the paint system simply eases the dull and repetitive mechanics of creation. When Gerbarg uses such a system, she "paints" directly on the computer screen with the help of two hardware peripherals: a graphics tablet—a flat electronic "tablet" made of plastic and metal, about the size and shape of a drawing tablet—and a stylus that somewhat resembles a ballpoint pen. As Gerbarg strokes the stylus across the tablet, corresponding strokes of color appear on the computer screen.

Gerbarg needs only one stylus—a command or two to the system will alter the color or thickness of the strokes that appear on the screen. She can change the intensity of the brush stroke, producing lines in which any specified percentage of pixels (the picture elements, or dots, on the screen) is activated. Most systems can do some automatic drawing, producing a perfect circle or filling a closed figure with color.

Sophisticated paint systems also let Gerbarg draw a flower, for example, and make it part of her "paint box." Then a stroke of her stylus paints a line of perfectly repeated, identical flowers on the screen. She can also take portions of the full-screen image and move them

elsewhere without disturbing any other parts of the image. Some systems will reverse images, split images in half, and double them again and again. Gerbarg may even cycle automatically through colors so that she can sit back and watch as the computer paints abstract screen images with a succession of random color combinations. Finally, she can choose at any time to save a particular image on disk before experimenting further with it on the screen.

Compare this with an artist painting with a medium such as watercolor. Once it's done, the watercolor image is there, fixed and finished, mess or masterpiece. With a computer-based paint system, however, an artist has most of the flexibility of the traditional media, a number of automatic image-transforming tools, and an infinitely "soft" or flexible image that is never ultimately fixed until the artist is satisfied.

Custom Software Tools

While Darcy Gerbarg and other artists frequently depend on standard paint systems, others use custom computer image-making systems. Like the paint systems, such custom computer tools typically do not require any particular programming skills on the part of the artist. But while a paint system is generally so open and flexible that the artist almost entirely defines his or her own individual style, some custom systems tend to define a style enough so that the artist can be seen as painting "in the school of" the creator of the tool.

Artist Ruth Leavitt has achieved a characteristic style with a custom program written by computer scientist Jay Leavitt. The software lets the artist define colorful geometric shapes in three-dimensional perspective and then twist, expand, contract, and otherwise manipulate the shapes at will. For Leavitt, painting with the computer takes on some of the plastic qualities of sculpting with clay. Her final images seem at once both solid and fluid, possessing bold color and rhythmically distorted geometry, a vision of uncut gems taken from deep beneath the Earth's surface.

Although Leavitt sometimes transforms her screen images into stills through photography, she often records the full artistic process of image manipulation on videotape, producing marvelous abstract animations. In other words, she uses her computer system to experiment with form and dimension and then relies on traditional sculpting techniques to capture the final form in a less forgiving medium such as wood, metal, plastic, or Plexiglas.

Texture Mapping: A Versatile Custom Tool

Another artist's use of custom software represents a serendipitous collaboration of art and science. Computer artist David Em uses software tools developed at the National Aeronautics and Space Administration's (NASA's) Jet Propulsion Laboratory by computer scientist James Blinn. Blinn originally developed the software to generate scenes of interplanetary space and the surface of planets and moons based on data sent back to Earth by NASA's Voyager space probes, but Em has found other uses for it.

Using Blinn's software, Em can quickly define a number of solid geometrical shapes—the computer performs the necessary calculations to display these in three-dimensional perspective. Em then patterns the shapes using a

David Em's distinctive painting style is a product of an innovative computer process called texture mapping.

process known as *texture mapping*. Invented by Blinn and others, this process involves describing a flat texture or pattern (such as a grid) that the computer paints, or "maps," onto the surface of a geometrical solid, following its three-dimensional perspective.

While Blinn's texture mapping was originally designed to display detailed images of the surfaces of planets and moons, Em uses the system to clothe spheres, toroids (doughnut-shaped solids), cones, pyramids, and other solids with bright, woven patterns. Other tools in the custom system enable Em to split a screen into perfect mirror images, to turn portions of an image upside down, to move parts of an image, to tilt a scene in three dimensions, and to stretch an image in any of its three dimensions. In addition, Em can merge two separate images by defining the percentage of pixels from each image to be activated.

The result is a very distinctive and evocative painting style, conjuring a universe of strange forms and deep perspective, suggesting at times the feeling of outer space and at other times a feeling of inner space, of a strange, echoing, hollow world from deep within the psyche. Though the style is distinctly David Em's, it is marked by the nature of Blinn's custom-designed set of software tools. Looking toward the future, one can see such custom software becoming prototypes for commercial systems. The capabilities now available only through custom programming could before long become standard tools.

Creative Programming

Going beyond those who use the computer solely as a tool, the artist with programming talent has some special control over the machine and the images it produces. Such an artist can reach inside the machine during the very act of creation so that programming itself becomes an integral part of artistic creation. The talented programming artist can manipulate images to produce wholly original effects that lie on the far edge of what others only dream.

Duane Palyka was trained as both an artist and a mathematician. Currently a senior staff member at the New York Institute of Technology, Palyka, perhaps more than any other contemporary computer-using artist, directly applies his programming skills to the creation of his art. If other artists can be said to paint on the computer screen, Palyka paints on the inside of the computer, within the program itself.

Some of Palyka's best-known images are based on the three-dimensional computer modeling of a human female form. The original program was created by Ed Catmull, who described the form of a live model as a series of mathematical and numerical definitions of basic three-dimensional shapes. By calculating highlights, shadows, and hidden (not ordinarily seen) portions of these forms, Catmull's program will display the figures from any point of view and with any hypothetical light source.

In Palyka's *Picasso 2,* shown opposite, one can see these figures that the artist has texture-mapped in various ways. Palyka further enhanced some of the figures by altering the original program so that it displayed a portion of the normally hidden sides. Instead of having the computer assign no illumination to the hidden surfaces, he experimented with various illuminations to add the interesting complexity one sees in the figures. Continuing to modify the original program definition, Palyka exploded the second figure from the left by altering the interconnecting definitions in the code that created the original form, causing the individual geometric shapes and curves to move outward.

Thus, Palyka's abilities as a programmer have given him a wide range of artistic options that are in some ways more immediate than those offered by predetermined software systems. The computer program itself is his palette, and he experiments with the program's parameters just as a painter might experiment with various mixtures of colors to create the complex and intriguing images that define his art.

Programmed Creativity

So far we've seen artists who use the computer as a relatively straightforward tool—a fast, efficient, but rather dumb assistant that can carry out assigned tasks but is virtually incapable of making artistic decisions. But there is a more radical way in which artists are using computers, a way that corresponds to the automatic music-composition programs some composers use. In these cases, the computer actually participates in the creative process, making its own aesthetic decisions based on the artist's definitions.

Harold Cohen is one of a few artists who rely on computers but do not necessarily work with images on the video-display screen. Although he has now begun working with sophis-

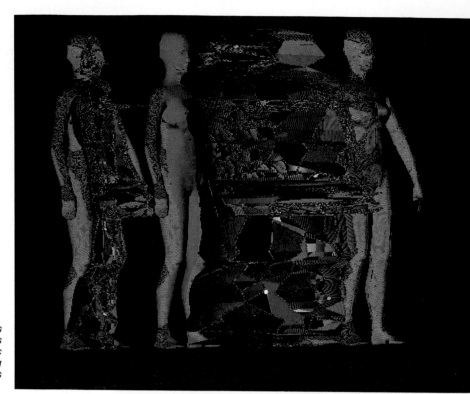

Duane Palyka applies his programming skills to expand his artistic abilities in producing such complex works as this Picasso 2.

ticated plotters, a number of his earlier works were created with a computer-controlled robotic "turtle" that draws images with a pen as it moves across sheets of paper spread across the floor. Many of these are mural-sized works, and the process of the turtle's drawing has itself been featured in several museum exhibits. Cohen frequently took over where the turtle left off, adding color to the line drawing.

Unlike any of the other artists discussed so far, Cohen has given a significant degree of artistic control to the computer itself—the machine is actually making what we might well describe as aesthetic choices. But how can this be? The very notion of programmed creativity seems a paradox.

Clearly, the computer is not making creative choices as a human artist would. The machine does not have a personality that could generate basic, general ideas and feelings about aesthetics and the act of drawing. But the computer can act in response to an artifact of human creativity embedded in the program, and in its response carry out actions that are unpredictable and often delightful.

In creating the drawing program for his computer-controlled robotic turtle, Cohen called upon his own experience as a painter and artist to define a hierarchical list of drawing instructions. The instructions direct the turtle to close figures at certain points, to respect the integrity of figures, to distribute figures in a certain fashion across an open field, to define shading in a certain way, to distinguish between the inside and the outside of a figure, to find open space and move toward it, to draw by keeping the pen down, and to move without drawing by lifting the pen up.

If Cohen were to place the turtle in precisely the same spot at precisely the same heading at the beginning of each drawing, the program ought to produce precisely the same drawing each time, for it includes no randomizing elements. However, the interactions between the dissociated subprograms are so complex that the computer-controlled turtle produces an original, distinctive drawing every time. Once they have been colored, the final images are often disconcertingly evocative, like expansive contemporary cave paintings.

In several ways, Cohen's art reminds one of the images produced with the programming

Harold Cohen

A computer made aesthetic decisions in creating this work based on Harold Cohen's instructions.

language Logo; and given Logo's growing popularity, especially in schools, it's likely that we'll see variations on this theme. It's true, of course, that Cohen's software could be sold commercially, but the drawing program he has developed represents only one example of the vast creative potential that remains to be explored. Judging by Cohen's accomplishments, one can foresee a day when artificial aesthetics will be just as provocative a subject as artificial intelligence is today.

Breaking Down the Walls

Although this article has focused on the use of computers in the visual arts, it's no secret that computers are used as creative tools by professional artists in music, writing, sculpture, film, choreography, animation—you name it. A few naive folks imagine Computer Art as a high-tech style of visual production involving weird, otherworldly shapes, sharp edges, and metallic colors, perhaps accompanied by fingernail-on-the-blackboard music. But in fact, Computer Art does not exist in the way that Op Art, Pop Art, or Machine Art does. Indeed; art produced by or with the assistance of a computer is not a style or a fad or a movement. Computer-based art may be disturbingly strange or comfortingly familiar, realistic or abstract, symmetrical or

asymmetrical, geometrical or not. It may not include any particular indications that a computer was involved at all.

Unlike a car, paintbrush, atomic bomb, or any other fixed and frozen piece of technology that possesses only a couple of specific uses, the computer is a universal tool with universal applications. Modern computers are so adaptable that they have begun to stretch the traditional limits of the visual arts, and similar developments are happening in virtually all of the other arts as well. But at the same time that today's technology is stretching these traditionally defined limits, it is also to a large extent dissolving them.

Take artist John Whitney, for example. Using a computer system, he has created a visual art—a style of abstract animation that is a visual equivalent of music. Whitney's animations move like brief chamber concerts or symphony fragments, flowing visually in lucid, abstract images through dissonance to consonance, from discord to harmony.

Artist Aaron Marcus has used computer systems to create a "visual poetry" that depends as much on the appearance of the language as it does on its denotative and symbolic content. The 19th-century French poet Guillaume Apollinaire can be credited with first

Radioactive Jukebox, *by Aaron Marcus, is a dramatic example of the artist's compositions using computer systems to create interpretive "visual poetry."*

establishing the idea of "concrete poetry," poetry that attempts to produce meaning both with words and with the images of the words. Modern computers make image manipulation so easy that even words themselves (their size, proportion, position, color, and style) become plastic, defying once and for all the rigidity of the typesetter.

Then there's interdisciplinary artist Ann Sandifur. With the aid of a personal-computer system and an inexpensive music synthesizer, she has created a massive concrete sculpture in Spokane, Washington's, Metro Hall. But it's not just sculpture—it's also music, visual art, kinetic art, and environmental art. Sound compositions on the synthesizer directly control light-emitting fiber optics; overhead lights; image projectors; and a series of valves, photo sensors, and stepper motors that in turn control a visually fascinating, continually recirculating flow of colored sand. Meanwhile, optical sen-

sors on the roof of the building can respond to aspects of the weather by creating a kind of weather music via the synthesizer. At the same time, vibrations moving through the concrete influence the dispersal of the colored sand, which separates according to color-coordinated grain size.

As these and many other examples illustrate, the computer is having a profound impact on all of the arts. Drawing on new inspiration and creative energies, contemporary artists using the machines have taken us beyond traditional limits and definitions to make uniquely modern artistic statements. The most exciting aspect of this burgeoning creativity is that the computer is just now becoming widely accessible as an artistic tool. And while it's impossible to say whether the computer will be the tool of the next Picasso, it's certain that it will unleash the Picasso in many who never thought of themselves as artists □

REINVENTING THE COMPUTER

by Tom Alexander

A wave of technological change is poised to sweep over the computer industry. Faster and cheaper computers will allow users to do things they can't today—operate a typewriter by voice, for example. Companies and nations alike will face the opportunities and dangers that always accompany a major innovation. The stakes are high: the new technology will affect all information-age businesses, ranging from electronic-mail networks to computer manufacturing, which are expected to have worldwide revenues, in today's dollars, of up to $500 billion a year by 1993.

The transformation will be based on one fundamental idea: that the way to speed up computers is to divide the labor among many inexpensive data-processing devices rather than continue the present quest for ever faster single processors made with ever more exotic materials and techniques. Called parallel processing, the new approach is analogous to mass-producing shoes with unskilled labor on assembly lines instead of handcrafting them with skilled workmen one by one. Over the next few years, United States, Japanese, and European industries and governments will spend some $10 billion on advanced computer research, including parallel processing.

Even Supercomputers Have Limitations

The demand for faster but cheaper computers grows continuously. Sales of "supercomputers"—fast, specialized, hand-built, and expensive number-crunchers (possessing rapid numeric computation capabilities)—have been taking off. Cray Research Incorporated, a Minneapolis, Minnesota, company, has received more and more orders for supercomputers over the past few years. The burst of sales was ignited by technological advances that made possible deep price cuts—as much as $5 million on a $10 million Cray—and put the machines within reach of more users.

Aircraft and automobile manufacturers have begun to use simulations performed on supercomputers in place of wind tunnels and machines that smash parts to determine their strength and durability. Pharmaceutical companies are using computers to develop new drugs with molecules derived from quantum theory, which predicts how atoms will interact, instead of relying on the random mixing and testing of substances. Oil companies are constructing computerized 3-D (three-dimensional) models of underground oil and water movements to

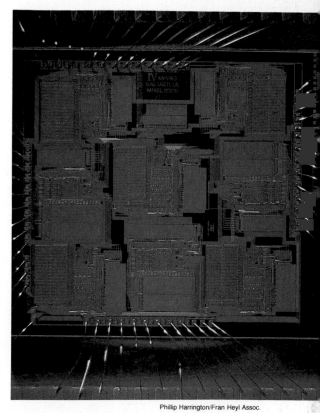

Phillip Harrington/Fran Heyl Assoc.

Opposite: Researchers fit a robot hand with 12 intercommunicating computers to test concepts of parallel processing. Above: A chip with eight processors.

determine how to exploit oil fields. Digital Productions, a Los Angeles, California, company that turns out feature films and television commercials, used a Cray to simulate in vivid detail the surfaces of alien planets that appear in the movie *The Last Starfighter*.

Today's supercomputers are too slow for many potential tasks. Some jobs now take weeks or months—for example, simulating the airflow around an entire airplane in flight. Users have identified additional applications that would take hundreds or thousands of times longer; one would create a minutely detailed model of a fusion reactor's interior at work.

Improvements in Current Design Still Inadequate

Unfortunately, performing these tasks will be impractical as long as computer makers stick with the present dominant design—the "von Neumann architecture," named for the Hungarian-American genius John von Neu-

A technician uses an infrared scanner to detect possible problems with a Cray supercomputer at a General Motors research laboratory. Today's supercomputers just aren't fast enough to perform many complex tasks.

Hank Morgan/Rainbow

mann, who helped develop it near the end of World War II. In the von Neumann approach, a single main-processing unit calls forth programmed instructions and data from memory in sequence, manipulates the data as instructed, and either returns the results to memory or performs other operations. With only one processor at work, the pace of computation is set by the speed of the processor's electronic circuits. Circuit speeds, in turn, are limited by the agility of transistor switches, the rate at which electricity flows through wires, and the intense heat produced by tiny fast-acting chips. Conventional supercomputers require expensive cooling to keep them from burning up. The circuit boards in the forthcoming Cray-2 are immersed in a liquid coolant in order to keep them at room temperature.

The big computer and semiconductor-circuit makers have been exploring exotic new technologies to speed up the von Neumann computer with faster switches. This can be done by making integrated-circuit chips of gallium arsenide, a semiconductor material, instead of silicon, or by using devices called Josephson junctions, named for British researcher Brian Josephson. But gallium arsenide has proved brittle and difficult to transform reliably into

workable chips. Josephson junctions must be cooled to within a few degrees of absolute zero ($-273.15°C$ or $-459.67°F$). If these technologies are employed to speed up the traditional von Neumann architecture, tomorrow's faster computer may wind up priced out of the market. That perception was behind a recent decision by International Business Machines Corporation (IBM) to scale back its Josephson junction development.

In any event, these new technologies would be inadequate for many potential computing tasks. "In my opinion, we are already within a factor of 10 of the top speed achievable with a von Neumann machine," says Bill Buzbee, a computer scientist at the Los Alamos National Laboratory, one of the big buyers of supercomputers. A formidable barrier is what IBM's eminent computer scientist John Backus—inventor of the FORTRAN programming language, among other things—has identified as the "von Neumann bottleneck." That is the single channel along which data and instructions must flow between a conventional computer's central processor and its memory. Like a constriction in a pipe feeding raw material to a factory, the von Neumann bottleneck can limit the pace of production.

Parallel Processing

The faster, smarter, and cheaper alternative to von Neumann's architecture, many designers agree, is parallel processing. The latent advantages of parallelism have long been recognized; even von Neumann was impressed by discoveries in the 1940's about how animal brains process information in a parallel manner. Had electronic hardware not been so costly in his day, he might have designed a machine more like a brain.

That economic constraint no longer applies. A technology called VLSI (for "Very Large-Scale Integration") makes it possible to reproduce computer circuits with hundreds of thousands of transistors on a single tiny silicon chip almost as easily and cheaply as printing pages of a book. This capability affords designers a tantalizing way around the von Neumann bottleneck: put many processors on a single chip. Processors could operate simultaneously on different parts of a problem and even specialize in performing particular operations at great speed. Another type of parallelism, called active or associative memory, can immensely speed up certain computing tasks, such as retrieving information from data bases, by eliminating the role of the central processor in searching through memory. In essence, each piece of data would be stored with its own tiny processor, smart enough to respond when a centralized computer calls for that item.

System Specialization to Come

Parallelism will probably spawn many specialized types of computers with different species of processors connected in a variety of ways. Inherently general-purpose, the von Neumann computer relies on software programs to let it perform many different kinds of jobs. But almost any computational problem can be solved more rapidly with special-purpose hardware that uses a minimum of software. In addition, prices of hardware have plunged, but software costs have not, and software now accounts for seven of every ten dollars spent on computing. Now that the cost trade-off has swung in favor of hardware, much of the complex software may be replaced by specialized parallel machines. Certain types of machines will do the number-crunching, while others will control robots, search data bases, understand written and spoken language, and even see.

Cray and Control Data Corporation, another Minneapolis company, already turn out supercomputers based partly on parallelism. The Cray-1 and Control Data Cyber 205 embody a basic von Neumann architecture to which are attached banks of simple processors that carry out arithmetic operations on large collections of similar data, called vectors and arrays. One type of vector might consist of a continuous series of readings from scientific instruments—such as barometric pressures at many points around the world, which are often

A parallel processor used for oil prospecting saves time and money at Exxon's Research Production Company.

Hank Morgan/Rainbow

used in constructing weather maps for forecasting. In addition, several companies build array-processing attachments for general-purpose computers. With an array processor costing less than $500,000, a user can soup up his $300,000 Digital Equipment Corporation VAX computer system to about one-tenth of the $7 million Cray-1's performance—an attractive proposition for those who can't afford the Cray.

Array processors and other high-speed computing devices are leading to what Cornell physicist and Nobel laureate Kenneth Wilson calls "the computerization of science." They are replacing experimental apparatus in fusion energy, advanced physics, astronomy, biology, chemistry, and aeronautics. The trend has spilled over into industrial research and design. At General Motors, engineers study engine knock with computer models of pressure waves that occur in a car cylinder after fuel vapor ignites.

Today's number-crunchers won't work for tasks in which each processor executes a different program but nevertheless must exchange information with other processors. A machine for understanding speech, for instance, might need one processor to pick out sounds, others to identify words and parts of speech, and still others to search for meaning. Each processor would constantly make guesses and compare notes with other processors to resolve the ambiguities and confusions of human expression. That way they could distinguish the different meanings of words in "Time flies like an arrow" and "Fruit flies like a banana."

A mobile robot will probably use separate processors for navigation, propulsion, and for operating each joint of a manipulating arm and hand. These would have to consult with each other and with processors in charge of vision, which will dissect scenes into specific features such as color, texture, and lines, and pass the findings on to higher processors that can recognize these as the elements of known objects.

Programming Obstacles Foreseen

At present, programmers must spell out in excruciating detail everything they want a computer to know and do. Some experts think parallelism will eventually make computers easier to program. But for the moment scientists are baffled about how to program parallel machines at all. Massachusetts Institute of Technology (MIT) computer scientist Michael Dertouzos says parallel machines can fall into a "deadly embrace," a paralysis that ensues when one processor must wait for data from another, which in turn waits for another, and so on. A parallel system caught in this predicament might wind up working more slowly than a von Neumann machine—or not at all.

And how do you break up sequential problems in mathematics or logic so that they can run concurrently on multiple processors? Just as nine women can't cooperate to produce a baby in one month, parallelism can't reduce the time it takes to solve a problem that must be approached in a series of steps taken one after the other. But other problems, including some now usually performed sequentially, can be broken into discrete parts that could be solved more quickly by a series of processors working in parallel than by one computer alone. For example, parts of a long column of figures can be distributed among processors for addition, with subtotals then being combined.

At the University of North Carolina at Chapel Hill, computer scientist Gyula Mago and others are working on parallel systems that automatically reduce a complex problem to many primitive operations that can be executed simultaneously. In Mago's reduction machine, as it is called, each processor is given a special task to perform—say, addition or multiplication. A complex formula might be fed into the computer, and as it percolates through the network, each processor would perform its particular function as needed, just as specialized circuits in animal brains apparently do.

Reprogramming thousands or even millions of parallel processors to perform each new application would be impractical. So each processor might be permanently programmed to perform a limited repertory of tasks. Ultimately, programming such a machine to solve a new problem might require an operator to do no more than type in necessary equations and push the start button.

Imitating Human Memory

Some proponents of parallelism hope that it will make possible machines that learn things on their own—computers able to do jobs no programmer knows how to tell them to do. These proponents argue that the von Neumann computer is an awkward vehicle for biological-style intelligence. For example, computers and people do arithmetic differently. People don't actually add the numbers two and two, as a computer does; instead they associate the mem-

Above: A computer simulates the style and aerodynamics of a car design. Right: This realistic image of a Pontiac Fiero was made by a supercomputer. Parallel processors will perform even more intricate simulations than those shown here at very high speeds.

Top: Hank Morgan/Rainbow; Above: Digital Productions

orized phrase ''two plus two'' with the word ''four.'' Far more complex associations probably lie at the heart of human perception, recognition, generalization, learning, and intuition—things difficult to explain even to ourselves, much less spell out for an obtuse machine. What conceivable sequence of instructions, for example, could tell a machine how to recognize a face in a crowd?

The key to association in the human mind appears to be massive parallelism in which billions of items in memory are stored in conjunction with their own specific processors—cells called neurons. Human memory consists of a vibrant network of processors comparing notes with other processors and singling out similarities, learning relationships, and generalizing about concepts. Teuvo Kohonen and his colleagues at Finland's University of Technology have imitated human memory in a machine that

Malvin Kalos stands beside the Ultra—the parallel-processor prototype he is developing at New York University.

can distinguish human faces from one another, even faces viewed from perspectives the computer hadn't seen them from before.

Other researchers have developed parallel concepts that enable computers to learn as humans do through exploration, observation, and trial and error. At the moment, these concepts take the form of simulations on conventional von Neumann computers, and for that reason, are limited and simple. Using only a few processors, Andrew Barto and associates at the University of Massachusetts at Amherst have simulated a neural net that learns by trial and error the manipulations necessary to balance a broomstick on end atop a moving cart.

One ambitious active-memory project is the Connection Machine, invented by Daniel Hillis, an MIT graduate student. In its ultimate form, the machine would consist of perhaps a million or more processors, each with a relatively small memory and about as much power as the processor in a home computer. The links among the machine's processors can be altered to construct different parallel architectures in different applications, ranging from medical diagnosis to robot vehicles. The Connection Machine is being developed at a new private company, Thinking Machines Corporation of Waltham, Massachusetts, which has already fabricated prototypes of some necessary VLSI chips.

More brainlike still is a concept being explored by researchers Geoffrey Hinton and Scott Fahlman of Pittsburgh's Carnegie-Mellon University and Terrence Sejnowski of Johns Hopkins University. As in neuron networks, the machine they envision will have processors with memory distributed throughout the network. The researchers hope this will permit the machine to deal in "fuzzy" concepts, including generalizations and analogies, that conventional computers find difficult. Distributed memory should also provide redundancy and resiliency like that of animal nervous systems, which can suffer the loss of many memory cells without totally losing recollection of an item—the image of grandmother's face, for example.

Race Is on for Computer Dominance

Perceiving competitive opportunities in the potential break with conventional computing, many of the world's computer designers have raced back to the drawing boards. The Japanese were the first to understand that what's at stake is dominance of computer hardware and software. This is the industry that best exploits what advanced countries have to sell—the knowledge in the heads of highly educated people, rather than the strength of their muscles. With the fortunes of entire nations, not just companies, at risk, the race to dominate these "information technologies" has become an international competition in which governments encourage and subsidize the participants.

Japan's much-publicized fifth-generation computer project is aimed at developing parallel machines that can perceive their surroundings and recognize, manipulate, and draw inferences from non-numerical symbols—words, sentences, and visual or aural patterns. "We're thinking about computers that will have everyday non-numerical applications—processing and understanding text, making judgments, giving advice," says Kazuhiro Fuchi, director of the project. He says that these yet-to-be-developed computers will do many jobs secretaries do today. "The cost of having a human secretary will be greater than having a fifth-generation computer," he adds. "Only rich or high-level executives will be able to afford secretaries."

Europe also aims to seize the moment of technological transition to chop into the computer dominance of the United States. In Britain, government, industry, and universities are collaborating on advanced computer developments. The government will put up nearly $300 million over the next several years, and companies are expected to match that sum. The European Community and some 200 Western European companies, including Siemens and Britain's General Electric, are putting together a five-year, $1.1 billion effort called the European Strategic Program for Research and Information Technologies (ESPRIT). It will cover advanced-computer technology, from fundamental semiconductor research to parallel hardware and artificial-intelligence software. Most of the work will be done by companies and universities.

U.S. hopes for maintaining the lead in computers depend on a variety of government and private projects. The Pentagon's Defense Advanced Research Projects Agency (DARPA) has launched a Strategic Computing program on which it plans to spend $600 million in the first five years. Nominally aimed at exploiting promising advances in microelectronics, computer concepts, and artificial intelligence, DARPA's project is also designed to stimulate broad corporate and university research in these technologies through research contracts. One of the project's goals is a robot vehicle able to navigate autonomously over roads and through woods at 56 kilometers per hour (35 miles per hour), guided by artificial vision and other senses. DARPA hasn't publicly specified a mission for such a device, but whatever uses the robot vehicle might have on land, the sensory, navigational, and computational talents involved would obviously be useful in unmanned air, space, or underwater craft with reconnaissance or destructive missions.

Vast Opportunity Competitors

At the moment few parallel computers have reached the market. The Cray X-MP (the "MP" stands for "multiprocessor") merely connects two Cray-1's in the same box. The Cray-2, which appeared on the market in 1985, has four processors, each more powerful than the Cray-1. Control Data recently formed a little company called ETA Systems to develop a parallel supercomputer 20 times faster than any present machine. Denelcor Incorporated of Aurora, Colorado, offers an ingenious design—at up to $8 million per machine—that allows users to hook together as many processors as they need.

Most research on parallel processing is still being done in universities where more than 70 novel concepts are being investigated. Just about every major computer maker in the United States is also pursuing parallel research in some form. They include such surprising participants as Goodyear Aerospace, which recently developed a 16,384-processor machine for the National Aeronautics and Space Administration (NASA) to use in processing images transmitted from earth-surveying satellites. A harbinger of new technology aborning is the recent sprouting of little companies started by university professors and defectors from old-line computer companies.

One revolutionary aspect of parallel computing is that it will probably open many more niches for competitors to develop machines to handle specific tasks, just as Floating Point Systems has done with machines for high-speed calculations in engineering and science. Most likely it will take years for the real world to sort out which concepts are practical and economic—and which companies will make investors rich. But in the next decade specialized parallel machines will begin nibbling at the market for general-purpose computers like IBM's mainframes, giving many little contenders in many countries a shot at growing big□

Electronic Arts

INTEGRATED SOFTWARE
by Carol Anne Ogdin

Personal computers (PCs) are marketed as productivity-enhancing tools for the white-collar worker. But despite vendor (seller) claims emphasizing how easily novices can perform analysis, compose reports, or prepare graphics, the sad fact is, few of the available software products are really that easy to use.

Single-Function Software Inconvenient

Until recently, PC software was designed to address only one application at a time. Word processing, electronic spreadsheets, data storage and retrieval, and graphics have been implemented as if the others didn't exist or were wholly unrelated.

Each function, however, can be made

more valuable when integrated with one or more of the other functions. But should a person try to merge a graph or a spreadsheet model into a report prepared under a word-processing program, the difficulties of real-life PC use quickly become apparent.

Such individual programs were a boon in an era when the available PCs had only 64 kilobytes (K) of memory and a few hundred thousand bytes of diskette storage. (One byte equals eight binary bits of data, and is equivalent to one alphabet character or one digit. One kilobyte, or K, equals 1,024 bytes.) But memory capacities have increased since those days, and most new PCs offer 128K or more of memory and 5 or 10 megabytes (one megabyte equals 1,000,000 bytes) of nonremovable-disk data-storage capacity.

This increase in memory came just in time for users, who had become weary of inconvenient and complex independent application programs, and began demanding integrated products. Today's personal computers give them the memory capacity necessary to run this new generation of software.

Integrated Software Allows Merger of Programs

The basic difference between the old single-function software and integrated-software systems can be found in the external and internal behavior exhibited by each type of program. Simply put, external behavior is behavior that is observable and directly controllable by the user—the allowed keystrokes and commands, the menus (lists of program options) and displays, for example. Internal behavior refers to the methods the computer uses to store and retrieve data, or the format by which information is placed on the disk.

Individual programs that are developed independently generally don't exhibit similar external behavior. Therefore, users who want to utilize two or more of these programs must struggle to remember a variety of different, often conflicting, rules.

For example, the same command can mean two entirely different things when used in the context of two separate software programs. This inconsistency is more than just a nuisance; the user frustration it causes could very well subvert the productivity that these products are designed to enhance.

Integrated software, on the other hand, merges two or more application programs into

Lotus Development Corporation

Symphony, a versatile program, combines financial, word-processing, graphics, and other capabilities.

what could be called a seamless whole. Successful integration provides the user with two or more heretofore independent capabilities with apparently single external behavior and shared internal data-storage rules.

Three Categories of Products

But the trend is toward even more functional integration. At a minimum, these integrated products are styled after the common desktop activities performed by white-collar workers, such as word processing, electronic spreadsheet, graphics, data management, and communications.

Some products offer such additional features as personal-scheduling calendars, project-management aids, and telephone calling and answering assistance. In fact, most activities carried out by today's professional will be offered as components of some integrated system within the next few years.

The available or imminent integrated-software offerings tend to fall into one of three categories: expansion products, which extend popular products to include more capability; structured products, which combine multiple software capabilities under one consistent set of

The most sophisticated versions of integrated-software products feature multiple windows, like those shown here in samples of the DesQ (right) and Topview (below) systems. The windows emulate a desk-top work station.

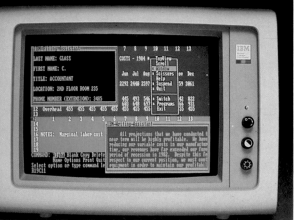

Top: Quarterdeck Office Systems; Above: IBM

rules; and metaphor products, which function as the electronic equivalent of a desktop.

Because working backward to integrate existing programs has proved impractical, new families of software products have been implemented instead. Most of this integrated software has been designed for the IBM PC (International Business Machines Corporation's personal computer), IBM XT (IBM's more advanced PC), and compatible systems because these PCs dominate the market, and the demand for software for them is brisk. And since most integrated-software products are modular, users can save money by using them because they have to buy only those capabilities they actually require, while being confident that other capabilities can be added as needed.

LOTUS 1-2-3

Lotus Development Corporation's phenomenally successful product called 1-2-3 is a good example of an expansion version of integrated software. It includes all the features desired by an experienced user of electronic spreadsheets, plus extensive graphic-presentation capabilities that work from spreadsheet-supplied data.

There are numerous other spreadsheet features that are valuable in their own right, but the graphics capabilities are especially attractive when compared with the independent graphics previously available.

A product like 1-2-3 is a natural outgrowth of users' experience with earlier programs. And if a user felt "pinched" by that generation's limitations, an integrated product that expands on those time-tested concepts can be a natural source of relief. Lotus, for instance, strove to make the program convenient and easy to use, going so far as to include a special template that surrounds the IBM PC's ten function keys to aid the user.

Software Families in Demand

In an earlier time, the vendor of a wide range of software products might have offered separate, independent programs for word processing, spreadsheets, graphics, and other functions. Today's broad-range suppliers, on the other hand, have been urged by their customers to offer structured families of products, which are usually offered on separate diskettes. The members of the software family have been designed to exhibit consistent behavior.

At the heart of these products is a common way of storing and retrieving data on disks and diskettes. Because the packages each rely on that common method for data management, internal data consistency and the capability for data sharing are inherent. At the same time, designers have imposed rules about how data are accepted from and displayed to users, so the components of the integrated family appear to behave similarly.

Most of the vendors with new offerings in the marketplace have adopted this approach. Simply explained, it integrates a range of well-understood applications already in use. The internal- and external-behavior rules have been standardized so that the same basic concepts of menus, commands, and cursor controls are retained in each application package.

The ITSoftware System

Take Martin Marietta's ITSoftware, for example. Each of the ". . . IT" modules reads and writes standardized data files on diskettes and hard disks. KeepIT, the data management/storage and retrieval program, implements displays and commands that assist the user in creating, querying, and reporting from data files. When the user moves to a different ". . . IT" program, the other external behavior will follow that of KeepIT's. The internal behavior (data structure) is strictly consistent in all the products.

The KeepIT program's external behavior is based on familiar menus that state applications in simply understood terms and one- and two-letter commands that permit access to applications. The simple language and coding configuration allow the user to communicate with the machine by using simple keyboard commands.

Each package (KeepIT, WritIT, etcetera) contains a directory of its programs. The KeepIT family is composed of nearly 50 individual programs to which the user gains access through the menus provided by the KeepIT master program.

Other family members can be added as needed, but the programs are separate and independent. The user must be responsible for remembering what generic group of capabilities are being utilized. There isn't an overriding master program to which control always reverts for moving data, for example, from CalcIT to WritIT.

Further, extensive data-conversion programs are provided so data can be exported to and imported from other popular products, such as 1-2-3, Multiplan, VisiCalc, and myriad word-processing systems. Of course, Martin Marietta would prefer customers to adopt CalcIT and WritIT modules, in which case the conversion programs aren't needed.

The ITSoftware solution addresses the integration issue alone, and the implementation is "plain vanilla." No exotic graphics displays, special peripherals, or extremely large memories are required. This low-risk approach means that users who are already comfortable with terse menus and letter commands can achieve integration without incurring significant hardware expense.

Investigate Options in Choosing Products

However, choosing to adopt a particular family of integrated modules is a double-edged sword: The price one pays for integration is the loss of the option to buy from a variety of different vendors to achieve the best performance-cost ratio. This is particularly frustrating if one selects a vendor's integrated family only to find that some of the modules are not yet available.

It's worth the effort to determine whether a family is based on a standardized set of modules

A woman uses one module in the standardized family of ITSoftware products, which complement one another.

Martin Marietta

dure, comes from the algorists, who in turn took their name from Al-Khowarizmi, a ninth-century mathematician. In some countries, computing by "algorism" was even forbidden by law during the Middle Ages. Not until paper became abundant in the sixteenth century did the new method finally replace the crude Roman system.

Calculating with Arabic numerals on paper, or with the help of primitive mechanical devices made of wheels and levers, slowly replaced counting boards in Europe. Meanwhile the abacus became the preferred way of calculating in Russia and Eastern nations. In its contemporary form of beads sliding on rods, it goes back at least to fifteenth-century China, and appeared in Japan in the next century.

A National Pastime in Japan

And so matters remained until the advent of the hand calculator. Today, just as U.S. educators debate how long children should do math drills with pencil and paper before being given access to a calculator, Japanese teachers argue over when to wean their students from the abacus. In both countries, traditionalists argue that unless children first understand the underlying logic of mathematics, they'll never understand what a calculator is doing.

But abacus education, which has been part of the grade-school curriculum in Japan for more than a century, has now been relegated to 10 hours of instruction in the third grade. Even that introduction is enough to intrigue thousands of children with the delights of the *soroban*. They flock to special schools, called *juku*, for hour-long training sessions three times a week; the cost is around $10 a month. Some 60,000 such schools have sprung up all over the country as a result of this intense interest.

National *soroban* championships are an annual tradition. For the past several years, the hands-down winner has been Eiji Kimura, a senior in business administration at Kyoto Industrial University. His love affair with the abacus began at age eight, when he attended his

Eiji Kimura (right) performs complex calculations in his head by visualizing the sequences used on an abacus.

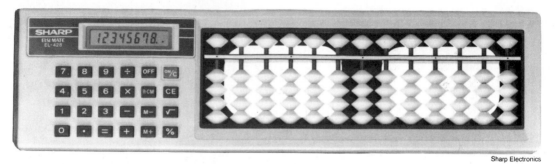

Sharp Electronics

This calculator with a built-in abacus appeals to many Japanese as a perfect blend of tradition and technology.

first *juku*. Two years later he had reached a fourth-degree level (on a scale of 10), and he won his first national championship at age 16. Kimura practices with ferocious intensity for two uninterrupted hours every day, and can perform feats that flabbergast his rivals and even his teacher. He can add 15 12-digit numbers in 20 seconds, and in less than four minutes can perform 30 multiplications, each a 12-digit number times a six-digit one. Thirty comparable long-division problems take him three minutes.

Math Wizard Performs Amazing Mental Feats

All this takes place faster than human fingers can flick the beads of an abacus, because Kimura has attained such a state of mathematical supremacy that he now performs his calculations in his head by visualizing the sequences used on a *soroban*. Here's how he mentally multiplies 256,436 by 1,297,584: "First divide both figures in two parts—256,436 as 256 and 436, and 1,297,584 as 1,297 and 584. Then multiply 436 by 584 and write down the last three numbers. Next multiply 436 by 1,297 and 256 by 584, add them up, and write down the last three numbers. Then multiply 256 by 1,297 and write down the first seven numbers. Now put them in order—the seven numbers first, followed by the three numbers from the second stage of calculation, and finally the three numbers from the first multiplication."

In other words, he immediately breaks multiplication into (256,000 + 436) × (1,297,000 + 584). The whole operation takes him eight seconds. Says he: "I have an abacus in my head, although the image isn't a clear one. When I see a number, I instantly draw mental images of beadlike things."

Division is Kimura's favorite subject, although he concedes that such formidable problems as 3,457,046,665,864 divided by 9,853,796 give him the faintest of headaches: "Sometimes I cannot see the beads clearly in my head. That's when I have trouble. I sometimes see numbers falling apart." Kimura's mentor-coach, Masaharu Yamamoto, likens his pupil's state of intense concentration in mental calculation to that of Zen meditation—not an ecstatic state, but a state of detachment or letting go. Kimura says, "It's not that I don't hear anything. I hear people speaking, but only a few words stick to my memory. Things just don't disturb me."

Integrating Tradition with New Technology

Many mere mortals, both Asian and Western, experience something of the same soothing feeling while working on an abacus. Watching the little beads slide up and down, a child gets an excellent idea of what arithmetic is all about, and how numbers correspond to objects in the real world. Many Western mathematicians and scientists like to use the abacus because of its many sensory charms—the changing visual patterns, the pleasant clicks, the tactile sensation. Perhaps they also enjoy the way the abacus links them to earlier times and other cultures. Perhaps they find a perverse satisfaction in rebelling against the growing, often ugly, complexities of modern life.

Even Japanese calculator manufacturers seem to understand this reluctance to abandon sliding beads for silicon chips. The Sharp Corporation produces an array of calculators that contain small, built-in abaci. Most owners use the calculator for multiplication and division, but are more comfortable doing addition and subtraction on the abacus. Sharp has sold more than 1.5 million of these hybrids in the past decade, a good omen for the survival of a noble tradition □

EARTH
SCIENCES

REVIEW OF THE YEAR

EARTH SCIENCES

EARTHQUAKES AND SEISMOLOGY

The year 1984 was marked by widespread earthquake activity. The largest quake struck Soviet Central Asia on March 21, affecting an 800-kilometer (500-mile) area and causing widespread damage and many casualties. The earthquake measured 7.1 on the Richter scale, a widely used indicator of an earthquake's severity, with a magnitude of 7 or higher on the scale signifying a major quake.

In the United States an earthquake of 6.2 Richter magnitude occurred on April 24 on the Calaveras fault zone. Centered about 19 kilometers (12 miles) southeast of San Jose, California, the quake caused $7.5 million in damages. Another strong quake (5.7 magnitude) rocked a wide area of central California and western Nevada on November 22, but there was no major damage. An earthquake that sounded like a "sonic boom" jolted parts of Wyoming, Utah, Montana, Colorado, Nebraska, and South Dakota on October 18. Measuring 5.5 on the Richter scale, it damaged buildings 320 kilometers (200 miles) apart in Colorado and Wyoming. And, on April 21, a 4.1 magnitude quake rocked the Lancaster, Pennsylvania, area—an area not considered "earthquake country." Motion was felt in a six-state area, but there were no injuries or major damages.

Meanwhile, studies of seismic-sensitive areas continued, with geologists watching for activity along the New Madrid fault, which slices through parts of Arkansas, Missouri, Tennessee, and Kentucky. The site of the devastating New Madrid earthquakes of the winter of 1811–12, this fault seems to spawn strong quakes every 40 to 80 years. Scientists believe that a repeat of the 1811–12 quakes would cause the worst natural disaster in U.S. history.

VOLCANOES AND VOLCANOLOGY

In late March, Hawaii's Mauna Loa volcano erupted for the first time in nearly nine years. Lava "curtains" spewed more than 180 meters

Top: Road-crew workers and geologists inspect a bridge in California that was damaged during an earthquake on April 24, 1984. Left: Frank Garcia discovered a spectacular wealth of fossils at Apollo Beach in Florida.

Top: AP/Wide World; Above: Richard Shepherd/Orlando Sentinel

(600 feet) in the air along a fissure almost 5 kilometers (3 miles) long. Although lava flows advanced toward the city of Hilo, there were no injuries or severe property damage. Within two days, Kilauea volcano, situated on Mauna Loa's southeast slope, also erupted, marking the first time the two had erupted together since 1868. Meanwhile, Mount St. Helens in Washington showed renewed activity on March 30, shooting an ash plume more than 4,500 meters (15,000 feet) skyward. The great lava dome within the crater also continued to grow. ■ Elsewhere several major eruptions jolted Mount Erebus, the largest of Antarctica's five active volcanoes.

Future volcanic activity seems possible in several calderas—the scars of past cataclysmic eruptions. The ground beneath Long Valley caldera near Mammoth Lakes in California continues to inflate, and the land under the caldera in Yellowstone National Park inflated about 1.7 centimeters (0.67 inch) a year from 1923 to 1983. In both areas there may be volcanoes brewing due to "hot spots"—plumes of molten rock rising from deep within the Earth.

EARTH STRUCTURE

Thanks to some newly developed techniques, scientists are learning more about the movements and structure of the Earth's crust, the forces that power crustal movements, and the interior of the Earth.

Improved echo-sounding techniques allowed geophysicists to make profiles of the Earth's crust from records produced by reflected seismic waves. They discovered a great suture near the present Georgia-Florida border; the suture is believed to have formed millions of years ago when the continents moved, taking their present shape and position. Seismic records also indicated that North America is splitting open along the Rio Grande rift zone that slices north and south through Colorado and Mexico. This rift is widening about 0.1 centimeter (0.04 inch) a year.

The crust lies on a dozen rigid plates that make up the lithosphere, or outer layer of the Earth. These huge plates, or slabs, ride and drift on the underlying mantle, and their movements are associated with volcanic eruptions, earthquakes, mountain building, and seafloor spreading. Seismic tomography, a new technique similar to CAT scanning used in medicine, has now made it possible to map the mantle in three dimensions. This mapping has revealed that hot semiliquid rock moves upward within the mantle and suggests that the entire mantle provides the energy that makes the crust-bearing plates drift and the ocean floors spread.

Meanwhile, Russian geologists are probing deeper into the Earth by means of cores from the world's deepest borehole. This superdeep test, being performed near the Arctic Circle on Kola Peninsula, has already reached a depth of more than 12,063 meters (39,576 feet)—far deeper than any previously known test.

GLACIOLOGY

Scientists have long speculated that melting of the polar ice caps, predicted as a consequence of warming of the Earth's climate, would cause a rise in sea level—with possible catastrophic effects. Recent studies now contradict this. New research suggests that there would probably be little increase in melting—even if the climate of the Earth should warm—because other changing climatic and moisture conditions could result in increased snowfall in the high, cold interior of Antarctica. The behavior and movement of the west Antarctic ice sheet are important in studies of glaciology and world climate. Researchers are now using airborne radar soundings to determine the ice's thickness, the topography of the base of the glacier, and the internal physical characteristics of the ice sheet.

In Alaska, geologists studying the Variegated Glacier have learned much about the cause of "surging glaciers." Unlike normal slow-moving ice masses, surging glaciers periodically accelerate rapidly, sometimes threatening lives and property. Researchers now believe that periodic surges result when changes in the shape and motion of the glacier inhibit drainage of water along the glacier's base, causing an increase in water pressure beneath the glacier, which, in turn, affects its base and causes the ice to slide very rapidly.

PALEONTOLOGY

One of the richest known fossil deposits was discovered during the year—in Florida's Tampa Bay Apollo Beach area. About 60 species—including now-extinct camels, ground sloths, mammoths, saber-toothed cats, and tapirs—were dated at 1.5 million to 1.9 million years old.

Dinosaur studies also continued during the year. Soviet scientists discovered a complete dinosaur egg and numerous fragments in the Fergana Valley in central Asia. Estimated to be about 105 million years old, it is the first such discovery in Eurasia. Meanwhile, in Montana, paleontologists unearthed a fossilized dinosaur still in its egg. It is only the second such specimen to be found. The structure of the 75-million–year-old embryo suggests that the creature may have been warm-blooded; this supports the belief of some paleontologists that dinosaurs, unlike modern reptiles, were warm-blooded.

WILLIAM H. MATTHEWS III

William A. Garnett

Mounds of Mystery

by George W. Cox

Above: In Oregon, Mima mounds stand out clearly from the smoothness of surrounding wheat fields. Right: The rippled landscape of Mima Prairie in Washington.

Certain phenomena in nature seem to demand an explanation the instant you see them. Consider, for example, the case of Mima mounds. Early explorers and settlers found these curious earth mounds, as big as 2 meters (6 feet) high and 50 meters (160 feet) across, dotting grassland areas of western North America in numbers ranging from 1 or 2 to more than 20 per acre. In 1817, when William Darby saw these "mounts of earth" on the coastal prairies of western Louisiana, he wrote, "these hillocks have given birth to many speculations; all perhaps wide of the truth; the most reasonable hypotheses ascribe them to a kind of mole." The pioneer western naturalist, Joseph Le Conte, who saw mounds on the West Coast in 1874, also remarked on the range of hypotheses. "Some have supposed that they are Indian burial mounds," he wrote, "veritable cities of the dead. Others . . . artificial mounds, upon which were built huts of Indian villages. Still others . . . that they were in fact large fishnests." Le Conte made an astute observation: "a phenomenon so widespread must be attributed to the action of a widespread agent."

Features Typical Over Wide Range

Mima mounds are indeed widespread. They are found from western Washington, southern Saskatchewan, and northwestern Minnesota south to northern Baja California and north-central Sonora and east to coastal Texas and Louisiana. Across this broad range they go by several different names. Along the Gulf Coast, and northward into eastern Oklahoma, they are termed pimple mounds, leading some observers to facetiously describe mounded grasslands as pimpled plains. In the northern Great Plains, the designation is frequently prairie mounds, and in California, where I have been studying them since 1979, they have traditionally been known as hogwallow mounds. The name *Mima* is taken from Mima Prairie, south of Olympia, Washington, and is an Indian name that seems to have won out against what were probably more prosaic competitors.

Mima mounds can be seen in a variety of physical settings—from sea level, in areas bordering salt marshes in California and Texas, to lower alpine-tundra habitats in the Sangre de Cristo Mountains of southern Colorado—but there are none in the southwestern desert or in regions originally covered by forest. They are found on residual soils over all major types of bedrock, on alluvial (clay, silt, sand, gravel, or other organic particles carried by running water) deposits and old lake beds, on glacial moraines (accumulations of earth and stones), and on the sandy soils of Pleistocene and Recent barrier islands.

The mounds themselves, however, have certain common features. They are made of sandy, loamy, or silty soil—never of heavy clay—and often contain gravel and small pebbles. Larger rocks are found on surfaces between mounds, where they sometimes form

Terry Domico/Earth Images

dense pavements. Mima mounds are most fully developed on level sites, where they are nearly circular, but they also are found on steep slopes, and in these places they are sometimes elongated in the downhill direction. One of the most constant features of the mounds is that they are always found in places whose soil has some sort of shallow basement layer—bedrock, hardpan (compacted soil), densely bedded gravel, heavy clay, or a permanent water table. This impermeable layer is usually less than 30 centimeters (12 inches) below the surface and often causes severe waterlogging of the soil during the rainy season.

Theories on Origin Abound

In more than a century and a half of scientific observation, more than 30 theories on how Mima mounds were formed have been proposed, but none has been proved. Many of these theories have purported to explain mounds in specific locations, despite Le Conte's admonition that they are widespread. Probably not coincidentally, individual theorists have often favored explanations that depended on their special area of knowledge—soils, hydrology, geology, climatology, botany, or zoology. Some of these theories have been serious and scientific, others more fanciful. On hearing a description of the mounds of Mima Prairie, distinguished geologist Alexander Agassiz reportedly identified them unhesitatingly as the large nest mounds of a type of sucker. The nests, he theorized, had once been located underwater and now were exposed.

There were other suggestions—Mima mounds were credited to Indians, falling trees, buffalo, ants, mud volcanoes, and other peculiar mechanisms. Most of these ideas have been discarded. What remain are four serious scientific hypotheses.

The erosion hypothesis suggests simply that the mounds are residual high points left by water or wind erosion. According to some versions of this hypothesis, wind or water previously removed soil and other matter from the surface, leaving the mounds behind. Other adherents of this idea say that the erosion occurred underground, when minerals dissolved and were removed by deep drainage. Mounds have been protected from erosion by trees or clumps of shrubs, they say, and have not been worn down by drainage because they are far from deep drainage channels.

The second major hypothesis attributes Mima mounds to wind deposition. It suggests that mounds are no more than coppice dunes—material deposited by the wind around trees or shrubs that have long since disappeared.

The frost-sorting hypothesis usually argues that mounds are the product of intense freezing and thawing processes that occur in cold climates. In such regions today, variations in soil structure, moisture supply, or plant cover create cells that alternately expand and contract during freezing and thawing cycles. These cells sometimes heave up into low mounds. All three physical hypotheses usually assume that mounds are fossil features, formed at a time when the climate was drier or colder than it is now.

The Latest Hypothesis

Most recent, and most complicated, is the fossorial (burrowing)-rodent hypothesis, presaged perhaps by William Darby, but first brought to the general attention of the scientific community in 1942 by mammalogists Walter Dalquest and Victor B. Scheffer. Based on observations at Mima Prairie and several other locations in western Washington, Dalquest and Scheffer postulated that Mima mounds were formed by pocket gophers or similar animals that tunnel outward from their nest sites, causing the backward displacement of soil. They suggested that the mounds are found where such mammals nest year after year. The nests, and thus the mounds, are at a fixed distance from one another because of territorial requirements. Those who subscribe to this hypothesis note that the shallow basement layer in the soil becomes waterlogged in wet weather. Fossorial rodents, such as pocket gophers, can survive only in high spots where the soil is well drained. If such spots exist, the animals establish their nests in them every year. Since gophers usually dig their foraging tunnels outward, they continually displace soil toward the nest. The soil they mine is pushed backward through the tunnel system before being deposited on the surface or packed into an abandoned chamber. Backers of the rodent hypothesis argue that, over decades or centuries, this gradual translocation of soil built mounds.

Pocket gophers, and many other animals as well, are known to frequent Mima mounds. All Mima mound areas in North America lie within the range of one or another species of pocket gopher, and careful examination of mounds almost always reveals the characteristic surface heaps of these animals—piles of fresh soil that look like small mine tailings. In most of the eastern Great Plains, the plains pocket gopher is the resident species; south of Corpus Christi, Texas, it is replaced by the South Texas pocket gopher. From the western prairie provinces and upper plains states through the Rocky Mountains and Columbia Plateau, the northern pocket gopher is the principal mound inhabitant. The Mazama pocket gopher frequents the mound prairies of the Pacific Northwest, and the valley pocket gopher, the hogwallow country of California and neighboring areas of the Southwest. Excavation of Mima mounds shows that pocket gophers locate their nests and food-storage chambers in the mounds but also tunnel into the areas between the mounds when these are not waterlogged.

Mounds Used by Many Animals

Many other animals also use Mima mounds. Since they are often the only well-drained spots in a flooded landscape, mounds become important refuges for species trying to escape floods. The deep, well-drained mound soils are ideal places for animals such as ground squirrels to build their nests; one or two species of ground squirrels are found in mounds in every region of the West. Several species of mole also inhabit Mima mounds, throwing up surface heaps more volcanolike than those of pocket gophers. Foxes and skunks commonly locate their dens in them. Badgers and coyotes visit the mounds when hunting for prey, and they dig winding furrows that follow pocket gopher tunnels. When they

Top: Jeff Foott; Bottom: George Cox

Many real and fanciful theories have been put forth to account for the origin of the mysterious mounds. One promising hypothesis suggests that pocket gophers (left) and other burrowing rodents are to blame. Below: A stand of fir trees thrives in the well-drained soil of a Mima prairie.

have cornered pocket gophers or ground squirrels in their chambers, the predators sometimes excavate deep pits. I recently examined a plot of land on the Aransas National Wildlife Refuge in Texas and found that all of the ten large mounds there had been excavated by coyotes that evidently were hunting gophers.

Other animals migrate to mounds seasonally. In a study at Waubun Prairie in northwestern Minnesota, John Tester, of the University of Minnesota, found that certain Mima mounds—particularly those surrounding a shallow prairie pothole—were overwintering sites for almost all of the Manitoba toads. For several years Tester and his students encircled selected mounds with drift fences that directed emerging toads into cage traps. Once their age and sex had been recorded, the toads were marked and released in order to make their way to their pothole-breeding area. Each spring anywhere from 150 to more than 3,000 toads emerged from individual mounds. The marked toads tended to return to the same mounds year after year. Adults were more diligent in this effort than juveniles, but the overall return rate was about 92 percent. One reason the animals seemed to prefer mounds as overwintering sites

was the looseness of the porous mound soil, presumably a result of activity by other animals. On the surrounding prairie the soil was dense and covered by a thick, almost impenetrable turf. Another important factor was that the mounds were deep and well drained. Using radioactive tracers to monitor some of the hibernating toads, Tester found that they had dug down from 45 centimeters (18 inches) to more than 130 centimeters (50 inches), where temperatures were just above freezing. During the winter some individuals went even deeper as the freezing level approached them.

The Manitoba toad is probably not the only animal to use mounds this way. In mounds on the coastal mesas near San Diego, California, the Pacific rattlesnake overwinters in the tunnels and chambers of pocket gophers. In the spring some snakes can be seen basking at the openings of these tunnel systems. John Tester also suspects that the jumping mouse hibernates in the Minnesota mounds.

Mound-Created Basins Ecologically Vital

In California, Mima mounds are part of a habitat that is of major importance to plant and animal life. There the high density of mounds—com-

During the rainy season, basins between mounds fill up with water and support diverse plant and animal life.

George Cox

A cross section of a Mima mound reveals many small rocks, which may have been moved there by rodents.

George Cox

monly 6 or more per hectare (15 or more per acre)—creates many small, closed basins within mound fields. These basins fill up with water during the rainy periods of winter and spring, creating temporary ponds or vernal (springtime) pools. The pools are rich in endemic (local) plant species and temporary pond organisms with wide, highly discontinuous ranges. More than 100 California plant species inhabit these pool basins. Many germinate and begin to grow underwater but complete their life cycle after the pool has dried up. Several frog and toad species breed in the basins, but the invertebrate life, obviously rich, has as yet been only partly surveyed. Several years ago, for example, I spotted an unfamiliar colonial organism growing in a pool, attached to some dead weeds. Stalked and branched like a tiny tree and about 1 centimeter (0.5 inch) high, this organism proved to be a colonial ciliate protozoan. (A ciliate protozoan is a tiny animal that has minute, hairlike projections called cilia.) Its known world distribution includes only three other localities—France, Hungary, and central Mexico.

The vernal pools in California have become the subject of controversy, for they are rapidly being destroyed by urban and agricultural development. This controversy is what

first brought Mima mounds to my attention, since whatever formed the mounds also produced the pool basins. If vernal pools are to be conserved, we need to know whether the mounds and their basins are a stable product of some ancient geomorphic process or a dynamic landscape maintained by some ongoing mechanism. I therefore set out to test the major hypotheses of mound origin.

African Mounds Add Weight to Rodent Theory

Since the beginning of my study of Mima mounds, I have been interested in the hypothesis attributing them to animals. This explanation has been controversial, but of the four major hypotheses, it has received the strongest support. In 1949, seven years after Dalquest and Scheffer decided that Mima mounds must be the work of pocket gophers, geologist W. Armstrong Price studied mounds in the Gulf Coast and the Great Plains and came to the same conclusion. Five years after that, Rodney J. Arkley and Herrick C. Brown looked at Mima mounds in the central valley of California and on the Columbia Plateau. They, too, concluded that mammals had probably built the mounds. I communicated with all of these scientists when I began my own study, and they supplied me with information that they used to resolve the question for themselves.

In thinking about the physical hypotheses, I realized one critical difference between them and the fossorial-rodent hypothesis. If any of the physical hypotheses is correct, mounds should be present on most continents and presumably in some places where no burrowing animals can be found. One simple way to disprove the rodent hypothesis, I realized, would be to find Mima-type mounds that don't have animals living in them. Victor Scheffer pointed out the importance of this test in papers published in the 1950's.

Reflecting on this, I remembered an experience I had in Kenya, Africa, in 1978. As I was traveling in a safari van between Nanyuki and Nyahururu in the central highlands, I was surprised to notice that the landscape was pimpled with mounds much like those near San Diego.

At the time this was only of passing interest to me. Now, however, I wanted to visit the place again, so I returned to the site with Christopher Gakahu, a mammalogist at the University of Nairobi. We examined several mound areas in the Aberdare Highlands near Nyahururu. The mounds were indeed similar in size, spacing, and structure to Mima mounds of North America and possessed a shallow basement layer of laterite (a product of rock decay that is red in color) hardpan. Furthermore, they were inhabited by a species of mole rat that is closely convergent to the pocket gopher in size, morphology, and behavior. To me, this provided strong evidence that, in Kenya at least, the fossorial-rodent hypothesis could not be ruled out. And the presence of the mole rat in mounds so far away from the western United States seemed more than a coincidence.

Compositional Studies Support Rodent Idea

But this evidence, however encouraging, didn't prove anything. The most direct way to approach the problem seemed to be to examine the mounds themselves. Was there anything about their structure or composition that would indicate that they had been formed by rodents, rather than by erosion, deposition, or frost sorting and heaving? Could some explicit test be done?

In the San Diego area, I saw the opportunity for such a test. There the soil in mound areas contains a great deal of gravel and small pebbles. Considering this fact, I started to compare what each of the four hypotheses implies about the number and sizes of rocks in the mounds. If the erosion hypothesis is true, mounds are simply high spots of the original soil, and rocks of all sizes should be found in them. The wind-deposition hypothesis, which argues that mounds are made up of dirt and sand, presupposes no rocks in the mounds. Finally, if the mounds were formed by freezing and thawing cycles, rocks of all sizes would have been forced to the surface and to the perimeter of the mounds themselves.

But implicit in the fossorial-rodent hypothesis, I realized, is a very specific, and contrary prediction: certain rocks—those small enough to be moved by rodents—will be concentrated in the mounds. Pocket gophers, in moving soil toward the tops of mounds, would also move small rocks, but leave larger rocks untouched. The key to the puzzle thus seemed to be in analyzing the contents of the mound soil.

To determine this, I took soil samples along mound-basin transects in the Miramar Mounds National Landmark in San Diego. I found few large rocks in the soil, but a heavy concentration of rocks smaller than about 5 centimeters (2 inches) in diameter. This concentration of small rocks in the mounds contradicts the erosion hypothesis, which suggests that large rocks should be in the mounds too, and both of the other physical hypotheses, since they imply that no rocks at all should be concentrated in the mounds. Only one hypothesis is left unscathed—the one that says small rocks, those that rodents can move, should be found in great quantities inside the mounds.

Soil-Moving by Gophers Examined

To test whether pocket gophers actually move soil the way we imagine, my assistant Bruce Kingsbury and I put soil plugs containing 11-gram (0.4-ounce) iron cap nuts in active pocket tunnels at the edges of mounds. We then used a metal detector to find the cap nuts after the animals had cleared the soil plugs. This experiment demonstrated that pocket gophers have a strong tendency to move soil in the direction of mounds. Some of our metal markers were moved more than 5 meters (15 feet) onto the mounds.

Despite these results, we cannot yet estimate how long gophers might take to build a mound. We don't know enough about how fast mounds lose soil by erosion or even how much soil pocket gophers can move in a given period of time. From the data available to me, I calculated that a gopher could move as much as 9½ tons of soil a year, but rates may be anywhere from 1 to 10 tons. We also don't have a clear picture of how the size of a mound or where on the mound a gopher is working affects its tendency to move soil toward the mound center. However, assuming that erosion is zero and that the animals excavate soil at rates similar to those determined by other scientists for the northern pocket gopher in Utah, we have calculated that the average mound on the Miramar Mounds National Landmark could have been built in as little as 110 years. We hope to obtain data in the near future that will permit us to estimate the time needed for mound formation.

An Obvious Conclusion

Our studies of San Diego–area mounds have revealed that they are not limited to the coastal mesas—the level marine terraces on which most of the city is located. Mounds cover many low hills adjacent to the coastal mesas and large valleys, and dot poorly drained valley floors and wet alluvial fans in inland locations. They also appear in many mountain meadows. Since Mima mounds in other parts of western North America are restricted to areas of original grassland, we believe that all of the California sites were originally covered by grassland. If so,

Mima mounds may aid us in understanding the changes in vegetation that have occurred since California was settled by Europeans.

The Mima-mound phenomenon has spawned strikingly divergent scientific hypotheses. But I believe one now dominates the field. Although all the die-hard theoreticians of Mima-mound formation will probably not throw in the towel immediately, the evidence is now hard to dispute.

So far, I have found Mima mounds only in parts of North America and East Africa with fossorial rodents such as pocket gophers and mole rats. Similar mounds are also widespread in South Africa and have been reported recently from Argentina, two regions with still other groups of fossorial rodents similar to pocket gophers. Furthermore, at least in San Diego, the composition of mounds suggests that their soil has been moved by pocket gophers; our experiments do not support the scenarios of mound formation outlined in the erosion, wind-deposition, and frost-sorting hypotheses. I am planning further studies of mounds in Africa and South America, and I believe the evidence already points to a conclusion. Fossorial rodents are the builders of Mima mounds, the largest, most widespread landscape features produced by any mammal other than man □

This huge expanse of hogwallow mounds, as the bumpy formations are called in California, lies in Merced County.

George Cox

Tim McCabe/SCS

THE SALT of the EARTH

by Janet Raloff

Irrigated agriculture was born more than 6,000 years ago in the Mesopotamian floodplain of the Tigris and Euphrates rivers in Asia. Part of what would later be known as the Fertile Crescent, this region once fed a population of between 17 million and 25 million people and gained renown as a net food exporter. So much of the region is now desert, however, that even though its population is only about half what it once was, it must import large quantities of food. What transformed this fertile delta into desert? There are, of course, a number of reasons, but many experts believe that salt should head the list.

A Long-Ignored Problem

The problem of soil salinity is as old as irrigation. Although it is not widely appreciated outside those regions that are severely affected, low visibility in no way diminishes its stranglehold on arid farming. Today, as in ancient Mesopotamia, many of the world's most productive farmlands are in jeopardy of "salting out."

Salt is crippling agricultural production not only in North Africa and the Middle East but also in North America, South America, Australia, and Asia—including China and the Soviet Union. Determining the exact acreage involved is difficult, but some of the estimates are alarmingly high. For example, Georg Borgstrom, retired professor of food science and human nutrition from Michigan State University in East Lansing, stated that based on studies published over the past few decades, ''at least 50 percent, and presumably now close to 65 percent, of all irrigated land will be destroyed by salt before the end of the century.''

''We're just reaping the results of not paying attention to the problem for the past 100 years,'' maintains Stephen Rawlins, a member of the staff setting priorities for the U.S. Department of Agriculture's (USDA's) Agricultural Research Service. ''As long as the problem is 10 years or more away, we don't worry about it. But time is up now and salinity must be dealt with.'' Moreover, with most of the best land for irrigation already under the plow, Rawlins says, ''we can no longer afford to farm our land till it salts out and then abandon it for some new tract.'' Helping to create a crisis, he believes, is the fact ''that we're starting to come up against a food crunch in many of these older irrigated areas—like in Pakistan and India.''

Salinity Troubles in San Joaquin Valley

All water, even ''fresh'' rainwater, contains some dissolved salts. Rain may acquire some salt from pollutants in the air. River water and

snowmelt accumulate some from the rock beds they erode. And soil contributes some to whatever water percolates through it. Though plants may find low levels of some salt constituents beneficial, salt concentrations upward of 2,000 to 3,000 parts per million (ppm) are generally toxic. (Rainwater has on average 10 ppm salt, while seawater has 35,000.)

On croplands where rainfall is plentiful and drainage good, salt will be regularly flushed through the soil and out to the ocean via rivers and subterranean passageways. Where rainfall is low, salts may never flush out of the root zone. And where drainage is restricted or nonexistent, saline pockets of groundwater will develop over time. However, salt hazards frequently go unnoticed until farmers decide to transform arid zones into oases of productive croplands through irrigation.

That's exactly what happened in California's San Joaquin Valley, where large-scale irrigated agriculture began developing around 1870. Bordered by three mountain ranges and the delta of the Sacramento and San Joaquin rivers, it is one of the most important agricultural areas in the world. The 400-kilometer (250-mile)-long valley produces close to $5 billion worth of crops annually. In fact, three of its eight counties head the nation in farm marketings. But with rainfall averaging only 35 centimeters (14 inches) a year in the north and a mere 13 centimeters (5 inches) annually in southern and western stretches, high productivity is sus-

SCS

The white areas in this aerial view taken in Colorado show residual salts that have been deposited by subsurface flows of highly saline irrigation drainage.

Many farmers must resort to building costly evaporation ponds such as this one to contain salty wastewater.

tained only with irrigation.

As a result of that irrigation, however, 200,000 hectares (500,000 acres) of the region's 2 million irrigated hectares (5 million acres) are already seriously affected by salt, according to Gerald Horner, an agricultural economist with the USDA's Economic Research Service in Davis, California. Figures compiled for the state of California predict that within 15 years, the affected acreage could double.

Report Projects Deteriorating Situation

The region's rich soils built up over millions of years through the erosion of its surrounding mountains. Rock particles settled out in the order of their size, with the largest forming light, permeable soil in a perimeter about the valley floor. Rain and snowmelt carried the tiniest particles to the valley trough, eventually creating five layers of virtually impermeable clay. Today the most salt-affected regions lie atop that clay, some of which is only 4 to 12 meters (12 to 40 feet) below the surface. With no natural drainage, water entering the valley stays put until it evaporates or is pumped out.

A 1979 analysis of the situation by the U.S. Department of the Interior's Bureau of Reclamation, the California Department of Water Resources, and the State Water Resources Control Board noted that typical irrigation water there contains salt in concentrations of about 350 ppm; "but even this low concentration means that about 1 to 1.5 tons of salt are being applied to each irrigated acre annually. Since [water] evaporation from the soil and transpiration through plant tissues (collectively termed evapotranspiration) extract essentially pure water, nearly all the salt content of the applied water is added to the soil." Moreover, the report says, when two major new water projects "reach their expected ultimate deliveries into the valley of about 5 million acre-feet [one acre-foot is the volume of irrigated water that would cover one acre (0.4 hectare) to a depth of one foot (0.3 meter)] per year, the salt being imported to the valley [via irrigation water] will total about 2 million tons each year. This is enough to cover almost 1,800 acres [730 hectares] with a layer of dry salt a foot [0.3 meter] deep."

Evaporation Ponds Necessary but Troublesome

In the beginning, salt will stunt a plant's growth. When levels get high enough, the plant simply dies. In order to keep salts from building up in the plants' fragile root zone, excess irrigation water—more than the crops actually need for growth—must be applied periodically to wash, or leach, salts deeper into the soil profile. But with an impermeable clay layer under much of the San Joaquin Valley, this salty leachate will eventually build up to waterlog the root zone in toxic brine (a strong saline solution) if drainage isn't provided.

For many farmers, however, installation of drains won't end their problems. Typical annual drainage volumes in the valley have been running about half an acre-foot—or 617,000 liters (163,000 gallons)—per acre irrigated, according to Horner. That means that even a small farmer will generate millions of liters of wastewater—drainage so salty that it frequently defies reuse for any other purpose. The seemingly intractable and growing dilemma is what to do with it.

Explains Horner: "We can't use the natural water sources because half the valley is a closed system [having no natural outlet] and the other half has been closed because of water-quality constraints. So what we're doing now is building evaporation ponds." Horner estimates that affected landowners—primarily those farming the valley's trough—must use anywhere from 5 to 10 percent of their acreage for these evaporating ponds.

And what isn't immediately obvious, he points out, is that the cost of retiring land to concentrate saline drainage goes beyond the mere land removed from production. Not only must the ponds be lined to keep the saline leachate from escaping, but landowners must also build a conduit (a tubular, enclosed passage) network of subsurface drains and a pumping system to transport that drainage water into the ponds. "So when your land has a drainage/salinity problem, your fixed costs might double," Horner says. Given the grim economic picture facing most farmers as it is, he says, these ponds will probably be enough to make those who had marginal operations "go under."

In addition, new research indicates that the ponds may create a hazard to wildlife. A report issued in August 1984 by the Bureau of Reclamation notes that toxic levels of selenium—a natural trace mineral in soil—have built up in some San Joaquin Valley drainage water being stored in its Kesterson Reservoir. The heavy-metal pollution was signaled by birth defects and high rates of fetal mortality among local waterfowl.

Tim McCabe/SCS

A cotton field shows crop failure in California's Imperial Valley due to the high salt content of the soil.

Imperial Valley Farmers Also Face Difficulties

Imperial Valley, another of California's prime agricultural regions, is also suffering serious salt problems. According to Myron Holburt, former chief engineer with the Colorado River Board of California in Los Angeles, "In Imperial Valley, farmers have installed over 28,000 miles [45,000 kilometers] of drainpipes, at a cost of over $72 million," in an attempt to manage the salt being deposited onto their fields by irrigation water.

Holburt says the Colorado River, a primary source of water for Imperial Valley farmers, is classified as highly saline for irrigation purposes. If irrigators aren't careful in managing its use, he warns, they might be forced to switch to more salt-tolerant crops, which as a rule are less profitable.

In comparison with the San Joaquin, Imperial is a small valley. Yet drainage water coming off fields in this closed basin "amounts to somewhere in excess of 1 million acre-feet a year," explains James Rhoades, research leader in soil and water chemistry at the U.S. Salinity Laboratory in Riverside, California. "For sake of perspective," he adds, "this is about the water supply of the nation of Israel—not a small volume.'' But unlike the San Joaquin farmers, Imperial Valley growers at least have somewhere to send their saline drainage for permanent disposal—the man-made Salton Sea.

Study Describes Worldwide Problem

Salinity problems similar to California's are occurring in areas throughout the western United States. A graphic portrait of salt's international dimensions is conveyed by a recent 97-page study out of the Washington, District of Columbia, office of Earthscan, an information agency of the London, England–based International Institute for Environment and Development.

It found, for example, that:

• roughly half the irrigated land in Syria's Euphrates Valley has become saline to the point where crop losses now total an estimated $300 million annually;

• between one-quarter and one-half of all irrigated lands in South America are affected by salinization, ''and the problem is increasing as fast as new lands are being brought under irrigation'';

• in India, 35 percent of all irrigated land is seriously saline;

• and in Pakistan, where 80 percent of all croplands are irrigated, a third of the irrigated total—or 5.2 million hectares (12.8 million acres)—is already experiencing severe salt problems, and another 16 percent is threatened with salinization by high water tables. In fact, the report says, another ''250 acres [100 hectares] go out of production every day [in Pakistan] because of salinity.''

Salt-affected Lands Defy Quantification

Citing figures by the United Nations Food and Agricultural Organization (FAO), Earthscan reports that today ''about 120 million hectares (300 million acres)—half the world's irrigated land—suffer from reduction of crop yields due to salinization.''

Not everyone accepts that number. Among those who differ is Harold Dregne, a senior land-resources adviser to the Agency for International Development (AID) in Washington, District of Columbia, and a renowned scholar on desertification (of which salinity is a primary cause). Dregne has compiled his own statistics, and they indicate that such a figure represents merely the area ''continually threatened with waterlogging and salinization'' to the point where desertification could result. But Dregne also admits that arguing over the statistics is rather pointless because even the best figures ''are very imprecise—educated guesses really.''

On that, Jan van Schilfgaarde agrees. Van Schilfgaarde, who until September 1984 directed the U.S. Salinity Laboratory, notes that the more widely quoted statistic—that 30 percent of irrigated arid lands are salt-affected—''came from a coffee-hour discussion here at the lab 25 years ago.'' Though to this day everybody quotes it, he acknowledges, ''we have no statistics to back it up.''

A farmer opens an irrigation ditch to water his wheat field in Pakistan, where salinity problems are severe.

Kay Muldoon/World Bank

Georg Gerster/Photo Researchers

In Colorado, a technician using a special tool takes a core sample of soil to test its salinity.

Rhoades, now acting director for the Salinity Laboratory, points to one of the primary reasons the problem has thus far defied quantifying. "One has to take many soil samples to get something representative of an area—not only across the landscape, but also with depth." What's more, he notes, "a soil's salinity changes with time: as the water table goes up and down, as a farmer changes from one crop to the next, even as he changes [irrigation or tillage] practices. So there is a tremendous sampling requirement." And at perhaps $25 per analyzed sample, he says, "you can see that accurate sampling has been essentially prohibitive."

Rhoades has been working on new technologies to make sampling quicker, easier, and less costly. But the fruits of his labors are still so new that they have not yet been used to do any serious salinity mapping on a large scale.

Salt Control Should be National Priority

Further complicating quantification of salinity is the fact that "many farmers don't even recognize they have a problem until it gets so grossly bad that it's obvious," explains George Stem, chairman of the Soil Conservation Service's Salinity Assessment Leadership Team (SALT). Stem says, "You could lose 5, 10, or even 15 percent of your productivity while you're developing a salinity problem"—a loss that is within the normal variation that could occur from year to year just due to changes in temperatures, rainfall, or farm-management practices. In fact, unlike most blights, "there aren't any real symptoms" to low levels of soil salinity, notes Rawlins of the Agricultural Research Service. "The crops just grow worse—not quite as big."

But a national soil-salinity assessment—the first in the United States—was initiated by the USDA's Soil Conservation Service in late 1984. Stem is hoping that its results will convince policymakers in Washington, District of Columbia, that controlling salinity should be a national priority.

It's ironic, Stem says, that although controlling salinity is essential to conserving soil quality, the Soil Conservation Service has given salinity "very little recognition in terms of our national problems." He attributes that in part to the perception that salinity is a regional problem affecting only the western U.S. He suggests that another reason for salinity's low profile within the Soil Conservation Service's action plans is the agency's focus on controlling erosion. Stem maintains that while erosion is unquestionably a serious problem that shows no regional preferences, in many ways it can also be less devastating than salt: "Even if you have erosion for 50 years," he says, "you still generally can produce something on your land. But you let the salinity problem get bad, and boom—your productivity is gone."

Stem also believes that, "without question," the salt problem will only be getting bigger. And to illustrate his point, he notes that serious salinity problems are beginning to develop for the first time in the eastern part of the United States. By overdrawing groundwater, he says, several Atlantic and Gulf Coast states are beginning to get saltwater intrusion into what were formerly freshwater aquifers—sources of water for both drinking and irrigation.

Economic and Political Obstacles Abound

So what are the prospects for the future? "In theory, soil salinity is a reversible problem anywhere," according to Dregne. Except where the

A once-fertile field in California where alfalfa thrived is now fissured and crusted with salt.

soil is heavy clay, he says, "you can cleanse any problem if you have enough low-salt water to flush through the soil and as long as you have drainage" to carry away the salty wastes. The rub is that "it gets to be expensive."

In Egypt's Nile Delta Valley, for example, where the Aswan High Dam has eliminated the periodic flooding that used to wash salts out of the upper topsoil, a drainage system is now being installed at an estimated cost of $1 billion, Dregne says. "And that will take care of only a part of a small valley." The cost of contending with the San Joaquin Valley's most serious crisis—no place to permanently dispose of highly saline drainage—could also prove to be massively expensive. One proposal that has been suggested—to pipeline drainage over the mountains for ocean disposal—could cost $44.7 million annually. A less expensive option, to dispose of it in the ocean via San Francisco Bay, has met with continuing vehement political opposition on environmental grounds.

In fact, most analysts now consider politics and economics to be the leading obstacles to controlling salinity. Take the "equity issue," Stem says. The Colorado River is the leading source of irrigation water for the Southwest. At its headwaters, salt concentrations are only about 50 ppm. By the time they reach California, however, they have increased twentyfold. Even though upstream users may have contributed substantially to the downstream salt loading, they resent being asked to pay for cleaning up California's water, Stem says. Similarly, California farmers resent having to pay the costs of managing salts washed downriver to them. Economist Horner believes the attitude is building, at least in California, that if a farmer can hold out long enough from taking corrective action, eventually the federal government will step in with subsidies. He says many farmers seem to be banking on the assumption that Congress won't let the nation's most productive farm districts salt out.

Dregne has observed that in many other regions, especially developing countries, irrigation farmers frequently cannot afford the technology to manage salt better, or they lack the education and guidance to put that technology to effective use.

These socioeconomic and political problems tend to be far less manageable than the technological ones. And that's why few experts expect to see the salt problem effectively harnessed in their lifetime □

DEEP-SEA STORMS

by Victoria Kaharl

Our second night at sea, the marine geologists aboard the research vessel *Knorr* gathered in the chief scientist's cabin to look at photographs of the ocean bottom. The photos were taken by "Pogo," a strobe-equipped camera mounted on a steel frame that bounces across the seabed, each bounce triggering the camera's shutter. Pogo snapped its first shot at 5:50 P.M., after a two-hour journey by winch to the bottom nearly 5 kilometers (3 miles) below, and by 9:00 P.M., the slides were ready to go.

The geologists could hardly contain their excitement at the bumps and lumps on the screen before them. "Look," I. N. (Nick) McCave shouted. "A fairy ring." In his clipped Oxford accent, McCave explained that the strange mound with five symmetrical holes was apparently made by an animal, perhaps of the phylum *Echinodermata,* which includes starfish and other five-sided creatures. Another slide.

"Oh!" said Charles Hollister. And another. "Ah," McCave chimed in, pointing his bare foot to make a long shadow across the screen. "Go back, Charley, go back!"

HEBBLE Dispels Myth of Deep-ocean Tranquility

The researchers aboard the research vessel *Knorr* are hunting for telltale signs of something that until recently was not thought to exist—an extraordinarily strong current, or "benthic storm," on the bottom of the deep sea. People had long believed that "the deep waters are a place where change comes slowly, if at all," as the famed ecologist Rachel Carson wrote in her classic *The Sea Around Us.* But the results of the High Energy Benthic Boundary Layer Experiment (HEBBLE), of which this cruise is part, have helped dispel the notion of a tranquil abyss (a deep chasm). Deep and dark it is; calm and unchanging it is not.

Since HEBBLE's modest beginning in 1979, some three dozen scientists of varying disciplines have participated in the project, which is funded by the Office of Naval Research. The experimental site is in the North Atlantic about 725 kilometers (450 miles) off the coast of Massachusetts. There project scientists have detected massive, fast-moving storms sweeping along the bottom. They have been recorded moving at speeds of up to 75 centimeters (30 inches) per second—about one knot—exerting a force equal to a 97-kilometer (60-mile)-an-hour wind on land.

Surface Eddies Considered Cause of Storms

Storms can carry a ton of sediment a minute, causing dramatic changes in the seafloor—scouring it in some places, depositing enormous loads of clay and silt in others. "A benthic storm is very much like a blizzard," says Arthur R. M. Nowell of the University of Washington, codirector of HEBBLE. "The visibility goes to zero. Then the weather clears and you can see small ripples of mud in striking patterns much like drifts of snow around fences and trees after a real whiteout [a blizzard that dramatically decreases visibility]."

Photos: Woods Hole Oceanographic Institution

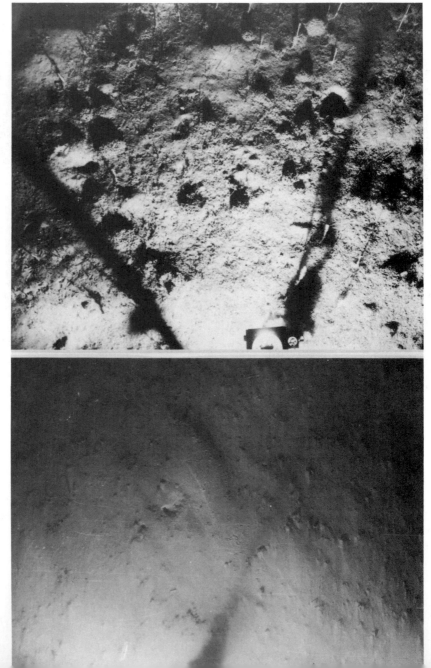

Sediments show signs of disturbance from bottom-dwelling animals during tranquil times in the deep sea (right). But when big benthic storms rage through the region, the seafloor is swept smooth (bottom).

Scientists are not yet able to predict when benthic storms will appear, although preliminary data put their frequency at about every two to three months. The storms last from a few days to two weeks and can affect areas tens of kilometers (1 kilometer equals 0.6 mile) wide.

What causes the storms is also still uncertain. However, Charles Hollister, codirector of HEBBLE and senior scientist and dean of Woods Hole Oceanographic Institution, claims researchers are "very close" to an answer. Their results appear to link the storms to the nearby Gulf Stream and the surface eddies it sheds—rings of swirling water hundreds of kilometers across. The kinetic energy (energy related to motion) of these eddies is somehow transferred downward and generates a current that joins and reinforces the normal current on the seafloor, which in the HEBBLE area is unusually strong for the deep sea. This enhanced current becomes a storm when it grows strong enough to lift copious amounts of bottom sediment.

Evidence that energetic surface eddies combine with stronger-than-normal bottom currents to generate benthic storms is "too strong to be coincidental," says Hollister. This link is also bolstered by the fact that the largest sediment drifts on the seafloor are found in the coupled areas. Thus, Hollister says, it may be possible to identify other areas likely to experience benthic storms by sandwiching world maps showing areas of strong bottom currents with those showing energetic surface eddies. "When you do this, you find that the proper conditions exist in numerous areas," he says. "These include the entire northwestern part of the North Atlantic basin and vast areas off the coast of South Africa, Argentina, and New Zealand."

New Data Could Provide Industrial Benefits

The discovery of powerful benthic storms, which the scientific community is only now beginning to appreciate fully, will likely have far-reaching implications. The storms may become an important factor in the design and placement of virtually any object meant for abyssal depths in potentially stormy areas.

For example, Hollister says the storms might be able to sweep sediment out from under seabed telephone cables, causing them to "strum," weaken, and fail. Trouble with telephone cables in the deep sea is rare, according to American Telephone and Telegraph Company (AT&T) senior engineer Jeff Ewald. In-

Suki Coughlin

HEBBLE researchers hunt for tiny marine organisms in samples of mud retrieved from the ocean floor.

deed, the company's transatlantic cables have experienced only minor problems over the years. But AT&T has recently received some "inexplicable" transmission signals from its TAT-7 transatlantic cable that skirts the HEBBLE experimental site, says Hollister, who has been investigating trouble with telephone cables for two decades. He suggests that this "may not be a coincidence." However, Ewald will say only that AT&T is interested in evaluating HEBBLE results "as they might affect our cables in the North Atlantic."

Lessons about sediment dynamics—the movement of mud—may also be applied to problems in coastal waters. "It's surprising that we know more about sediment dynamics in the deep sea than in the shallower waters of the continental shelf," Nowell says. "But until HEBBLE, nobody had ever conducted such intense sediment-transport studies anywhere in the ocean." The information could be used to boost the efficiency of dredging operations and improve the structural stability of pipelines, bridge footings, and other structures emplaced on the bottom. "If we could come anywhere near to accurately predicting the seafloor's response to underwater forces such as currents," Hollister says, "we could save millions of dollars in dredging fees and marine construction and repair costs."

Storms May Disturb U.S. Navy Defense Systems

The U.S. Navy is interested in benthic storms because of its charge to patrol and protect home waters, according to Commander Joseph Spigai, former HEBBLE program manager of the Office of Naval Research. "The navy is very interested for a variety of reasons in knowing about the stability of the ocean bottom," he says. "Does it shift around? And if so, how often and where? We think this has some potential applications to our national defense."

Among the navy's ocean-bottom structures and "one of the primary systems that may be affected" by the storms, he says, is the Sound Surveillance System (SOSUS). This is an array of hydrophones used to listen for enemy submarines in the North Atlantic. "Scouring of the bottom may disturb our sensors," Spigai says. "There's a chance that they might be covered and uncovered by the moving sediments."

The listening posts may face another problem as well: HEBBLE investigators theorize that the turbulent storms must be noisy. "As long as the key to locating submarines is listening for the noise they generate, any sound produced by a storm might muffle the acoustic signature of an enemy sub," says Nowell. Spigai agrees that the storms "may mask other noises that the navy might be listening for," adding the comment "that's about all I can say on the matter."

HEBBLE Prompts New Avenues of Oil Exploration

Benthic storms are also causing geologists to reexamine their ideas about where to search for new reserves of oil. They know that petroleum forms in areas of the seafloor where massive deposits of sediment rich in organic material accumulate quickly, at least by geologic standards. According to the conventional view, the organic-rich sediments—largely the remains of aquatic plants and animals that live near the surface—drift steadily down from above and remain where they hit bottom. But the power of storms to redistribute sediments adds a new

wrinkle. Hollister speculates that the areas where ancient storms deposited their sediment loads would have been favorable sites for the formation of oil-bearing rock. Thus, by learning more about how benthic storms work and where they occur, geologists might be able to "look down paleocurrents" to find new oil fields.

The researchers hope to provide clues for petroleum exploration in another way as well. At the HEBBLE site, a certain type of microscopic hard-shelled amoeba—called foraminifera—is more primitive and abundant than similar fauna in apparently storm-free areas. Fossils of these "forams" are also found in oil-bearing rocks in the North Sea and even many places on land. Oil-company geologists sometimes use these fossilized forams as markers to help them identify potential reserves. "But forams might become even more useful if we knew more about how they lived in the ancient seas," says Michael Kaminski, a Woods Hole–Massachusetts Institute of Technology graduate student. "Therefore, I'm trying to use the present as a key to the past. By studying the forams that live in the mud at the HEBBLE site, we may get a better understanding of the kind of environment that oil-bearing rocks formed in many millions of years ago."

Scientists Question Effects of Ocean Dumping

Perhaps the most important question raised by the discovery of benthic storms, however, is their potential effect on hazardous wastes that may be consigned to the sea bottom. "When most toxic and radioactive pollutants enter the ocean, they look for fine grains of sediment to call home," says Nowell. "Indeed, sediments scavenge pollutants very effectively—just like Maalox [a popular brand of antacid used to neutralize stomach acidity]." Thus, storms that move about huge quantities of sediment might move pollutants as well.

For example, the United States and several European nations are studying the feasibility of burying high-level radioactive wastes from nuclear-power plants beneath the seafloor. "However, the HEBBLE site and others like it might be [extremely] poor places to put something that you don't want to see again," says HEBBLE biological-oceanographer Dave Thistle of Florida State University. One problem is that bacterial activity at the HEBBLE site is unusually high for the deep sea. The storms apparently bring in fresh supplies of oxygen and nutrients—ideal for bacterial growth.

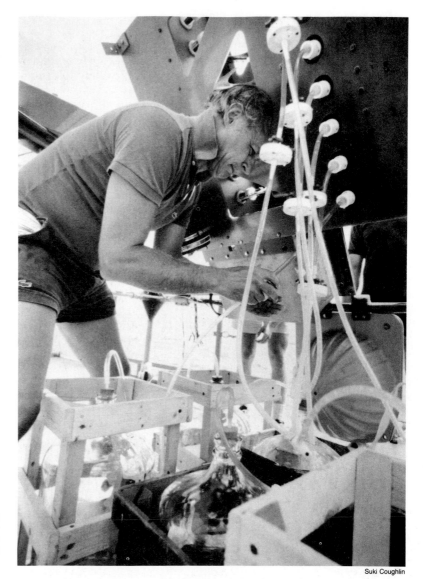

Geologist I. N. McCave takes a sample of sea-water collected from the deep to determine its sediment concentration.

Suki Coughlin

"These bacteria are perfectly willing to mobilize sediments carrying pollutant materials, including metals and radionuclides [radio-active atoms]," says Thistle. "Then the question is whether there is a way for the pollutants to move up the water column." The answer may be yes. He says pollutant-laden bacteria might be eaten by larger bottom-dwelling creatures. Some of the materials excreted by these animals, such as egg cases and fat globules, are buoyant enough to rise to the shallower regions where humankind's food fish live. Thistle stresses, however, that this is still just theory. The HEBBLE researchers have planned more studies of the role bacteria play in mobilizing

sediments. If it turns out that bacteria can start pollutants on their way into the food chain, then Thistle says potentially stormy areas probably should be avoided as waste-disposal sites.

But Hollister says there is another way to look at the waste-disposal question. Storms could actually dilute the wastes to safe levels by dispersing them over a broad area. While such a strategy for disposal may ultimately prove to be acceptable, the HEBBLE researchers caution that for now there are more questions than answers. "Before the seafloor is selected as a final dumping ground for any hazardous wastes, we must be able to make reliable predictions about how they will behave over the long

The HEBBLE instruments are designed to withstand the harsh conditions of the benthic environment.

term,'' says Nowell. ''But our mathematical models of sediment dispersion still need verification. They're based at present on numbers that essentially are guesses.'' The hope, of course, is that HEBBLE will provide the ''numbers'' needed to improve such predictions.

A Radical Notion

The idea that currents in the deep ocean probably move much faster than suspected was proposed early this century by a German physical-oceanographer named George Wust. But the concept, which he inferred from data on bottom temperature, pressure, and salinity, met with resounding skepticism.

In 1962 Charles Hollister, then a graduate student at Lamont-Doherty Geological Observatory in New York, got his first glimpse at what he thought was a storm-swept seabed while looking at a photograph taken by Lamont geologist Maurice Ewing. Hollister could not accept the conventional reasoning that the rip-

ples and sculpted mounds in the photo had been caused by some earth-shaking geologic event thousands of years ago, possibly during the last Ice Age. He speculated that something powerful and recent had scoured the seabed and created the ripples.

In 1964 Hollister took his own pictures in the same general area of the North Atlantic that would become the HEBBLE experimental site. The photographs showed more of the same—ripples, mounds, mud waves—and further confirmed his theory. For the most part, however, the scientific community adhered to the traditional notion of a tranquil abyss. Other investigators periodically reported data that indirectly suggested the presence of swift currents in the deep sea. But as late as 1978, there still wasn't enough evidence ''to shake a stick at,'' says Tom Pyle, HEBBLE's first navy-program manager and now chief scientist of the National Ocean Service. So when Hollister proposed HEBBLE, ''it was a real gamble,'' says Pyle.

Special Instruments Needed for Deep-sea Work

If HEBBLE was indeed a gamble, it started paying off almost immediately. In the summer of 1979, scientists on the first research cruise found deep-sea currents faster than anything even they had imagined. The researchers filtered hundreds of liters (1 liter equals 0.26 gallon) of seawater for suspended sediment. Cloudy or muddy samples would indicate the presence of currents powerful enough to lift the fine sediment from the bottom. A reading of 100 to 500 micrograms (one microgram equals one-millionth of a gram) of sediment per liter would have sufficed to show turbulence; their samples yielded up to 12,000 micrograms. ''It was astounding,'' recalls Lamont's Wilf Gardner.

Part of the challenge for HEBBLE researchers has been to develop instruments that can operate in the deep ocean—an environment, says Hollister, that is more hostile than the Moon. ''There's no rust on the Moon because there's no oxygen,'' he explains. ''There's no saltwater to short-circuit your electronics. Saltwater eats metal. In the ocean, animals tend to eat everything they can find. You put a piece of wood or metal down there on the bottom and it becomes a condominium; everybody wants to move in.''

The project required sensors that could withstand 45,150 kilograms per square centimeter (7,000 pounds per square inch) of pressure and near-freezing temperatures while taking measurements continuously for hours or days. The instruments had to be stable enough to endure the jostlings and vibrations from the ship and the bottom blizzards, yet delicate and sophisticated enough to detect the intricate fluctuations of turbulent water and tiny particles of suspended sediment. "It was a tall order," recalls I. N. McCave of the University of East Anglia in Norwich, England.

If an instrument was available but unable to function in the deep ocean, the HEBBLE engineers adapted it for abyssal depths. If a needed instrument didn't exist, they designed and built it. One invention born of necessity, for example, is the Benthic Acoustic Stress Sensor (BASS). Conventional meters used to measure ocean currents rely on mechanical rotors, which can interfere with the flow of water and throw off results. BASS uses sound waves to measure currents. It also does what no other instrument can do—measures water speed and direction twice a second. These instantaneous measurements allow scientists to calculate precisely the stresses that a storm exerts on the bottom when it lifts the sediment.

The instruments are affixed to large steel and fiberglass tripods that free-fall to the abyss. A storm triggers a microprocessor on one of the tripods—called Master BASS—which then acoustically alerts the other sensors to switch themselves on. After a storm, Master BASS orders the sensors to turn off in the same way. Without such "intelligent" remote control and selective sampling, the instruments' recording devices would reach capacity in a matter of hours and their batteries would be quickly used up. Acoustic commands also summon the tripods back to the surface. Flotation spheres—large glass balls encased in brightly colored plastic—give the tripods the buoyancy they need for their long upward journey.

Seafloor Laboratory Provides New Insights

A new phase in the project began in the summer of 1985 when the research vessel *Knorr* returned to the HEBBLE site carrying a special cargo. Until then, studies relied on cameras and various instruments to monitor conditions at the seafloor. But that summer's cruise featured the debut of SeaDuct—an 1,815-kilogram (4,000-pound) "laboratory" of pink fiberglass and glistening aluminum that was lowered to the seabed.

SeaDuct is allowing investigators for the first time to create controlled currents on the bottom and to measure how the sediments respond. These tests, says Hollister, are providing vital information about the behavior and effects of benthic storms. Indeed, SeaDuct, along with the other HEBBLE studies, will enhance our very meager understanding of the vast, sunless underworld that is perhaps the least-known and least-studied region of our planet□

A worker adjusts an instrument on SeaDuct—a self-contained, unmanned, deep-ocean laboratory.

Woods Hole Oceanographic Institution

When North Becomes South

by Subir K. Banerjee

One December day in 1538, João de Castro's compass needle pointed the wrong way. It happened near Bombay, India, on an uncharted island in the Arabian Sea, where de Castro, the viceroy of Portuguese India, had dropped anchor to take his bearings. He later recorded these observations in his diary:

[As I placed] my compass upon a great rock to see the orientation of the island, the rose suddenly turned around showing the north where the south was before. When I saw this I supposed that the rose was off its pivot, and took the compass from the rock to put it right. As I took it, suddenly it turned round, and the north went back to its proper place! Concluding that this strange occurrence must be caused by the nature of the rock, I put down the instrument and took it up many times, and each time it repeated the performance. Very astonished at this incident, I wandered nearly all over the hill, putting the compass down on every rock, but it made no variation. I only found one boulder near the other of a like nature, but there the rose did not make so complete a turn.

Unusual Occurrences

As it turned out, João de Castro's islet was not the only source of disorienting rocks. Specimens found in India during the 19th century, and in France and Japan during the first years of this century, had the same effect on compass needles. A number of scientists attributed this property to some peculiar mineral composition, while others thought the electromagnetic properties of lightning might be to blame. Still others insisted that the rocks held a deeper significance, perhaps offering clues to the geologic history of the planet. Not until 1963 was the argument resolved.

A Theory Takes Hold

That year, two research groups convinced most geophysicists that the rocks are evidence of a past reversal in Earth's magnetic field, vestiges of a time when the northern magnetic pole resided where the southern is today. According to this view, these volcanic rocks are "fossil magnets" that faithfully recorded the intensity and direction of the global magnetic field prevailing at the time they cooled and hardened. What won this theory acceptance was the finding—reached independently by teams from the U.S. Geological Survey, in Menlo Park, California—that rocks from widely scattered parts of the world but of about the same age display reverse polarity. Further dating studies indicated that Earth's poles have flipped as many as 25 times during the past 5 million years—on average, once every 200,000 years. The last such flip, however, happened 730,000 years ago. We are, it would seem, long overdue for a magnetic reversal.

Reversal May Result in Major Disruptions

When it happens, it could disrupt activities around the globe. Not only will hikers be misled by their compasses, but the magnetic guidance systems of missiles, spacecraft, airplanes, and ships could also go haywire. Bacteria, insects, fish, and birds that use the magnetic field to orient themselves will probably have trouble finding their homes. World climate might even change: normally, radiation particles from the Sun remain at the outer extremities of the magnetic field, hundreds of kilometers above the Earth's surface, as they migrate toward the northern and southern magnetic poles. During a reversal, with the field temporarily weakened, the particles might pass through the upper atmosphere, providing nuclei for the formation of ice crystals and, ultimately, vast banks of ice clouds that would spawn cold, rainy weather.

There is no cause for concern that such calamities will occur without warning. Only a few decades ago, scientists thought that magnetic reversals happened almost instantaneously, but we now believe them to be the culmination of centuries of gradual geomagnetic change. To be sure, the ultimate source of that change is still somewhat mysterious; it lies deep within the Earth, in ever-changing patterns of

Opposite: Francis Bacon, Landscape, *1978*
Opposite: Marlborough Gallery Inc.

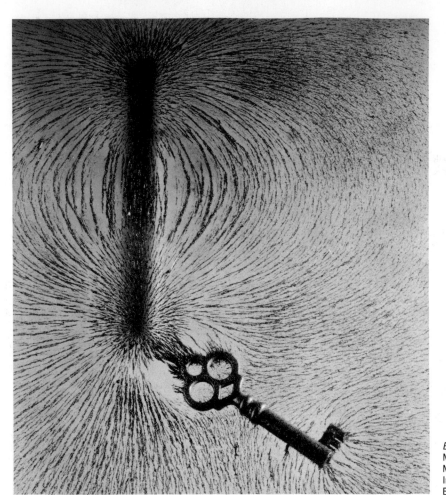

Berenice Abbott, A Metal Key Changes the Magnetic Pattern of Iron Filings Around a Bar Magnet, c. 1939–61

churning molten iron. Nonetheless, geophysicists are unraveling the mystery, modeling the process with greater precision in an attempt to define the telltale signs of an imminent reversal.

And some of those signs have recently been observed, suggesting that the Earth may be headed toward another magnetic reversal. It is unlikely that our grandchildren or their grandchildren will live to see it; the poles probably will not reverse themselves for another 2,000 years or more. Still, in the life cycle of our planet, that is but the blink of an eye; in terms of geologic time, we may be moments away from the next magnetic reversal.

Origin of the Term "Magnet" Obscure

The word "magnet" comes from the Greek term for magnetite, a strongly magnetic oxide of iron, but thereafter the word's derivative be-

comes less certain. The poet Lucretius ascribed the term to Magnesia, the ancient Greek province (in what is now Turkey) in which the mineral was mined. But the Roman naturalist Pliny the Elder traced the name to Magnes, a shepherd "the nails of whose shoes and the tip of whose staff stuck fast in a magnetick field while he pastured his flocks."

Pliny's use of the phrase "magnetick field" was accurate in an entirely unintended sense. Today we know that any magnet, whether magnetite, an industrial electromagnet, or a paper clasp that sticks to the surface of a refrigerator door, is surrounded by a magnetic field—a miniature version (complete with a positive and negative pole) of the one that envelops the Earth. Like Earth's magnetic field, any magnet's field can endow certain metals (and other minerals, to a lesser extent) with magnetic fields of their own. Thus did the English come to call magnetite "leading stone," or lodestone; a thin, lightweight piece of iron stroked with magnetite becomes magnetized and can then serve as a compass needle, its negative pole attracted to Earth's positive pole.

Magnetic Behavior Tied to Various Sources

The Chinese, not the English, were first to harness the directional properties of magnets. Around the first century B.C., delicately balanced magnetite spoons, free to swivel on plates of finely polished bronze, were in use—not for navigating but, rather, for divining the future course of events. By the 12th century, though, the Chinese were using a more conventional compass for more conventional purposes. It consisted of a straw 2.5 to 5 centimeters (1 to 2 inches) long pierced at right angles by a magnetized steel needle of the same length to form a cross. When floated in a bowl of water and protected from the wind, the needle aligned itself with the northern and southern poles.

Among the first to try to explain the behavior of the needle was Pierre de Maricourt, a 13th-century Frenchman who wrote in Latin under the name Petrus Peregrinus. De Maricourt speculated that the needle's tendency to point north was related somehow to the fact that the North Star, alone among celestial bodies, remains fixed in the heavens. He was on the right track: according to present-day theory, the polarity of the magnetic field results from the rotation of the Earth about its axis—which also, of course, is what makes the heavens appear to revolve around an immobile North Star. But de Maricourt's intuition went unrecognized. Most of his contemporaries thought that there must be strongly magnetic mountains near the North Pole attracting the needle. Critics of that view pointed out that travelers had seen mountains with magnetic ores (principally magnetite) all over the world and that, moreover, no such mountains had been observed in the Arctic Circle. But the belief held.

Early Investigations of Magnetic Phenomena

Three hundred years after de Maricourt's treatise appeared, Robert Norman, a distinguished instrument maker in London, England, wrote a small book on the same subject called *The Newe Attractive*. Norman was intrigued by the fact that the south end of a compass needle had to be weighted with wax to keep the north end from dipping. He investigated this puzzling phenomenon by first balancing an unmagnetized needle

in a perfectly horizontal position and then magnetizing it. He thus showed that the north-seeking end dipped only after the needle was magnetized. Since magnetization had not altered the weight of the needle, he concluded that it dipped because the center of magnetic attraction—the "pointe attractive"—lay inside the Earth, not on its surface, as de Maricourt's critics had believed. After Norman's discovery, sailors realized that the farther they sailed from the equator, the more their magnetic needles inclined. Thus, a specially constructed compass (a "dip needle"), free to move vertically, could be used not only to determine direction but also to judge latitude.

In 1600, less than 20 years after Norman's work, William Gilbert, who was physician to Queen Elizabeth I of England, codified the sailors' findings in a Latin treatise called *De Magnete*. Gilbert constructed a "terrella," a model of the Earth, from lodestone, and also made a "versorium," a tiny magnetic compass needle. With these miniature replicas, he showed that a compass points north when held over the terrella's equatorial regions, but that it both points

The wineglass experiment, from The Newe Attractive *(1581), by Robert Norman*

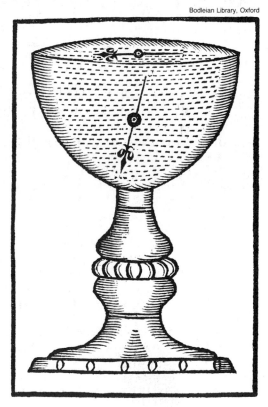

Burndy Library

Experiment on magnetism, from De Magnete *(1600), by William Gilbert*

north and dips when held near either end of the globe. He then charted precisely the continuous change in the angle of the needle's inclination as the compass moved from northern to southern extremes, and concluded that the Earth, like the terrella, must have an internal "magnetic dipole"—that is, a positive and negative pole.

It hardly matters today that Gilbert incorrectly believed the Earth to be made of magnetite. He rightly observed that the Earth has many of the properties of a giant magnet. Still, as the German physicist Carl Friedrich Gauss would show in 1838, the Earth also has magnetic properties that are not so easily explained.

Dipole and Nondipole Fields

Between the time of Gilbert and Gauss, various observers had uncovered data at odds with Gilbert's simplified view of the world—regions where the magnetic field was stronger or weaker than his spherical lodestone would have suggested. Gauss expanded this empirical base by giving world travelers magnetometers (instruments that measure the intensity of a magnetic field) and asking them to report their readings. He then sought to explain the irregular peaks

and valleys in the topography of the geomagnetic field. Using mathematical analysis, he concluded that the Earth must contain a number of magnetic dipoles: a dominant dipole, running from one end of the globe to the other, and several minor dipoles, each extending from the core of the planet to some region on its surface.

We now know, thanks largely to the magnetic-satellite mission (MAGSAT), which the National Aeronautics and Space Administration (NASA) launched in 1979, that Gauss was right. Ninety percent of the geomagnetic field is of the strength and orientation that would be produced by a giant bar magnet running along Earth's axis of rotation. The remaining 10 percent consists of smaller fields surrounding six to eight such "magnets," which, instead of pointing to the North Pole, point to such places as Outer Mongolia, Europe, central Canada, central Africa, the southern Indian Ocean, and the South Atlantic. These minor dipoles, by a curious choice of words, are called nondipole sources.

In reality, neither the major dipole nor the minor "nondipoles" are conventional magnets.

Most geophysicists believe that both the dipole and nondipole fields are generated by the movement of molten iron in Earth's core, thousands of kilometers beneath the surface. Like a bowl of porridge, the core is hottest at its center. From its depths, liquid iron wells up to the crust, where it cools and then sinks again, creating eddies about 160 kilometers (100 miles) in diameter.

The Dynamo Theory

The most widely accepted theory as to how these eddies give rise to powerful magnetic fields rests on one major assumption: that the interior of the planet, at some time in the distant past, received a dose of magnetism from an external source—the Sun, perhaps, or some other celestial body. (Billions of years ago, in its youthful ''T Tauri'' phase, the Sun, it is thought, had a much stronger magnetic field than it has today.) Given this primer, the rest follows from the law of physics: molten iron, like any electrical conductor, generates electricity when moved through a magnetic field. This electricity intensifies the magnetic field, which in turn intensifies the electricity; the cycle then begins anew. A similar process underlies the workings of self-exciting dynamos (generators) in bicycle headlights powered by the motion of the wheels. Hence the name of this hypothesis: the dynamo theory.

But how do the numerous eddies—there may be as many as 50, swirling every which way—create a magnetic field that points overwhelmingly in one direction, roughly parallel to Earth's north-south axis? The answer, most geophysicists now think, is that the Earth's spin imposes order on the system by twisting the paths of some of the iron eddies, mainly those with an east-west alignment. The ''tops'' of these currents—the arcs that run closest to Earth's surface—point north-south instead of east-west, while eddies with a north-south alignment are only slightly affected. Thus, the planet's rotation imparts a predominantly north-south orientation to the entire system, which otherwise would have no pronounced net alignment. The result is a north-south magnetic field.

But random forces still make their presence felt. The dipole does not line up exactly with Earth's axis of rotation but, rather, wobbles slowly around it; each end of the magnetic axis migrates across the surface of the Earth at a speed of about 8 kilometers (5 miles) per year.

Sometimes this axis coincides with Earth's spin axis, and sometimes it is 10 to 15 degrees away. (For decades now, the difference has been roughly 11 degrees.) But paleomagnetic measurements of dated archaeological samples, sediments, and rocks show that when averaged over 10,000 years or more, such angular departures cancel out to zero. So the dipole that dominates the geomagnetic field is indeed parallel to Earth's axis of rotation, just as Pierre de Maricourt believed in the 13th century.

Iron-Eddy Model Accounts for Polar Reversal

Slight wobblings of the geomagnetic field are one thing, but 180-degree flips are quite another. How can such radical change be explained? The answer lies in the eddies. Those whose tops flow mainly north produce magnetic fields pointing north, and those with tops flowing south produce fields pointing south. The net direction of Earth's magnetic field depends simply on which type of eddy is more populous.

This iron-eddy model suggests that we will have some warning before the magnetic poles flip. If a reversal will come only when southerly eddies outnumber northerly eddies, then it should be preceded by a narrowing of the gap between the two, as southerly eddies grow in number and northerly eddies decline; in other words, the present magnetic field should weaken before it is reversed.

Michael Fuller, of the University of California at Santa Barbara, stumbled upon evidence reinforcing this expectation while studying the paleomagnetic record in the Nisqually Valley, near Mount Rainier, in Washington. He discovered that rocks at the northeast end of the valley had cooled during a time of normal polarity, while those at the southwest end had cooled earlier, when the poles were reversed. In the middle was rock that had recorded the transition from normal to reversed polarity. By taking samples across a distance of 305 meters (1,000 feet), Fuller showed that the first sign of a reversal is indeed a slow and continuous decrease in the intensity of the existing magnetic field. Rob Coe, of the University of California at Santa Cruz, has corroborated this with a study of ancient reversal recorded in the layers of basalt from Steens Mountain, in Oregon. He found that the geomagnetic field gradually decreased to less than 10 percent of its original strength before accelerating toward a reversal, and then, after the 180-degree flip, slowly gained strength.

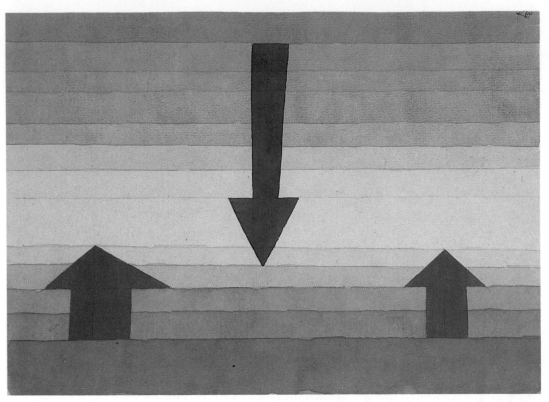

Paul Klee, Greeting, *1922*

Scientists Seek Signs of Impending Change

In 1976 my students and I began to examine layers of sediment in lake floors that might contain signs of an impending reversal. We found samples from Elk Lake, in Minnesota, to be faithful and subtle records of geomagnetic history. Not only is this material rich in magnetite, which indicates both field direction and intensity, but it also comes in laminations—one black-and-white couplet for every year over the past 10 centuries. (This striped pattern forms because the plant remains of summer darken with age, while the winter's inorganic layer lightens.) These laminations allow us to date fossil magnets far more accurately than radiocarbon methods would permit.

The muds and clays in Elk Lake indicate that although the intensity of the geomagnetic field has fluctuated since peaking 4,000 years ago, it has weakened overall. If this trend continues at its average rate, the field's intensity will drop to 10 percent of its peak value 2,000 years from now. Still, we cannot predict a reversal of Earth's poles in the year 3984 for sure.

In the first place, we lack data from other parts of the world. The possibility thus exists that what we see at Elk Lake is merely the dying gasp of a single nondipole eddy situated 3,200 kilometers (2,000 miles) beneath Minneapolis–St. Paul. Other researchers will have to study continuous geologic records embedded in ancient lake floors around the world to give us a global picture of the past several thousand years of change in the magnetic field.

Random or Long-term Forces to Blame?

A second source of uncertainty is more fundamental. How the relative populations of northerly and southerly eddies are determined is still unclear, and some geophysicists argue that it will forever remain that way—that random forces are responsible and that the struggle between the two kinds of currents for control of the magnetic field is thus intrinsically no more predictable than the flip of a coin. Others contend that there is some long-term force behind the reversals. For example, Helmuth Schloessin, of the University of Western Ontario, in

London, Canada, and John A. Jacobs, of Cambridge University, contend that magnetic reversals are linked to what we might call the Earth's "respiration." For hundreds of thousands of years, the theory goes, Earth's core "inhales" such metals as crystallized iron, after which it begins to "exhale" silicate slag. It is during the transition between inhalation and exhalation that the iron eddies are thought to shift systematically, thus effecting a magnetic reversal.

If some such force indeed underlies magnetic reversals, then the trend we have documented in the Elk Lake sediments may reflect

Paul Klee, Fluctuating Equilibrium, *1922*

Paul Klee Foundation, Museum of Fine Arts Berne

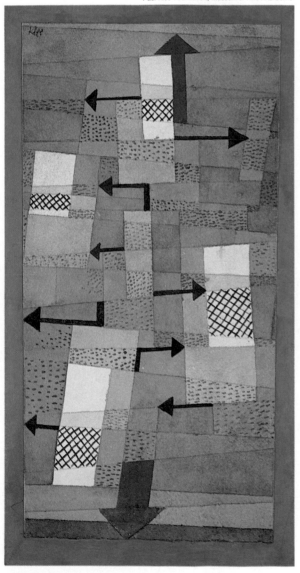

that force and is likely to continue. But if randomness alone is responsible for the ever-shifting coalitions of northerly and southerly eddies, then the trend is not a trend at all; it is no more likely to continue than to abate, just as a coin that has landed tails five times in a row has only a 50 percent chance of landing tails on the next flip.

A Matter of Debate

Thus, geophysicists today find themselves in the position of an investor who wants to know when the stock market will dip down to the 900 level. One thing is certain: there will be some warning, because the Dow Jones Industrial Average will have to pass through 925 before reaching 900. But what are the chances that the warning will turn out to be a false alarm, that the market will reverse itself somewhere between 925 and 900? And in estimating those chances, does it help to know whether the market has fallen rapidly to the 925 level or whether it stagnated at that level weeks ago?

The answer depends on the investor's model of the stock market. If he believes that long-term forces underlie trends in the Dow Jones average, then he can conclude with confidence that past trends will continue. But if he believes that the market's behavior is essentially random, then he doesn't care whether the market has fallen to 925 or risen to it. Either way, the chances are 50–50 that it will fall tomorrow.

The interpretation of our data from Elk Lake hinges on precisely the same question. We know that the magnetic field there is at about 40 percent of the peak strength it reached 4,000 years ago. And we know that it has been dropping—not steadily but erratically, like the stock market—over the past several thousand years. Does that mean that the chances are better than 50 percent that it will fall further next year? The answer depends on which side of the debate you take, whether you think the ongoing struggle between northerly and southerly eddies is guided by randomness or by some consistent underlying force. We are still waiting for evidence that will decisively favor one side of the debate or the other. Presumably, the answer will come before the next magnetic reversal. But perhaps it will not. If in the year 3984 birds begin to fly north for the winter, and hikers get lost in the woods with uncommon frequency, then a blow will have been struck against the adherents of randomness □

ENERGY

REVIEW
OF THE
YEAR

ENERGY

By 1984 the crisis in energy availability had all but disappeared, but the ramifications of the costs associated with assuring the availability of energy were still in evidence.

PETROLEUM

In the United States the cost of oil climbed by 60 percent between 1978 and 1984. Energy conservation—fostered by the high cost of most fuels—brought about the biggest changes in the nation's energy security. In a June 14, 1984, speech, U.S. Department of Energy (DOE) Secretary Don Hodel pointed out that oil consumption in the United States was down 10 percent compared to 1980, and oil imports were down 33 percent. At least as important, he added, "Our suppliers have been diversified." Whereas close to 18 percent of the nation's total oil

supplies in 1980 came from the Persian Gulf, that figure was just 3 percent by 1984.

Stockpiling of oil in the Strategic Petroleum Reserve also increased energy security. In 1984 the Reserve had 400 million barrels—an amount equal to 80 days worth of U.S. imports from all sources, 200 days worth of imports from members of the Organization of Petroleum Exporting Countries (OPEC), and a supply able to meet current demands if Persian Gulf sources were halted for 800 days.

The energy conservation that offered consumers some security from supply disruptions had the opposite effect on suppliers. OPEC member states haggled over how much they could raise oil prices and cut their production, so as to regain the cartel's once preeminent influence on setting oil prices. The cartel's problems began when many major non-OPEC oil producers—including Great Britain, Mexico, and Canada—began underbidding OPEC nations, taking away their business. Unwilling to let their economies suffer, individual OPEC member states countered by "cheating"—cutting deals to sell their oil at below OPEC rates or increasing the volume of their production above their OPEC-set quotas.

These falling oil prices discouraged costly exploration for new oil. Although Shell Oil

Company refused to call its $400 million investment in mid-Atlantic Ocean exploration a failure, it decided in September to abandon drilling there—at least until oil prices rise. The same month oil companies failed to bid on leases to federal lands in Georges Bank on the Atlantic Outer Continental Shelf, and the government decided not to even bother opening bidding on other tracts. ■ Meanwhile several big oil companies spent 1984 prospecting in their competitors. In April a proposed merger of Chevron (formerly Standard Oil Company of California) and Gulf Oil won conditional approval from the federal government. One month later Mobil Oil Company was granted a much-sought green light to acquire Superior Oil. And in July, Texaco Incorporated was given the needed general go-ahead to acquire Getty Oil Company.

COAL

Both production and consumption of coal in the United States increased in 1984, setting all-time records. However, all wasn't rosy for coal producers. Although it successfully fought off attempts to regulate the emission of pollutants believed to contribute to acid rain formation, the National Coal Association reported concern that these controls would come—and that when they did, coal's low-cost image might be tarnished. Moreover, the U.S. Department of the Interior continued its moratorium on the issuing of new leases for the mining of coal on federal lands. Finally, in mid-1984, developers gave up efforts to build the proposed 2,900-kilometer (1,800-mile) ETSI coal-slurry pipeline. Its goal to deliver Wyoming coal to mid-South and Gulf Coast electric utilities met insurmountable lobbying and litigation by the nation's major coal hauler, the railroads.

SYNFUELS

The nation's first commercial-scale coal-to-gas-to-electricity power plant, the Cool Water Coal Gasification Program in Daggett, California, announced on May 21 its first significant production of electricity from synthetic natural gas. Eventually, the project is expected to meet the electrical needs of 100,000 people.

The Great Plains Coal Gasification Project near Bismarck, North Dakota, another commercial venture to produce synthetic gas from coal, also began phasing into full-scale operation during 1984. In April the U.S. Synthetic Fuels Corporation (SFC) announced its intent to issue a 10-year price guarantee for the plant's pipeline-quality gas, making it, along with the

Cool Water project, one of only four to have received support from the SFC.

The SFC was established in the wake of the Arab oil embargo as a federal "bank" to foster creation of synthetic oil and gas. However, the U.S. General Accounting Office (GAO) reported in July that the corporation was falling short of its congressionally set goal of encouraging the production of 500,000 barrels of crude-oil equivalent per day by 1987. Though political pressures hobbled some activities of the SFC, the GAO found the main factors thwarting its goal were "changing economic and energy conditions"—namely, an oil glut, worldwide recession, and falling oil prices.

NUCLEAR

For the nuclear industry 1984 was a transitional year. Following several years of very depressed activity, three new plants commenced operation and six more received initial authorization to phase into full power. With 87 operable reactors in the United States, nuclear generation of electricity grew to roughly 14 percent of the nation's total. On the down side, for the sixth straight year, there were no new orders taken for U.S. nuclear power plants. Although nearly complete, the Zimmer plant in Ohio was canceled; construction of the Marble Hill plants in Indiana was halted; and the Tennessee Valley Authority scrapped four scheduled reactors.

SOLAR ENERGY

The solar industry had a banner year. For the first time sales of solar equipment topped $1 billion in the United States, with more than half of those sales going for nonresidential installations. The world's first commercial-sized central-station solar-cell power plant operated by a utility was dedicated on July 13. PV 1, the one-megawatt photovoltaic power project of the Sacramento, California, Municipal Utility District, has computerized clock-driven controls that rotate the photovoltaic arrays to follow the sun. ■ Construction was completed on another facility— the 6.5-megawatt Carrissa Plains solar-energy generating station in California. Owned, built, and operated by ARCO Solar Power Production Incorporated, it was designed for unmanned operation.

Efforts to improve solar technology also continued. The DOE announced testing of an experimental crystalline silicon solar cell able to convert a record 18 percent of the sun striking it to electricity—2.5 percent more than the previous record. And, ARCO began marketing Genesis, a high-power amorphous (noncrystalline) silicon solar-electric module, which is billed as a major stepping-stone to low-cost amorphous technology for electric-power generation.

JANET RALOFF

THE REALITIES of a FUSION FUTURE

by T. A. Heppenheimer

Every second, over 4 million tons of hydrogen fuse in the heart of the sun. This dynamic fusion process releases the vast amounts of energy that reach us in the form of light and heat. Yet trying to re-create this union, governed by the laws of physics here on Earth, has turned out to be the most difficult technical problem physics has ever faced.

Huge Reactors Surpassed by Smaller One

Nevertheless, fusion is deemed so important that the U.S. Department of Energy is funding to mammoth devices just for research. The Tokamak Fusion Test Reactor (TFTR) at Princeton University in New Jersey is housed in a building five stories tall, 46 meters (150 feet) long, and more than 30 meters (100 feet) wide. Its magnetic coils sprawl over huge ring supports that are 9 meters (30 feet) across. And at Lawrence Livermore National Laboratory near Oakland, California, there is the Mirror Fusion Test Facility (MFTF). It features a steel cylinder larger than a Boeing 747 fuselage; at each end is a "yin-yang" magnet (in fact, two magnets in one) as tall as a two-story house and weighing nearly 400 tons. These gigantic assemblages are designed to fuse atomic nuclei less than one trillionth of a centimeter in diameter. (One centimeter equals 0.4 inch.)

These behemoths stand as testament to the idea that bigger is better. Today that strategy is being challenged by Alcator C, the Massachusetts Institute of Technology's (MIT's) fusion device. While Livermore's MFTF is larger than an airliner, Alcator is smaller than one of the engines. Its experimenters recently stole a march on Princeton by achieving a key goal of fusion years before it can even be matched by the TFTR.

A Developmentally Difficult Source of Power

For more than 30 years, the prospect of fusion power has tantalized energy researchers. Its two fuels are deuterium and tritium, the heavy isotopes of hydrogen. (Isotopes are atoms of a chemical element that have the same atomic number but that differ in atomic weight.) One very promising factor is that deuterium can be produced from seawater in amounts sufficient to last for millions of years. According to former congressman Mike McCormack, the leading energy expert in the House of Representatives in the 1970's: "The development of fusion power will be the most important energy event since the controlled use of fire."

How can we light this fire? Fusion means the fusing together of nuclei; if a deuterium nucleus touches a tritium nucleus, they will release their energy. But both nuclei carry electric charges and repel each other strongly. To overcome this, the nuclei must have a good deal of energy; in other words, they must be very hot—at least 100 million degrees Celsius (180 million degrees Fahrenheit).

The challenge of fusion is twofold: Physicists must produce extremely high temperatures and then hold the hot, seething gas called plasma in some sort of container. No ordinary bottle will do. The plasma cannot be allowed to touch a wall because it would swiftly lose its heat. But at 100 million degrees Celsius, the plasma can be held by magnetic fields. Building such a magnetic crucible, called a "magnetic bottle," is no easy task. Physicist Edward Teller said over 30 years ago that containing a plasma with magnets would be like trying to hold a blob of jelly by wrapping rubber bands around it.

Beyond Break-even

During the past three decades, physicists' ambition has been to heat a plasma and confine it long enough to achieve a combination of factors known collectively as the "Lawson criterion" (after the British physicist John Lawson). This criterion is that the plasma must reach a certain density and be confined by the magnets for sufficiently long to reach a "Lawson number" of 6×10^{13}. For instance, a density of 10^{14} particles per cubic centimeter (0.06 cubic inch) and a confinement of 0.6 seconds would meet the criterion because the Lawson number is obtained by multiplying these two figures together.

Then, at 100 million degrees Celsius, a plasma would put out as much energy from fusion reactions as there was energy being fed in to heat it. This condition is known as break-even. If the plasma could be even better confined (by being made denser while being held within the magnets for longer times), it would put out more energy and need less heating. At a Lawson number of 3×10^{14}, the plasma would ignite. It would then need no outside heating but would keep itself hot with its own reactions.

Two Distinct Designs

Still, as Teller and others foresaw, it has been very hard to keep the plasmas from escaping from the magnetic fields. In 1968 it was considered a major advance when the Soviet Union announced test results from a fusion device they called a "tokamak"—a Russian acronym for "toroidal (doughnut-shaped) magnetic chamber." They achieved a Lawson number of 5×10^{11}, about 100 times less than would be needed for break-even. Even so, that accomplishment was enough to give a major boost to fusion research.

During the 1970's, amid widespread predictions of energy shortages, the U.S. Department of Energy increased its fusion budget ten-fold and approved building the TFTR and the MFTF. The TFTR was built to use tritium, which is radioactive and requires special facilities for its handling. The MFTF reflected a different approach: rather than hold its plasma within a doughnut-shaped chamber, it was designed to test what are called magnetic mirrors. These cause escaping plasma to bounce back into a long tubular chamber, as if reflected from a conventional mirror.

These huge devices also differ in the design of their magnets. The TFTR features a conventional magnet design: a doughnut-shaped chamber wound with current-carrying copper coils that produce magnetic fields. Such magnets are relatively inexpensive to build, but they call for large flows of power when operating. Livermore opted for magnets that feature superconductors (substances that completely lack electrical resistance at ultralow temperatures), which would be chilled with liquid helium and carry huge electric currents with little loss of resistance. But while saving on the electric bill, these proved very costly to build. Each yin-yang magnet has over 48 kilometers (30 miles) of

The Mirror Fusion Test Facility at Lawrence Livermore National Laboratory features a colossal magnet assemblage.

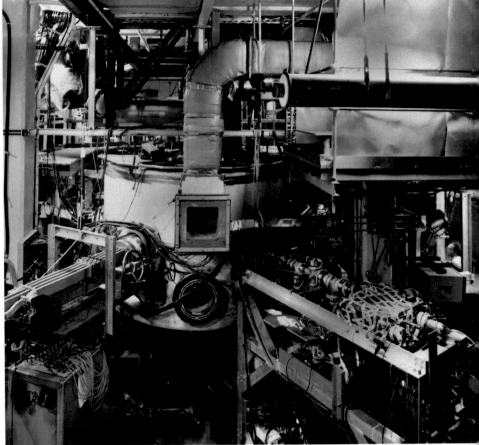

Although scientists at the Massachusetts Institute of Technology did not exhibit a true fusion reaction with the Alcator C tokamak, at right, they proved that a plasma could be confined in order to produce fusion energy.

Mark Strand/North Dakota State Univ.

superconducting cables, at a cost of $60 per meter ($18 per foot). The casing around each magnet is made of stainless steel up to 13 centimeters (5 inches) thick, and takes a year and a half to build.

As the equipment has become ready, the experiments have pushed both people and facilities to the limit. "We are living on the hairy edge," said Dale Meade, head of the experimental division of the Princeton Plasma Physics Laboratory. "The name of the game is to push parameters, to push the frontier. These guys live in a very high-pressure world. And it's not just for weeks. It's for years."

Technicalities Hamper Progress

Many of the problems stem from the extreme conditions encountered within the equipment. To study the plasma, researchers use lasers so powerful that during the few billionths of a second that they are flashing, they are putting out a burst of light with the momentary power of all of New York City. Close by are photodetectors (devices used to measure the intensity of radiant energy) more sensitive to light than the photographic plates of an astronomical telescope.

While the plasma may have a temperature of 100 million degrees Celsius, only a short distance away is a magnetic coil cooled with liquid helium to just above absolute zero ($-273.15°$ C or $-459.67°$ F).

It is no wonder, then, that progress in fusion has been slow. In 1978, when Princeton experimenters using a tokamak called PLT first achieved a temperature suitable for fusion, it was hailed as the outstanding fusion accomplishment of the decade. But that experiment had featured a rarefied plasma that would heat up readily; its low density meant a low Lawson number of 3×10^{11}. Achieving the break-even Lawson number has been far more difficult.

A New Fuel-injection Technology

Physicist Ron Parker at MIT had other ideas. He was running a fusion-research program built around the Alcator C tokamak, which was small and compact, and he was running it on a shoestring budget. His offices and laboratories were in a group of yellow brick buildings that once had held a bakery and warehouse.

In 1977, under Parker's guidance, an early version of Alcator reached a Lawson number of

3×10^{13}, halfway to break-even. Then in 1982, when Parker was ready to push ahead with a set of improvements that just might take them all the way, he received a shock. The U.S. Department of Energy intended to cut off his funding.

The Department of Energy strategy was to use the money to accelerate the pace of larger experiments such as the TFTR. "A budget like Alcator, if it were absorbed into the TFTR, would just about make it burp," says Parker. Harold Furth, director of the Princeton laboratory, decided, as did several institutions, to help out. He agreed to make the largest contribution toward freeing $9.5 million for MIT. That was still less than MIT had had the previous year, but it meant that Parker could go ahead.

The key to his hopes lay with a new technique for injecting fusion fuel into the plasma. All fusion reactors are continuously fed, continuously leaking. Gas is injected, flashes into plasma, is momentarily confined by the magnets, then leaks away to be replaced by new fuel. The techniques of fuel injection represent high technology in their own right. The usual way has been to puff in little wisps of deuterium gas. Instead, Parker was out to use a piece of equipment called a pellet injector, which had been developed at Oak Ridge National Laboratory in Tennessee under the direction of aerospace engineer Stanley Milora.

This shoe box–size injector operates something like a four-barrel derringer pistol. Inside the gun mechanism, deuterium is liquefied to a temperature close to absolute zero and drained into four holes in a disk, where it is chilled further and frozen. This forms four tiny fuel pellets, each the size of a pinhead. Then the disk is rotated to align the four pellets with four barrels aimed at the plasma. When a valve is released, puffs of helium gas shoot the pellets into the heart of the plasma, where the temperature is in the millions of degrees. The pellet then evaporates like a snowball in a fire, but when it does, it makes the plasma denser, which is critical in the effort to achieve a high Lawson number.

Alcator's Problems Pressure Researchers

As the MIT researchers were preparing for their first tests in the spring of 1983, a problem cropped up. A number of magnet coils in the Alcator had become weak through long use. This meant buying a whole new set. Parker put the job out for bids and got a low bid of $100,000 from a small outfit in Los Angeles,

California. No one knew much about them, but one of Parker's colleagues had had some magnets built there, so he gave them the order. After a while he sent a couple of engineers to have a look. They were astounded at what they saw.

"It was a big old warehouse with bats flying around and owls and wildlife living there," says Parker. "It looked like a scene from an Indiana Jones movie." The company was operating through permission of the bankruptcy court. Still, this shop wasn't doing a bad job; they had the proper equipment. When their coils reached MIT, they worked well. The only problem was with a couple of coils that were dirty and had to be rebuilt. They had animal hairs in them.

Now Parker found himself up against a deadline. He wanted to carry through the experiment with the pellet injector in time for the November 1983 conference of the American Physical Society—the main meeting of fusion researchers. By late September they had rebuilt their tokamak using the new coils and were ready to go ahead. But after two weeks they faced another problem. People smelled something burning inside the Alcator.

All tokamaks are built around a large electrical transformer, which induces a current in the plasma to heat and help contain it. While putting in the new magnet coils, the MIT people had also put in a new transformer core. But it wasn't working properly; some of its insulation was burning. Fortunately, they still had the old one and could use parts of it for repairs. "A lot of us were getting pretty discouraged," Parker recalls. "But we stuck to it."

On Wednesday, five days before the conference, they were ready for the big push. Parker himself took over the control panel of the Alcator, sitting in a swivel chair and adjusting dial settings as he set up the experiment runs. He kept his crew working till late in the evening, struggling to reach a record. The following day they were at it again. There was a general sense that the data would be good, but until they were analyzed, no one could really be sure—so they kept on pushing. Around 5:00 on Thursday afternoon, a new test gave what looked like the best data of all. Still Parker wasn't satisfied; he set up another test, only to hear a loud bang that shook the floor. Everyone knew that was the last test they would run before the conference. That's when Steve Wolfe, an expert in plasma physics, sat down to calculate their Lawson number.

John Peoples and Joseph DiBartolo

Above: Technicians install the vacuum vessel and coil assembly of the Tokamak Fusion Test Reactor. Below: The Alcator C's innovative fuel-pellet injector.

MIT

Unexpectedly Good Results

By noon on Friday, just three days before the conference, Wolfe had the result: a whopping 8×10^{13}. This was a momentous occasion. The MIT researchers, however, had not demonstrated a true fusion reaction. They had heated their plasma to only 18 million degrees Celsius (32 million degrees Fahrenheit), a comparatively low level, and they had worked only with plasmas of deuterium; tritium, being radioactive, would have called for special equipment. But Parker's group had overcome the most difficult part of the problem. After 30 years of effort, the world of physics could now be shown what it had sought: a plasma confined well enough to produce fusion energy.

A few weeks after Alcator set its record, the TFTR in Princeton gained its own success. Its builders had been using a theory that predicted how long it should confine its plasma, and they expected a confinement of 0.1 second. When they ran the experiments, the TFTR proved to be holding its plasma three times longer. The plasma density was still rather low, and the Lawson number was 8×10^{12}. Still, the plasma confinement was better than expected, and the temperature was about 20 million degrees Celsius (36 million degrees Fahrenheit).

This was a bonus—it meant that the goal of ignition, of kindling a true fusion fire, was suddenly much closer. The TFTR had been built to achieve only break-even; the more difficult goal of ignition was to come in some future device. But when Princeton's Harold Furth presented his TFTR results at another conference, he remarked that a machine of the TFTR's size, with magnets that were more powerful, would be able to reach ignition.

Success with Inertial-Confinement Fusion

There was good news from other areas of fusion. All along, the main effort has been going into building a "magnetic bottle" to confine the plasma. For years, however, researchers at several laboratories have been pursuing a different approach, called inertial-confinement fusion (ICF). Rather than confining a diffuse gas by using magnets, this method calls for enclosing the fuel as a frozen ice within a glass sphere the size of a grain of sand. This microsphere would then be zapped with an intense and powerful beam from a laser or similar device. With this momentary burst focused on the outer layers of the sphere, its inner layers would heat up and compress; for some trillionths of a second, the center of the sphere would reach the conditions at the center of a star. In mid-May 1984, scientists at Sandia National Laboratories in Albuquerque, New Mexico, announced they had succeeded in focusing a beam of ions so sharply that it could be used to drive fusion targets. And not far from the

INESCO

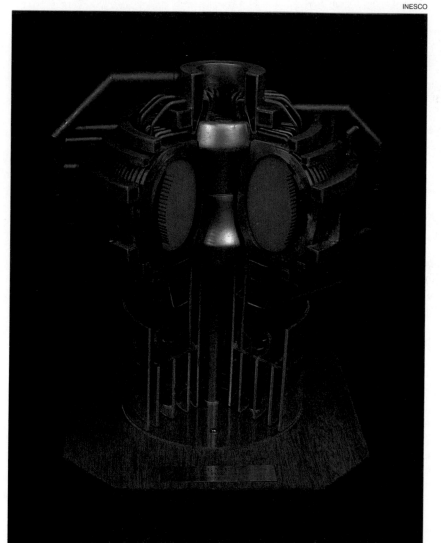

This model of a Riggatron reactor, which would actually fit on a tabletop, represents a novel, small-scale approach to the design of fusion devices.

MFTF, other Livermore scientists were readying Nova, the world's most powerful laser, for initial shots on ICF targets in early 1985.

Fusion's Future Not Viewed Favorably by All

Yet ironically, just as fusion research was gaining these successes, its future was being questioned in a most dramatic way. One of Parker's close associates, Lawrence Lidsky, published an article in the October 1983 issue of MIT's *Technology Review* and set forth his challenge: "Even if the fusion program produces a reactor, no one will want it." He warned that "the costly fusion reactor is in danger of joining the ranks of other technical 'triumphs,' such as the zeppelin, the supersonic transport, and the fission-breeder reactor, that turned out to be unwanted and unused." In Lidsky's view, any such reactor would be based on such designs as the Princeton and Livermore behemoths, the TFTR and the MFTF, and would be too expensive, complex, and unreliable to serve as a basis for commercial fusion power.

Lidsky's arguments were not new. A number of experts had long been setting forth their own views on how fusion should develop, views that could answer Lidsky's objections.

One viewpoint came from Hans Bethe, a Nobel laureate whose work in the 1930's on nuclear reactions in stars laid the groundwork for the start of fusion research. Bethe agrees that fusion reactors based on the TFTR and the MFTF will not succeed as producers of electricity, but in his mind that is not important. Rather, he argues, the proper role for the first fusion reactors will be to produce nuclear fuels for the world's existing nuclear reactors.

Another view comes from the utility industry. Clinton Ashworth, of Pacific Gas and Electric in San Francisco, California, says the power companies will not want to build giant, expensive fusion plants right away but will want to start small.

Small-scale Riggatron Reactors

Then there is the approach of Robert Bussard, who was chairman of International Fusion Energy Systems Company (INESCO), a privately funded fusion firm, before its financial collapse in August 1984. Formerly a senior director of the fusion program in the U.S. Department of Energy, Bussard's views strike to the heart of Lidsky's argument. Bussard prepared detailed designs, based on MIT's Alcator C, to show that fusion reactors can be small, cheap, and readily

disposed of when they wear out. These designs are called Riggatron reactors. They take their name from the Riggs National Bank of Washington, District of Columbia, which gave INESCO a credit line to help it get started. They have featured important contributions from Bruno Coppi of MIT, who helped design the original Alcator tokamaks, as well as from Carl Weggel, formerly of MIT, one of those who designed the magnets for Alcator C.

The key to it all is Bussard's background as an inventor of highly compact nuclear systems. The problem in such devices is to carry away their huge quantities of heat, and this is the area in which Bussard made his professional reputation during the 1950's. Indeed, to him the problem of designing his Riggatrons was more an exercise in heat transfer than in nuclear physics. This shift in viewpoint allowed Bussard to propose fusion-reactor designs of breathtaking smallness. At the same fusion conference where MIT's Ron Parker announced his success with Alcator C, Robert Jacobsen, INESCO's former technical director, presented the designs for five experimental Riggatrons. The largest was no bigger than a compact car. The smallest would fit on a table. Any of them, if successful, could put out about 2 million kilowatts (one kilowatt equals 1,000 watts) of fusion power, continuously, for a month; then it would be used up and replaced. By contrast, when the TFTR achieves break-even, it is to produce 30,000 kilowatts in two-second bursts. Still, as of now, no one can be sure that any of these approaches will show the way to fusion's future.

No Seawater Yet

Today, then, while the fusion community can look with pride upon hard-won successes, these achievements do not open the door to commercial power plants capable of using seawater as their source of fuel. Rather, they open the door to a new set of challenges, in which it must be shown that fusion can go beyond being a brilliant scientific achievement, and actually serve to build power plants that people will want to buy and use □

SELECTED READINGS

"Pro fusion and con fusion" by Michael Kenward. *New Scientist*, October 4, 1984.
The Man-Made Sun by T. A. Heppenheimer. Little, Brown & Company, 1984.
"The engineering of magnetic fusion reactors" by Robert W. Conn. *Scientific American*, October 1983.

SAILING TO SAVE FUEL

by Leslie Ware

It is the mid-1800's. The age of sail. Captain Ahab of the *Pequod*, chasing a whale, cries, "Forward there! Set all sail and keep her to the wind!"

Now it is the 1980's. The age of high technology. Captain Lane Briggs of the *Norfolk Rebel*, chasing smaller fish, pushes a button. His 320-horsepower diesel engine kicks in. But what's that he's doing? Hoisting sail, 130 square meters (1,400 square feet) of it.

Sail Power Finds Renewed Favor

After Ahab's time, the captains of most commercial vessels pushed throttles and listened to the pulsing drone of engines. Now the winds are shifting, and an old, evocative sound—the fluttering of sails—can occasionally be heard above the engines' drone.

The cause of this rediscovery of sail power is not romantic but economic. It has been estimated that the world's shipping fleet gulps 730

Opposite: A computer automatically trims sail on the Shin Aitoku Maru, Japan's first wind-powered oil tanker. Right: This sail-assisted schooner, called Norfolk Rebel, yields substantial savings in fuel to owner Lane Briggs.

Jesse A. Briggs

million barrels of petroleum a year—representing about 3 percent of the world's demand—at a cost of about $30 billion. If 20 percent of the world's merchant marine fleet hoisted sail, it is said, its fuel bills would drop by $3 billion a year.

A barrel of Bunker C fuel oil, used by many commercial ships, sold for $2.70 in 1973 and $29.28 by the beginning of 1983. It hasn't taken long for people in some quarters to realize that wind is a lot cheaper than Bunker C. Admitting that commercial ships can't rely on wind alone, they have formed organizations to promote "sail-assist," the use of sails to supplement engines. They've tested all manner of rigs (arrangements of sails and masts)—some aren't even true sails—on everything from fishing boats to huge cargo ships. And they've saved fuel. In a 1981 report for the U.S. Maritime Administration, Wind Ship Development Corporation predicted fuel savings of 20 to 30 percent for sail-assisted ships.

Enthusiasts Exchange Information

In 1982 sail-assist promoters held the first American conference on sail power, and a year later, they held an international conference on sail-assisted commercial fishing. In the fall of 1983, Jacques Cousteau, looking to replace his ship Calypso, tested the waters with his own unusual rig. As the president of one sail-assist company says, "It's a burgeoning situation."

Oil prices have stabilized recently, but that hasn't taken the wind out of the sails of advocates like John Shortall III, an engineering professor at the University of South Florida whose special interest is commercial fishing boats. "I think this is just a temporary plateau," he says. "I spent twenty years in the energy field before this. If the Middle East blows up and Iran goes even crazier than it is, it's a whole new ball game."

Lane Briggs, for one, is ready to play ball. Briggs, the owner of Rebel Marine Service—a Norfolk, Virginia, towing and salvage company—has formed Sail Assist International Liaison Associates, a nonprofit corporation that serves as a clearinghouse for information and helped put on the conferences.

Briggs got into sail-assist by accident. In 1975 he was operating a motorized tug when the local marina staged a sailboat race. Any participant was welcome to free crabs and beer. Briggs was game. He attached an old piece of canvas to his boat, "used a pahchute [parachute] for a spinnakuh [spinnaker—a large triangular sail]," he says in a deep southern drawl, and sailed the course. A week later, while towing, he raised the sail on a whim. The boat sped up, and Briggs had an idea. He hired a naval architect to build the 15.5-meter (51-foot) schooner Norfolk Rebel, launched it in May 1980, and has been fishing, towing, salvaging, and toting cargo ever since.

Using a grant from the National Marine Fisheries Service, Briggs tracked his fuel consumption: A 47-kilometer (29-mile) trip under the engine alone consumed 106 liters (28 gallons) and took three and a half hours. The same trip with sails hoisted and engine going at fewer revolutions per minute used only 30 liters (8 gallons), although it took a half hour longer.

Three Distinct Types of Rigs

Briggs has traditional-looking sails aboard *Norfolk Rebel,* but there are various schools of thought on how to harness the wind. Builders can fit existing ships, adapt historical technology using modern materials, or use totally new approaches to wind propulsion. Some rigs are so strange Ahab wouldn't know what to make of them.

"When it comes to these sail schemes, I think they're all winners," says Lloyd Bergeson, the president of Wind Ship. "I love 'em all." Bergeson, a plainspoken man in his sixties, started Wind Ship in the old shipbuilding town of Norwell, Massachusetts, in 1979, after sailing to Norway alone. He was worried about the buildup of carbon dioxide in the atmosphere, and on that voyage pondered using computers to predict how ships would perform if they were to use more wind and less fuel.

Of the sail schemes Bergeson professes to love, he loves three best. The wing sail, made of fiberglass and a honeycombed fiber, looks a little like an airplane wing mounted on end. Its mast rotates to catch the wind, and its flaps feather when the wind isn't worth catching. Wind Ship has tested scale models with encouraging results.

In 1981 Wind Ship put the second of Bergeson's favorites, a cat rig—the familiar triangular cloth sail—on *Mini Lace,* a 65-meter (214-foot) freighter belonging to a Greek shipping firm. The skipper can furl the 273-square-meter (2,940-square-foot) sail and shift the boom (the stout pole that hits you on the head) by remote control from the bridge. One windfall: Once, when *Mini Lace*'s engine failed, the sail brought her into port on schedule.

The third rig explored by Wind Ship, along with Windfree, Incorporated, of California, is variously known as a spins'l, Flettner rotor, or Magnus effect cylinder. It protrudes like a smokestack from the deck of the yacht *Tracker*.

A gas-powered hydraulic motor rotates the cylinder at varying speeds depending on the wind's force. What makes *Tracker* move is the

The freighter Mini Lace *harnesses the wind with a typical triangular cloth sail known as a cat rig.*

Tracker's *strange-looking rig is a rotating cylinder that makes use of the wind's force to drive the boat forward.*

Magnus effect, which occurs when any body rotates in a current of gas or liquid. As the cylinder spins in the air current, it creates a low-pressure area that acts as a vacuum and draws the boat forward, at the rate of six knots (almost 11 kilometers [7 miles] per hour) in a 15-knot breeze. It is the equivalent of a 56-square-meter (600-square-foot) sail.

The cylinder is a remake of a rig demonstrated by German physicist Anton Flettner in the 1920's. Ironically, his large rotor ships lost out to motor ships as fuel became cheaper.

Wind Ship has computed the fuel-consumption rates of its three rigs: At six knots, the wing sail saves 32 percent, the cat rig 26 percent (*Mini Lace* saves $57,200 a year while going 5 percent faster than she would otherwise), and the rotor 20 percent after one deducts for the fuel needed to spin the cylinder.

Improving Upon Traditional Designs

In October 1983, Jacques Cousteau and a crew of five left Morocco for New York aboard *Moulin à Vent* (''Windmill''), a 20-meter (65-foot) catamaran with a rig that looks somewhat similar to *Tracker*'s. Cousteau's ''aspirated cylinder'' has vents that can be covered by a flap positioned by an on-board computer.

The rig worked well until 50-knot winds and huge waves caught Cousteau east of Bermuda and tore the cylinder from the deck.

Frank MacLear thinks he shouldn't bother. MacLear, head of the naval architecture and engineering firm MacLear & Harris, says, ''I can't take the aspirated cylinder and Flettner rotor terribly seriously.''

He is all for modifying something a bit more traditional—the for-and-aft rig that most people think of when they hear ''sailboat.''

Sailors have been using this rig for centuries, MacLear argues. "Why go invent a new mousetrap?" He improves upon tradition in two ways, though. He subtracts the boom and adds enough automation that by pushing a button, a person can furl sails at the rate of 9 square meters (100 square feet) per second, a parlor trick in pleasant weather but vital when a storm threatens. Others agree that, whatever rig, automation is necessary if sail-assist is to burgeon further: The cost of hiring extra deckhands can cancel out fuel savings.

MacLear & Harris has a contract to design two sail-assisted cruise ships, with an option for two more. MacLear thinks they may give sail-assist impetus: "Our cruise ships may actually show the way, show what people have been loath to experiment with. When people see what sail does on these ships—see that they use maybe half the fuel—it may lead to more development of commercial sailing."

If Frank Shallenberger has his way, we will see ships that look rather like the old square-riggers. In 1972 Shallenberger, a retired professor from Stanford's business school, built a 4-meter (13-foot) boat and equipped it with "DynaShip" sails, based on a square-rig designed in the 1950's by German engineer Wilhelm Prölss. "We met, got along well, and I purchased the rights to represent the idea in the Americas," says Shallenberger, who is now president of DynaShip Corporation in Palo Alto, California.

Despite the modest scope of Shallenberger's first experience with DynaShip sails, he proposes to use them on bulk carriers ranging in size from 84 to 238 meters (275 to 780 feet). A full-sized DynaShip has not been built yet, but based on computer simulations, speeds will average 10 to 12 knots with the engine used 15 percent of the time.

Barriers Hamper Widespread Development

Trying to interest American shippers in building sail-assisted vessels has been difficult, Shallenberger says: "We haven't been successful because in the early seventies [1970's] the price of oil was low. There was a vastly overbuilt fleet anyway, and the shipping industry is quite reactionary. Then the price of oil rose, and we thought it would force them to go to other kinds of ships, but it just put them in deeper trouble.

Moulin à Vent, *Jacques Cousteau's catamaran with a rotor like* Tracker's, *worked well until a storm ruined the rig.*

Now they can't afford new ships—at least that's what they say.''

Operators of small commercial vessels—fishing boats, for example—have the same problem. Although putting sails on a fishing boat is ''eminently practical,'' according to the University of South Florida's John Shortall—especially for fishermen who go 320 kilometers (200 miles) offshore for snapper and grouper and stay out two weeks—there are only about 100 sail-assisted fishing boats in the United States.

Bernie Arthur of Skookum Marine Construction, Incorporated, in Port Townsend, Washington, has built approximately 45 fishing boats with sails since 1974. In the past couple of years, he has watched high interest rates and short financing terms reduce demand. A fisherman who sees that a sail-assisted boat will save him money in the long run, Arthur notes, ''has to liquidate his business to afford one.'' Coast Guard regulations, union problems, Federal Trade Commission (FTC) restrictions, and difficulties with insurance are seen as further barriers to the spread and large-scale development of sail-assist.

Japan Leads the Way

Asked what can be done to boost their cause in the United States, sail-assist advocates point to Japan, which is probably spending more money developing commercial sail than any other country. Although large wind-powered vessels in the United States are most often found sailing blue pencil lines on architects' drawing boards, Japanese companies have built five large motor vessels with sails.

The first, the 66-meter (216-foot) oil tanker *Shin Aitoku Maru,* was launched in 1980. It is equipped with two rigid cloth sails stretched over hinged steel frames. A computer automatically trims sail and controls the propeller, keeping the ship's speed constant.

In her first two and a half years of operation, *Shin Aitoku Maru* used 8 to 10 percent less fuel than conventional ships. And crew members were less green—they reported a more comfortable ride.

''We have to mount things on the scale of the Japanese,'' Lloyd Bergeson says, ''and then slug it out with them. That's what I'm trying to do,'' he adds, sounding like a weary prize fighter, ''but I'm just a little guy.''

The ''big guys'' in Washington are being accused of sitting on their wallets, despite the

DynaShip

A novel ship design developed by DynaShip Corporation uses aerodynamically efficient aircraft-wing sails.

Maritime Administration's contract for the Wind Ship study and the National Marine Fisheries Service's aid to Lane Briggs. ''I like Reagan,'' says Frank MacLear, ''but you've gotta spend more on research. . . . There should be tax credits, all kinds of stuff, even if they don't want to give money out.''

Unpredictable Future for Sail-Assist

Are sails on the horizon? In part, the answer depends on the attitude of those in a position to help the cause of sail-assist. MacLear asks ''a few brave, venturesome, or altruistic businessmen or entrepreneurs'' to step forward.

Bergeson seconds this. ''As you know, or maybe you don't know,'' he growls, ''very few people think, and per capita, the number of thinkers is down since the days of TV. And bankers don't think. And shipowners don't think. And politicians don't think. For steamships to replace sail took how long?'' I confess ignorance. ''Well, you have to guess.'' Fifty years? ''It took well over 100 years,'' he booms. ''So how long do you think it will take sail-assist to significantly dent the infrastructure, even though it's logical and would increase profits?'' □

Stephen Homer

TAPPING FUNDY'S THUNDERING TIDE

by James Dodson

It's awesome when the tide rushes out," said Michael Dadswell. "You close your eyes and you'd swear you were in whitewater rapids. Violent whitewater rapids! That violence is what makes Fundy so unique, and so alluring. For decades people have dreamed of harnessing that power and making it their own."

Dadswell, a youthful, dark-haired Canadian fishery biologist, swiveled his eyes out over the vast, coppery mud flat of Minas Basin, a finger embayment (a bay or a formation resembling a bay) in the upper reaches of the Bay of Fundy, on Nova Scotia's western side. It was low tide. Fishing boats sat marooned on the

mud where the sea had vanished. The bay's edge glittered hypnotically several hundred meters beyond. In all, it was a vista of serenity.

Tides Have Awesome Power

But it was also the calm before the storm. For the Bay of Fundy is a land of extremes. And in six hours the highest tides in the world would come pounding in to inundate the entire coastal area.

Twice each day the Atlantic Ocean surges into the bay's entrance like water being forced into a 96-kilometer (60-mile)-long funnel. As the tides squeeze into the bay's narrower and shallower upper estuaries (an estuary is a river-

Opposite: A strong tide creates whitecaps as it passes Cape Split near the future site of the Minas Basin dam.

fed waterway that meets the ocean), there is no place for the water to go but up. So the tides rise—sometimes to an incredible 16 meters (54 feet).

As much as 184,000 cubic meters (6.5 million cubic feet) of water rush into or out of Minas Basin each second—ten times the flow of the Mississippi River into the Gulf of Mexico. At the top of the surge, the sheer physical power of the incoming tide has been calculated to have the brute force of more than 8,000 freight locomotives or 25 million horses.

Dam May Have Deleterious Effects

Harnessing this raw power with a hydroelectric dam has been a dream of engineers since 1910. But now the dream is moving beyond the plans and blueprints. Technical problems have been solved. Money is available, billions of dollars. New England is forecasting a growing need for electricity. The development is poised for launching.

But the story is not that simple. Scientists are now finding that harnessing the tide may flood coastlines, decimate fisheries, and disrupt bird migrations.

Dadswell was drawn to the Bay of Fundy in 1976 when he and other scientists met to discuss the ecological effects of a giant dam proposed for construction across one section of the bay. It would be one of the world's largest—14 stories high and 8.5 kilometers (5.3 miles) long—and contain 128 turbines. These would produce 4,560 megawatts (1 megawatt equals 1 million watts) of power—over three times the output of Hoover Dam on the Colorado River; enough power to place it among the top 10 hydroelectric plants in the world, all without the pollution of coal-fired plants, or the controversy of nuclear-power plants.

The Tidal Power Corporation (TPC), a venture owned by the Nova Scotia government, estimates the dam will cost $6 billion, take 10 years to build, and help revitalize the economy

Each day when Fundy's tides recede, many local residents turn out to dig for clams in the exposed mudflats.

Stephen Homer

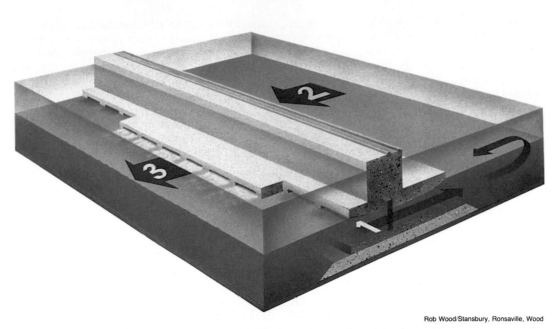

A schematic shows how the tidal hydroelectric dam proposed for the Bay of Fundy would generate power. The incoming tide (dark blue) from the bay would rush through the dam's open floodgates (1) to the basin side. When the water level peaks at high tide (light blue), the gates would close to trap the water in the basin (2). Once the tide starts to recede, the water would be forced through the dam's turbines (3), generating electricity.

of an underdeveloped section of Canada. But Dadswell and other scientists are concerned. Pointing to Economy Point, a promontory (a prominent mass of land) at the mouth of Cobequid Bay in Minas Channel, Dadswell said: "Just imagine the terrific tides pouring through here, carrying fish so thick, it's a bit like fish soup. The water sloshes them back and forth, in and out with the tide all summer long. If there is a dam in the way, they'll be run through the turbines time and time again. We're talking about millions and millions of fish.

"And that's not all," Dadswell continued. "Closing off this end of the bay will certainly alter a unique habitat for migratory birds that make this their one stop in a long flight from South America to the Arctic Circle."

Other scientists fear that a dam that size could alter tidal patterns as far south as Boston, Massachusetts, causing flooding of farmlands and towns. It has even been suggested that Portland, Maine, might have to rebuild its sewer system entirely.

Proponents of the big dam say some of these fears are debatable. But, as Dadswell points out, "If we hadn't started asking questions and seeking answers, God only knows what kind of mess we might already be in."

Fortunately, the scientists and the developers have entered an alliance—albeit an uneasy one—to investigate and discuss these problems. And part of the process is to study the impacts of a small-scale trial project that is already operating on an arm of the bay.

How Power Is Produced

For almost five decades the desire to harness Fundy's tides has kept its currency because tidal power was thought to be alluringly clean, safe, and free of pollution. After the dramatic jump in world oil prices in the 1970's, a government-funded study was made of tidal power. The conclusion was that electricity could be economically produced.

There are only a handful of tidal-power operations in the world—one in the Soviet Union, one in France, and several in China—but none of them comes close to the Fundy project in size and scope. Its operation, though, is fairly orthodox. Every 12 hours, the rising tide would be admitted through open floodgates in the dam. When the water crests, the gates close. Then, as the tide reverses, the trapped water escapes through turbines, making electricity.

Power would be generated only about 12 hours a day—in the two periods when the tide is receding. Conventional hydroelectric plants on rivers are able to generate around the clock, but only during seasons when stream flow provides adequate water. The Fundy dam would generate during only part of each day, but it would not be affected by drought or other disruptions that can plague river dams.

Bay Alteration Would Disrupt Tidal Rhythms

Inevitably, the big dam will alter the area's landscape. The structure would at all times retain a minimum level of water behind it, a level higher than the current low-tide mark. Likewise, the front of the dam would turn away some of the incoming tide, acting as a partial barrier that would effectively shorten the length of the bay.

This could have significant consequences. Just as the outgoing tide has nearly finished its exit from the basin, the incoming tide shoves it back. If the bay were shortened by the barrier of the dam, say scientists who cite complex principles of hydraulics (the science that examines the practical uses of liquid in motion), the variation in the tides would then be magnified—not just in the Bay of Fundy, but in the Gulf of Maine to the south, all the way to Massachusetts some 400 kilometers (250 miles) away.

A model of the phenomenon, constructed by oceanographer David Greenberg of the Bedford Institute of Oceanography in Dartmouth, Nova Scotia, showed how tinkering with the shape of the bay would concentrate the tidal rhythms. Tides, Greenberg postulates, would run significantly higher as far south as Cape Cod, Massachusetts.

Using Greenberg's model, oceanographer Peter Larsen, working out of Bigelow Laboratories at Boothbay Harbor, Maine, corroborated previous estimates that an 8-kilometer (5-mile) dam at Minas Basin would raise high tides and lower low tides by about 15 centimeters (6 inches) throughout the Gulf of Maine. In ocean terms, that amount doesn't sound like very much. But Greenberg, Larsen, and other scientists see the danger of higher high tides inundating farmlands, contaminating wells, and damaging valuable salt-marsh habitat. Conversely, lower low tides could create impassable channels and require that piers be extended.

Scientists Examine Dam's Effect on Fisheries

Alarm over the tide problems brought further action. "Within a year of the 1976 conference," Dadswell says, "several scientists organized the Fundy Study Committee and agreed to look more closely at various aspects of the project. By then we knew a lot more about the potential consequences of building the dam. But we'd just scratched the surface."

Since 1978 Dadswell has worked as a researcher with the Canadian Government's Department of Fisheries at St. Andrews, New Brunswick. He studied fish in the Bay of Fundy—their feeding, spawning, and migratory patterns—and how changes in environment might adversely affect their populations. Dadswell at first accepted the traditional view that the upper bay, where the dam would be built, was a barren place, a watery desert whose turbid waters and widely exposed mud flats were essentially empty of life.

Then he made a shocking discovery. "I was told by a fisherman that American shad—larger relatives of herring—were feeding in large numbers in the upper bay each summer."

By tagging the fish, releasing them, and awaiting calls from fishermen, Dadswell was able to confirm that the Bay of Fundy was a destination for shad, which traveled there from freshwater rivers all up and down the U.S. East Coast. At a peak migration, according to his calculations, as many as 150,000 of the commercially valuable fish could drift with each tide into an embayment like Cumberland Basin. Over a summer, that could represent anywhere from 5 million to 15 million shad passing through, probably one-third of the East Coast shad population. The significance was ominous: a large-scale hydroelectric project could spell disaster for those fish. U.S. fishery managers mirror Dadswell's concerns. Through the Atlantic States Marine Fisheries Commission, they have sent letters to the Canadians, the U.S. Congress, the U.S. State Department and other federal agencies, and conservation organizations, warning them of the proposed development in the Bay of Fundy and its threat to U.S. fisheries.

Alerted to this problem by Dadswell, TPC has been looking for possible ways to avoid it. "We might be able to keep fish out of the turbines," explains George Baker, executive vice president of TPC, "and we might have to if mortality is high. We think mortality might in fact be less than 1 percent per passage through the turbines."

Dadswell was working with his own data, however. "I calculated that we could be looking

Stephen Homer

A Canadian Wildlife Service biologist tags a sandpiper to study how the dam might affect migratory birds.

years the Canadian Wildlife Service (CWS) has recognized the upper bay as an important feeding ground for several species of migratory shorebirds, including large numbers of semipalmated sandpipers, sanderlings, dunlins, and several kinds of plovers and short-billed dowitchers.

Taking a closer look at the situation, Perter Hicklin, a CWS biologist, found that the birds use Fundy's mud flats as a vital fueling stop—their single stop in most cases—on their 9,700-kilometer (6,000-mile) migration over the ocean from South America to the Arctic Circle and back. Each August, Hicklin found, millions of birds mass in the upper bay and feed in a frenzy on a small translucent crustacean locally known as "mud shrimp." There they fatten themselves for up to 20 days, roughly doubling their weight before striking out again. Hicklin's estimates place 70 to 90 percent of the arctic breeding population of semipalmated sandpipers in the upper bay over the feeding cycle. This finding draws attention to an issue of major concern.

The big question: If vital feeding grounds are flooded by the water retained behind the dam, will the birds find new feeding grounds? And if they do, will those grounds be rich enough in food to provide the high fat content the birds need to complete their migration? Hicklin concludes that alterations in the composition of the bay might throw the ecosystem out of kilter. The dam could starve many migrating birds to death.

A Matter of Trade-offs

The Tidal Power Corporation, aware of these concerns, has met each environmental issue head-on, hoping that an open debate will reduce the distortion in reporting on the issues. "We realized from the beginning," George Baker affirms, "that what we are talking about is a balance of trade-offs. If we can't confront the serious questions people like Mike Dadswell have and ease those concerns, item by item, or if the facts bear out the theory that tides may be affected by a 6-inch [15-centimeter] margin along the New England coast—and if that proves simply unacceptable to the Americans—well, then, we're smart enough to know this thing won't go."

Baker, a key figure in the 1976 meeting, admits there will be negative effects if the dam is built. But he suggests that the positive impacts have been overlooked: there would be a steady supply of electrical power to the United

at anywhere from 10 to 50 percent fish mortality," he says, "and it isn't just confined to the American shad populations. We're talking also about salmon and striped bass. On any given day, millions of fish would go through those turbines. Some people are speculating the entire American shad fishing industry could be devastated. Even if the actual kill rate only works out to, say, 20 percent, the shad fishermen down as far south as Georgia and Florida are going to suffer consequences."

Migratory Birds May Be Disturbed

Dadswell's concerns about the shad are echoed poignantly by other environmentalists. For

States, at reasonable rates; no Persian Gulf conflict could possibly interrupt this flow of energy; thousands of jobs would be created over a 10-year period; and some studies indicate altered marine environments in the upper bay might actually prove beneficial—new aquatic habitats would be created that could be beneficial to certain forms of life, and closing off the bay would provide some flood and erosion control, and reduce crop damage from storms.

Baker goes on to say that no one clearly knows yet what the negative or positive impacts will be. "We're engaged, at this moment, in trying to find out," he says.

Pilot Project Provides Useful Model

In the spring of 1984, TPC began letting water through a small-scale tidal hydroelectric plant it had constructed near the mouth of the Annapolis River, which empties into the Bay of Fundy near the town of Port Royal, Nova Scotia. The dam's single turbine is the first tidal generator to be installed in North America, and will produce about 50 million kilowatt-hours (1 kilowatt equals 1,000 watts) of electricity per year,

enough to supply the power needs of a community of 9,000 people.

Baker believes the Annapolis pilot dam will answer some crucial questions quickly, including the effects on farmlands. Estimating the impact on fish could take longer.

So for now, an air of restraint and cooperation prevails in the debate arena on the big dam. "It benefits us all to know exactly what the other side is thinking and worrying about," says George Baker. "That way, there aren't any huge terrible surprises."

Michael Dadswell agrees. "There was a time when people who wanted to build the dam would have gone ahead and done it and to [heck] with the consequences. History books are filled with people's mistakes that cost the environment dearly. But this time we got a break. We've had a chance to step back and look at this thing closely. For that reason alone, this may be one of the rarest opportunities for environmentalists and developers to come together and work on some very old issues—the tides, and how to properly and safely exploit them" □

This small-scale tidal power plant in Nova Scotia will provide valuable data before the big Fundy dam is built.

Union Switch & Signal

Train dispatchers can help railroads save fuel by optimizing the schedules and speeds of the trains in their command.

old question: Can the locomotive diesel engine run successfully on different, less expensive fuel? Several railroads experimented with residuals and other low-grade fuels in the 1950's and 1960's. But with the standard number 2 diesel fuel costing less than 2.6 cents per liter (10 cents per gallon) at the time, they had little economic incentive to use substitutes. The situation is considerably different today, even though the price of diesel fuel has dropped appreciably below its 1982 peak of 28 cents per liter ($1.05 per gallon). Railroaders have two good reasons for investigating alternative fuels. They would like to know what sources of fuel they can use in an emergency if petroleum supplies are again restricted, and they hope to develop fuels to supplement or replace number 2 diesel as it becomes scarcer and more expensive.

Researchers at the Southwest Research Institute in San Antonio, Texas, are looking at three broad alternatives in a program sponsored by the Association of American Railroads. One is the class known as "off-specification distillates"—fuels that offer less power than the standard diesel variety. Another class consists of alcohols, vegetable oils, powdered coal, and distillates from shale, tar sands, or coal. Finally come the hybrids: mixtures of diesel fuel and water or alcohol or carbon.

Synthetic Crude Oils Show Most Promise

So far, research has proved that diesels can run on a number of alternate fuels. Synthetic crude oils seem to give the best performance. But whether alternates can really compete with diesel fuel remains uncertain. Some alternative fuels contain impurities, such as manganese and ash, that would increase maintenance costs. With others the diesel engine does not start easily or run smoothly enough. According to T. N. Pratt of EMD, petroleum distillates will continue to predominate as railroad fuels for years to come. But their quality will gradually fall and prices will rise, making synthetic crudes from shale or tar sands, and distillates derived from coal, increasingly attractive toward the end of the century.

Other Power Sources Under Investigation

If railroad executives are considering alternative fuels, can other types of locomotive power be far behind? In fact, railroads have already tried nondiesel locomotives. Union Pacific operated a number of oil- and coal-fired gas-turbine electric locomotives in the 1950's and 1960's, and U.S. and Canadian railroads have run passenger trains powered by aircraft-type gas-turbine engines. Engineers at the Jet Propulsion Laboratory (JPL) have studied the possibility of using the adiabatic (no heat loss or gain) diesel engine, which eliminates the cooling system and uses energy in exhaust gases. Other schemes include resurrecting the Stirling engine—an external-combustion system invented in 1816 that can, in theory, burn any type of fuel—and designing new coal-powered locomotives.

These proposals have so far generated little enthusiasm among railroad officials. The reasons are obvious. Coal-fired locomotives would need a complete new support structure, including coaling and watering stations, and maintenance shops. Even electrification, a more feasible way of using coal energy that is already in small-scale operation, short-circuits on the ground of huge capital requirements—although it seems likely to be adopted for some of the most heavily used freight lines by the end of the century.

The Era of Diesel Dominance

Overall, the diesel-electric locomotive seems certain to remain the dominant form of railroad motive power in North America, at least until the year 2000. But just as diesels have evolved considerably over their first 50 years, they promise to continue to change in the next few decades. Bombardier, Incorporated, the Mont-

real (Canada)-based company, is now testing a diesel locomotive that uses alternating-current traction motors. They are more rugged and more easily maintained than the conventional direct-current motors, and can develop more power in the same-sized package. EMD and GE have both introduced computer-aided design techniques, and plan soon to market new locomotives that feature microprocessor-based controls. The controls will increase the reliability of locomotives, in part by reducing the need for mechanical relays. New controls will also make troubleshooting simpler and thus keep locomotives on line more of the time.

Toward Greater Self-reliance

Not too far in the future is the likelihood of computerizing the actual operation of locomotives and their handling of trains. In fact, high-speed passenger lines in Japan are already using computerized trains. On-board computers, fed with data on the motive power, characteristics of the train, and nature of the roadbed, run the trains with little intervention from engineers.

Diesel-electrics that will become available in the next few years will therefore have adapted to the new environment of more costly fuel. They will be more reliable. They will be able to haul heavier loads faster, when necessary. And they will be able to reduce fuel costs further through an enhanced ability to burn alternative fuels. The diesel that pulled propulsion technology up from its 19th-century roots will continue to haul it reliably into the 21st century □

As diesel-electric locomotives evolve technologically, they will become even more reliable and energy efficient.

THE ENVIRONMENT

REVIEW
OF THE
YEAR

THE ENVIRONMENT

During 1984 a series of catastrophes brought forcefully to world attention the dangers of unwary environmental management. In the worst industrial accident in history, massive leakage of the gas methyl isocyanate, used in making pesticides, from an American-owned chemical plant in Bhopal, India, on December 3 killed over 2,000 people and injured many thousands more. The tragedy in India came only a fortnight after an explosion of household gas at a storage facility near Mexico City killed 450 people and forced the temporary evacuation of 100,000. Concurrently, one of the worst famines in recent history was besetting Ethiopia and adjacent areas of Africa, with a death toll estimated at year-end at 100,000 and with the lives of additional millions threatened.

Various factors figured in the calamities. The first two raised obvious questions about industrial safety measures. The Ethiopian famine culminated several years of drought. But a common environmental thread in all the episodes was the element of land use. In both India and Mexico, the high casualty rates were attributable to questionable urban planning that produced inordinate concentrations of population in hazardous industrial zones. In Africa a basic cause of the dire food shortages was long-term disregard for the importance of cropland and timbered areas, which has caused an inexorable process of "desertification."

The year also saw renewed concern about possible environmental consequences of nuclear warfare, and on the domestic scene the United States continued to face problems stemming from chemical and poisonous wastes, acid rain, and other pollution.

BHOPAL INCIDENT

In the early morning of December 3, 1984, a worker at a Union Carbide pesticide plant noticed abnormally high pressure readings on a storage tank holding the ingredient methyl isocyanate. Efforts to correct the problem were too late. A white gas began seeping from the tank and started spreading—carried by northwesterly winds to Bhopal, where thousands of workers and their families were sleeping in shantytowns. People ran into the streets, coughing, screaming, vomiting, defecating, and losing their vision—a nightmare that ended for many with collapse and death. A comprehensive tally indicated there were more than 2,000 dead and perhaps some 100,000 left with permanent injuries including blindness, brain damage, sterility, and kidney and liver damage.

In the aftermath of this unparalleled disaster many questions were raised. How could it happen? Were safety precautions adequate? Were the personnel at the plant properly trained to handle this dangerous and highly unstable chemical? Could it happen elsewhere—in the United States, for example, where a Union Carbide plant similar to the Bhopal facility operates in West Virginia? Why was such a facility in a densely populated area?

Answers to some of the questions finally came. In the midst of its "Green Revolution," and eager for increased amounts of pesticides and fertilizers to enhance crop productivity, the Indian government granted Union Carbide a license to manufacture pesticides at the Bhopal facility. At that time the surrounding area was not densely populated, but in the following years many thousands moved near the plant. The Indian-managed facility was equipped with safety features—not as many as are common in many U.S. plants—but at least one safety device did not work properly that night. In addition the pressure gauge had gone well beyond the danger point before it was noticed. But the basic cause of the disaster remains unclear: Was it a change in temperature, impurities in the tank, a minuscule crack, or possibly, as Union Carbide chairman Warren Anderson hinted at in an early 1985 news conference, sabotage?

NUCLEAR WINTER

The possibility of worldwide desolation from atomic warfare stirred scientists and officials. The U.S. federal government launched a $50 million research program to explore the theory that large-scale detonation of missiles could create a global pall of smoke and soot that would obscure the sun, causing a "nuclear winter" with severe temperature drops and bringing the extinction of plants, many animals, and possibly even humans. This could be caused, it was calculated, by the explosion of warheads totaling less than half of the current weapons' stockpile of the United States and the Soviet Union. (See "Nuclear Winter" on page 278.)

CHEMICALS AND POISONOUS WASTES

Problems stemming from chemicals and poisonous wastes dominated the national scene. The pesticide ethylene dibromide (EDB), widely used in grain-derived food products, was found to have a cancer-causing potential. This discovery led the Environmental Protection Agency (EPA) to ban its use as a grain pesticide. Although the EPA said the nation did not face "a public health emergency," large quantities of packaged foods were withdrawn from grocery shelves in a number of states.

Controversy continued over acid rain, "yellow rain," and Agent Orange. Although researchers failed to find evidence of health effects from exposure to Agent Orange, a defoliant used in Vietnam that contains minute amounts of dioxin, seven chemical companies settled for $180 million in a class-action suit by thousands of Vietnam veterans claiming maladies resulting from exposure to the chemical. Further litigation against the federal government is expected.

The nature of "yellow rain"—a supposedly toxic powder observed in battle areas of Southeast Asia, Afghanistan, and Iraq—remained a mystery. The U.S. government has suggested that yellow rain represents a new sort of chemical warfare, involving compounds called tricothecene mycotoxins, developed by the Soviet Union. But a 28-nation scientific conference was unable to resolve a contradictory theory that the powder could be of natural origin, such as bee droppings.

Amid widening evidence that acid rain is affecting all sections of the United States and parts of Canada, the Reagan administration adhered to its position that drastic measures to reduce smokestack emissions would be premature. (Such emissions are precipitated by rain into harmful acids.) However, nine northeastern states won a federal court ruling that the EPA had failed to respond adequately to their complaints of fallout from midwestern industrial plants. And New York, the first state to address the acid rain problem directly, enacted a law requiring a 30 percent reduction in sulfur dioxide emissions by 1991.

PUBLIC OPINION AND GOVERNMENT ACTION

In what conservationists called the first major environmental legislation of his presidency, President Reagan signed into law amendments to the 1976 Resource Recovery and Conservation Act imposing far more stringent regulations on the handling and disposal of toxic wastes. However, Congress deferred until 1985 action to renew the basic air-pollution, water-pollution, and safe-drinking-water laws and to expand significantly the size and scope of the "Superfund" for cleaning up hazardous-waste sites.

There appeared to be growing public support for environmental issues. A Gallup poll found that 61 percent of a national opinion sampling favored giving precedence to environmental protection even at the risk of curbing economic growth.

GLADWIN HILL

The Pantanal:
Wondrous Wildlife Region at Risk

by Vic Banks

"The Pantanal has the greatest concentration of fauna [animal life] in the Americas," says Dr. Maria Tereza Jorge Pádua, the former director of Brazil's National Parks and Equivalent Reserves, and recipient of the 1982 Getty International Conservation prize. She is talking to me in her research office in Brazil's capital, Brasília. "People outside of Brazil know only the Amazon. It's a shame because the Pantanal is a very important ecological place . . . but the *contrabandistas* [illegal hunters] are doing much more

Photos by Vic Banks

The unpaved Transpantaneira "highway" is the only major road that stretches across the lush vegetation of South America's Pantanal wilderness.

[damage] to it than [they are] in the Amazon." The issue Dr. Pádua describes is one of the most important conservation battles emerging from South America in the 1980's. A spectacular wildlife region barely known to scientists, let alone the general public, the Pantanal is being robbed of its rare animal life in virtual silence.

A Wildlife Paradise

The Pantanal is about 1,800 air kilometers (1,000 air miles) northwest of Rio de Janeiro. It lies between Bolivia and the state of Mato Grosso in Brazil along the Rio Paraguay. When seasonal rains swell the river's waters to flood proportions, they create an immense network of lagoons and marshes. As a result the Pantanal forms one of the largest gathering grounds for wading birds in the Western Hemisphere. So incredibly rich is this birding area that the Pantanal is purported to have rookeries (nesting colonies) that cover several square kilometers, densely packed with tens of thousands of roseate spoonbills, wood ibis, great egrets, and magnificent jabiru storks.

The few scientists who know the Pantanal claim that it is much more than an avian (bird) paradise. Because of the region's unique mosaic of habitats comprising rivers, lakes, marshes, grasslands, and forests, many geographically unrelated animals can be found living close together there. Jaguars, anacondas (large, constricting snakes), giant river otters, and millions of caimans (crocodilians) all live in the Pantanal. These diverse animals coexist with herds of feral (wild) horses and Indian cattle, which graze freely across the huge, privately owned ranches that ring the Pantanal.

Poaching Escapades Conducted Flagrantly

Dr. Pádua hands me a wildlife calendar from her desk. It's not your typical collection of aesthetic animal photographs. Instead, each month's picture depicts an exploitative venture that is currently going on in the Pantanal. Dr. Pádua flips to the December illustration—a huge pile of caiman skulls towering higher than the man standing next to it. A sad sigh escapes her lips as she says, "I've felt impotent to do anything about this illegal trade. It's increased so tremendously in the last [several] years. We estimate more than 500,000 caimans a year are killed in the Pantanal alone, but one newspaper in São Paulo [a huge, industrial city on Brazil's southeast coast] claimed that more than 2 million skins a year go across the Bolivian border." The skins are then shipped worldwide to garment centers, where they are turned into apparel for the high-fashion industry.

Dr. Mauro Reis, president of Brazil's forestry service, claims that the poachers are well organized and have connections reaching high-level government officials. They ship illegal wildlife products across vast open lands between Bolivia and Brazil without punishment. Some outlaws use aircraft to conduct smuggling operations from isolated jungle airstrips, bringing animal skins into Bolivia and carrying drugs out. Some other lucrative, illicit activities include collecting rare birds and monkeys for the pet trade and depleting the local rivers and tributaries of vast quantities of exotic fish. In recent years these destructive pursuits have reached shocking proportions, causing damages estimated in excess of $100 million, much to the outrage of many people.

Outcry Over Destruction Prompts Expedition

In an effort to quell some of the growing public outcry, Brazil's President João Figueiredo paid an unprecedented visit to the Pantanal late in 1983. About four months after his visit, he ordered the Brazilian Army into the Pantanal in an attempt to slow, if not stem, the wildlife destruction there. Since the government was interested in better informing the public of these protective efforts, I was able to join a small expedition fielded by the forestry service on a journey deep into the heart of the Pantanal.

Perhaps part of the reason the Pantanal is so poorly known to outsiders is its remote location. My field assistant and I flew more than 970 kilometers (600 miles), from Rio de Janeiro to Brasília, where we had to obtain detailed information and necessary permits to enter the Pantanal. From Brasília we flew another 800 kilometers (500 miles) to Mato Grosso's capital city, Cuiabá. Here we met the rest of our party at the forestry-service headquarters. Dr. Paulo S. Benedito, the regional forestry official, introduced us to an army colonel who had just returned from the Pantanal on a raid. They showed us a storeroom that was filled with seized weapons and other contraband: stacked like so many rags next to the weapons were the skins of jaguars, ocelots, jaguarundis and other South American cats, giant river otters, anacondas, caimans, and howler monkeys. This disturbing haul of pelts, according to Gaspar Locha, our driver, was considered "nothing."

This confiscated collection of animal skins is tragic testimony to the magnitude of the illegal wildlife trade.

Above: Hidden among some plants, a group of young capybaras tries to stay out of sight while a jaguar hunts nearby. One of the capybara's primary predators is the caiman (left).

A Fascinating First Day

The next morning we were up before 5:00 A.M. packing our diesel truck with an aluminum motorboat in tow. By sunrise we were well on our way toward Poconé, a little town founded in the 1600's that serves as the northern gateway to the Pantanal.

Up until the 1970's, about the only way to travel the Pantanal was by horse, motorboat, or small plane. Then work began on the building of the Transpantaneira highway, which is intended to connect the Brazilian towns of Cuiabá and Corumbá that are nearly 500 kilometers (300 miles) apart. In 1973 slightly more than one-third of this highway was completed between Poconé and the Cuiabá River. The rest of the Transpantaneira through the Pantanal remains to be completed, but for 200 pothole-ridden kilometers (120 miles), this red dirt "highway" provides an amazing journey through a wildlife wonderland.

In seeming indifference to our fast-approaching vehicle, numerous packs of capybaras (large South American rodents that resemble enormous guinea pigs) blocked the road, wallowing in mud-filled ruts. Out across the marshy fields, wild horses grazed right next to dozing caimans, and flocks of birds pecked the muck in search of food. I was surprised to see a flock of screaming monk parakeets form a green cloud as they raced through the sky, then quickly disappear into a huge nest hanging from a nearby tree.

At midmorning Gaspar stopped the truck by a stand of palm trees so we could stretch and take a break. My pocket thermometer read 42° C (108° F) in the shade. Carlos, our expert naturalist, walked over to a stand of coconut palms, where he found two neatly cut halves of coconut seeds. Others lay scattered about the ground at the base of the trees. He motioned for us to quietly follow him into the forest. "Kaaaaa . . . Kaaaaa" broke the silence as we squinted skyward for the source. The deafening shrieks and a flash of dark blue feathers in the branches proved to be hyacinth macaws—the largest parrots in the world, and increasingly sought by bird collectors. Three of the magnificent birds flew among the coconut palms. "Just one of these [parrots]," noted Carlos, "is worth more than $5,000 in the United States."

A painted heron keeps an eye out for fish while wading in one of the many marshes that cover the area.

At dusk we reached a remote forestry outpost near a flooded field. Our guides, quick to cool off from the long ride, plunged into the stagnant water, oblivious to any threat from caimans or razor-toothed piranhas (small carnivorous fish). Ten minutes later, using bacon on a hook, we caught some of these vicious little fish right out of the "swimming hole." Cooked with coconut milk and hot peppers, they were fantastic. And so had been the first day of our trip.

The Cycle of Life

Even in the absence of the sun, it was oppressively hot and the night air was perfectly still. An incessant cloud of insects fluttered around my face. Carlos noticed my obvious discomfort and was sympathetic. "Ah, but Victor," he mused, "it's *primavera* . . . springtime. It's not like your North American season that comes alive with rains and warmer temperatures. Here in the Pantanal the rains have already come and gone, a sea of water has evaporated in just a few months. Each day the sun grows hotter, drying the lagoons and marshes. New animals are born but they [compete with] older ones [for resources]. Food and especially water are harder to find. It's a time of great stress for these animals. Some won't survive. You'll see . . . that's the way nature is in the tropics."

During the next few days, it became apparent that Carlos knew the environment well. Fields of mimosa grass were green and luxuriant. Blossoms opened everywhere. We even saw a capybara sunning itself on a little island less than 1.5 meters (5 feet) from its natural predator—a large caiman. But these peaceful scenes changed abruptly when our party crossed the 117th wooden bridge along the Transpantaneira. Beneath it we could see the evaporating remnant of what had once been a huge lake. Now the lake was reduced to the size of a swimming pool, and more than 60 caimans cruised through the shallow water. The surface rippled constantly as if a light rain were falling. A closer look revealed that thousands of fish, mostly piranhas and spotted catfish, were rising to the surface in a desperate effort to gulp oxygen. Closing in from distant trees were countless caracaras (large, long-legged hawks), black hawks, herons, egrets, and black-headed vultures. They began to congregate on the grass at the water's edge when one especially hungry caracara overcame its caution and flew to a little sandbar less than 1 meter (3 feet) from a group of caimans. The bird defiantly walked into the

An immense nesting colony of wood storks looks like a clump of strange, white trees in this aerial view.

murky water, picked up a floating fish, and plopped back on the bank. It tossed its head back in triumph and let out a raspy trill. Then the feeding frenzy began. Everywhere wings and feathers blurred the line between sky and water. It was a primeval scavenging scene reminiscent of East Africa.

Once again the tables had turned on the hapless piranhas, transforming predator to prey. Caimans were everywhere with jaws agape, packed full of fish. Nature, however, would be a great equalizer. When the fish supply was

exhausted and the relentless sun dried up the pool, it would be the caimans' turn to endure. They would be forced to crawl across the parched ground in search of other lifesaving water holes. Only the hardiest would survive until the next rains came.

An Official Park at Last

More important than weeding out weak animals, explained Arne Sucksdorff, a famous Swedish filmmaker whom we later met in Cuiabá, was that this annual ebb and flow of water replenishes the poor soil with fresh nutrients from the richly laden rivers and tributaries. Sucksdorff, who won an Oscar award for one of his wildlife documentaries, fell in love with the Pantanal more than 18 years ago and decided to stay. He regards this region as an international treasure that is being tragically plundered.

To protect some of the important wildlife habitats remaining in the Pantanal, authorities decided to expand a small and extremely isolated biological reserve, the Caracara, near the Bolivian border. In 1974–75 wildlife-management experts were invited from both Brazilian and United States research organizations to study the area and to recommend larger boundaries that would incorporate realistic territories for such endangered mammals as the jaguar and the giant river otter. By 1980 Parque Nacional do Pantanal was officially established. But critics say it requires a tiresome eight-hour boat ride to get there from the Transpantaneira highway. And, in high-water years, the park has none of the spectacular animals that live along the unprotected highway.

Protectors' Lives Threatened

Dr. Pádua acknowledges that conserving the Pantanal has carried a legion of frustration. "Today Brazil has 24 national parks and 10 biological reserves that are fully protected, at least on paper. But in reality," she points out, "there are just 620 park rangers to patrol 20 million hectares (49.4 million acres). Even poor people build small farms there now to do slash-and-burn farming. So many people today just want to develop the country, and our decision-makers seem not to understand our work. They say we are a stone in the shoe of progress—they don't like us." Dr. Pádua has been threatened numerous times and can no longer visit the place she loves to study without armed guards.

Arne Sucksdorff helped draw national attention to the plight of the Pantanal by writing articles about the poachers. He has even chased outlaws single-handedly far into the swamplands. For his trouble Sucksdorff's family has been terrorized, and he still receives repeated death threats. Even now there is an armed guard posted at his house every night.

Rookeries Teeming with Birds

Before starting off on the last leg of our trip out of the wilderness, we had the opportunity to borrow an aircraft and get a panoramic view of the Pantanal. We were especially hoping to spot one of the many giant nesting colonies that the area is famous for to those who have visited there.

From high in the air, we had a truly incredible view. The entire horizon was a sea of green, interspersed now and then by brown rivers and grasslands. The Transpantaneira appeared as a red gash through the land and was practically the only sign of human presence to be seen. Nearly an hour passed before the pilot banked the plane to the right and pointed to a large patch of all-white trees in the distance. It was clear that what made the trees seem white was the sheer number of birds roosting amongst their branches. The pilot slowed the engine and maneuvered right above the treetops. Thousands and thousands of storks, egrets, herons, and other birds were nesting on every limb.

Luckily the pilot was able to land the plane on an adjacent cattle pasture. A local cowboy agreed to take us to the rookery in a small boat. When we arrived, Gaspar estimated that the nesting ground was nearly 1.6 kilometers (1 mile) long. We used the boatman's machete to clear a path through the vines and dense undergrowth. Up close, some of the tallest trees seemed like high-rise apartments for birds with different species living at different levels. Some of the nests were under construction, while others already contained hatchlings. Caracaras and vultures roosted alarmingly nearby, watching intently for a moment's chance to make off with any young bird. The dynamics of these immense rookeries pose fascinating scientific questions.

Tourism a Last Resort

Unfortunately, channeling resources to answer such questions, in light of Brazil's shaky economy, would be considered a luxury in these times. Even basic equipment that is essential for national-park survival must go without funding: trucks, boats, radios, guard posts, signs. To date, international conservation groups have been unable to include the Pantanal in their priorities. As a last-ditch effort, local authorities have turned to tourism to help bring attention to the Pantanal. By appealing to the world traveler, the Brazilian government is taking a considerable risk with the future of this remarkable wildlife sanctuary. But considering what damage has already taken place there, is there any doubt which is preferable: 500,000 caimans killed for their skins each year, or the attraction of 500,000 tourists? □

These western white pines infected with blister rust will eventually be replaced with disease-resistant seedlings.

THE COMEBACK OF WESTERN WHITE PINE

by Louise Kingsbury

One or two healthy pines among hundreds, even thousands, of diseased trees. Twenty-five years of patience and determination. Supplies of colorful cloth bags to hold cones. And "a little biological good luck." Those were the key elements in a massive restoration of western white-pine forests that a generation ago were hopelessly lost to the disfiguring, killing cankers (erosive sores brought on by disease) of white-pine rust.

Breeding Blister-Rust Resistance

The first phase of a U.S. Forest Service research and development program that began in 1950 has culminated in three seed orchards in Idaho that will eventually produce enough disease-resistant western white-pine seedlings to plant 4,050 to 8,100 hectares (10,000 to 20,000 acres) per year. The seed orchards—two at Lone Mountain northwest of Coeur d'Alene and the third at the Forest Service's Coeur d'Alene Nursery—contain nearly 9,000 carefully bred trees. Over 65 percent of the seed from these trees is expected to produce trees that will resist intense exposure to the rust fungus.

A low percentage of resistance? "Not when you consider that before we started this research, in some places we had up to 10,000 infected trees for every completely rust-free one," says Richard T. Bingham, the now-retired forest geneticist who headed the blister-rust resistance program for 25 years.

"We lost the white pine from about half of the 2 million acres [810,000 hectares] of good pine stands in the Inland Empire of northern Idaho, northeastern Washington, northwestern Montana, and south-central British Columbia," says Bingham. "Because of our research, we may eventually be able to replace whole forests that were killed by blister rust."

The program, under the direction of the Forest Service's Intermountain Forest and Range Experiment Station in Ogden, Utah, is based on crossbreeding western white pines that are genetically rust-resistant. The goal from the program's beginning was the rapid and economical development of planting stock that is sufficiently resistant and otherwise adapted for Inland Empire planting.

"The first phase of the program satisfies a somewhat limited goal, that of merely helping to return western white pine to Inland Empire forests," says Bingham. "The second phase, which began in 1967, is aimed at producing stock that is successively faster growing, better adapted, and even more resistant."

Pine Important to Wildlife and People

This long-term program, which has occupied practically the entire careers of some scientists, will restore one of North America's most beautiful trees to sites ranging from sea level to 3,050 meters (10,000 feet). Western white pines grow 30 to 50 meters (100 to 165 feet) tall. Their narrow, conical crowns encircle tall, straight trunks that may be 0.9 to 2 meters (3 to 7 feet) or more in diameter. Cylindrical cones that can reach 0.3 meter (1 foot) in length dangle below limbs sporting slender, bluish green needles. Mature trees are 100 years old, and some are known to live 500 years.

The western white pine is important to wildlife, providing considerable cover. Seeds are sought by squirrels, mice, and various birds. Bears sometimes claw the trunks in spring to reach sweet sapwood.

The tree is also valued by humans. Healthy western white pine, like its cousin the eastern white pine, comes close to being an ideal timber-type conifer. Although rarely used as construction lumber, because it is neither strong enough nor cheap enough, it is a staple for molding, shelving, window frames, inside trim around doors, fancy cabinet work, and many other building needs. It is prime material for wooden matches, toothpicks, pattern making, and the whittler's carving knife.

Characteristics of the wood have made western white pine one of the most valuable trees of the Pacific Northwest. The wood is light brown and light in weight. It is soft enough so that nails do not split it; the grain is so straight that the wood slices easily. As finish sash and trim lumber, the wood continues to command very high stumpage and lumber prices. It is more than acceptable in mixed-species paper pulp.

Forests Saved from Lumbermen but Not Disease

Early lumbermen, after depletion of much of the eastern white pine, moved west to discover that western white pine grew in great abundance in a relatively short amount of time, and was even larger than the eastern variety. The Inland Empire's primeval white-pine forests might also have been cut away, except for the advent of conservation. Under the direction of President Theodore Roosevelt and the first Forest Service chief, Gifford Pinchot, vast forest reserves were established.

But there was no protection from blister rust, which was introduced in the early 1900's from infected seedlings imported from France and Germany. Just as chestnut blight and Dutch elm disease bring certain death to some eastern hardwoods, blister rust kills western white pines. And it spreads quickly. In 1937, only 15 years after the rust's entry into Idaho, the disease had infected about 15 percent of the white pine of the St. Joe National Forest.

"By the 1940's the infection had climbed to over 95 percent in some areas of the St. Joe," says Bingham. "Without any doubt, the white-pine blister-rust epidemic in the Inland Empire stands was the world's most spectacular bar none."

Control Program Abandoned for Resistance Plan

A multimillion-dollar federal rust-eradication program in the 1930's had failed to stop the disease from spreading, as it had in the eastern and Great Lake States. Even though alternate plant hosts for the rust—such as currant and gooseberry bushes—were first attacked with chemicals, then uprooted by the millions, some rust spores simply caught the wind and infected new trees. A later chemical attack using antibiotics on rust cankers proved to deter but not stop the

Top: A branch infected with blister rust is covered with the killing cankers that are typical of the disease. Right: A large canker on this branch was destroyed by a resistant reaction in the pine's bark, thus halting the spread of the disease.

rust, and control work was finally abandoned in 1968.

"Due to some farsighted leadership in the old blister-rust-control organization, we had already started resistance work in 1950," says Bingham. "We could see that genetics had solved agricultural problems and improved stocks such as corn and wheat. Why not trees too? True, trees take a long time to reach maturity and produce seeds for basic studies of disease resistance. But by the 1950's agriculturists and early forest geneticists had provided enough knowledge about disease resistance so that we could start this project."

In 1950 four U.S. Department of Agriculture units began a project planned to last to the turn of the century. The units were the Spokane Office of Blister Rust Control (now defunct) of the Bureau of Entomology and Plant Quarantine in Washington, and three Forest Service units—the Northern Region, the Northern Rocky Mountain (now part of the Intermountain) Forest and Range Experiment Station, and the California (now Pacific Southwest) Forest and Range Experiment Station. In charge were Bingham, research forester Anthony E. Squillace, and forest geneticist John W. Duffield.

Laborious Efforts Rewarding

The scientists began by isolating individual rust-free western white pine—that is, trees that stood as lone survivors in stands composed almost totally of multicankered pines that had been exposed to the disease for at least 20 years.

These lone trees probably had something else going for them besides luck. "It seemed that at least some of them must have been genetically resistant," says Bingham. "The heavy rust attack and the few survivors provided a little biological edge to get us started."

Summer after summer, Bingham, Squillace, Duffield, and field-workers would scour forests, traveling deep into the backwoods looking for rust-resistant trees, and then crossbreeding them. They literally wore out the bottom branches of some often-climbed trees as they pollinated cones and covered them with protective individual bags. During the 25-year research project, the crews climbed well over 5,000 trees without even one serious falling accident.

Occasionally, hungry squirrels would break into cone bags that had been carefully placed over the developing cones to prevent consumption by insects. In April or May over several years, as soon as snowmelt permitted, cone bagging would begin. Yet a cone beetle and two types of cone moths would occasionally beat the field crew to as much as 25 percent of the cones.

Once control-pollinated seeds were in hand, they were sown in a nursery. Seedlings were artificially inoculated with the rust when they were two years old, and were evaluated for various resistance reactions and overall level of resistance. The scientists rejoiced when seedlings resisted artificial exposure to the disease, and they studied the various means by which the seedlings expressed resistance.

By 1957 the scientists had such encouraging results that they looked for additional funding, and for adequate laboratory, nursery, office, and arboretum space, along with land for seed orchards, in order to accelerate research and developmental work toward practical production of rust-resistant nursery stock.

Researchers Aim to Breed Ever-Hardier Stocks

The slow, evolutionary process and the years of crossbreeding and testing are paying off. After the Forest Service officially abandoned blister-rust control work in 1968, some managers saw that as the abandonment of the western white pine as a future valuable resource. Recently,

After pollinating the cones of a rust-resistant pine, a forester covers them with bags to keep out unwanted pollen.

Researchers are trying to breed ever-hardier planting stocks of western white pine at U.S. Forest Service nurseries.

however, given the progress of the resistance program, the Forest Service's Northern Region resurrected management of western white pine.

"Everybody wants the resistant nursery stock," says Bingham, "including federal and state governments and private companies. Even though some 1 million seeds are being produced annually, the limited amount of planting stock is almost being fought over. That's exciting for us!"

Meanwhile, phase II work, which began in 1967 and overlapped phase I, seeks even higher and more stable resistance in planting stocks. Currently, phase II is under the technical direction of the Intermountain Forest and Range Experiment Station and the Northern Region. Funding comes from an eight-member cooperative called the Western White Pine Tree Improvement Committee, which is part of the Inland Empire Tree Improvement Cooperative. Current members are the Forest Service units; the University of Idaho; the Department of Lands, state of Idaho; Burlington Northern Timberlands; Port Blakely Mill Company; the Coeur d'Alene tribe, Bureau of Indian Affairs;

Diamond International Corporation; Idaho Pines Timber Associates; Potlach Corporation; and St. Regis Paper Company.

Project has Far-reaching Effect

The Forest Service's blister-rust research might help solve similar problems around the world. White-pine blister rust is an international problem, especially in Europe, where eastern white pine—once a favorite exotic forest tree—is now eliminated by the rust. Many nations have sent their scientists to the United States to study the Intermountain Station's program. Through the International Union of Forest Research Organizations (IUFRO), the Forest Service has western white-pine materials under test in Germany, France, and other countries.

In the end, it is the patience of the researchers that may be the most remarkable aspect of this successful program. Quick solutions are often sought for many of society's problems. Here the devotion of a quarter of a century to just one phase of a project that is scheduled to continue to the year 2000 is a mark of people with foresight and a global view of ecological and environmental matters □

Lowell Georgia/Photo Researchers

HARD TIMES HIT THE BAY by William McCloskey

C aptain Wadie Murphy of Tilghman Island, Maryland, "follows the water,"
as the saying goes, on Chesapeake Bay.
Every winter, he harvests oysters aboard his
venerable wooden skipjack, the *Sigsbee,* and in
other seasons he catches crabs and fish. It is a
ritual that many Chesapeake watermen have followed for decades. Today, however, Murphy
and his fellow watermen fear that their traditional way of life may be dying, as the
once-beautiful waters of the bay grow ever more
impoverished.

Catches Shrink Year after Year

With more than 11,100 square kilometers
(4,300 square miles) of water and an astonish-
ing 13,000 kilometers (8,100 miles) of shore-

line, the Chesapeake Bay is the largest estuary
(a river-fed waterway that meets the ocean and
is affected by its tides) in North America. Watermen like Murphy refer to this national treasure, which stretches 320 kilometers (200
miles) inland from southern Virginia to northern
Maryland, simply as "The Bay," as if there
were no other. The familiar form of address is
fitting for a waterway that has been, to centuries
of watermen, a home, a livelihood, and a capri-
cious mistress.

 The bay produces 33 percent of the U.S.
oyster catch, and 50 percent of its tasty blue
crabs. Not long ago, the bay also supplied 2.7
million kilograms (6 million pounds) of striped
bass annually (on bay waters the species is
known as "rockfish"). But over the past de-

cade, the catch of prized striped bass has plummeted by 90 percent to a mere 270,000 kilograms (600,000 pounds); ominously for the future, current counts of young striped bass are at record lows. Another cause of great concern: the bay's recent oyster catches are just one-third the sumptuous averages of 30 years ago.

Says Marylander Willie Roe: "I look at the bay now and it makes me sick. There were so many things I loved to do, and now they're gone." Adds a seafood broker in one of the bay's fishing towns: "I'd have been out of business the last few years if I'd relied only on local catches." As Captain Murphy of the *Sigsbee* puts it: "No matter how hard you work any more, you can't get ahead with such scarce catches. I'll tell you what's going to happen—local people will have to get out."

People Lured to Area in Droves

At present, though, more and more people are flocking into growing towns and second homes on bay shorelines. Since 1950 there's been a population increase of nearly 50 percent in the bay's 166,000-square-kilometer (64,000-square-mile) drainage basin, which stretches over six states. The amount of land classified as urban and residential has tripled, replacing forests and pastureland. Approximately 180,000 Maryland and Virginia licenses are now issued annually to owners of sail and motor-driven pleasure boats, which indicates the lure of the bay to urbanites. On a breezy summer weekend, motorboats buzz everywhere like mosquitoes. Often, bay vistas are colored less in watery green than in whites from taut mainsails or reds and yellows from billowing spinnakers.

Patrick Lynch, an easygoing man whose red beard shows streaks of gray, has for 30 years piloted ships from distant ports up the 270 kilometers (170 miles) of Chesapeake Bay channel to the inland seaport of Baltimore, Maryland. He remembers that when he started, the shores of the bay were dark at night except for small permanent communities and an occasional light from a farmhouse or beach cottage. "Now," he says, "it's a line of lights most of the way—houses, power plants, mercury-vapor lamps."

For those who measure beauty by mountain vistas, the Chesapeake Bay seems an unlikely place to stir the devotion people feel for it:

flat topography, marshes on the Eastern Shore, sandy beaches, and small bluffs on the western side. But the bay, whose width ranges from 5 to 35 kilometers (3 to 22 miles), is sized on a human scale. "For all its size and gross statistics," writes William W. Warner in his Pulitzer-prizewinning *Beautiful Swimmers: Watermen, Crabs and the Chesapeake Bay,* "it is an intimate place where land and water intertwine in infinite varieties of mood and pattern."

The bay proper runs through the eastern parts of Maryland and Virginia, fed by some dozen major rivers and 40 lesser ones. The rivers flow from the bay's shore states—plus Pennsylvania, Delaware, West Virginia, and even New York—into the vast drainage basin. Counting its rivers, the bay touches, and is affected by, approximately 90 percent of Maryland and 60 percent of Virginia.

A Rich Historical Heritage

The Chesapeake's history goes back as far as we care to follow. In the Pleistocene Era some 3 million years ago, the bay was a riverbed of the

This magnificent estate on the bay's Eastern Shore is one of many residences that now line the waterfront.

Susquehanna. Earlier, some geologists contend, it was another full-fledged bay. The first permanent English settlement in the New World, established in 1607, was Jamestown, located on the James River of the lower bay in Virginia. The colony's founder, English explorer Captain John Smith, responded to the gentle climate and scenery, and the abundance of game, by calling it "a faire Bay . . . with fruitful and delightsome land" where "Heaven and earth never agreed better to frame a place for man's habitation."

Captain Smith may have discovered the bay for Europe, but his colony wedged itself into an existing Algonquian society of some 200 villages. The Indian heritage survives in some of the beautiful, evocative names of the rivers—the Potomac (which flows through Washington, District of Columbia, before emptying into the bay), the Patapsco (which flows through Baltimore), the Patuxent and Rappahannock, all of which originate in the Appalachian Highlands. On the flat Eastern Shore are the shorter, seafood-rich Choptank, Nanticoke, Pocomoke, and Wicomico.

As they enter the bay, the rivers bear the imprint of the settlements along their shores. The Susquehanna, the bay's major tributary, carries chemical-laden runoff water and silt from Pennsylvania's industries and farms. Maryland's refineries and chemical plants leave their marks on the Patapsco. The James bears the wastes of two Virginia cities, Norfolk and Richmond.

Bay Called Giant Protein Factory

Because of its size and number of tributaries, the bay is considered one of the most complex marine systems in the world. Fresh water pours in from the rivers while salt water enters on tides from the ocean, creating a continuous flow of fresh and salt waters from opposing directions. In the salty mouth of the Potomac, at Piney Point, Maryland, the water is hospitable to oysters. But the Potomac is virtually fresh water less than than 120 kilometers (75 miles) upriver, where finfish (true fish) spawn. Given the length of the bay, river waters to the north end remain fresh, usually unaffected by the sea.

The salty ocean water, being denser than fresh, enters the bay in the deeper layers. It also mixes. Thus, every section of the bay has its own stirring of nutrients through the waters, its own pattern of salinity and flow, its own balance of plant and animal life.

Except for the channel that allows inland Baltimore to be a major seaport, the bay is relatively shallow. In the past, depths of 5 to 9 meters (15 to 30 feet) made it easy for sunlight to penetrate the water and reach aquatic plants; dissolved oxygen from the atmosphere could mix in bottom-flowing waters. The light and nutrients stimulated microscopic plants and animals at the bottom of the food chain, which in turn attracted and sustained the larger creatures. Particularly on the Eastern Shore, shallow water has been able to foster the growth of submerged grasses.

The bay supports some 2,700 species of animal life. For people, the variety of edible bay life is exhilarating. It includes mollusks (oysters and clams); crustaceans (crabs); catadromous fish (those that spawn in the sea) including menhaden (herringlike marine fish), eels, sea trout, flounder, bluefish, and croakers (also called hardheads); and anadromous fish (those that lay eggs in fresh water but live part of their lives in the ocean) including scarce shad, striped bass, and herring. To these can be added the waterfowl—ducks, geese, and swans—that winter in the bay during seasonal migrations south from Canada. In all, it's "a great big protein factory," in the words of Baltimore's literary sage, Henry L. Mencken, for whom few pleasures of the flesh surpassed those of eating oysters on the half shell and steamed crabs.

Aquatic Vegetation Suffers Substantial Decline

Concerned by the protein factory's dwindling productivity, Congress in 1976 called on the Environmental Protection Agency (EPA) to prepare a long-term, $25 million study to seek scientifically based answers to some key questions: How serious is the bay's decline, what are its causes, and what can be done about it? During the process of completing the study, scientists have begun to unravel the complex puzzle, which Larry Schweiger, a regional executive of the National Wildlife Federation, calls "one of the greatest environmental challenges of our time."

One subject of the study is the aquatic grass that grows in the bay's shoal water, especially in regions less than 2 meters (6 feet) deep. This submerged vegetation feeds and shelters waterfowl and a host of tiny organisms; it also helps to stabilize the floor of the bay and prevent erosion. In 1971 researchers examined 26 areas of the bay likely to support submerged vegetation, and they found abundant grass in 81 percent. But by 1980 vegetation grew in only 38 percent of the same areas. Concluded scientists Robert Orth and Kenneth Moore, who work at the Virginia Institute of Marine Science: "We believe that the observed vegetation decline is unprecedented in the bay's recorded history."

Among the causes of the grass decline are blooms of algae and tiny phytoplankton, which use up oxygen in the water after they die and begin to decompose. It has long been known that deeper portions of the bay lack oxygen in summer, but researchers discovered that there has been a fifteenfold increase since 1950 in the oxygen-depleted regions.

Excess Nutrients Upset Ecological Balance

Blooms of algae also block sunlight, preventing it from reaching the underwater vegetation. But why are the algae blooms and phytoplankton increasing? Scientists are convinced that the cause is a flood of excess nutrients, especially nitrogen and phosphorus, which sweep into the bay in runoff water from farms and residential lawns, and which pour forth from sewage-treatment plants throughout the bay's vast drainage basin. (It hasn't helped the bay either that, as a money-saving measure, Virginia sewage-treatment plants have recently been allowed to

Right: Waterman Edward Abbott, who has seen catches of blue crab and other species decline vastly in recent years, is concerned about the Chesapeake's future. Below: Many waterfowl take refuge in one of the area's protected remaining wetlands.

pour out greater concentrations of phosphorus than originally intended.)

Because it stimulates algae, the heavy dose of nutrients puts a great strain on the underwater plants, and on the creatures dependent on those plants. Traces of herbicides from farms and lawns in bay water appear to be too weak to damage healthy vegetation, but for plants deprived of nutrients and sunlight, the traces of herbicides may become a fatal "last straw."

Judging from core samples of local sediments, the decline of underwater vegetation has no counterpart in recent bay history, so it cannot be dismissed as part of a natural cycle. According to Larry Hindman, manager of the Maryland State waterfowl program, the redhead duck, which feeds on the leaves and stems of aquatic grasses, was abundant through the 1960's but now mostly migrates elsewhere. Its population in the upper bay dropped from a counted 100,000 in 1955 to less than 1,000 in 1983 (the count is believed to include less than one-third of the full population). Other waterfowl once equally dependent on bay vegetation have made interesting adaptations. Canada geese and whistling swans have "abandoned the bay for feeding," says Hindman. They now graze in nearby farm fields, but return to the water to roost. Their population is increasing. Canvasback ducks, not suited to walking on land, have remained in the rivers but switched their diet from eel grasses to soft-shell clams. But the canvasback population is in general decline because shellfish and invertebrates that live in bay grasses are also declining.

Bay Serves as Trap for Toxic Substances

In another finding new enough to be startling, the EPA study revealed that the bay is a sink that traps and keeps toxic materials within its boundaries, rather than a tidal flush that eventually sends wastes out to the ocean. Sediments in the upper and middle bay show growing levels of toxic metals and synthetic-organic materials. What goes in, stays in. This adds new concern to such events as the disastrous contamination of the James River (a lower-bay tributary) by the organic chemical Kepone. And it makes all the more timely ongoing monitoring of toxic chemicals produced by industry: the Johns Hopkins University Applied Physics Laboratory in Maryland, among other groups, has been studying the interaction between toxic substances and bay organisms. Researchers are divided on the question of chlorine's impact on fish eggs, but the substance is harmful to shellfish larvae.

Farm fertilizer receives a large share of the blame for the presence of excess nutrients in runoff waters, but lawn washes flowing from suburban drains also bear a goodly share of chemicals, and this source of runoff has increased along with the urbanization surrounding the bay. One Sunday in the spring of 1983, Richard Klein, coordinator for Maryland's Save Our Streams program, released several bucketfuls of trout into Stony Run in Baltimore, a small stream that rambles into the Patapsco River. "A dead, degraded urban stream," says Klein, "that probably hasn't seen trout for 200 years. Now the lead and zinc levels are probably five to ten thousand times greater than back then."

According to Klein, 2 out of every 10 automobile owners change their own oil and dump it into the nearest storm drain; during rains, the drains also carry the runoff of pet droppings ("You'd be surprised how much!" says Klein), lawn fertilizers, pesticides, and copper dissolved from rainspouts.

Cleanup Efforts Require Major Commitment

As for the impact of farm runoff, one proposed solution is the creation of 9- to 30-meter (30- to 100-foot) buffer zones of heavy cover crops to filter water beside streams. Another is low-till farming, which reduces plowing and potential erosion of silt and fertilizer into bay tributaries; silt buries bay vegetation and smothers soft-shell clams.

Farmers in Pennsylvania might feel no direct concern for the quality of water in the distant Chesapeake Bay. Still, as one Susquehanna Valley farmer, George Wolff, puts it: "Lost fertilizers are dollars that are leaving us."

Any sacrifice of productive cropland to protect the bay would probably require governmental payments to growers. Farmer Wolff suggests a partial solution, which he has used successfully on many of his lands for the past 10 years: namely, use of a so-called chisel plow after the autumn harvest. As Wolff explains, a conventional moldboard plow churns the stubble underground, leaving the fragile surface exposed to water and ice. But a chisel plow throws the stubble in ridges; the spiky surfaces catch water and cause it to percolate into the ground. Besides keeping fertilizers in his fields, Wolff sees another payoff—the ground holds moisture longer during a dry spell. He calls chisel plowing "conservation tillage," and swears by it.

Photos: Lowell Georgia/Photo Researchers

Above: A sizable share of chemical runoff comes from suburban developments along the bay's shorelines. Right: An area resident calls attention to the problem.

To begin the work of implementing policies based on the EPA's findings, a Maryland-Virginia-Pennsylvania governors' conference held in December 1983 produced a commitment to "work together" to clean up the bay. As Maryland governor Harry Hughes put it: "The bay produces more marine life than any other body of water in the world, other than the Atlantic and Pacific oceans, and if that doesn't say that this is a national treasure, I don't know what will."

The conference led to a subsequent release of new money for bay cleanup by the three state legislatures as well as by the EPA. The 1984 funding was relatively modest for the scale of work to be accomplished—but all parties understood it to be a beginning. As Governor Hughes wisely pointed out, the job of restoring the bay's water quality will require at least 10 years of dedicated effort.

"It's easy to talk about the bay's problems,

NOW MORE THAN EVER ooo SAVE THE BAY!

and difficult to do anything about them," observes Lynn Greenwalt, former director of the U.S. Fish and Wildlife Service and now a National Wildlife Federation official. "To reverse the current situation and prevent further deterioration, we must improve enforcement of existing laws that govern the operation of sewage-treatment facilities. We must also greatly increase our efforts to control farm runoff at its source. That means people must be willing to change their habits, and it means a greater financial commitment—perhaps a billion dollars or more over the next decade. It will be worth every penny; everyone benefits from a productive bay."

The Way of the Watermen

Meanwhile, the complex ebb and flow of life on the Chesapeake Bay continues. The anadromous fish have fallen on bad times, due, apparently, to the inability of the young to survive the present water quality in the middle bay. But the catadromous fish appear to be doing well in the lower region of the bay. Menhaden, for instance, continue to provide Virginia with one of the world's most abundant sources of fish meal.

And long-term efforts continue. In April 1983, I rode with Captain Russel Dize aboard his skipjack *Kathryn* to plant new oysters. Each year, Maryland seeds millions of bushels of oyster shells—the tiny free-swimming oyster larvae, called spat, need a surface to settle on and grow. At the one-year growth stage, the state hires watermen to dredge and tong the spat-bearing shells into boats and transport them to a number of new sites. The work is a continuing effort to keep the bay productive, whatever the forebodings about water quality and high nutrient levels.

In the blue, rainy dawn, black shapes of skipjacks and smaller patent-tong boats glided ahead and astern of us, each maneuvering for position. Soon the dredges were bringing up a

A huge flock of Canada geese passes a marina while migrating to the bay, where the birds will spend the winter.

Watermen make their livelihood on Chesapeake Bay, using long tongs to harvest oysters from the deep.

Medford Taylor

load per minute, which the busy men emptied and shoveled without stop. Despite blowing, chilly rain, their oilskin raincoats and sweaters peeled off quickly. The pitch was feverish and very exciting, but also like a picnic in the presence of potential abundance.

At the edge of the bay, hand-tongers stood on the gunwales of small, open boats and maneuvered 9-meter (30-foot) shafts. Rakes at the bottom of these scissorlike instruments dug into the heavy shells as the men lifted them hand over hand to the water's surface. Hand-tonging is one of the true back-busting ways to make a living, but the skill is second nature to most bay watermen.

"Follow the water?" one hefty hand-tonger told me. "Wouldn't have it no other way."

All the boats on that blowy day carried their spat far up the Choptank River. Within three years of the move, the spat become harvestable oysters. There can always be a future—that is, if people care and plan for it □

SELECTED READINGS

"Chesapeake Bay's underwater forests" by Elizabeth G. Macalaster and Robert J. Orth. *Sea Frontiers,* March–April 1984.
"Chesapeake Bay anoxia: origin, development, and significance" by Charles B. Officer et al. *Science,* January 6, 1984.
"The changing Chesapeake" by Michael Wright. *The New York Times Magazine,* July 10, 1983.
Beautiful Swimmers: Watermen, Crabs, and the Chesapeake Bay by William W. Warner. Atlantic Monthly Press, 1976.

Stephen M. Voynick

Mine-Poisoned Rivers

by Stephen M. Voynick

When Captain Zebulon Pike led his United States Army mapping team west in 1806, he followed a rushing mountain river into the unexplored central Rockies. Forty years later another army explorer, Colonel John C. Frémont, followed the same river nearly to its headwaters. Both filled their journals with reports of the river's great beauty and the abundance of game along its banks. Pike went so far as to refer to the upper sections of the river as "the Terrestrial Paradise."

Pristine River Meets Tragic Fate

The river was the Arkansas, which empties into the Mississippi after a 2,300-kilometer (1,430-mile) journey across half of Colorado, Kansas,

Oklahoma, and Arkansas. The Arkansas begins as snowmelt in a 3,660-meter (12,000-foot)-high alpine basin near the Continental Divide in central Colorado. Its clear, icy waters begin as a small torrent splashing across the tundralike meadows. After dropping to timberline, the Arkansas races downward through dense stands of aspen, pine, and spruce to emerge 22 kilometers (14 miles) later in a broad 3,050-meter (10,000-foot)-high mountain valley. Even though the Arkansas there has not yet really begun its long journey, it is already a major water resource. It serves as a fishery, a recreational river for rafters and kayakers, and a source of water for downstream drinking and irrigation use. It is both sad and hard to believe that when those crystal headwaters enter that first high mountain valley so near its source, the Arkansas falls victim to one of the nation's most destructive and yet most readily accepted forms of water pollution—metal-mine drainage.

Arkansas River Degraded by Frontier Mining

Metal-mine-drainage pollution in the West is widespread and common in the United States; in 10 western states where frontier mining played a major role in development, approximately 6,440 kilometers (4,000 miles) of streams and rivers suffer from the characteristic symptoms of excessive acidity and heavy-metal contamination. Among Colorado's 725 kilometers (450 miles) of mine-polluted streams, the upper Arkansas is a textbook example not only of the history and origins of the problem but also of the local apathy that discourages cleanup action.

The pristine upper Arkansas that Pike and Frémont knew survived only until 1860, when gold was discovered in a tributary—California Gulch. After four years and $4 million in gold, the miners departed in search of richer gravels. They left behind denuded forests, lifeless gravel heaps, and a gulch that contributed a steady stream of mud and silt to the Arkansas River.

Those first pollutants were mild compared to those that soon followed. After an 1877 strike of rich silver-lead minerals, the dying little gold camp was renamed Leadville. Within two years it had exploded into the biggest, richest, and wildest silver camp in the West. In only 12 years, hundreds of underground mines had produced 6,000 tons of silver and several million tons of lead. An unusually diversified mineralization sustained the local mining economy into the 20th century; during both world wars, Leadville was a major producer of zinc, lead, and copper.

Drainage Tunnels Transport Toxic Waters

Leadville's miners were always fighting a severe underground water problem. In 1906 they completed construction of the Yak Tunnel, a 6.4-kilometer (4-mile)-long haulage-drainage

A ways downstream from the confluence of the Arkansas River and California Gulch, the stream is biologically dead.

Stephen M. Voynick

waterway that drained over 97 kilometers (60 miles) of both abandoned and active underground mine workings. Disposal of the troublesome mine water was simple and convenient; it drained by gravity into the already ravaged confines of California Gulch, then emptied into the Arkansas. In the frontier philosophies of land use, such drainage disposal was a necessary, logical, and "natural" part of mining.

Another drainage project was begun during the World War II mining boom. By 1953 the 3.2-kilometer (2-mile)-long federally constructed and owned Leadville Drainage Tunnel was completed. Technically, it was a success, draining an initial 15,140 liters (4,000 gallons) per minute; practically, it was another federal boondoggle, since it drained only abandoned or inactive mines. Like the Yak, the Leadville Drain dumped its highly acidic and heavy-metal-laden effluent into the Arkansas.

Today Leadville's mining district has only two active mines. It also has 26 square kilometers (10 square miles) of old mine dumps; acres of slag (refuse from the melting of metals) heaps from long-gone smelters (furnaces used to recover metals from their ores); and over 645 kilometers (400 miles) of abandoned, collapsed, and flooded underground mine workings. And, of course, Leadville has two drainage tunnels

that silently and faithfully continue to perform their intended job. Every day, water from rain and snowmelt percolates downward through shafts and fractures into the underground labyrinths. After its destructive chemistry has been completed, the water is collected in the two drainage tunnels and efficiently routed into the Arkansas River.

Sulfides to Blame

Sulfide minerals, the primary commercial ores of most base metals, are the culprit in the metal-mine-drainage problem. Metal mining is basically a process of penetrating a protective oxidized surface layer to reach and extract lower sulfide ores. Thus exposed, these sulfides react with water and oxygen to produce sulfuric acid and other metal compounds or free metal ions. Zinc, lead, copper, and silver sulfides, while releasing free metal ions, do not contribute significantly to acidity.

The most problematic mineral is iron sulfide, or pyrite. Although not a primary ore of iron, pyrite is extremely common and closely associated with the occurrence of base- and precious-metal minerals. The oxidation of pyrite produces enormous quantities of both sulfuric acid and iron ions. As the highly acidic mine water is released into normal streams, dilution

Colorado Mountain History Collection

Stephen M. Voynick

Left: Runoff from mines in this 1920's photo of Leadville still drains directly into the Arkansas River. Above: Sulfide minerals are the major problem.

raises the pH (the pH scale is a system used to express acidity and alkalinity, with values running from 0 [most acidic] to 14 [most alkaline]); this decrease in acidity causes the iron to precipitate out as iron hydroxide, or "yellow boy," discoloring the water and clogging streambeds and banks.

Alarming Statistics

Heavy-metal content of water is conventionally expressed in micrograms (one microgram equals one-millionth of a gram) per liter, a measure meaning little to most laypeople. As an example of acceptable metal-content levels, the U.S. Public Health Service drinking-water standard is a maximum of 300 micrograms of iron per liter. An iron content exceeding 700 micrograms per liter is considered detrimental to fish and other aquatic life. The water in California Gulch, which has a pH of 3.6 (extremely acidic), contains 45,000 micrograms of iron per liter; 60,000 micrograms of zinc per liter; 30,000 micrograms of manganese per liter; and abnormally high levels of copper, cadmium, and lead.

These levels, computed against mean flow rates, may be expressed in more understandable—and far more frightening—figures. The approximate combined mean flow of the Yak Tunnel and Leadville Drain is over 12 million liters (3 million gallons) per day. The two tunnels discharge about one ton of heavy-metal pollutants into the Arkansas River every day, a rate that has been continuous for over 30 years.

Negative Impact on Plant and Animal Life

With the exception of stunted grasses that cling tenaciously to life on its fouled banks, California Gulch is devoid of life. Its flow has an alarming effect on the Arkansas. Below the mouth of California Gulch, the iron content of the main flow of the Arkansas River—a level that reflects the contents of the other heavy metals—is 15 times higher than the standard. Local ranchers complain that the pollution creates foaling complications and other problems in their livestock. Flora and fauna are adversely affected for 24 kilometers (15 miles) downstream; the fish count is very low, their growth is retarded, and their flesh contains unusually high amounts of a spectrum of heavy metals. In contrast, the Arkansas River above Leadville is prime habitat for a variety of trout species.

Traditional Views Hard to Overcome

Local western attitudes regarding mine drainage remain shrouded in the antiquated land-use concepts of the frontier. In Leadville the Arkansas has served as the historic and traditional disposal method of mine drainage and smelter wastes. The rationale is that if the Arkansas sufficed during the frontier, it will also suffice today.

The Yak Tunnel drains much of the acidic and heavy-metal-laden effluent from Leadville's mining district right into the Arkansas River.

Stephen M. Voynick

The use of simple dilution to eliminate or neutralize pollutants is, fortunately, fairly effective, thanks to the numerous clean tributaries that complement the Arkansas. The downstream biological effects are chronic rather than acute, helping to sustain old delusions over the adequacy of dilution. Only unusual events, such as that which occurred on February 23, 1983, focus outside attention on the continuous pollution. An inspection crew working within the Yak Tunnel reportedly collapsed a wooden retaining bulkhead. The poisonous orange torrent that rushed into California Gulch discolored the Arkansas for 64 kilometers (40 miles) downstream, necessitating the shutdown of a pumping station diverting drinking water to the city of Colorado Springs.

Cleanup Responsibility a Complex Issue

The upper Arkansas is among the Environmental Protection Agency's (EPA's) national sites for potential hazardous-waste cleanup through the $1.6 billion Superfund program. Until very recently, Superfund recognition had been merely honorary, not effective. Internal chaos disrupted the EPA while other factors unique to

mine drainage hindered initiation of cleanup action.

The focus of EPA attention was on those cleanup projects where cost sharing was possible, meaning those sites of relatively recent origin. But most metal-mine-drainage pollution is not the product of the modern mining industry, but of countless inactive or abandoned mines. Origin of this pollution may often be traced back to the 1870's. Since that time most mining properties have undergone complex legal transitions; they have been sold, traded, consolidated, or abandoned and allowed to lapse back into the public domain. Current mine-property ownership may be easily determined, but fixing legal pollution responsibility has been a very uncertain matter.

Obstacles Discouraging But Action at Last

Unlike those of industry, most mine-pollution sites are geographically isolated and culturally insulated; they are not visible in a manner that appalls, infuriates, or directly threatens the masses. Apathies seem strongest where pollution is worst—those places where men, like their fathers before them, still mine for a living.

If the Yak Tunnel could be moved, say to the nearby resort town of Aspen, and the drainage poisons allowed to dump into the Roaring Fork, apathy would be replaced by an uproar of outrage that would echo across the entire United States.

There is no simple solution to the mine-drainage-pollution problem. The most direct and inexpensive approach—simply "plugging" the drainage tunnels—would threaten adjacent clean groundwater supplies. Miners have their own reasons for opposition; plugging would raise water levels within the mining districts, dimming the eternal hope that abandoned mines will someday produce again.

In August 1983, the first ray of hope appeared for the upper Arkansas. As a direct result of the tragic pollution spill six months earlier, Congressman Ken Kramer (Republican-Colorado) took the problem directly to the regional EPA headquarters in Denver, Colorado, and got results. The EPA has allocated $175,000 for a 10-month two-part study of mine pollution in the Leadville sector of the upper Arkansas. A "remedial investigation" will determine sources and extent of pollution; a follow-up "feasibility study" will seek alternatives for a long-term solution.

In a related move, the Department of the Interior recently awarded the state of Wyoming $24.7 million to aid in the reclamation of 44 abandoned mines.

A National Problem

In history, origin, and the vague matter of current responsibility, metal-mine-drainage pollution is unique. Unless it is brought to the special attention of our elected representatives, it will be accorded only low priority on the long EPA list of modern industrial pollution. Nor will the problem just go away; there are enough exposed sulfide minerals in abandoned mines and mine dumps to produce a steady flow of acidity and heavy-metal contamination for centuries.

Responsibility for cleanup will never be imposed on the private sector; metal-mine-drainage pollution is a national heritage, sort of a deferred payment for the reckless glories of frontier mining. The problem is national in scope; exposed sulfides have ruined many streams in the East, particularly in the coal-mining regions of the Appalachians.

The upper Arkansas River has long served as a model of mine-drainage pollution; now, perhaps, it will serve as a model for cleanup.

Stephen M. Voynick

In stark contrast to the beauty in the background, California Gulch carries a toxic torrent of pollutants.

The cost will not be cheap; the most likely solution will be a million-dollar purification plant to treat the combined effluents of the Yak Tunnel and the Leadville Drain. On a national scale, mine-pollution cleanup costs become staggering; a 1980 estimate exceeded $7 billion.

Like many western rivers, the Arkansas can never be restored to the pristine state it was in when Pike and Frémont saw it, but it can be a clean river and a prime fishery again. The first step—recognition of the uniqueness of the problem—has already been taken. Mine-drainage pollution needs attention now. To continue to sit back as one ton of heavy-metal contaminants is dumped daily into the clear waters of the Arkansas and other rivers like it is much more than a national problem. It is surely a national disgrace □

HEALTH
AND
DISEASE

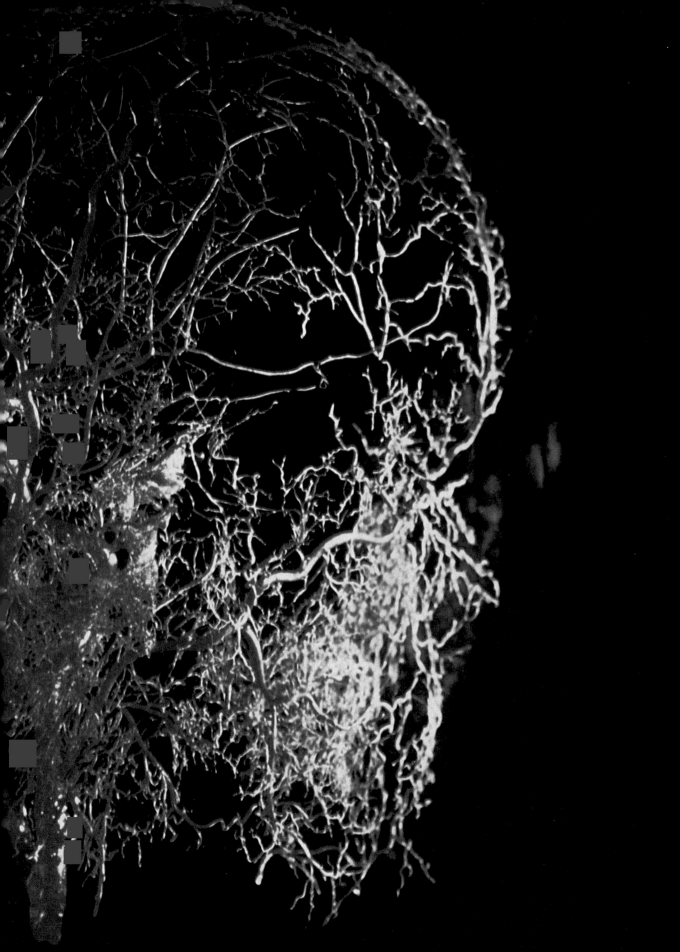

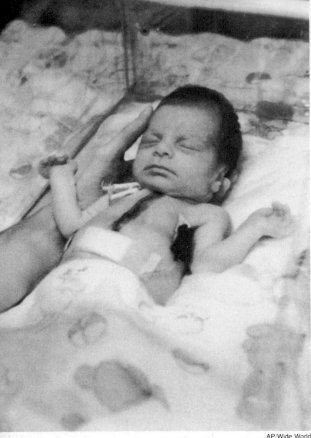

REVIEW
OF THE
YEAR

HEALTH AND DISEASE

Heart disease is the nation's leading killer, and the most dramatic recent stories in medicine involved radical experiments to save the lives of people whose hearts were destroyed by different forms of cardiac disease. One experiment involved an attempt to give a baboon heart to an infant girl known as Baby Fae who was born with a common heart defect. The other experiments involved the use of artificial hearts, one under bizarre circumstances. At the same time use of the new antirejection drug cyclosporin helped improve survival rates for those with heart transplants.

Other important events of the year included advances in understanding Acquired Immune Deficiency Syndrome (AIDS) and Alzheimer's disease and improvements in the treatment of severe burns and Tourette's syndrome.

An infant girl known as Baby Fae, who received a baboon-heart transplant in a highly controversial and publicized experiment, died 20 days after surgery.

BABY FAE

An attempt to give a baboon heart to Baby Fae became one of the most controversial medical experiments in recent years. Debates extended beyond the science of the experiment to focus on its ethics and the way the doctors and the hospital where the experiment was carried out chose to disclose facts about the case.

Shortly after her birth on October 12 in Barstow, California, Baby Fae developed signs of heart failure, and on October 19 she was transferred to Loma Linda University Medical Center. There doctors diagnosed her problem as hypoplastic left heart syndrome. In this birth defect, which occurs about once in every 3,000 live births, the left side of the heart is much smaller than the right, resulting in a biologically functionless heart. Until recently, and with rare exceptions, babies born with this defect did not survive beyond a few weeks.

At Loma Linda, pediatric surgeon Leonard L. Bailey had spent seven years experimentally transplanting hearts from one animal species to another in hopes of developing a way to transplant animal organs to humans. Dr. Bailey decided to try to save Baby Fae with his technique. His hopes were based on two crucial points. One was the immaturity of the infant's immune system, and the second was the antirejection drug cyclosporin. Dr. Bailey's belief was that Baby Fae's immature immune system would allow her to accept the baboon heart as her own and that cyclosporin would ward off any attempt to reject the animal organ. He said that he believed his was the only team experimenting with cyclosporin for animal-heart transplants in infants.

It took Dr. Bailey five hours to transplant the baboon heart on the 14th day of Baby Fae's life. The infant surprised most people by her early course. She developed good color, breathed easily without the aid of a mechanical ventilator, and took bottle feedings. Four days after the procedure she became the longest-surviving human recipient of a transplanted animal heart.

Then, a little more than two weeks after she underwent the highly experimental procedure, Baby Fae took a turn for the worse and her new heart and her kidneys began to fail. Despite reports by Loma Linda spokespersons that she was rallying with the aid of additional and stronger medications, Baby Fae died 20 days after receiving the baboon heart. Dr. Bailey initially attributed her death to complications from an apparent rejection reaction; however, later—

but still preliminary—autopsy results did not show the physical evidence typical of organ rejection.

The experiment not only caught the medical community by surprise, but it also made it difficult for experts to comment because Dr. Bailey had published so little of his research data in medical journals. "No doubt there has been a tremendous victory accompanying this loss and you'll understand more about that when the data is public," Dr. Bailey said. When a report appears it could stir further debate because some Loma Linda spokespersons have hinted that the team found new immunological markers in the newborn period that could be critical for future transplant surgery.

The Baby Fae experiment was widely debated, with some physicians pointing out that an alternative method of treatment for Baby Fae was available—namely, an experimental two-step palliative procedure developed by Dr. William Norwood that has had limited success to date.

Officials of the U.S. National Institutes of Health (NIH) issued a report on Dr. Bailey's experiment saying that his team had overstated Baby Fae's chance for survival but had

adequately informed her parents of the risks and alternatives. The report criticized Dr. Bailey's team for not searching for a human heart transplant instead of a baboon one. Dr. Bailey said he had not sought a human heart because his team's "entire research endeavor had been aimed at" transplanting animal hearts. In responding to the report, Loma Linda officials promised that they would seek a human heart before attempting a second animal heart transplant.

ARTIFICIAL HEARTS

Surgeons who performed experimental artificial heart implants also found themselves in the middle of public disputes. After a nearly two-year lapse since the first permanent Jarvik 7 artificial heart was implanted—in Dr. Barney B. Clark by Dr. William C. DeVries, at the University of Utah—a second was implanted in late 1984 and two more in early 1985, at Humana Hospital Audubon in Kentucky. ■ And an Arizona surgeon implanted a different and unauthorized type of artificial heart in a desperate attempt to save the life of a 33-year-old auto mechanic. A few days

Artificial-heart recipients William Schroeder (left) and Murray Haydon (right) shake hands at Humana Hospital.

UPI/Bettmann Newsphotos, Strode/Humana Inc.

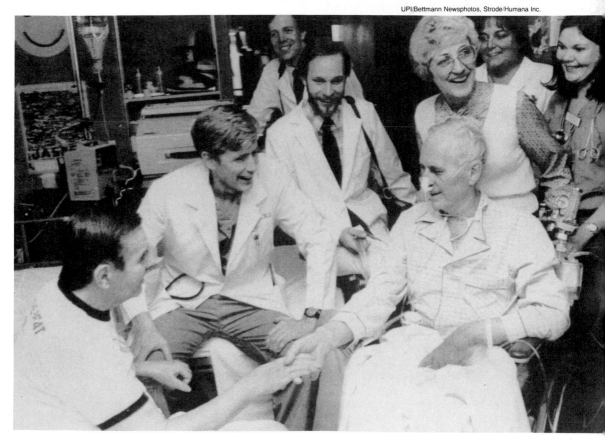

later the U.S. Food and Drug Administration (FDA) gave approval to doctors at the Hershey Medical Center in Pennsylvania to implant another type of artificial heart—known as the Penn State heart—on a temporary basis.

The resumption of activity with artificial hearts occurred after Dr. DeVries moved from the University of Utah hospital to the Humana hospital, lured there by Humana's offer to fund up to 100 artificial-heart implants. DeVries' move and Humana's offer triggered remarks from some medical leaders who felt that Humana was the wrong setting for testing the artificial heart. However, in November the FDA gave DeVries approval to carry on his research at Humana. On November 25 he implanted a Jarvik 7 heart in William J. Schroeder, a 52-year-old retired worker whose own heart had been destroyed by heart attacks and diabetes and had not been helped by coronary bypass surgery.

Mr. Schroeder made what his doctors called an "amazing" recovery. In an interview on December 9, an exuberant Schroeder said he felt "really good" and "super." But four days later Schroeder suffered a stroke that destroyed much of his memory and impaired his speech. Months later he could no longer remember the name of President Reagan, who, two days before the stroke, had called to congratulate him on his recovery.

Mr. Schroeder became the longest survivor on an artificial heart. He was the first to use a 5-kilogram (11-pound) portable battery pack to power his heart, and in April 1985 he left the hospital to live with his wife in a specially equipped apartment near the hospital.

The third implant of a Jarvik 7 heart occurred in February 1985 when DeVries implanted it in 58-year-old Murray Haydon, whose heart had been destroyed by a disease called cardiomyopathy. When Haydon awakened in the recovery room, he asked a nurse to turn on the television so he could see how he was doing. He has made steady progress since, marred somewhat by a second operation to plug a tiny leak through which blood was seeping into his chest cavity and by some breathing difficulties.

In April 1985 the first implant of a Jarvik 7 to take place outside the United States was performed on an unidentified middle-aged Swede at the Karolinska Institute in Stockholm. That same month Jack C. Burcham became the fifth U.S. recipient of an artificial heart. He died 10 days after the surgery from bleeding complications.

Though all recipients of the Jarvik 7 heart encountered major complications, they showed that humans could live with an artificial heart and that both the device and the body could adjust to each other.

The early implants were followed by a bizarre implant at the University of Arizona Medical Center in Tucson involving 33-year-old Thomas Creighton, whose heart had been destroyed by heart attacks and cardiomyopathy. Creighton underwent a heart transplant but the new heart failed, and his surgeon, Dr. Jack O. Copeland III, called for an artificial heart to keep Creighton alive until another human heart could be found for transplant. Two staff members from the University of Utah carried a Jarvik 7 heart in a chartered jet to Tucson. That device was not used, however, because the Utah team arrived about three hours after a team from St. Luke's Hospital in Phoenix, Arizona, where Dr. Kevin Cheng had developed a significantly different type of artificial heart called the Phoenix heart. Twelve hours was the longest the Phoenix heart had ever been tested—and that was in a calf. Dr. Copeland implanted the Phoenix heart and reported that it worked flawlessly for 11 hours in Creighton's chest. After that a human heart was found for Creighton and a second transplant took place, but complications soon occurred and Creighton died shortly thereafter.

The FDA had not approved the Phoenix heart, and officials initially criticized Dr. Copeland for violating federal law in using the device, but they recanted after the public showed strong support for Copeland. An official of the drug agency said that the implant of the Phoenix heart "was a unique emergency" and "it may well not have been possible" for the doctors involved to have called the FDA for prior approval. Nevertheless, some experts called for government action to prevent the Arizona case from setting a precedent whereby any doctor can do any experiment on a dying patient and justify it for that reason.

AIDS

The epidemic of AIDS continued in the United States, still largely confined to four high-risk groups: homosexuals, intravenous drug users, hemophiliacs, and Haitians, but with increasing concern about its possible spread to other groups. Epidemiologists focused on the large number of cases occurring in Zaire and nearby African countries, and preliminary results of their studies showed that AIDS could be spread heterosexually and in significant numbers.

■ Meanwhile, in the United States, the FDA licensed a test to detect evidence of the AIDS virus in blood. Some 200 cases of AIDS have developed among recipients of blood transfusions and blood products [such as Factor VIII used by hemophiliacs]. The blood test was developed as a result of research conducted at the National Cancer Institute by a team headed by Dr. Robert C. Gallo after he reported finding a virus that he called HTLV-III as the cause of AIDS. His report

Vaseline-gauze-coated patches of skin, first cultured in test tubes, grow together on the badly burned abdomen of a young boy at the Shriners Burn Institute in Boston, Massachusetts. The grafts grow well without being rejected because the initial patches came from the boy's body.

Shriners Burn Institute

came one year after a French team headed by Dr. Luc Montaigner at the Pasteur Institute reported finding an AIDS virus that it called L.A.V. Subsequent research showed that both viruses are the same, but precisely how the virus causes AIDS and what other cofactors may be needed to produce the disease remain mysteries.

ALZHEIMER'S DISEASE

Researchers added two more pieces to the sketchy jigsaw puzzle of Alzheimer's disease. This disease usually appears in the fifth or sixth decade of life and causes progressive loss of mental functioning. Often called "premature senility," the dementing disease is related to more than 100,000 deaths each year in the United States.

A team headed by Dr. Antonio R. Damasio at the University of Iowa reported pinpointing the damaged areas of the brain that appear responsible for the memory loss linked to Alzheimer's. According to a study of five patients who died of Alzheimer's, the physical damage is confined to a surprisingly small and anatomically specific area of the brain—two key areas in the hippocampus, which is a small area in the temporal lobe that is necessary for making and cataloging memories.

In the autopsy study, most damage to the hippocampus was in the entorhinal cortex, an assembly area for information coming into the hippocampus; and in the subiculum, an assembly area for data coming out of the hippocampus and dispersed to other areas of the brain. As a result of the damage, the hippocampus is isolated from the rest of the brain. Even within these two areas the damage was very selective, affecting only certain parts. The selective nature of the damage is a surprise because most doctors had thought the progressive memory loss resulted from damage to nerve cells in scattered areas throughout the brain.

Meanwhile, in studies done independently at

Harvard University on the brains of six Alzheimer victims, researchers found a basic biochemical abnormality in Alzheimer-diseased brains. The research team, headed by Dr. Charles A. Marotta, found markedly diminished production of new protein in the brain cells damaged by Alzheimer's disease. The reduction in new protein presumably interferes with brain function. The defect involved overactivity of the enzyme alkaline ribonuclease, resulting in loss of control of normal protein-making activities. This biochemical finding is compatible with the anatomical findings of the other study, and together the findings are helping to solve the puzzle of Alzheimer's.

TEST-TUBE SKIN TO TREAT BURNS

Doctors at the Shriners Burn Institute in Boston, Massachusetts, took tiny patches of skin from the bodies of two severely burned brothers, grew the patches into large sheets, and then grafted them back over the burns. The skin patches were induced to grow first in test tubes and later on large strips of gauze in the laboratory. Doctors applied waves of grafts of the test-tube skin to replace more than half of the skin areas on each of the boys, who were burned over 97 percent of their bodies. The skin that grew on the boys was smooth, shiny, and soft, and it functioned well and did not have the rejection problems inherent in transplanting skin to the patient from the body of another person.

TOURETTE SYNDROME

The FDA approved the use of a drug called pimozide to relieve some of the most severe symptoms of Tourette Syndrome, a rare disease that often begins in childhood and that causes involuntary movements, uncontrollable vocal sounds, and, frequently, the involuntary shouting of obscenities. The drug will be available to those among the estimated 100,000 sufferers who do not benefit from another drug—Haldol.

LAWRENCE K. ALTMAN, M.D.

229

Illustrations (3) by Arnold Roth

The DEATH of DIETING

by Paul Ernsberger

R uby Greenwald was a 19-year-old new mother in suburban Chicago, Illinois, when her weight problem started. Her doctor put her on a diet, and she quickly lost the extra pounds. But several months later, the pounds were back—plus a few more.

The Yo-yo Syndrome

There was another diet. This time it was harder; there was more to lose. "While my children were growing up," says Ruby, "I lost and regained dozens of times: down 30 pounds, up 45; down 45, up 55, always creeping upward.

I've spent thousands of dollars and tried every diet program, book, and pill; acupuncture and hypnosis, too. They all worked—at least for a while. I'm part of the success statistics of a dozen weight-loss programs. And look what I have to show for it!'' Ruby gestures indignantly at her 300-pound body.

Ruby is a ''yo-yo dieter,'' and she's not alone. In a survey of 15,000 readers of a major women's magazine, 42 percent of the overweight readers said they were on-again, off-again dieters. They lose weight, then gain. They are always dieting even when they're gaining. They struggle and fail—and hate themselves. And as they diet, their weight baseline continues to rise.

Lose-Gain Swings May Cause Real Harm

Some of them have even figured it out—crash dieting is bad for them. But do they know how bad? It's not just that these diets don't work. Crash dieting sets up a yo-yo pattern of loss and rebound gain that can make you heavier. For some time, researchers have known that severe calorie restriction forces the body to respond as if to starvation conditions: It conserves energy by lowering the metabolic pacemaker. The biological stage is set for regain on less food. But beyond upsetting the weight-control system, any sequence of severe diets also has health consequences, which only now are being recognized.

In my laboratory at Northwestern University, we have found in animal tests that the feast-fast cycle itself can cause a distinct form of high blood pressure. This ''dieter's hypertension'' develops over the course of sizable lose-gain swings and eventually becomes set. In humans, this may lead to congestive heart failure, rather than the heart attacks and kidney disease common to other forms of hypertension. Doctors know overweight people are twice as likely to have hypertension as lean folks, but they thought the problem was the extra weight.

My colleagues and I have evidence that the cause is not in the poundage but in a dieting pattern. And we believe we've found an explanation: norepinephrine. This potent stress hormone is the link between body metabolism and blood pressure.

The Vicious Cycle of Overcompensation

The research trail goes back more than 40 years. In 1938 British scientists found that laboratory rats deprived of food and then allowed to feed

freely quickly regained weight and became heavier than rats that had never dieted. They called this rebound ''overcompensation.''

Other early studies found that as weight goes down, we lose both fat and protein, but regained weight is largely fat. Children recovering from serious malnutrition often regain until they become obese. But even if the youngsters' weight is controlled, their body-fat content will be unusually high. Cattle raisers have capitalized on this research. By underfeeding animals before fattening them, they have a cheap way of increasing the fat content of beef.

Overcompensation may be fine for tender, marbled steak, but an expanding waistline is not what 50 million dieting Americans have in mind. True, some people lose five to 10 pounds, regain the same amount, and never go beyond. Heredity probably protects many from overcompensation. But for a large proportion of dieters, the biological cards are stacked against dieting: Cutting calories turns out to be the great fattener. The five-year follow-up records of almost every type of diet program show one-third to one-half of the dieters gained back more weight than they lost.

Overcompensation is kicked off by a profound dietary shock to the system—perhaps a 20 percent loss of weight—and it is fueled at cellular and hormonal levels. During a diet, fat cells shrink; they never disappear. When normal eating is resumed, the fat cells don't just fill up with fat. They multiply—even doubling in number—and refill. The new fat cells are forever, and they encourage your body to accumulate more fat. For wild creatures threatened with periodic famine, such a biological program offered protection. But in a world of mechanized work and overabundant food supply, this ever-upward effect only compounds the problem. The body can now store more fat; the next diet will be harder. And failed diets—not just obesity—can sabotage health, even kill.

Feast-Fast Pattern Boosts Blood Pressure

Jean Mayer, a pioneer in obesity research and president of Tufts University, put laboratory mice on a feast-fast schedule and found that yo-yoing shortened their lives.

Other researchers put swine through wide weight swings. The animals developed high blood pressure and heart disease.

And epidemiologists have long observed that overweight people are particularly prone to hypertension. But when they tried to determine how extra pounds boost blood pressure, they came up against an apparent contradiction. Fatty breeds of laboratory animals have normal blood pressure, whereas specially bred high-pressure rats are actually quite svelte.

It's clear that severe dietary restriction lowers blood pressure regardless of weight at the outset. And it always drops before applicable weight is lost.

If fat tissue is not closely linked to hypertension, than why, I wondered, are fat people so prone to high blood pressure? Fat animals don't ordinarily have hypertension. But when they gain weight, the increase is slow and steady. Most overweight Americans tend to go on and off diets. I began to suspect that wide up-down weight swings might themselves be responsible. So I decided to fatten normal laboratory rats and then send them crash dieting. Once, twice.

Sure enough, before the third yo-yo cycle was over, the animals developed mild high blood pressure. Mild in degree, that is, not in

effect. Even borderline hypertension involves a hormonal assault on the heart that may lead to heart failure.

The Norepinephrine Connection

My research has traced this effect to the nerve cells that manufacture norepinephrine—the "fight or flight" hormone. Normally, when the brain signals danger, these cells step up production of norepinephrine. This hormone, in turn, speeds heartbeat, constricts blood vessels, and raises blood pressure.

These nerve cells also respond to another kind of stress—overeating. If you overindulge during holiday feasting, your norepinephrine output will increase, triggering metabolic systems that "burn off" the extra calories.

Norepinephrine activation of these "energy-wasting" systems may be the reason most of us can overeat without gaining weight. It also explains why overfeeding can lead to small increases in blood pressure: The norepinephrine that fans the metabolic fires is the same norepinephrine that speeds the heart and drives up blood pressure.

Thus, the body has a natural system linking blood pressure and calorie control. For reasons still unknown, repeated feast-fast cycles make norepinephrine-producing nerve cells perma-

nently hyperactive. As animals go through more swings of the yo-yo, blood pressure no longer drops during dieting, perhaps because permanent blood-vessel changes keep pressure up.

A critical role in this disruption may be played by an area in the hypothalamus believed to be a brain control center for appetite, insulin levels, and metabolism, plus blood pressure. If we remove a certain part of this area—the paraventricular nucleus—from a rat, blood pressure drops but the rats get fat.

Life-shortening Consequences

There's good reason to believe this animal research applies directly to people. Inadvertently, during World War II, the siege of Leningrad (the German encirclement of this Soviet city) turned the city into a natural laboratory for observing the effects of severe dieting, however involuntary. As a result of the German blockade, millions of inhabitants were unable to get adequate supplies of food. The proportion of hospital beds taken up by patients with disease related to hypertension fell from a prewar 10 percent to 2 percent in 1942.

When food supplies were restored, the prevalence of high blood pressure quadrupled over prewar levels and 50 percent of all hospital admissions were hypertension-related. The

Roger Ressmeyer/Wheeler Pictures

Exercise may be the only effective way for people to break away from their yo-yo dieting patterns and shed weight permanently.

symptoms of high blood pressure in Leningrad were identical to those typical of overweight people: Heart failure was common, but not heart attacks or kidney disease. And they appeared in normal-weight people as well as in the over-weight. An epidemic of congestive heart failure peaked a year or two after the siege, about the time people had regained their prewar weight.

A more deliberate study in Los Angeles, California, indicates that loss-regain cycles in-deed shorten life. At the Wadsworth Veteran's Administration Hospital, Dr. Ernst J. Drenick put obese men on a total fast for 30 days or more. After release from the hospital, they regained the weight—and more. After losing and regaining again, the men were in trouble: 80 percent eventually developed diabetes; fully 25 percent died, mainly of heart disease. Their death rate was up to 13 times higher than that of equally obese nondieters in large studies in Nor-way and Denmark.

A Need to Revise Hypertension Therapy

The norepinephrine connection casts doubt on the medical practice of treating obese, mildly hypertensive patients by handing them a diet. "Get that weight off," the doctor orders. And the patient slinks off to try again. But failed dieting probably caused the hypertension in the first place.

Fat or thin, patients with mild hypertension should avoid a drastic calorie cutback. Instead, they should monitor the food they eat: Avoid salt, sugar, saturated fats (red meat and butter, for example), and excessive alcohol; increase potassium, calcium, polyunsaturated fats (vege-table oils), fiber, and fish.

Above all, they should opt for gradual weight loss through vigorous exercise. Exercise doesn't just burn off fat; it has a special advan-tage in this case.

When hypertension patients take norepi-nephrine-blocking drugs—such as the popular beta-blocker propranolol—blood pressure drops but weight may go up. Regular aerobic exercise, on the other hand, resets metabolic thermostats. The result: both blood pressure and weight head down.

Beating the Body's System with Exercise

Does the weight boomerang spell futility for all attempts to lose weight? Certainly not. But it means that we must work with our biochemis-try, not at cross-purposes. Dieters' hypertension will disappear with time—provided weight

Jim Carson

stays constant, either high or low. It seems to take about two years, though recovery is in-creasingly delayed with each cycle.

The critical factor in breaking out of the cycle is not diet. It's exercise. It's both a cure and an alternative to yo-yo dieting.

The benefits of aerobic exercise do not stem from weight loss per se. Physical activity subtly resets the systems that control metabo-lism and regulate weight. Exercise can lower dieters' high blood pressure in part by allowing norepinephrine production. And it can strengthen the heart, which may have been weakened by protein loss during dieting.

Crash dieting, with its wide weight swings, is making Americans fat and, worse, sick. The modern compulsion to be thin is thwarted at every turn by nature's determination to protect the human body from starvation. On the other hand, we are designed to be active. When we run, hike, swim, or dance, we are giving expression to a biological need. Nature ap-plauds—and doesn't notice we are losing weight □

Jim Pozarik/Gamma Liaison

PREVENTING OSTEOPOROSIS by Alice Kahn

Osteoporosis is the most common major health problem among older women. It involves a loss of calcium from the bones, which leads to an increased risk of fractures, especially of the pelvic bones and the lumbar vertebrae of the lower back.

Osteoporosis, literally "holes in the bones," affects 25 percent of postmenopausal women, and as the proportion of older people in the population has increased, it has received new attention. But younger athletes, particularly distance runners, may also develop osteoporosis.

Bone-Mass Decline Greatest in Older Women

Growing interest in the condition has also raised new questions about the advisability of estrogen-replacement therapy (ERT). This fe-

male sex hormone has been maligned by many women's health advocates for increasing postmenopausal women's risk of endometrial (uterine) cancer. But ERT is now enjoying new popularity because it helps prevent osteoporosis.

The calcium in bone is constantly being replaced with calcium dissolved in the blood. Through this process, called "remodeling," the calcium in the normal adult skeleton is entirely replaced every 10 years. After age 35, however, bone mass begins to decline. If steps are not taken to preserve it, women over 50 lose about 10 percent of their bone mass per decade. Men over 50 lose bone mass at about half that rate. Osteoporosis is rarely diagnosed until pain, a fracture, and/or disability reveal an advanced stage of the condition. By 60, women suffer 10 times as many forearm fractures as men.

A Debilitating Condition

Osteoporosis often weakens the vertebrae of the back, which then collapse under the weight of the body. Collapsed vertebrae may cause pain (if the ribs come to rest on the hipbones), or a noticeably curved spine ("dowager's hump"), and/or permanent height loss of up to several inches. Vertebral collapse may also lead to spinal compression fractures, which affect one-quarter of white women over 60. It's not cute being a "little old lady."

Osteoporosis-related hip fractures can be even more serious. Hip fractures have become the 12th-leading cause of death in the United States, and the falls that usually cause them have become the number one cause of accidental death in elderly white women. Emotional cost aside, the nation now spends more than $1 billion a year on acute care for hip fractures.

Preventive Nutrition

Because osteoporosis involves the depletion of calcium from the bones, a diet rich in this mineral is an important preventive. As people age, the intestines slowly lose their ability to absorb calcium. Older people should consciously increase their calcium intake. To obtain sufficient amounts of the mineral, Rosetta Reitz, author of *Menopause: A Positive Approach,* recommends these calcium-rich foods: whole grains, fresh fruits and vegetables, nuts, seeds, and fish. She also suggests eating foods rich in vitamin D, which aids calcium absorption. She advises avoiding foods rich in phosphorus—particularly red meats, which deplete calcium.

Calcium supplementation is another way to obtain the mineral and sustain bone mass. *Medical Self-Care* drugs editor Joe Graedon suggests that postmenopausal women consider a supplement of 1 or 2 grams of calcium a day. Women with a family history of osteoporosis might consider taking calcium by age 35. A vitamin D supplement is also a good idea.

Significant Risk Factors

In addition to nutritional factors, other osteoporosis risk factors include: being slender, lack of exercise, smoking, heavy alcohol use, heavy coffee consumption, corticosteroid drugs (such as cortisone), lack of exposure to the sun (for vitamin D), and loss of natural estrogens due to early or surgical menopause (premenopausal hysterectomy). Anglo-Saxon and Asian women are at higher risk than black and Hispanic women, with Jewish women in between.

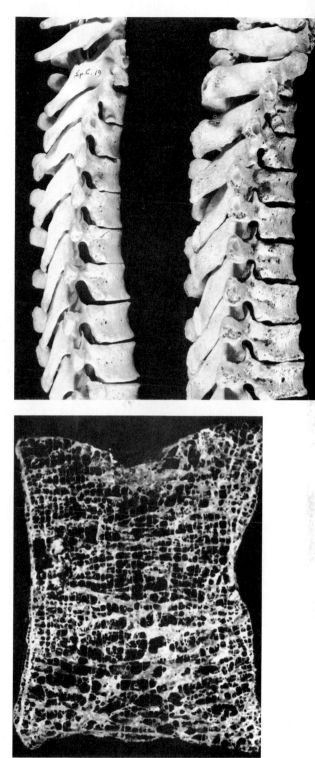

Top: Terri Landers/Union Memorial Hospital; Above: Center for Climacteric Studies

Top: The spine of a healthy woman (left) is noticeably different from the porous, brittle spine (right) of a woman with osteoporosis. Above: A vertebra ravaged by osteoporosis shows massive loss of bone density.

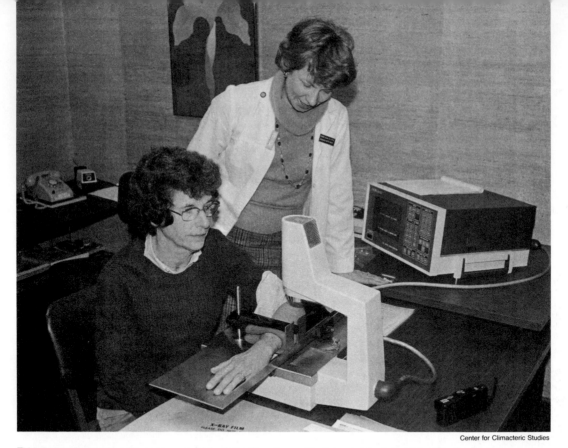

This single-photon absorptiometer accurately determines bone density and detects bone loss earlier than X rays.

Thus, the portrait of a woman at high risk for osteoporosis is a slender white woman who smokes, drinks alcohol and coffee frequently, leads a sedentary indoor life, and eats a diet lacking in calcium.

Although exercise helps maintain bone mass, excessive physical activity may contribute to its depletion. Some women distance runners develop amenorrhea; their periods cease, apparently due to "ovarian shutdown." Ovaries that shut down also produce less estrogen, making women with amenorrhea candidates for early osteoporosis unless they take calcium supplements.

The Estrogen-Replacement Controversy

Estrogen retards bone loss. Estrogen production declines with age, especially after menopause, and as a result, bone loss accelerates. Estrogen-replacement therapy (ERT) can help maintain bone mass and prevent osteoporosis. But ERT has been controversial because it also increases the risk of uterine (endometrial) cancer. It has also been linked to gallbladder disease, benign liver tumors, blood clots, high blood pressure,

and breast tenderness. Women with histories of blood clots, undiagnosed vaginal bleeding, fibroid-uterine tumors, liver disease, or breast or uterine cancer should not take estrogen. However, the combination of estrogen plus progesterone has been shown to reduce these risks.

Other women must weigh the risk of living with years of pain and disability from osteoporosis against the risk of developing serious health problems, primarily endometrial cancer, a disease that with careful monitoring can be detected early and treated successfully through hysterectomy. Clearly, this lesser-of-two-evils choice involves identifying those at highest risk for osteoporosis. But in the final analysis, the choice is a personal decision.

One Woman's Choice

Mary Ann Williams fits part of the risk profile for osteoporosis. She is 58, slender, and white. She smoked for 20 years, but quit more than 10 years ago. On the other hand, she has been a swimmer and hiker all her life, and has always eaten a well-balanced diet, both of which help prevent bone loss. Williams is a professor of nutrition at the University of California's San Francisco Medical Center. She knows a great deal about bone loss in older women. For more than 10 years, she has lived with osteoporosis.

Until 1974 Williams enjoyed good health. In her late 40's her physician suggested she take estrogen to avoid menopausal symptoms. She dismissed the estrogen recommendation as nonsense. She knew that the hormone was associated with endometrial cancer and other health problems. Then one day she developed a severe pain in her hip. The pain progressed to the point where she could not walk. Since she'd always been physically active, the disability was devastating.

An X ray indicated a deformity at the end of the femur (thighbone), and in 1976 she had total hip-replacement surgery. Her leg muscles atrophied (degenerated) as a result of her illness, surgery, and recovery. But she regarded the operation, now routine but new at the time, as a miracle because she was able to return to swimming and walking. She became determined never to be disabled again.

After her operation she reluctantly tried estrogen replacement, but stopped because it caused unpleasant breast tenderness. She decided to pursue the alternative course for bone-mass retention: exercise and dietary calcium supplementation.

A New View of Calcium Consumption

Williams explains that she grew up at a time when people believed that adults didn't need much calcium, an era from which we are just emerging. Adults' recommended daily allowance is currently 800 milligrams (mg), the amount in about three cups of milk. Unfortunately, the average North American woman consumes only about 450 mg of calcium a day—often because low-calorie diets limit high-fat foods, many of which are rich in calcium.

The 800-mg figure may be conservative. Recent research suggests that premenopausal women (after age 35) should probably ingest about 1,000 mg a day to build up their bone mass. And because of the hormonal changes of menopause, postmenopausal women probably need 1,500 mg a day to maintain what nutrition-

As osteoporosis progresses, the collapse of spinal vertebrae results in a loss of height from the upper part of the body.

From Stand Tall, © 1982, Triad Publishing Co.

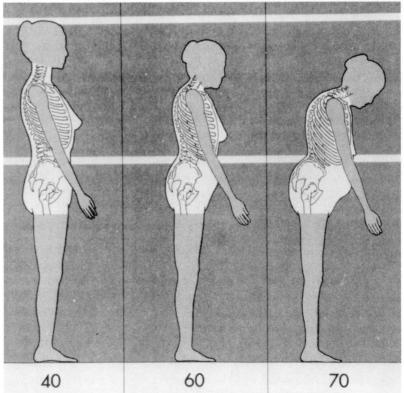

40   60   70

ists call a "positive calcium balance." According to Dr. Morris Notelovitz, coauthor of *Stand Tall: The Informed Woman's Guide to Preventing Osteoporosis,* "Twenty-five years of a negative calcium balance can consume one-third of a woman's skeleton." The message to women is clear: Eat more calcium.

When Mary Ann Williams looked at the prospect of consuming five glasses of skim milk a day (or the equivalent), she also considered what the added calories might mean (not to mention problems like constipation and gassiness that some people experience from that much milk). It was difficult to consume 1,500 mg of calcium from her diet and still control her weight. In addition, there were other dietary considerations. Some foods encourage calcium excretion, including those high in sodium, fiber, oxalates (in some green vegetables), and phytates (in cereals and bran). Furthermore, fasting, heavy coffee consumption, megadoses of vitamin A, and high-phosphorus reducing diets (such as red meat and diet sodas) further accelerate calcium depletion. In light of this complex situation, Williams decided that a semivegetarian diet with two glasses of skim milk and 800 mg of calcium lactate supplementation each day was the best solution for her.

A Difficult Decision

In 1982 Williams' physician informed her that she had lost 2.54 centimeters (1 inch) of height since menopause, a strong indication of progressive osteoporosis. He advised estrogen. He said that if she took a low dose cyclically—that is, 25 days on, then one week off—and combined it with 10 or 12 days of progesterone, her cancer risk and estrogen side effects would be greatly reduced. He added that she might bleed, but said that a biopsy for endometrial cancer could be performed quickly if that happened. (Most doctors recommend a routine endometrial biopsy—a cancer examination of tissue from the uterine lining—before starting ERT.)

The prospect of bleeding, biopsies, and even a small risk of endometrial cancer frightened her. She was angry that her physician did not appreciate her fear of cancer. On the other hand, she felt tormented by a fear of returning to the level of disability she'd known with her hip problem. She was also concerned about spinal collapse: "They can't fix backs, you know."

She consulted another doctor, who told her that the latest evidence suggested that combined estrogen-progesterone treatment decreased cancer risk considerably, and if uterine cancer occurred, it was usually treatable. Williams weighed the cancer risk of taking estrogen against her family's tradition of long-lived, though shrunken, women. In the end, she decided that her fear of cancer and subsequent hysterectomy was not as great as her fear of years of physical disability due to osteoporosis. She began taking estrogen with progesterone, and found that her previous breast problems did not recur.

"Sure, taking hormones is unnatural," Williams says, "but so is living to ages we didn't live to before. This is an experiment, and I won't know for sure until the end if this approach is better or worse than any other. But I just decided that estrogen's cancer risk wasn't as great as its benefit of preserving bone."

What's a Woman to Do?

Until the final verdict is in, until we have accurate methods of predicting osteoporosis risk and detecting it in its early stages, what should women do? Dr. R. Lindsay, a longtime osteoporosis researcher, writes, "Despite the obvious protective effects of estrogen therapy, the true incidence of osteoporosis is unknown, and the provision of preventive therapy to all postmenopausal women is inappropriate."

Unless you are in a high-risk category (for example, early or surgical menopause), the best osteoporosis preventives include regular weight-bearing exercise, such as walking or jogging, and a high-calcium diet, with supplementation after the mid-30's. Osteoporosis is yet another reason to avoid smoking, crash-dieting, and excessive use of coffee and alcohol.

But many questions remain unanswered. How much calcium is really enough? How much physical activity is enough? What are the real trade-offs between estrogen's endometrial-cancer risk and its effectiveness in preventing bone loss? At present, scientists simply do not know. The uncertainties are enough to drive a woman to drink. So set 'em up, Joe—four glasses of skim milk, straight up□

SELECTED READINGS

"Osteoporosis, calcium and estrogens" by Roger W. Miller. *FDA Consumer,* November 1984.

"Boning up on osteoporosis" by Joan Arehart-Treichel. *Science News,* August 27, 1983.

Stand Tall: The Informed Woman's Guide to Preventing Osteoporosis, by Morris Notelovitz, M.D., and Marsha Ware. Triad Publishing, 1982.

Wilhelm Bosl

Myths and Truths About Baldness

by Benedict Leerburger

In the late 1880's, a man was arrested in Des Moines, Iowa, for selling a medicine that failed to grow hair on a judge's bald head. The phony hair-growing tonic was a foul-smelling liquid made from dissolved lime and cow manure. The salesman argued that hair was simply a crop, and to make it grow, you had to improve its "soil." This unorthodox baldness "remedy" was not that unusual; for ages men and women have been trying all kinds of treatments in an effort to cure hair loss.

Hair-Loss Ideas of the Ancients

Attempts to grow hair on balding heads have been ongoing for thousands of years. An ancient Egyptian prescription believed to cure baldness called for a mixture of lion, hippopotamus, crocodile, goose, snake, and goat fat. Another Egyptian formula used dogs' paws, dates, and

donkeys' hooves as the prime ingredients. The early Greek physician Hippocrates, who is considered the father of medicine, claimed that baldness could be cured by making a pungent ointment from a blend of opium, essence of roses or lilacs, and wine or the oil of unripe olives.

In the fourth century B.C., Aristotle stated that baldness was caused by excessive sexual activity. Although the great Greek philosopher, bald himself, did not pinpoint the exact cause of baldness, he hit upon one of the factors that is now known to affect both hair growth and hair loss—male hormones called androgens.

The Hormone Connection

Since Aristotle's time, many people have associated virility, or manliness, with having hair. In the Bible, for example, Samson lost his strength when Delilah cut off his long hair. English jurists still wear the traditional white wigs of old as a symbol of justice, dominance, and strength.

One of the first to link "manliness" with hair growth on a scientific basis was James B. Hamilton, a Yale University anatomist. Since androgens are produced in the testicles, Hamilton was interested in the relationship between hair loss and men who could not produce androgens due to castration. In the 1940's he studied more than 100 castrated men and discovered that more than half of them had a full, healthy head of hair. It is now known that a male of any age with a full head of hair who is castrated cannot become bald because castration destroys the production of androgens. If a man is castrated after the normal balding pattern has commenced, the castration will stop the balding process. No one, however, would logically suggest castration as a cure for baldness!

Following Hamilton's work, other researchers experimented with the female hormone, estrogen, to study the relationship between hair growth and hair loss. Their findings showed that men injected with large doses of estrogen did, indeed, develop more hair on their heads and bodies. However, the use of estrogens as a hair restorative is unpredictable at best and, in some cases, may result in unpleasant side effects or may even cause cancer.

Today there is scientific agreement that androgens are a major determinant of baldness among individuals with a hereditary predisposition to hair loss. Although most men naturally possess substantial amounts of this hormone, women have androgens as well. The baldness-producing effects of androgens are tempered by women's ample supplies of estrogen until menopause, at which time declined production of this hormone is less able to negate the effects of androgens.

The Life Cycle of a Hair

It has only been in the past few decades that scientists have fully understood the details of hair growth and balding patterns. Normally, hair comes and goes in a three-step cycle of growth, resting, and shedding. The average person has approximately 100,000 hairs on his or her head. Oddly, the number of hairs varies with color, with redheads having slightly less than average and blondes having slightly more. Ironically, the natural shedding of about 40 to 100 hairs daily is a sign of a healthy scalp.

Every hair grows out of a long, narrow pocket of skin cells with a bulblike root in the scalp known as a follicle. A typical hair has a growing cycle of about two to six years, and grows in length up to 2.54 centimeters (1 inch) each month during this period. The hair then enters a resting phase that lasts for several months. (At any one time about 15 percent of the hair on a person's head is at rest.) Finally, a new hair begins to grow and pushes up from the root of the healthy follicle, causing the old hair to fall out.

During the regular growing-resting-shedding cycle, healthy follicles shed their hairs periodically but continually produce new ones as the old ones are lost. However, a variety of factors—including an inherited susceptibility to androgens—may cause the follicles to cease making new hairs, and may ultimately result in *alopecia,* or baldness.

Both Men and Women Affected

The most common type of alopecia, male-pattern baldness, does not usually begin until a person is in his 20's. By age 30, one-third of all men have receding hairlines; by 50, one-half show partial hair loss; and by 65, two-thirds are noticeably bald.

Women are also subject to hair thinning, although rarely do they become totally bald. Women frequently suffer temporary hair loss soon after childbirth (known as *postpartum alopecia*) or after discontinuing birth-control pills. While a woman is pregnant or taking oral contraceptives, more of her hair stays in the resting phase. Therefore, after delivery or discontinuing the Pill, the hairs that should have been shed do so at once. Although this hair loss is temporary, 50 percent of all women start losing their hair permanently after menopause, due to decreased production of estrogen.

Significant Causes of Hair Loss

Besides the factors already discussed, other significant causes of baldness include: viral, bacterial, or ringworm infections; certain cancers; radiation overdoses; and serious burns of the scalp. All of these factors may cause follicle destruction, resulting in permanent hair loss.

Certain causes of baldness may produce only temporary hair loss. Some of these are as follows:

• Cosmetic damage, such as the frequent wearing of tight ponytails and braids; excessive use of heat when drying hair; and excessive

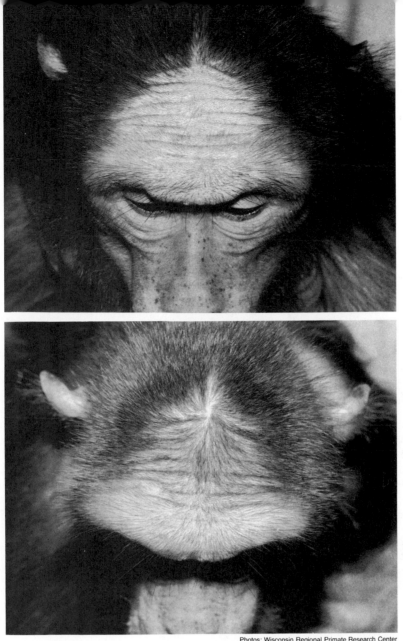

Photos of a stump-tailed macaque taken before and after eight months of treatment with the drug minoxidil prove that hair growth was stimulated on the forehead of a female who had become bald with age. Researchers have tested the drug on both monkeys and humans.

Photos: Wisconsin Regional Primate Research Center

brushing, bleaching, or use of too-tight rollers or hair clips. The extent of the damage from these factors depends on how long the individual's hair has been abused.

• Illness characterized by long periods of high fever may lead to hair loss. A fever-induced hair loss is usually corrected without medication. When the illness passes, hair returns. Thyroid disorders can also cause hair loss. According to New York dermatologist Dr. Rhoda Narins, a blood test can quickly determine if a thyroid condition is to blame for hair loss, and any medical consultation regarding unusual hair thinning should include a thyroid test. Alopecia due to a thyroid condition is effectively reversible with drug therapy.

• Drugs, particularly anticancer drugs, can lead to a temporary loss of hair. When the treatment stops, the patient usually regains his or her normal head of hair.

• Stress, particularly a severe mental strain such as that following an accident or major surgery, can lead to partial hair loss or excessive shedding. Cases have been reported of soldiers losing tremendous amounts of hair within a few weeks following their battlefield experiences.

Recently, Dr. Giulia Perini of the University of Padua, Italy, evaluated a group of men and women who suffered from alopecia. He found that 87.5 percent of them had "been through a stressful life event in the 6-month period before the disease appeared." A major crisis such as divorce or the death of a loved one was experienced by two-thirds of the test patients. When the stress factors are eliminated, the person's hair usually returns.

Severe dieting, if resulting in caloric malnutrition, can lead to hair loss. Since hair itself is made up almost entirely of protein, it needs protein for nourishment. A lack of protein may cause the hair to enter its resting phase, followed by excessive shedding several months later. Anyone dieting strenuously should take care to ingest proper amounts of protein. Vegetarians should be sure to eat nonmeat sources of protein to prevent such problems.

Drug Grows Hair But Still No Sure Cure

Despite the fact that many unqualified "hair specialists" still try to sell ointments, salves, and lotions that they guarantee will grow hair, the American Medical Association has stated that "hair treatments and remedies claiming to prevent, postpone, correct [or disguise] baldness have been promoted for centuries and they all have one thing in common—they fail to grow hair."

In 1983, however, researchers at the Upjohn Company thought they may have stumbled across a "magic elixir." In their tests of a drug called minoxidil, originally developed to treat hypertension (high blood pressure), they discovered that the drug had an unusual side effect: patients were growing hair all over their bodies. The drug is currently being tested on both monkeys and humans. For example, Dr. Hideo Uno, a senior scientist at the Wisconsin Primate Research Center, reported in 1984 that minoxidil stimulated hair growth on the foreheads of stump-tailed macaques that had become bald with age.

Human tests on minoxidil were conducted at many medical centers in the United States during 1984. Subjects spread minoxidil on their bald spots twice daily for at least a year. Although the test results are still being studied, California dermatologist Vera Price noted that, "there is no question that minoxidil can stimulate [hair] growth in some patients." But some researchers have claimed that the yield is often nothing more than a fine peach fuzz.

Although there are, as yet, no sure cures for baldness, women who are losing hair may be able to stem the loss by a topical application of the hormone progesterone, which acts as an antiandrogen. For a postmenopausal woman with female-pattern baldness, which is usually hereditary, using progesterone is less dangerous than using estrogen. If a woman begins treatment with progesterone at the first signs of balding, the condition generally will proceed no further, according to Dr. Narins.

Unfortunately, men who are treated for hereditary baldness with progesterone may succumb to the same undesirable side effects that estrogen treatment can result in. While progesterone may stop hair loss, it may also produce female characteristics in men, such as breast enlargement. Research is now being conducted to develop a male antiandrogen that could arrest alopecia without side effects.

Cosmetic Alternatives

For the present, those with hairless pates will have to resign themselves to cosmetic alternatives. One of the most popular and traditional alternatives is wearing *hairpieces*. Hairpieces may be worn for extended periods of time, but they do trap scalp heat and may become uncomfortable after a while. They also require cleaning and styling, so a spare is almost a necessity.

A more permanent approach is *hair weaving,* a method in which a hairpiece is woven tightly to the remaining hair. The appearance may be very natural, but the weaving must be retightened at regular intervals as the natural hair continues to grow. The method may also cause the natural hair to fall out more quickly, from the tension on the bound hair supporting the hairpiece.

Another method of replacing lost hair is a *hair implant,* in which loops of nylon or other synthetic material are stitched into the scalp to anchor strands of real or synthetic hair. In June 1983, the U.S. Food and Drug Administration banned the sale of artificial hair fibers for scalp implantation because of the dangers of infection and scarring.

A safer medical alternative is the *hair transplant*. Tiny "plugs" of skin bearing healthy follicles are removed from the portion of the scalp where hair is growing, usually at the fringes. Plugs of barren skin are then removed from the bald scalp and replaced with the hair-bearing plugs. Although the transplanted hair

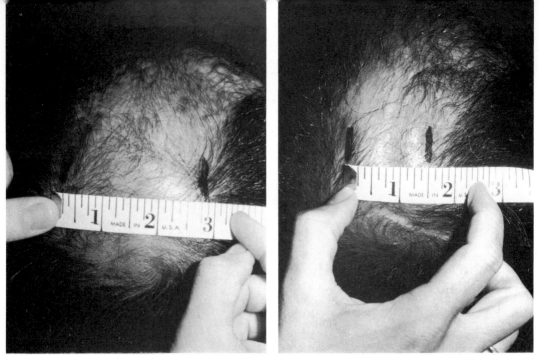

Photos (3): Richard Pilling

Scalp-reduction surgery substantially decreased the size of this man's bald spot. Hair implants will fill the gap.

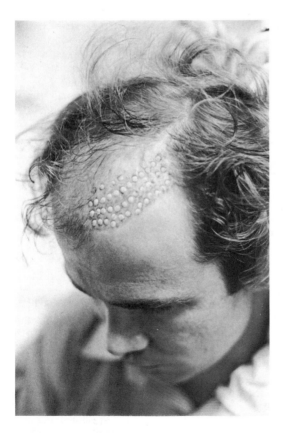

Rows of hair-bearing plugs of skin line the forehead of a balding man who just received a hair transplant.

soon falls out, new hair sprouts from the follicles in several months. One must have several hundred plugs transplanted for good cosmetic results, and the procedure can be quite costly.

Scalp-reduction surgery, a technique developed in Canada in the late 1970's, can reduce palm-sized bald spots to the width of one finger. This is accomplished by compressing the scalp together, removing the loose skin, and surgically stitching the scalp back together. The reduced bald spot is eventually filled in with hair from transplanted plugs. This "skin-tightening" technique cannot be attempted in many cases because the person's scalp is too tight for stretching.

Although people may try hormonal, cosmetic, or surgical approaches in a desperate effort to "banish" their baldness, the best that they can hope for is that someone will soon discover a real hair-raising remedy□

SELECTED READINGS

"When hair turns thin" by Deborah Blumenthal. *The New York Times Magazine,* March 13, 1983.

"Hair" by Luigi Giacometti, Ph.D. *American Health,* September–October 1982.

"Hair-raising happenings at Upjohn" [on minoxidil] by Lee Smith. *Fortune,* April 6, 1981.

All About Hair by Dr. Herbert S. Feinberg. Simon and Schuster, 1979.

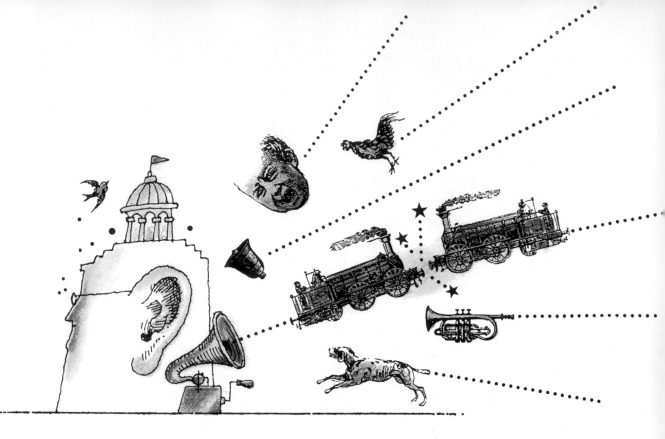

The Gift of SOUND

by Patricia Forsyth

For more than 40 years, Amy Sullivan lived in a silent world. Now she hears her grandchild's voice, a honking truck, a waiter reciting specials of the day. "All I can say is it's the difference between hearing and not hearing," Sullivan says. "It" is a multichannel cochlear implant—the tiny device surgically placed in her inner ear at Stanford University Medical Center in California.

The implant is medicine's latest assault on a kind of deafness that afflicts an estimated 200,000 Americans.

Historic Surgery Restores Hearing

Now in her late 60's, Sullivan lost her hearing in her teens. After her husband died in 1982, she sought help from her regular physician. "I didn't realize how helpless I was going to be when I was alone," she says.

Her doctor referred her to Dr. Blair Simmons, an ear, nose, and throat specialist at Stanford. In May 1983, she became the first recipient of the multichannel implant designed and developed in a unique collaborative effort by Simmons; Dr. Robert White, head of the university's department of electrical engineering; and associates.

During Sullivan's surgery, Simmons threaded a small cable of eight electrode wires into the cochlea, an inner-ear structure vital for hearing, and implanted a receiver through the skin and bone behind the ear.

Now sounds picked up by a tiepin-sized microphone clipped to a blouse are converted to electrical pulses by a computerized processor Sullivan wears in her brassiere. The pulses move along a wire to the receiver, which is connected to one of the cochlear electrodes. In turn, the electrode transmits the pulses to the brain via the auditory nerves. The result: hearing.

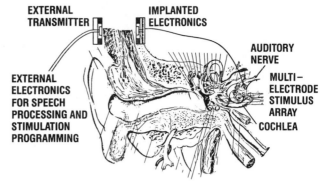

The multichannel implant consists of an external micro-phone that transmits sounds as electrical pulses, a receiver (left) implanted in the ear that picks up the pulses, and eight cochlear electrodes that then send the pulses to the brain via the auditory nerves.

A Boon to Wearers in Many Ways

Cochlear implants are not new. Single-channel models, with only one electrode threaded into the cochlea and with a two-part receiver (a coin-shaped outer coil lying on the skin juxtaposed [placed side by side] to an under-skin inner coil), were first used in the 1960's. Early models were plagued with technical problems, such as breaking wires, but the art has steadily improved.

Wearers cannot hear normally, Simmons cautions, but the implant helps in several ways. "Some deaf people can't modulate [temper] their own voices and end up speaking too loudly or softly and maybe atonally, flat," he says. "This is a definite help for them.

"Second, it's nice to know the car behind you is honking or a semitruck is about to pass you or the dog wants out," he says. "Also, it's more fun to be in a sound environment."

Finally, for most deaf people, the implant aids lipreading. "This is the big one," Simmons says. "For one thing, they're aware people are talking to them and turn to face them. And the ability to lip-read improves, especially with strangers."

Implant of No Use in Some Types of Deafness

The implants are medicine's attempt to substitute wire for the 30,000 hair cells—each sensitive to a different range of sound—that normally line the snail-shaped cochlea and convert sound transmitted from the middle ear to electrical pulses. When the cochlea fails from infection, drug toxicity, or other causes, "sensorineural" deafness results.

In true "neural" deafness, Simmons explains, the auditory nerves fail and the crucial link to the brain is cut. Even a cochlear implant is useless. The implant also is of no use to people with "conductive" deafness, whose damaged outer or middle ears prevent sound waves from reaching the cochleas. In such cases, conventional hearing aids often are helpful.

Ultimate Goal Is Simulating Normal Hearing

The greatest challenge facing researchers, Simmons says, is how to process the many frequencies of sound to yield something like normal hearing. There are several theories. "One is dump it all in and let the brain worry about it," he says. "That's the one-electrode approach. It works amazingly well, but it's not perfect.

"Then there's the preprocessing-necessary school of thought. That's us. You're not going to be able to duplicate the normal ear. You can't put 30,000 wires in." But sound can be chopped—or coded—into frequency segments, each of which will be carried by a different electrode, he says.

Most researchers think the multichannel model will outperform its simpler predecessor, Simmons notes.

Stanford's Innovative Setup

With two of its patients wearing these at the time of this writing, Stanford is one of three American centers approved for their testing. Outside the laboratory, a patient's processor is hooked to only one electrode, pending Food and Drug Administration (FDA) approval of multiple-electrode use.

Every week Sullivan and another wearer of the multichannel device, Linda Jansen, travel to Stanford for laboratory bouts with a computerized stimulator that can be hooked directly to the receiver behind the ear. Designed by Simmons' research team, including graduate students Neil Cotter and Dirk Van Compernolle, the stimulator is the only one in the country currently able to test eight channels simultaneously. During two-hour sessions with phonologist (speech-sound specialist) Dr. Laurel Dent, Sullivan and Jansen are tested on sound thresholds—how loud sound must be before they hear it—and on how well they can identify words and sounds and other hearing measures.

A Matter of Adjustment

So far, no sound heard by wearers—even in laboratory tests using all eight electrodes—is sensed exactly as it would be to a normal ear. For example, one implant patient, listening to a complicated jazzy beat, heard only the deep bass thump and identified the sound as a bouncing basketball. A wearer who once enjoyed country music does it again, but now hears only the rhythm.

Low-frequency sounds like a dog's bark or a knock at the door are relatively easy to code, Simmons explains. High-frequency sounds like human voices are another story. Sounds like running water or her car starting are much like she remembers them, Sullivan notes. An airplanelike sound turned out to be the lawn mower. But voices sound electronic.

"You have to get used to it," she says. "It's a metallic sound. It doesn't sound like a voice, but the words come through."

"It's like somebody talking under water," observes Jansen, in her late 30's, who lost her hearing in 1982. After receiving her implant in August 1983, she wore the device, called the Bioear, on her first day back at work as a computer operator at Signetics Corporation in Sunnyvale, California. "The phone ringing sounded like somebody talking," she says. "When I went home that night and was deep-frying shrimp, my shrimp talked!"

Jansen, who seldom wears her microphone and Bioear, says she is more frustrated than helped by sound from the single channel. "If the TV is on, the kids are fighting, or the phone rings, I can't distinguish one from the other," she says. "Everything sounds the same."

Before the implant is in place, the range a given person will hear cannot be predicted, Simmons says, and laboratory tests show that

Drs. Dent, Simmons, and White arrange some auditory-stimulation tests for a deaf patient with a multichannel implant.

Paul Fusco/Magnum

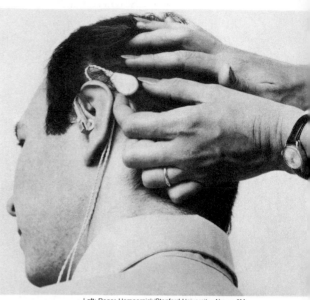

Above: A cable of electrode wires is clearly visible within a person's spiral cochlea. Right: A close-up view of some parts of 3M's cochlear-implant system shows the external transmitter held securely to the scalp by magnetic attraction to the implanted receiver.

hearing improves as a patient gains experience with the implant. ''No doubt, different people hear different sound quality,'' he says.

Sometimes background noise irritates. One wearer, a Montana rancher, complained of too much rustling and squeaking from his clothes and saddle. His Bioear was adjusted. Other patients, like a bulldozer operator who unplugs his hearing while working, appreciate the option of silence.

Technology Promising; for Now, Some Obstacles

Despite possible benefits, volunteers for implants are rare, Simmons says. ''Deaf pride is an incredible obstacle. People who have been deaf a long time have made adjustments. The people we see here have chosen to stay in the hearing world.''

Some volunteers hope knowledge gained through their participation will help others. Jansen's preschool neighbor, Karen, also is deaf. ''If this can help her and kids like her, it's worth doing,'' Jansen says.

Deaf communities are insular, but putting implants in young children might encourage them to stay in the hearing world, Simmons says. At this stage no implants are planned for children until more experience is gained from the adult volunteers.

Other objections to placing implants in young children include the risk of infection or development of scar tissue from repeated sur-

gery to replace broken implants, which may preclude later replacement by an improved model.

Because Stanford's new multichannel receiver passes through the skin—much more efficient and accessible than the older two-part receivers—infection could be, but hasn't yet been, a problem, Simmons says.

As in any surgical procedure, complications can arise. In spite of potential risks, Sullivan is enthusiastic about the implant. ''It's wonderful to be able to hear again,'' she exclaims.

''For conversation, oh boy, there's no comparison. I was tense all the time, and in a group I was helpless. Now I don't miss much.''

Jansen is less enthusiastic about the current state of the art, but says she has high hopes for the multichannel approach. ''This may not help me, but it may benefit your grandchildren or mine,'' she says □

SELECTED READINGS

''Implant brings sound to deaf and spurs debate over its use'' by Harold M. Schmeck, Jr. *The New York Times Science Times,* March 27, 1984.

''Sounds instead of silence'' by Denise Grady. *Discover,* October 1983.

''The electronic ear'' by Alison Bass. *Technology Review,* May/June 1983.

''Two-component hearing sensations produced by two-electrode stimulation in the cochlea of a deaf patient'' by Y. C. Tong and others. *Science,* February 25, 1983.

NEW PARTS for
DAMAGED BRAINS by Kevin McKean

Michel Tcherevkoff

With practiced hands, a laboratory assistant holds a struggling white rat half the size of a house cat while a scientist gives it a quick injection. The assistant lowers the animal into a glass cage. At first, the drug has no effect: the rat grooms and sniffs normally. Then the animal begins turning slowly to its left. The movement begins hesitantly, but soon the rat is circling steadily counterclockwise—a performer in a drug-induced dance that has a special significance for victims of the progressive and incurable paralysis known as Parkinson's disease.

Grafts Successful in Treating Disorders

The drugged rat circles because scientists have deliberately damaged a tiny part of its brain, thus simulating the degeneration that occurs during Parkinson's disease. In the late 1970's that brain damage would have been irreversible. Today scientists are learning to repair it by transplanting into a rat's brain a tiny sliver of brain tissue from a rat embryo to replace the deteriorated part. At Saint Elizabeth's Hospital in Washington, District of Columbia, where the circling experiment took place, transplants in test groups of rats have cut the circling rate in half, on average, and have stopped it almost entirely in some animals. Emboldened by the success of this and other animal experiments, surgeons in Sweden have begun to experiment with tissue transplants into the human brain for treating advanced Parkinson's disease.

Eventually, transplants may be used to treat other human nervous-system disorders. In laboratory animals, brain grafts have corrected hormone deficiencies resulting from brain damage, changed patterns of sexual behavior, reversed experimentally induced diabetes, and even restored youthful dexterity to aging rats. The results of these experiments have kindled hope that transplants may be developed to help a variety of conditions that are now untreatable, or nearly so, including Alzheimer's disease (senility), Huntington's chorea, and other degenerative brain diseases; developmental defects such as retardation; and even brain or spinal-cord injury.

Blood-Brain Barrier Deters Tissue Rejection

All that remains years away, in part because many technical problems must still be resolved. But even if transplants fail to cure or alleviate these disorders, they could answer—and indeed are already answering—many important questions about how the brain functions. Their promise is so great that "it almost borders on science fiction," according to Barry Hoffer of the University of Colorado Health Science Center in Denver, one of the earliest workers in the field. While the phrase "brain transplant" might suggest replacing an entire brain, Hoffer and other scientists have actually been grafting only minute amounts of tissue in order to stimulate a particular brain system, adjust the level of a certain chemical, or give some malfunctioning neural circuit a gentle "kick" to get it going again.

Their belief that such things can be done stems in part from the unusual nature of the brain, by far the most complicated organ in the body. The brain is peculiarly receptive to transplanted tissue because it is not subject to the same surveillance by the immune system as the rest of the body. It is protected by the so-called blood-brain barrier, a sort of biological fence. The barrier prevents drugs and other substances in the blood from escaping through the walls of blood vessels in the brain and getting into nerve tissue. It also somehow blocks the body's immune system from detecting the presence of foreign tissue. Thus, transplants into the brain are not so readily rejected as are new hearts, livers, or kidneys. About 90 percent of the brain grafts in laboratory animals "take" without the use of drugs to suppress the immune system.

A Key Problem Is Solved

The problem with brain grafts is not preventing rejection but making the transplanted tissue connect and function properly. Until recently this problem seemed insurmountable. But in the early 1970's preliminary experiments by a

After a tiny part of its brain was purposefully damaged, a drugged rat circles around involuntarily in a simulation of the progressive degeneration that occurs with Parkinson's disease. Recently scientists have learned to repair the damage by performing brain grafts.

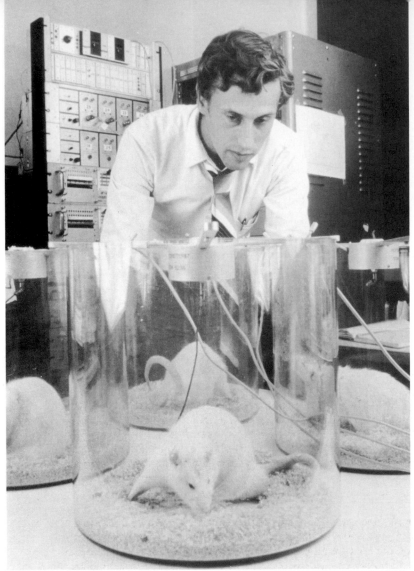

William Freed of the National Institute of Mental Health monitors the equipment he uses to record how fast his test animals spin.

John Bowden/DISCOVER Magazine, Time Inc.

handful of scientists, including Hoffer and two Swedes—Lars Olson of the Karolinska Institute in Stockholm and Anders Björklund of the University of Lund—showed that it could be solved.

Hoffer and Olson put slivers of brain tissue into the interior of a rat's eye—a site that shares the brain's protection from the immune system. Taken from a rat embryo, the tissue slivers were at the stage where they would normally have been establishing links with each other in the growing brain. (Tissue from mature rats would not have had this ability.) After the transplant, the grafted tissues went on to make a relatively normal connection. Says Hoffer: "We showed that there was enough inherent programming for the tissues to link up. Without that property, brain transplants would never work."

Knowledge of Parkinson's Disease Sparks First Transplant Effort

Encouraged by this success, researchers began to consider what human neurological disorders might be treatable by transplant. They focused on Parkinson's disease because it is one of the few for which the underlying mechanisms are at least partly known.

Scientists had learned in the 1950's that Parkinson's disease was associated with a deficiency of dopamine, one of the brain's neurotransmitters—chemicals by which nerve cells communicate with one another. Subsequent work showed that the deficiency was due to the death of dopamine-producing cells in an area near the center of the brain called the *substantia nigra* (Latin for black substance), a smudge of dark-colored tissue that mysteriously deteriorates during Parkinson's disease. The *substantia nigra* is tiny; it consists of only several hundred thousand dopamine-making cells, less than one millionth the number of cells in the entire brain. Yet their death can rob a person of voluntary movement. Observes William Freed of the National Institute of Mental Health (NIMH): "It is remarkable that the loss of a few hundred thousand nerve cells can put you at death's door."

Why does damage to a small area produce such disastrous effects? Because the *substantia nigra* plays a crucial regulatory role in the body's muscle movements. It does so by controlling the activity of a second, and much larger, brain area—the striatum—that seems to govern the initiation of voluntary movement. The nigral cells send their dopamine to the striatum, where it works something like a spark plug, igniting and setting in motion strong neural forces.

In Parkinson's disease, as the *substantia nigra* degenerates, the striatum is gradually starved of dopamine, which brings its activity to a halt. The drug L-dopa, which is used to treat Parkinson's disease, temporarily compensates for the loss because it converts to dopamine in the brain. But the drug has severe side effects, such as disruptions of heart rhythm, nausea, headaches, dizziness, and depression. It also loses its effectiveness after several years, and cannot halt the death of the *substantia nigra*.

The transplant scientists recognized that one way to treat Parkinson's disease might be to put a graft of dopamine-producing tissue near the striatum. But they needed a way to know whether the graft was functioning. For this, they turned to the circling rats—an animal experiment that gives direct evidence of dopamine levels in the living brain. The circling rats

enabled two groups of scientists—one that included Hoffer, Olson, Freed, and Richard Jed Wyatt of the NIMH; the other consisting of Björklund, Ulf Stenevi, and colleagues at Lund and at Cambridge University in England—to write a series of landmark papers in 1979 and 1980. Using slightly different surgical techniques, both groups were able to transplant *substantia nigra* tissue from rat embryos to restore dopamine levels and reduce or eliminate turning behavior in brain-damaged adult rats.

The First Experiments with Humans

Could something of the same sort work against Parkinson's disease? The researchers hesitated at first over the ethics of trying such an experimental procedure as brain transplants on human beings. "But we came to a point," Olson explains, "where we thought it was perhaps more unethical not to try." Two critically stricken victims of Parkinson's disease were chosen for the surgery, which was performed at the Karolinska Institute in 1982 and 1983. Instead of human fetal tissue, the doctors used tissue from the patients' own adrenal glands, which produce dopamine as a chemical intermediate in the process of making adrenalin. The first patient, a 57-year-old retired clergyman, did not improve visibly after his surgery, but was able to get along on less L-dopa. The second patient, a 46-year-old housewife, improved more substantially. Before surgery she had been almost completely paralyzed—often "lying like a statue" in bed, according to the surgeon, Erik-Olof Backlund. Afterward she regained some use of her arms and facial muscles.

Despite the undramatic results in these two cases, Backlund and Olson are hopeful about the technique. "We did the initial surgery on

1. In a healthy rat brain, the substantia nigra (blue) transmits the chemical dopamine (green) to the striatum (red), which helps govern muscle movement. 2. When substantia nigra is destroyed, the striatum is starved of dopamine and produces extra chemical receptors (black). 3. A dopaminelike drug (red squares) overstimulates the site, making the rat spin. 4. Dopamine balance is restored by a substantia nigra tissue transplant (purple).

George Kelvin/DISCOVER Magazine, Time Inc.

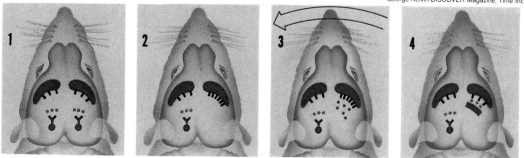

patients who responded poorly to L-dopa," says Olson. "But since the operation seems to cause no harm, we want to move to patients who respond well to the drug, because they might respond better to the transplants, too." Moreover, work with rats has since shown that success depends partly on where in the striatum the graft is placed. Says Backlund: "We would probably have done better had we chosen another site."

Promising Experimental Results Abound

Parkinson's disease is so far the only condition for which transplants have been tried on human beings. But work on laboratory animals is proceeding swiftly. At Mount Sinai Medical Center in New York City, researchers have used transplants of embryonic brain tissue to enable a strain of mice to manufacture a sex-related brain hormone that they had lost the ability to produce. A similar feat at the University of Rochester in New York restored to mutant rats the ability to make the water-regulating hormone vasopressin.

At Clark University in Worcester, Massachusetts, scientists showed that transplants from embryonic brains could also restore higher brain functions. They induced lesions (abnormal changes in organs or tissues due to injury or disease) in the frontal lobes, the part of the brain that in human beings is involved in planning and forethought. (It is also the part severed from the rest of the brain in the operation called prefrontal lobotomy, once considered a remedy for violent mental illness.) The lesioned rats lost their ability to learn to run a maze; the animals that received transplants regained much of that skill.

Researchers at Rockefeller University and Mount Sinai in New York City have used transplants to modify the sexual behavior of brain-damaged female rats. An experiment at the Weizmann Institute of Science in Israel showed that grafts of insulin-producing cells in the brains of rats could correct laboratory-induced diabetes.

In a particularly dramatic demonstration, Anders Björklund and his colleagues showed that some of the normal deterioration of aging could be reversed by transplants. The tests they used included one developed at Princeton University in which rats are placed on a slender wooden dowel suspended between two platforms. Says Björklund: "The young rats have no problem getting to their feet and walking to safety. But the aged rats either cling to the stick

A brain-damaged rat that has lost its ability to run a maze will regain its skill after receiving a brain graft.

Ira Wyman/DISCOVER Magazine, Time Inc.

or fall off." With transplants of fetal *substantia nigra* into the striatum, the older rats regained near-youthful performance.

Björklund and others are now trying to treat memory loss in aging rats by transplanting embryonic brain tissue into the hippocampus, a region of the brain known to be involved in memory. If they succeed, their research could lay the groundwork for a transplant for Alzheimer's disease, a progressive memory loss and dementia that afflicts 5 percent of all people above the age of 65.

Human-Tissue Sources Pose Ethical Problems

The successful animal work has already touched off debate over the ethics of using human fetal tissue for transplants in human beings. In June 1983, scientists, lawyers, and clergymen met near Boston, Massachusetts, under the sponsorship of the American Paralysis Association to argue the point. According to Boston City Hospital neurologist Thomas Sabin, one of the organizers, the consensus of the meeting was that human fetal transplants would be no problem so long as the tissue came, with the mother's permission, from fetuses lost by natural miscarriage. But other scientists do not agree. Olson, for one, says human fetal transplants are "out of the question" for ethical and practical reasons—among them the fact that there is no guarantee that spontaneously aborted fetuses would have healthy brains.

The use of other tissue sources would circumvent the problem altogether, and many investigators are working toward that goal. Björklund and his fellow researchers have had some success transplanting brain grafts from mice into rats—an interspecies transfer that would lead to quick rejection if any organ other than the brain were involved. The experiment has led to speculation that human transplant tissue might come from monkeys or apes rather than other human beings.

Another solution may be to establish fetal cell cultures from which transplants could be drawn. Perhaps the most elegant solution would be to avoid the use of fetal cells altogether by discovering ways to make adult brain cells grow and establish links with other cells. A major step in that direction came in 1982 at the University of California at Irvine, when Carl Cotman and his colleagues discovered that brain grafts survived best if they were transplanted about six to ten days after an initial surgical lesion was made in the brain. Cotman's team had no idea why.

Then they thought of a possible explanation: natural chemicals that promote the growth of nerve cells had accumulated in the wound during the intervening days. The theory seemed questionable at first, because it ran counter to the conventional medical dogma that the adult brain and spinal cord cannot regenerate. But subsequent work has borne the theory out, and Cotman and others are now trying to isolate this growth-promoting factor or factors. Says he: "We think we're tapping into the brain's natural response to injury."

Major Obstacles Still to Be Overcome

Cotman's work, like that of most transplant researchers, has been confined so far to the basic science of brain regeneration. His ultimate aim is to apply his knowledge to people with brain disorders. But the scientists face formidable obstacles. There is, for example, the problem of scale: the human striatum is a thousand times the size of a rat's. Does that mean that scientists would have to transplant a thousand times as much tissue into a human victim of Parkinson's disease as into a rat? Would transplants of that much tissue damage the host brain? Would they lead to a chemical imbalance and result in a mental illness like schizophrenia—sometimes linked to an excess of dopamine—that might not be detectable in animals?

In the meantime, there is a staggering number of victims of brain injury desperately seeking help; some 3 million Americans have been paralyzed by brain and spinal-cord injuries. Cotman and his fellow researchers get many poignant letters from patients volunteering for transplant operations that cannot be performed. For the present, brain transplants hold only promise. "We can't cure anything, and that's the plain truth," says Björklund. But researchers and patients nevertheless look forward to the day when the promise will be fulfilled □

SELECTED READINGS

"Brain-grafting work shows promise" by Gina Kolata. *Science,* September 23, 1983.
"Aged rats: recovery of motor impairments by intrastriatal nigral grafts" by Fred H. Gage et al. *Science,* September 2, 1983.
"A conversation with Richard Jed Wyatt" by Patrick Young. *Psychology Today,* August 1983.
"Fetal brain transplants: reduction of cognitive deficits in rats with frontal cortex lesions" by Randy Labbe and Arthur Firl, Jr. *Science,* July 29, 1983.

PAST, PRESENT, AND

FUTURE

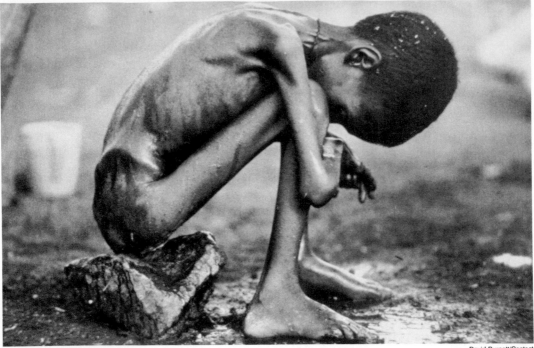

REVIEW
OF THE
YEAR

PAST, PRESENT, AND FUTURE

FOOD AND POPULATION

In 1984 world production of cereal grains—the major staple—increased by 8 percent, to about 1.78 billion metric tons. Population growth continued at an annual rate of about 2.5 percent, rising by nearly 120 million. And hunger persisted in those regions where it has become endemic— South Asia, sub-Saharan Africa, and parts of Latin America, as well as among disadvantaged groups in industrialized nations such as the United States. Food reserves remained at 18 percent, just over the 17 percent the United Nations (U.N.) Food and Agriculture Organization has determined to be the acceptable minimum.

The major problem for the 500 million chronically hungry people in the world continues to be access to the food produced, rather than shortfalls in production. Substantial numbers of malnourished people in South Asia continue to suffer, but there is no net food deficit there.

Pockets of malnutrition persist in Andean Latin America despite production increases in the region, and the number of people threatened by hunger in the United States has grown despite abundant crops. Nevertheless, the most severe food problems are in sub-Saharan Africa, where more than two dozen countries are facing their third or fourth year of crop shortfalls. Countries heavily affected by the drought and famine include Mauritania, Senegal, Guinea, Ghana, Kenya, Tanzania, and Mozambique—with a combined population of nearly 80 million.

Most seriously hit of the African nations is Ethiopia, where at least one-sixth of the population of 42 million is at risk. An intensive international relief effort is under way. Programs aimed at solving Ethiopia's typical sub-Saharan long-range structural problems are hampered by the lack of roads, trucks and other equipment, and support facilities as well as by governmental difficulties.

Africa also remains the continent with the highest population growth rate—nearly 3.5 percent. And it is the only region in the world where per capita food production has declined over the past two decades. More than two-thirds of the food consumed in Africa is grown there by poor farmers, 70 percent of whom are women, who are usually bypassed by traditional development-aid projects. The region also has the least adequate education and health care of any in the world.

The year was, however, marked by notable international attention to the problem of food security. The U.N. World Food Council, created in 1974 to monitor the recommendations of the U.N. World Food Conference of that year, held its tenth session in Addis Ababa, Ethiopia. The 36-nation body noted the lack of progress in some regions, rededicated itself to the global assault on hunger, and recognized in general that policies have to change in food-deficit countries if international supporting efforts are to be effective.

MARTIN M. MCLAUGHLIN

ANTHROPOLOGY AND ARCHAEOLOGY

In 1984 several important fossil finds provided new information on the origins and evolution of the human species, and studies of early human behavior were undertaken.

The fossilized bones of five skeletons of *Proconsul africanus,* a creature that lived about 18 million years ago and that scientists believe to be ancestral to both apes and humans, were discovered on Rusinga Island in Lake Victoria, Kenya, by an expedition led by Alan Walker of Johns Hopkins University and Richard Leakey of the National Museums of Kenya. The fragmentary skeletons were those of two adults that probably weighed about 25 pounds when alive, a young adult, a juvenile, and an infant. These discoveries will yield new data about *Proconsul* anatomy and growth.

The oldest known fossil bone fragment from a hominid, or early human, was discovered at Tabarin, near Lake Baringo, in northern Kenya. This new find pushes back the date of the earliest human fossils by another million years—to about 5 million years ago. The fossil, found by a team from Harvard University and the National Museums of Kenya, consists of a lower jaw fragment about 2 inches long and 1 inch wide bearing two molar teeth. Few fossils shedding light on human and primate evolution from 8 million to 4 million years ago have ever been discovered; hence this find is of particular significance.

The fossilized skeleton of a more modern individual, dating to 1.6 million years ago, was also recovered in Kenya, this one on the Nariokotome River near Lake Turkana in northern Kenya by an expedition led by Alan Walker and Richard Leakey. The bones indicate that the individual belonged to the human type *Homo erectus,* and this new find constitutes both the earliest and the most complete skeleton of *Homo erectus* ever recovered. *Homo erectus* is believed to have lived between 1.6 million and 400,000 years ago and to have been a direct ancestor of modern humans. Virtually the entire skeleton, except for the feet, was found. The individual was a male about 12 years old at the time of death. Analysis of the leg bones suggests that he stood about 5 feet, 5 inches tall, and that if he had grown to adulthood, might have stood 6 feet tall, thus suggesting that at least some of the ancestors of modern humans were much larger than has been thought.

New studies have been carried out on the behavior of our early ancestors. Reanalysis of archaeological sites dating back about 2 million years at Olduvai Gorge in Tanzania has suggested to some scientists that early humans may have lived less like modern hunter-gatherers than is generally assumed. Richard Potts of Yale University thinks that many of the sites that have been interpreted as "home bases," or base camps, where early humans lived and stayed between hunting expeditions may instead have been locations where hunters stored stone tools for use in butchering animals. Study of animal bones at the sites has shown that various carnivorous animals fed on the hunted creatures. This suggests that the humans may have taken only part of the available meat and left the butchering site to the scavengers. Real "home bases" may have developed later in human history, perhaps when mastery of fire enabled humans to protect their settlements from fierce predators.

Archaeological discoveries have also revealed new information about more recent humans. The excavation of a 3,400-year-old ship near the town of Kas off the southern coast of Turkey is expected to yield a wealth of data on the shipbuilding techniques and trade patterns of the Bronze Age. The ship, thought to be at least 65 feet long, sailed the eastern Mediterranean Sea around the time that Tutankhamen reigned in Egypt and the city of Troy flourished in Asia Minor. The cargo consisted of gold ornaments, pottery, and ingots of copper, tin, and glass.

An undisturbed 1,500-year-old Mayan tomb with walls painted in complex patterns and unusually rich grave offerings was discovered at Rio Azul in northeastern Guatemala. Buried in the grave was a male wrapped in a shroud, accompanied by a stingray spine used in bloodletting ceremonies, carved jade beads, and an elaborate set of ceramic vessels, including one ornate jar with a screw top—a very unusual feature—painted with symbols. Analysis of the different objects found is expected to reveal much about Mayan life.

PETER S. WELLS

Jungle Medicine

by Virginia Morell

Deep in the forests of Suriname, South America, one December night, Mark Plotkin found himself face-to-face with a jaguar. Asleep in his hammock, Plotkin suddenly had a vision of the powerful animal pacing into his hut, then purposefully striding up to him and staring him straight in the face. "It was so incredibly vivid," Plotkin recalls, "that I woke up trembling. I was covered in cold sweat." But the animal or his vision of it had departed. There was nothing but the night sounds of the Tirió Indian village, the wind rus-

tling the trees. Had the jaguar been a dream or reality? Plotkin, a Harvard University scientist who was seeking the herbal secrets of the village's shaman (witch doctor), decided his vision hovered somewhere between the two. The next morning he sent a message to the shaman: "I have seen the jaguar." The shaman's response was a smile and the cryptic reply, "That was me."

Witch Doctors' Knowledge Worth Tapping

Such an unusual experience is not extraordinary for Plotkin. Working to record the extensive knowledge of tropical plants possessed by South American Indians, he has participated in sacred tribal rites, watched healing ceremonies, and consumed ritualistic herbal concoctions, many of them mildly hallucinogenic. While he has not become a convert to the more exotic principles of witchcraft, Plotkin and his professional colleagues are discovering that tribal medicine men know a lot about healing plants that is of interest to modern physicians.

Plotkin is an ethnobotanist; he and others in his field around the world are using a combi-

Opposite: Scientist Mark Plotkin lived with the Tirió Indians to tap their knowledge of medicinal plants.

nation of anthropology and botany to study medicinal plant use by primitive cultures. Their studies are urgent, for as the Amazonian Indians, African nomads, and other primitive peoples are assimilated into Western civilization, their folklore and medical traditions are rapidly being forgotten. Furthermore, many of the plants they use are themselves endangered and may disappear before scientists like Plotkin can unlock the secrets of their usefulness.

In the view of ethnobotanists, that would be tragic. The witch doctors' knowledge of healing plants, they say, may hold the key to the creation of new drugs of benefit to us all. Most of the so-called "wonder drugs" of the 1930's to 1960's—such as digitalis for heart failure, reserpine for tranquilizers, and vincristine for treating leukemia—were derived from plants that had been used for centuries by native peoples.

Ethnobotanists Aim to Save Medicinal Heritage

South American plants could be the source of more such wonders. Curare, a sticky black substance made from the resin of a jungle vine, is used by natives as a fish poison; applied to the points of their arrows, it paralyzes the central nervous systems of their targets. Recently, it advanced surgical anesthesiology. An extract from the vine is administered as a muscle relaxant during surgery and is also useful in treating spasms caused by such diseases as tetanus and spastic paralysis. Another fish poison is the basis of rotenone, a highly effective, biodegradable insecticide.

Plants that the Indians have selected for use as contraceptives, arrow poisons, and cures for fever often owe their potency to alkaloids. These organic compounds form the basis of some 50 percent of modern medicines; they include such active agents as caffeine, nicotine, morphine, and quinine. The first plant-produced alkaloid known to science, morphine, was isolated from the opium poppy in 1806. Since that time, some 5,000 other alkaloids have been identified, greatly enhancing our ability to fight disease.

"The Indians have discovered many of the plants in the rain forest that contain active agents, or principals," says Plotkin. "There's a saying among the people of Suriname that goes, 'In the jungle, the Indian knows everything.' The Indians have depended on the forest for thousands of years to supply all their needs. But their knowledge of the tropical plants is rapidly

After throwing poisonous plants in a river to stun the fish, an archer takes aim and waits for his dinner.

Mark J. Plotkin

An Indian shaman in Suriname prepares a brew of herbal medicine to treat an ill member of his tribe.

Mark J. Plotkin

being lost. We are trying to save this heritage by doing what we call 'ethnobotanical salvage operations.' Basically this means that we are documenting the plants the Indians use and how they use them.''

New Field Credited to Harvard Botanist

As a defined field of study, ethnobotany has come into its own during the past 50 years. It was largely created by the great Harvard University botanist Richard Evans Schultes, who today oversees the Harvard Botanical Museum and the collecting adventures of his research assistants, one of whom is Plotkin. Schultes, a tall, white-haired man who works out of a simply furnished office decorated with photographs of tribal shamans and lush tropical scenes, lived and worked in the Amazon jungle from 1941 to 1954. During that time he collected 24,000 new plants, 5,000 of which he expects will one day prove beneficial to mankind.

"The Indians use 1,370 of these plants in some way, so that indicates that they have at least one active principal," says Schultes. "The Indians are actually quite sophisticated in their

analysis of what works and what does not. They basically use the trial-and-error method and will combine different plants to produce a desired result.''

One of the key desired results in various Amerindian cultures has been inducing hallucinogenic visions as part of their spiritual beliefs. They have traditionally sought out vision-producing plants. Yet for years many of these plants were regarded as mere legend by Western scientists. In 1936, however, Schultes tracked down the sacred intoxicating mushrooms and an inebriating morning glory that were used by Oaxacan shamans in Mexico. Since that date he has brought an additional 125 of these magic plants out of the realm of myth and into the world of science.

Researchers Join in Rituals to Test Hallucinogenic Plants

"Many of the hallucinogenic plants hold great promise as a source of new medicines," says Schultes. "Also, we know so very little about the functioning of our central nervous system. Hallucinogens allow us to duplicate and analyze the chemistry of hallucinations suffered, for example, by schizophrenics, and may help us map the chemical geography of the brain."

In the field, ethnobotanists are often invited to share in the Indians' vision rituals and to drink their hallucinogenic mixtures. Schultes has participated in many of these ceremonies and has probably sampled more hallucinogenic plant brews than a whole commune of 1960's flower children. Yet he has never experienced a hallucination. "I have seen colors and bright lights, but nothing like the Indians describe. I have never seen their gods."

Ethnobotanists participate in these vision quests because, as Plotkin observes, "It is the easiest way to tell if a plant actually contains an active principal. You can't say what the effects of a plant are if you just sit back and observe someone else taking it." Although most of these hallucinogenic brews prove harmless, others come close to being poisons. During a collecting expedition to the Kofán Indian village of

After drinking a beverage made from hallucinogenic plants, an Amazonian medicine man goes into a trance.

Victor Englebert

Santa Rosa, Colombia, Timothy Plowman of Chicago's Field Museum in Illinois heard about a potent drug that was used as a purgative and combined with other plants in a hallucinogenic beverage. He found an old man in the village who reluctantly agreed to mix up a powerful but "dangerous" brew from the bark of a tree. Plowman and his companion quickly swallowed a cupful of the bitter brown liquid, then sat down to observe its effects. A tingling sensation soon spread throughout his body, and then, although he was lucid, he began frothing at the mouth. Cramps knotted his stomach, waves of vertigo (dizziness) spun through his head, and eventually he could do nothing more than lie prone on the floor. Toward morning he and his friend managed to drag themselves away from this "strange place." But Plowman did not fully recover from the drug for two more days.

Nevertheless, he defends the experience. "These substances must be tested to find out if what the shamans tell you is legend or fact. This plant appears to have a powerful principal in it, one that seems to be a protein rather than an alkaloid, which is something new for us."

Tribal Trust a Must Before Secrets Shared

Ethnobotanists are constantly on the lookout for tales of magic drugs and legendary shamans. In their jungle sleuthing they approach native peoples much as an anthropologist does. "You have to spend time with the people, learn their language, live with them," Plotkin says. "When they get to know you and trust you and realize that you don't consider them 'stupid Indios,' then they often open up and share their knowledge with you."

On a trip to Suriname, Plotkin did exactly this and struck botanical pay dirt. "I flew into the interior to work with the Tirió Indians. But when I got there, I found six different tribes whose botanical lore had never been studied living in the same area. Each of these tribes has a different pharmacopoeia—they use different plants for different purposes—and I was able to collect a lot of information about it."

Plotkin was introduced to the shaman of the Tirió people and spent many days following him through the forest, collecting the plants he collected, and noting their uses. The shaman, a short, elderly man with steady, quiet ways, maintained a dour expression on all of their walks. "He didn't smile once," says Plotkin, "until I had my dream of the jaguar." Shamans

A shaman holding medicinal plants, feathers, and a
harmonica prepares to perform a healing ritual. Ethnobotanists are trying to document the wealth of pharma-
cological lore that such witch doctors rely on.

are credited with the ability to turn themselves
into jaguars, and Plotkin's vision acknowledged
this man's power, although Plotkin, who had
not taken any hallucinogen, has no idea of how
the shaman could have caused the vision.

Drug Companies Unwilling to Invest

Plotkin's research with the tribes in Suriname
netted him two possibly new and beneficial species: an unknown form of curare, used by the
river people, and a fish poison made from a vine
of the *Banisteriopsis* family. Yet it will likely be
years before a complete chemical analysis of
these plants is made. Although ethnobotanists
may bring back thousands of promising plants,
as has Schultes, they are essentially collectors
dependent on a chemist's laboratory to turn their
prized finds into useful products.

That dependence can be a source of frustration. Drug companies, intimidated by the expense and difficulty of researching ethnobotanical finds, have been reluctant to invest much in
that direction. Typical is the story of cancer
research. During the 1960's and 1970's, many
American drug companies actively sought new
plant species and special Indian cures in the
hopes of turning up an antidote for this feared
disease. But the search did not uncover any easy
solutions, and today these same companies are
concentrating almost exclusively on synthetic
drugs.

"It is, unfortunately, a question of the bottom line," says Schultes. "The companies were
not getting the returns they expected, so they've
gone back to working with synthetics. I think
they are missing the boat."

Association to Promote Promising Plants

In spite of the drug companies' reluctance to
pursue the possible benefits of the plant kingdom, the ethnobotanists continue their search.
In an effort to promote some of their most promising plants, several ethnobotanists have assembled to form the Beneficial Plant Research Association, headed by Plowman and Dr. Andrew
Weil, a Tucson, Arizona, physician. They are
actively researching such medicinal plants as
the root of *Heliopsis longipes*, used by the
Aztecs as a dental anesthetic; the bark of *Brun-
felsia grandiflora*, used as a treatment for arthritis; the sap of an Amazonian tree, *Croton*, that
stimulates wound healing and helps peptic ulcers; and the mushroom, *Lentinus edodes*,
which seems to stimulate the body's immune
system.

In an Amazonian rain forest, a Yanomami Indian tears the bark from a virola tree. The bark's hallucinogen - manifesting properties are due to chemicals that may prove very useful in developing many new medicines.

Victor Englebert

Their prized project centers on the South American coca tree, which Plowman describes as an "overly maligned plant." While acknowledging the harm that cocaine abuse has brought to our society, Plowman is quick to point out that cocaine is only one of many alkaloids in the coca leaf. In South America many tribes use a tea brewed from coca leaves for everything from a painkiller to a cure for altitude sickness and an antidepressant. Plowman's association is now actively working on developing an extract that might be useful for a variety of stomach ailments, and could alleviate motion sickness.

Plant Testing a Time-consuming Process

Research such as Plowman's is time-consuming and frequently frustrating. Even careful chemical analysis does not always assure that plants' active alkaloids will be found. In the 1940's Schultes learned that South American Indians use the sap of a tree belonging to the nutmeg family to heal fungal infections on their skin. Schultes dried out the bark and sent it off for analysis, but the chemists could not find any active principals in the dried sample. Recently, other scientists decided to test the bark again.

This time, however, they used fresh bark and discovered three compounds previously unknown to science. Two of these compounds have antifungal properties.

There are some 1,200 organic chemical constituents in plants, and 99 percent of these are never looked at. When an alkaloid is discovered, it is then tested on animals to determine exactly what it does. If it appears to be beneficial—the source of a new drug, for example—then it is subjected to a whole new round of tests until a final product is produced. The entire procedure from discovery of the plant to a packaged drug can easily take two decades of research.

But while the research is slow, the varieties of jungle plants and the numbers of native "doctors" who know how to identify and use them are diminishing at an alarming rate. Ethnobotanists, engaged in a meticulous science, must work at breakneck speed.

"The entire plant kingdom is really a chemical factory," says Schultes. "If we destroy the rain forests and lose these plants to extinction before we can analyze them for active principals, we may be missing out on a number of great remedies" □

Photos: J.K./Magnum

Gypsies

by Miriam Lee Kaprow

By ordinary standards, the behavior of the Gypsies I had come to study was unconventional. I was sitting in front of a Gypsy's house in Saragossa, an Aragonese city 130 kilometers (80 miles) south of the Pyrenees, in northeastern Spain. Paloma, a strikingly pretty woman of 25, strode over and grinned. She was beautifully dressed and wore a large gold medal on a heavy gold chain, gold rings, a gold bracelet, and gold earrings. Pointing to my own, smaller gold ring, she said, ''Give me that ring. It'll look real good on me. Are you going to give me that ring? You'd better watch out; there are lots of Gypsies around here who could do you a lot of harm.''

A Demanding Lot

Then Jon, who was 50, came out of the house, settled himself against a car, stared at me with his bright blue eyes, grinned, and said, ''Don't

you have a gift for me today? Why not? I'm poor, you're rich.'' Jon, who owned a station wagon, a television set, a washing machine, a phonograph, and a tape recorder, did not desist for the next eight minutes. ''Well? Where's my gift? *Por Dios* [By God], what a cheapskate you are!''

Twenty minutes later, inside Jon's house, his son's mother-in-law, Dolores, whipped my scarf off the table and said, ''This scarf's going to be for me, for me. Well, are you going to give it to me? I'm taking it; give it to me.'' Dolores left the house with scarf in hand, only to return with it 10 minutes later. ''There, take it, you cheapskate!'' Paloma, who turned out to be Dolores' daughter-in-law, came in and tugged at my pin. ''Give it to me. Is it gold? I'm so poor, my children don't have anything to eat; if you give it to me, I can get them food. What are you here for? Why don't you have a husband with you? Do you like sleeping alone? C'mon, give me that pin. What a cheapskate of a *paya* [non-Gypsy] you are.'' Amarga, Jon's wife, chimed in, "I'm going to send all my children to your house for lunch today. You give them food, you feed them. You watch out, they'll be there at one o'clock.'' She paused, and then added, "Gypsies can really be annoying, can't they?''

The Ultimate Anarchists

After I had lived among the Gypsies for six or seven months, this kind of behavior disappeared, but each new Gypsy I met asked for money, jewelry, or clothing, insisting that he (or she) was extremely poor or hungry, had lost his wallet, or needed something for his children. He went on in this vein until someone told him to stop "annoying a family friend.'' Long before the 23 months I spent in Saragossa were over, I recognized that the behavior of Gypsies was but one expression of their lack of commitment to conventional notions of propriety.

Not long after the Gypsies left their native India, probably in successive waves of emigration between the eleventh and fourteenth centuries, and fanned out through Europe and then the Americas, people began both to romanticize and to denounce them for caring too little about social status to become respectable—for being, in effect, antiestablishment. In Spain, where they arrived from France early in the fifteenth century, they have resisted assimilation, despite centuries of punitive laws and, after the late eighteenth century, "benevolent" schemes designed to integrate them. Like many other cultural minorities in the Western world, such as the Amish or the Hasidim, Gypsies have managed to stay apart from the larger society. But unlike the others, who were always more respectable in nonconformity, Gypsies have consistently flouted propriety. More than has generally been recognized, their decision to remain an enclave was deliberate; indeed, they might properly be called the ultimate anarchists. They are eminently successful as rule breakers. In fact, their anarchy may be one of the keys to their survival, for it has brought them a measure of prosperity and has spared them some of the perils that go with full participation in a nation-state.

Life in the Outskirts of Society

My conclusions about Gypsies come from field-work carried out between 1973 and 1976, when I lived in a section of Saragossa that I have called Barrio de la Arboleda (the name, like the names of all the Saragossa Gypsies mentioned in this article, is fictitious). In 1982 I made another trip to Saragossa. In all, I studied approximately 285 Gypsies in 47 households. (There are some 3,000 to 7,000 Gypsies in Saragossa, a city of about 700,000.) Like most other Gypsies in Spain, those in Saragossa are settled rather than nomadic, speak Spanish rather than any of the Gypsy languages, and in physical appearance and dress are indistinguishable from their non-Gypsy Spanish neighbors. But they have never participated fully in the institutions of the larger society. Some Spanish Gypsies choose to live in jerry-built (flimsy) shacks rather than in typical Spanish houses. In most cases, Gypsy children do not go to regular schools, nor do Gypsies run schools of their own. And they decline to register with Spanish authorities, so the government cannot issue them the national identity cards required by law and carried by nearly all Spaniards.

Gypsies are notorious nonconformists. Their children do not receive any kind of formal education.

The author discovered that Gypsies detest saving material goods so much that they discard leftover food daily.

Self-Employment Preferred

The crux of the Gypsies' relative autonomy has been, and continues to be, their work. They have worked chiefly for themselves instead of depending on the sale of their labor to others. And they have generally earned their living at work that is difficult to regulate and that provides the state with little or no tax revenue. For years, Gypsies in Spain sold horses and donkeys, worked as traveling sheep shearers, or pursued such occupations as acting and juggling. Of the Gypsies I studied in Saragossa, about one-quarter sold discount clothing at retail. Nearly one-quarter sold scrap metal and paper and supplemented their income with other work, often selling clothing or harvesting crops. Another fourth were self-employed in a variety of occupations, including whitewashing, raising livestock, and street performing. The rest were primarily wage laborers.

It is not so much the trades they choose but how they engage in those trades that distinguishes Gypsies from most workers in Spain. Self-employed Gypsies in the barrio rarely paid taxes; their places of business were movable, not permanent; they carried out all transactions in cash, even those in which thousands of dollars changed hands; their clientele was changing, not regular; and their stock turned over quickly. All these work characteristics were exemplified in the retail clothing trade, in which entrepreneurs bought several large lots of clothing at a time from wholesalers and sold them in the outdoor markets of the smaller cities.

No Interest in Material Goods

The Gypsies' work was virtually always labor-intensive, not capital-intensive. In most cases it was also profitable, a fact that will surprise those who think of Gypsies as leading a marginal existence. The scrap business—really profitable garbage picking—is a good example. Gypsy junk dealers usually had several relatives to help them and often pooled their efforts with close kin from other households. A group of this kind was likely to own a truck, while a person who collected scrap alone, often a widow or an elderly man, used only a handcart.

Indeed, Gypsies often lived well even if they worked fewer than five full days a week. And although many Gypsies made a profit, they never expanded their businesses. I knew three Saragossa brothers and their brothers-in-law who worked together as traveling whitewashers. Though they received more offers of work than they could possibly handle, they declined to subcontract jobs, taking only those they could complete themselves.

In short, the Arboleda Gypsies remained within the capitalist system but never participated fully in it. They were loath to accumulate material goods. Every Gypsy household threw away from three to twelve dollars worth of left-over food daily. Clothing, furniture, household objects, even cars, were used and replaced more rapidly than is usual among people who place a premium on profit making, saving, and inheritance.

Shack Dwelling a Social Problem

In housing as in work, their participation in the conventional institutions of the country was incomplete. Yet what of the fact that 60 percent of the Gypsy households I studied owned their own homes? Ordinarily, home ownership marks the solid citizen. But among Saragossa Gypsies, owning a house was a way of avoiding the scrutiny of the larger society. This was especially true of families who lived in shacks, or *chabolas*. The Gypsies built their own *chabolas* at a cost of about $400, using scrap materials that they put together in crazy quilt patterns. Most *chabolas* had from two to four rooms that were two or three times larger than rooms in ordinary houses. In the barrio (district) where I lived, the buildings had electricity but no running water; residents used a communal fountain instead. Portable gas stoves were used for cooking, wood-burning stoves for heating.

The very question of *chabola* dwelling—so controversial and so politicized in Spain that it bears a special name, *chabolismo*—highlights many of the disparities between what non-Gypsies believe about Gypsies and what Gypsies think about their own situation. For non-Gypsies, *chabolismo* is a social problem. The shacks are an eyesore, and the press characterizes them as unlivable, the usual epithet being *infrahumana*. But for the people who live in *chabolas*, this is not necessarily so. The inside of a *chabola* can be comfortable and even attractive. What's more, a shack is more valuable than a low-rent apartment in a municipal housing project because it can be rented, traded, or sold. It is important to remember that of the 15 Arboleda families who live in *chabolas*, only four could not afford conventional housing.

Shoplifting and Sponging Not Viewed as Wrong

The Gypsies' nonconformity was reflected not only in their work practices and housing but also in their values. Take shoplifting. Only two Arboleda families derived a major portion of their income from stealing, and few Gypsies took anything from stores or factories in their own neighborhoods. Yet petty theft did occur. Once, when I took several children to see the Christmas display in Saragossa's largest department store, they showed me, after we had left the

Many Gypsies choose to live in shacks as opposed to conventional houses. Here, some Gypsies load their caravan.

store, the things they had taken. There was no bravado or giggling; they were quite matter-of-fact and serenely confident that I would approve, as they knew their parents would.

A very different way in which the unconventionality of the Gypsies showed itself was in their agonistic (combative) relationships and in their demanding of gifts and favors. Among themselves, such behavior did not seem to be regarded as offensive. In fact, I once saw Jon's wife, Amarga, purposely turn teasing and sponging into a successful get-well visit. Amarga came to cheer up her sick brother-in-law Alfredo, who was 81. Catching sight of a swath of tarpaulin in his *chabola,* she began to cut herself a large piece, grinning with each slash and assuring her relatives, in a tone of mock consolation, that she would cut only a little more. Alfredo's wife, Elena, became more and more agitated and started to curse her. Finally, Amarga turned to Alfredo, who was recovering from a stroke and physically quite helpless. She offered him a cookie, lifted it to his mouth, and snatched it away several times as he tried to bite into it, before giving him the cookie at last. Everyone laughed. Even Alfredo was diverted and became far less depressed than

he had been all afternoon. Six years later I saw Amarga do the very same thing with Elena, who was ill and depressed. Amarga teased, begged objects, took them, goaded Elena, and snatched her money. Yet by the time Amarga left, Elena was out of bed and ready to go to the café.

Gypsy Nonconformity Has Substantial Benefits

Part of the reason for the Gypsies' rejection of conventional values is their persecution by society. Although Spanish law no longer excludes them from jobs, schools, housing, or public places, they rarely escape being stigmatized, no matter how well-off they may be economically, unless they become nationally famous entertainers or choose to conceal their background and sever relations with other Gypsies. Still, Gypsy nonconformity is more than a response to prejudice; maintaining only a tenuous relation to society has brought Gypsies significant benefits.

From the fifteenth century through the first third of the 19th century, Gypsies were the only minority in Spain to escape the jurisdiction of the Inquisition. Then and in later centuries, they avoided military service. We know from a letter

Decked out in festive clothing that most people consider typical Gypsy attire, three girls watch a local celebration.

written at the end of the eighteenth century by the minister of the navy, the Marqués de Castejón, that Gypsies were categorically refused entry into at least this branch of the armed forces. Not one of the Arboleda Gypsies served in the armed forces of either side during the Spanish Civil War of 1936 to 1939, and only a few of their sons and grandsons are fulfilling their compulsory peacetime service today.

There are other advantages to remaining separate. High on the list are the rewards of being one's own boss and choosing one's hours and conditions of work. There are economic benefits as well. In May of 1982, when Spain was in a period of high inflation and the unemployment rate stood at about 15 percent, the Gypsies I studied were living as well as, or better than, they had from 1973 to 1976, when there were more jobs and living costs were more moderate. The very occupations decried as major obstacles in the way of the "successful integration" of Gypsies have actually enabled these people to live through economic crises with no appreciable decrease in income.

Government Laws Disregarded

To the Spanish Government, the Gypsies' failure to conform has usually seemed like a problem. Government officials understand as well as do social scientists that the nonconformity of any minority group poses a threat to the nation because the group becomes a living example of successful disobedience. For centuries, authorities churned out hundreds of royal edicts and local ordinances designed to integrate this numerically tiny minority, which probably never exceeded more than one-half of one percent of the total population. Again and again, laws ordered Gypsies to give up their "disreputable" work as traveling jugglers, dancers, actors, or sheepshearers, and directed them to seek *labranza de la tierra,* which meant, in effect, to work as landless laborers. A few ordinances offered Gypsies the possibility of becoming servants, which should have seemed attractive because it allowed them to continue living in and around the cities. But the laws failed spectacularly—the Gypsies simply ignored them.

Poor Response to Efforts Aimed at Integration

Private citizens took up where the state had left off, trying persuasion where coercion had failed. Spanish voluntary associations formed to provide Gypsies with the benefits of the welfare state have proliferated. They seek to train Gyp-

Authorities have long tried to force Gypsies to give up their "disreputable" work as traveling entertainers.

sies for wage labor or for professional jobs, to promote literacy, to enroll Gypsy children in schools, to construct low-rent conventional housing, and, finally, to inscribe Gypsies' names in the national Civil Lists. These organizations nearly always legitimate [show to be justified] their status by proclaiming their independence of the state, by pointing out the injuries the state has done the Gypsies, and by emphasizing their own, pro-Gypsy position. Yet the organizations are committed to the very institutions and goals—the state, the class system, and assimilation—from which Gypsies have dissociated themselves. Not surprisingly, then, the response to most projects designed to help the Gypsies has generally been less than enthusiastic. As Gypsies have, in the past, thwarted the state's attempts at forced integration, so, in the future, they can ride out the schemes of more benevolent assimilationists □

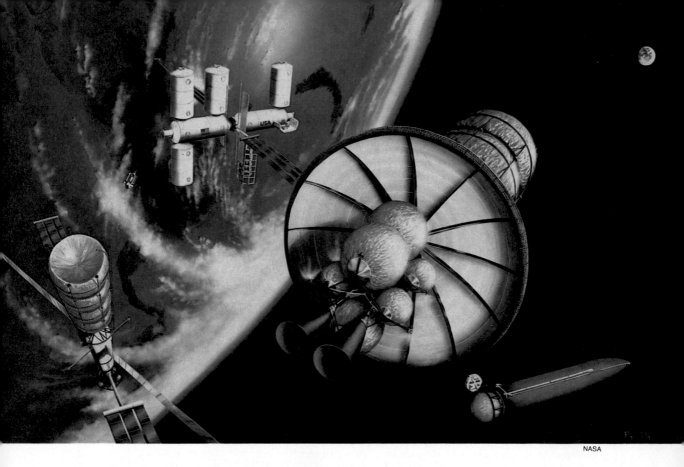

Lunar Base
by Brian O'Leary

On the 500th anniversary of Columbus's discovery of the New World, in 1992, the United States plans to launch its own new world into space. In 1984 the National Aeronautics and Space Administration (NASA) got the go-ahead to spend $150 million on a modular Tinkertoy assemblage that will constitute the first permanently manned American space station.

A Logical First Step

But that is just the first step in this new era of the Space Age. "The space station is a doorway," says George Keyworth, science adviser to President Reagan. "To what? The first obvious thing is a doorway to the Moon. I feel that the pluses pile up pretty high on our setting up a manned lunar station as the next major step for the United States in space."

This plan makes sense to many scientists. In their view, a lunar base is important to support further large-scale development in space.

One of the experts, physicist Gerard O'Neill, president of the Space Studies Institute in Princeton, New Jersey, points out that the energy cost of bringing materials from the Moon into space is less than 1/20th that of bringing them from Earth. And lunar materials can be used to construct giant Earth-orbiting structures: space industries, solar-power satellites for providing energy to Earth, space settlements, exploration vehicles, and fuel depots.

In April 1984, former NASA deputy administrator Hans Mark and a number of leaders in the space community held a closed conference in Los Alamos, New Mexico, about the lunar plan. Their speculation is that we could have an operational lunar base by 2007. Out of this conference came a NASA-sponsored technical symposium held in Washington, District of Columbia, in October 1984. Hundreds of scientists and engineers participated. Recently, several NASA study groups, three NASA funded and two funded by the National Science

Foundation (NSF), have looked at the possibility of a lunar base.

With the space station still on the drawing boards, these studies may seem premature. However, we need to know whether a lunar base is next in line because, explains David Criswell, consultant for the California Space Institute at the University of California, San Diego, "it will certainly affect the types of activities conducted at the space station."

Lunar Soil Valuable in Many Ways

It is clear that the government is going public with its vision, and the lunar base is at the top of its post–space station wish list. One of the most useful attributes of the Moon is its soil. The lunar dust will be immediately serviceable for covering over the human habitats and laboratories to protect the astronauts from cosmic rays, solar flares, and potential military threat. A 1.8-meter (6-foot) thickness of lunar dust provides the same protection against cosmic rays that we enjoy here on Earth. Simple heating of the lunar materials by a solar furnace can give us blocks for building, tiles, pipes, glass, ceramics, and concrete.

But the real value of lunar soil, the studies show, will become evident when we chemically process its pure elements for use on the Moon or in space. It is fortuitous that the raw lunar dust is largely made up of useful substances: oxygen (40 percent), silicon (20 percent), and metals (20 to 30 percent). Astronauts could use lunar oxygen for breathing or process it for water. They could fuel their rockets by making a propellant of liquid oxygen and liquid hydrogen. (It should be conceded, however, that many have serious doubts about the presence of hydrogen on the Moon, so it is likely that one component of the fuel would have to be brought from Earth.) Silicon could be fabricated into solar collectors, semiconductors (materials that can act as both electrical insulators and conductors), and glass. Metals could go into building large space structures. The key to becoming free of the Earth's gravitational field is to use lunar materials as much as possible.

Chemical-processing Plants Possible on Moon

Chemists have devised a number of feasible schemes for extracting pure elements in lunar processing plants. Each process involves physical separations—using solar energy to heat the materials—and chemical separations of the oxygen, silicon, and metals from their oxides through the use of reagents (substances used for their chemical or biological activities) such as hydrofluoric acid. Depending on which prod-

In this depiction of lunar mining operations, soil is processed before being converted to liquid oxygen.

NASA

ucts are needed, the processes call for a large number of complicated steps, but they are well known from terrestrial experience.

The plants would be self-contained units that recycle the reagents and churn out products whose mass is several times that of the processing machinery sent from Earth. According to the study by the Science Applications International Corporation (SAIC), one of the two commissioned by the NSF, a small pilot chemical plant weighing 1 ton could process 10 tons or more per year of lunar materials into oxygen, metals, and glass. The 10-to-1 advantage is important in the economics of becoming independent of Earth's resources.

Attaining Self-sufficiency

The ultimate goal is for a lunar base to become self-sufficient. This is a most ambitious goal, and some believe it is nearly impossible to reach. "I don't think we can cut the umbilical cord to Earth in the foreseeable future," says Rocco Fazzolare of the University of Arizona, a participant in one of the NASA studies carried out at a California Space Institute meeting held in La Jolla. "There are shortages of essential life-support materials on the moon. We must supply these materials and the spiritual needs of humans from Earth."

O'Neill and others are more optimistic. In exploring scenarios for a self-sufficient lunar base, they have kept in mind the realities of NASA's budget and assumed that all structures must be built using today's technology.

The key to rapid growth of lunar self-sufficiency is O'Neill's invention of a long, skinny, launching machine called a mass-driver. This electromagnetic motor, acting as a lunar catapult, will send payloads into space in a regular stream. The mass-driver accelerates the payloads to the lunar-escape speed (the minimum velocity a moving body must have to escape from the Moon's gravitational field and travel freely in space) of 2.32 kilometers (1.44 miles) per second, over a track 160 meters (175 yards) long, in less than a single second.

Mass-Driver to Transport Lunar Materials

The great acceleration is but another elegant application of the physics developed long ago by Sir Isaac Newton and James Maxwell. Ordinary coils, like those of an electric motor, carry current from solar panels along the mass-driver track. The astronauts will set up the coils in the

key positions along the track to generate strong magnetic forces that both levitate and accelerate each payload carrier as it passes by, one every two seconds. After the guidance is electronically fine-tuned, each payload would begin the long climb away from the moon to the collection point high above. After releasing its payload, the carrier would slow down and return to the starting point to pick up more.

The lunar materials would drift to a point 60,830 kilometers (37,800 miles) behind the Moon, to be caught by a cylindrical receptacle about 9 meters (10 yards) across. This special place, called L2, was selected because the mass-catcher can stay at that particular spot with the minimum consumption of fuel. The materials—as much as 1,800 tons the first year— would then be pushed gently to a stable high orbit around the Earth, where they would be processed into industrial products.

"We have confidence," O'Neill has written, "that mass-drivers are a highly efficient, low-cost, and reliable means of transporting large amounts of material into space." As proof of the concept's validity, a tabletop version in a laboratory at the Space Studies Institute has now reached accelerations of 100 times the peak acceleration of the shuttle. The model is full size, except for the mass of the carrier and the length of the track. Instead of using an entire carrier, which is shaped like a bucket, the researchers are accelerating the equivalent of the carrier's rim, made of lightweight aluminum wire. And instead of building a 160-meter (175-yard) track—shaped like a long, narrow tube, which the carriers slide through—they built just the first 53 centimeters (21 inches) of track, made up of 20 drive coils. When the machine is turned on, the carrier rim starts at rest and comes flying out 53 centimeters farther on at 400 kilometers (250 miles) per hour.

The researchers, though, still aren't satisfied. Says physicist Leslie Snively, of the Geostar Corporation in Princeton, New Jersey: "We are trying out new ideas to make the device simpler." Over the past few years, Snively and his associates, for example, have found ways to shorten the original required track length from 10 kilometers (6.2 miles) to its existing length.

The Moon has built-in advantages for the mass-driver. Says O'Neill: "The lack of any air resistance permits simple operations involving the high velocities and precise guidance that are required."

Robot Machines Will Release Ties to Earth

Plans for self-sufficiency also include self-replicating machines that fabricate more and more mass-driver components. "It appears possible," said former NASA administrator Robert Frosch in 1979, "to start with the investment necessary to put 100 tons of machinery on the Moon and after 20 years of machine reproduction to have an energy plant and manufacturing capability equivalent to the ability to manufacture 20 billion pounds, or 10 million tons, of aluminum per year. I believe that the technology is presently available [to build such self-replicating machines] and that the necessary development could be done in a decade or so."

The robot machines would in no way resemble R2D2 or C3PO of the movie *Star Wars* fame. Instead, they would be "dumb" special-purpose equipment that does simple tasks, as in an automobile-assembly plant. Two years of replication would produce 100 mass-drivers with a capability of handling over 100,000 tons of lunar materials per year. Within a few years,

A researcher tests a life-size section of a mass-driver—an electromagnetic catapult that will launch lunar payloads into space. Below: A full view.

the O'Neill scenario shows, solar-power satellites fabricated from lunar materials could deliver cost-competitive, environmentally compatible electricity to Earth via a low-density microwave link. A new multibillion-dollar industry will have begun, and humankind will have become free of its home planet at last.

Transfer Vehicles and Human Facilities

Essential to creating a lunar base is developing upper-stage rockets that could send personnel and cargoes beyond the low Earth orbits that space shuttles and space stations will be con-

Below: Wayne Sorce; Bottom: NASA

fined to during the 1990's. Called orbital-transfer vehicles (OTVs), these devices will tug payloads to and from geosynchronous orbit (that which occurs at the same speed as the Earth rotates) and on trajectories toward the Moon, asteroids, and planets. By 1996 NASA hopes to develop a fleet of reusable OTVs that would be periodically refueled at a space station. The OTV is clearly a prerequisite to sending people anywhere beyond the space station.

The SAIC scenario calls for a crew of six to eight in a modular base that closely resembles the space station in size and layout. Included would be a laboratory module for examining lunar samples, monitoring health, and producing food; a habitat module; an unpressurized resource, or utility, module; a small pilot chemical plant for processing lunar materials; a connecting module with an observation dome and air lock with access to the lunar surface; and two vehicles that at first serve as mass-movers and later become lunar rovers. As in the space station, each module would fit in the space shuttle's cargo bay and be about 4.6 meters (15 feet) in diameter and 12 meters (40 feet) long.

Typical crew might consist of the following: a commander-pilot, a mechanic-pilot, a technician-mechanic, a doctor-scientist, a geologist, a chemist, and a biologist-doctor. Crew members would rotate every two months, with transfers of three or four of them occurring between OTVs and lunar-excursion modules that rendezvous in low lunar orbit. This rather conservative scenario borrows technology from the Apollo spacecraft and the space station whenever possible.

Studies Make Use of Special Environment

The studies also describe experiments that would take advantage of the unique lunar environment. By using the Moon as well as the Earth as a stable platform for large antenna arrays, radio astronomy will be given a boost. The 386,200-kilometer (240,000-mile) average distance from the Earth to the Moon will provide a baseline for resolving detail in cosmic radio sources 30 times greater than it has been possible to do using antennas on either side of the Earth. The search for extraterrestrial intelligence will go forward, employing radio telescopes on the Moon's far side, and will be vastly more productive because the radio "chatter" from the Earth is blocked out. Lunar geology, which barely began in the American Apollo and Soviet Luna programs, and which could perhaps reveal the Moon's origin, would thrive at a permanent lunar base.

Some Scientists Debate Next Move

Despite the benefits of the Moon, not everybody thinks it should be our next stop. With oxygen so abundant here on Earth, why go to the Moon, where it is more expensive to produce? asks Fazzolare, the La Jolla study participant. We need instead to try to develop cheaper means of launching materials from Earth.

NASA

Orbital-transfer vehicles (OTVs) are a must in the creation of a lunar base. The devices would send people and payloads to and from geosynchronous orbit. Here, an OTV is being serviced near Earth.

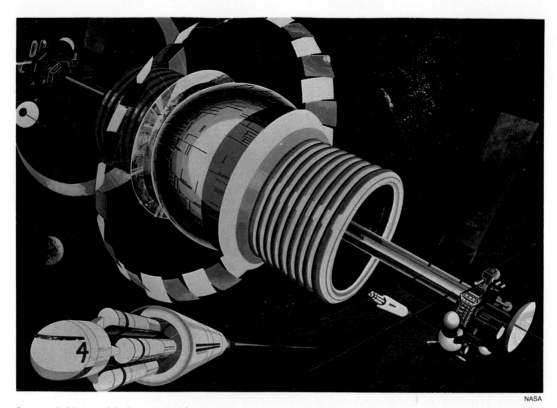

A space-habitat module is protected from cosmic rays by a spherical shell made of lunar industrial wastes.

Furthermore, the apparent lack of water on the Moon would make it necessary to send hydrogen from the Earth for life support and refueling. This objection would be partially overcome if some scientists' prediction that ice may be trapped in the permanently shadowed areas near the poles comes true. A lunar-geo-chemical-orbiter prospecting mission, planned for the 1990's, may solve the mystery. If the results are positive, we can envision a self-sufficient colony near one of the poles with a capacity for refueling all rockets that operate between low Earth orbits and out to other planets or asteroids. The base could even have full-time sunshine provided by solar collectors.

Nevertheless, the lunar debate is likely to continue. Many scientists, including Carl Sagan, appear to be more excited about going to Mars. Citing evidence that the Soviets are moving in this direction, Sagan proposes an Apollo-Soyuz type of joint mission to Mars. "Could we muster a mission with human crews for the sort of money repeatedly allocated for weapons systems on Earth?" he asks. "Astonishingly, the answer seems to be yes."

Apollo Astronaut Supports Lunar Plan

Whether it's our next step or not, a lunar base appears to be inevitable. One of the driving forces behind such a venture, according to part of the La Jolla study group, would be a desire to beat out the Soviets. Some feel that the first nation to get to the Moon will be likely to have the most control over how it's developed.

It is hard to believe that more than 12 years have passed since anybody has walked on the moon—an interval longer than the age of the entire space program at the time the first Apollo astronauts landed there. One of those men, Buzz Aldrin, recently reminisced about that historic moment. "It was [more than] 15 years ago," he said, "that I stood inside a cramped cockpit, looking out a triangular-shaped window, and watched as my colleague Neil Armstrong made the first footprint on the surface of the Moon. I heard him say, a second before anyone back on Earth did, that this was 'One small step for a man, one giant leap for mankind.'

"Today, I believe it is time we dare make the giant leap a reality for mankind. It's time to return to the moon—for good" □

Nuclear Winter

by Andrew C. Revkin

E arly in 1979 the U.S. Congressional Office of Technology Assessment (OTA) completed a 151-page report called "The Effects of Nuclear War." The first finding, set off in boldface, was: *"The effects of a nuclear war that cannot be calculated are at least as important as those for which calculations are attempted."* That has proved to be an unusually apt caveat (warning).

Now, several years after the OTA report, and four decades after the invention of nuclear weapons, the scientific and defense communities have suddenly learned of an aspect of nuclear war, overlooked by OTA and almost everyone else who had studied the subject, that could prove to be more devastating than any of the other effects—including the blast and radiation.

Ominous Factor Long Overlooked

The forgotten factor? Smoke. Government scientists had been studying the physical effects of nuclear explosions for decades, had produced massive volumes full of detailed observations, had scrutinized accounts of the atomic blasts at Hiroshima and Nagasaki, Japan, and the firestorms (fires so fierce and hot that their updrafts suck in air from all sides at near-hurricane force) at Dresden and Hamburg, Germany, and Tokyo, Japan. But no one had calculated the climatological effects of the globe-spanning pall of dark smoke that could rise from the thousands of fires ignited by a nuclear war. Indeed, with the exception of two neglected reports produced for the U.S. Government in the 1960's, the word *smoke* is hardly mentioned in the scientific literature.

A paper published in the Swedish journal *Ambio* in 1982 thus came as a complete surprise, stunning scientists and defense experts alike with its simple, ominous conclusion. Paul Crutzen, a Dutch atmospheric scientist, and John Birks, an American chemist, calculated in a rudimentary but convincing way that smoke from a nuclear war—several hundred million tons of it—"would strongly restrict the penetration of sunlight to the Earth's surface and change the physical properties of the Earth's atmosphere." And their calculations were based only on smoke from burning forests. When another research team considered smoke from burning cities, the forgotten factor took on even more significance.

Richard Turco, an atmospheric scientist at R & D Associates, in Marina del Rey, California, had been working with three researchers at the National Aeronautics and Space Administration's (NASA's) Ames Research Center, two of whom were former students of Cornell astronomer Carl Sagan, on the atmospheric effects of

dust raised by nuclear explosions. When Turco read an advance copy of the *Ambio* study, he immediately saw that smoke would be far more important than dust.

Turco reworked the *Ambio* calculations, adding in the smoke from burning cities. Along with the NASA group—O. Brian Toon, Thomas Ackerman, and James Pollack—and Carl Sagan, he put together a comprehensive analysis, including computer models, of the "global consequences of multiple nuclear explosions." The group, which soon became known as TTAPS (an acronym based on last names), discovered that the smoke could have a devastating effect on the Earth's climate.

Important Study Prompts Debate

The findings were so dramatic, in fact, that in late April 1983, more than 100 scientists were invited to a closed session at the American Academy of Arts and Sciences, in Cambridge, Massachusetts, to review the study. The physical scientists met first, testing the assumptions, dissecting the models, checking the data. Some adjustments and refinements were made, but the basic conclusions held.

Then the biologists took a crack at it. They extrapolated from the climatic effects to the impact on agriculture and ecosystems. The destruction wrought by nuclear war, they con-

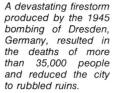

A devastating firestorm produced by the 1945 bombing of Dresden, Germany, resulted in the deaths of more than 35,000 people and reduced the city to rubbled ruins.

Illustrations: Julian Allan/Science Digest, © The Hearst Corp.

In this hypothetical chain of events, a fireball fills the sky over New York City seconds after a nuclear explosion (top). Secondary fires in combustible materials could then merge into one massive inferno (above).

than wood. In fact, Art Broyles, a physicist and fire expert at the University of Florida, estimates that even though these materials make up only about 5 percent of the fuel in cities, they would probably produce as much smoke as the rest of the fuel, which is primarily wood.

The individual clouds of smoke would coalesce after a week or two. Pushed by strong west-to-east winds, the smoke would form a uniform belt of particles girdling the Northern Hemisphere from 30 to 60 degrees latitude, a region that reaches from central Florida to southern Alaska. The weapons' blasts would also raise tons of dust into the stratosphere, where it could remain for years.

Chilling Aftereffects

The smoke—and, to a much smaller extent, the dust—would prevent all but a tiny fraction of sunlight from reaching the surface of the Earth in the Northern Hemisphere for weeks, possibly months. According to the TTAPS study, after a "baseline," or medium-size, nuclear war, in which warheads with a total yield of 5,000 megatons were exploded over a variety of targets, average surface temperatures would drop 60° F—below freezing even in summer—destroying agriculture, disrupting ecosystems, and making the postwar world a nightmarish mix of cold, dark, and starvation for those humans who survived the other effects. The study also projects the possibility that the high-altitude smoke cloud, and thus the cold and dark, could spread across the equator, plunging sensitive tropical ecosystems and the nations of the Southern Hemisphere into chilly twilight.

By blocking sunlight the smoke would disrupt the transfer of radiation from the Sun that creates and maintains Earth's equable climate. Most of the Sun's energy is transmitted as visible light. Sunlight penetrates the atmosphere and strikes the continents and the oceans, which, to varying extents, absorb the energy and heat up. The Earth radiates this energy back toward space as infrared radiation (IR).

Major Atmospheric Reversal a Possibility

Fortunately for humans and other life-forms, not all of the radiation escapes into space. If it did, the Earth would have a surface temperature below −17° C (0° F). The heat is trapped by the so-called greenhouse effect. As TTAPS explains, "The atmosphere generally acts as a window for sunlight but a blanket for heat." Carbon dioxide, water vapor, and the water in clouds all absorb some of the escaping energy. The air nearest the surface absorbs the most heat, giving Earth its 13° C (56° F) average surface temperature. But the air cools rapidly with increasing altitude, to about −55° C (−67° F) at the upper limit of the troposphere. The entire troposphere is stirred up and set into motion when the low, heated air masses rise—a process called convection. This is the main source of our weather: clouds, wind, and all kinds of precipitation.

Smoke has optical properties that make it a better blocker of sunlight than dust or water clouds. Visible light is transmitted at wavelengths of between 0.4 and 0.7 microns (one micron equals one millionth of a meter). A significant fraction of the particles in smoke are less than a micron in diameter. Dark particles of this size are ideally suited to absorbing energy at those wavelengths.

The result? If enough cities are burned—and according to one of the TTAPS scenarios, 100 cities will suffice—the atmosphere will be turned on its head. Sunlight will be absorbed not

The smoke from a nuclear war would prevent sunlight from reaching the Earth, causing surface temperatures to plummet.

A nuclear explosion near a city would rupture tanks of fuel and poisonous chemicals, creating a toxic wasteland.

at the surface but by the layer of smoke in the upper troposphere. The smoke and the troposphere will heat up, and the Earth below, deprived of up to 95 percent of its daily ration of solar energy, will cool.

The TTAPS group calls this the "antigreenhouse effect." One consequence of such a mass inversion would be a lack of convection. With few rising pockets of heated air, there would be little atmospheric turbulence, fewer storms, and thus less of the natural "scavenging" processes, including rain, that normally remove particles from the air. To make matters worse, as the smoke-laden air in the upper troposphere grew warmer, it would tend to rise even higher, taking it farther from the region of cleansing precipitation, perhaps as high as the stagnant stratosphere. The nuclear-winter effect, in Sagan's opinion, could thus be self-perpetuating.

Models Have Flaws, But Most Predict Big Freeze

The TTAPS researchers are the first to point out that their effort involved many assumptions. The model they used to chart the temperature profile of the atmosphere was one-dimensional, representing the average global atmosphere as a single column of air. The smoke for each of several dozen different war scenarios was assumed to be spread uniformly and instantaneously over the Earth. Rather than taking into account the oceans, which act dramatically to buffer any sudden climatic changes, separate computer runs had to be done for an all-water planet and an all-land planet (with 70 percent of Earth's surface being water, that is a large simplification). The simulations employed a feature common to such models—a fixed Sun—that leaves out any possible effect of the daily cycle of light and dark.

Despite these and other assumptions, subsequent two- and three-dimensional computer analyses have, for the most part, only mitigated the effects described by TTAPS. Coastal regions and islands would escape the brunt of the deep freeze but might be subjected to extraordinary storms as the warmer air over the ocean clashed with the cold air over land. Clear patches in the canopy of smoke, low-lying fogs, and other factors would lessen the effects. But only in a few cases have simulations failed to show significant, potentially destructive cooling of the Earth's surface.

Here are some of the other finds that have appeared recently:

• Michael MacCracken, at Lawrence Livermore, ran a three-dimensional global-circulation model (GCM) that showed a 25° F to 30° F drop in average surface temperature beneath the smoke cloud—half the TTAPS finding, but still catastrophic by any estimation.

• Vladimir Alexandrov, head of the climate-research laboratory of the U.S.S.R. Academy of Sciences, using a different GCM and a 10,000-megaton war scenario, reported a temperature decrease similar to MacCracken's.

• Starley Thompson, Curt Covey, and Stephen Schneider, at NCAR, running one of the most sophisticated climate models available, got results that support some of the TTAPS work, and they also observed a remarkable feature they called a quick freeze. The model produced patches of freezing temperatures that migrated at random across the globe as early as two days after a nuclear war. (TTAPS predicted the onset of freezing conditions after two or three weeks.)

MacCracken says the NCAR finding flags a major weakness in almost all the studies that have been done so far: "What we should be looking at is not the change in climate—the average conditions—but the change in weather, which is short-term, day-to-day fluctuations." A quick frost at the wrong time is all that is needed to destroy a year's crops.

Uncertainty Is Desirable

At this point, most of the climate-modeling researchers say one thing is clear: If enough smoke gets high enough, and stays there long enough, there will be significant surface cooling. But that is a big if.

In spite of the potentially enormous ramifications of nuclear winter, there are those who doubt it will affect public policy. But Dyson, Schneider, Sagan, and others still say the final effect will be positive: The very uncertainty that plagues research into the phenomenon is desirable. Schneider says, "A lot of the young guys who work with me ask, 'Is there any chance that I could make war more probable by these studies?' And the answer is there's always a chance. But the only way you make war more probable is by giving one side the belief it has a distinct advantage it didn't used to have."

According to Dyson, "the ideal answer" to the nuclear-winter question will be, "Yes, this may happen, and there's no way we can ever tell" □

SELECTED READINGS

"The climatic effects of nuclear war" by Richard P. Turco et al. *Scientific American*, August 1984.
"The climatic and biological consequences of nuclear war" by Herbert D. Grover. *Environment*, May 1984.
"Nuclear winter" by Anne Ehrlich. *Bulletin of the Atomic Scientists*, April 1984.

Virtually all crops in the Northern Hemisphere would be killed in the aftermath of a nuclear war.

Center on the Consequences of Nuclear War

PHYSICAL
SCIENCES

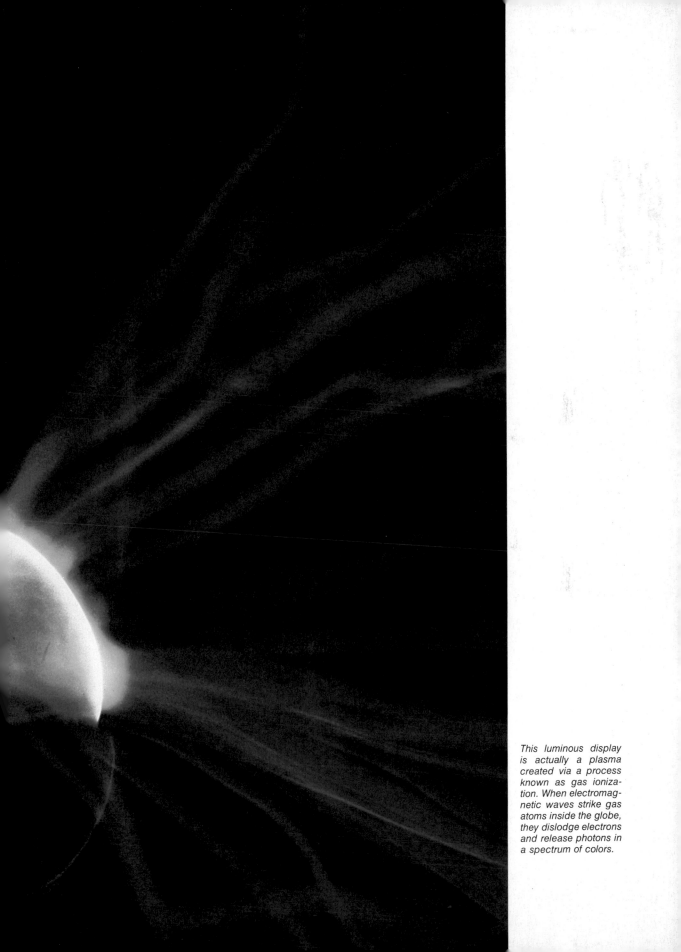

This luminous display is actually a plasma created via a process known as gas ionization. When electromagnetic waves strike gas atoms inside the globe, they dislodge electrons and release photons in a spectrum of colors.

REVIEW
OF THE
YEAR

PHYSICAL SCIENCES

PHYSICS

In 1984 scientists continued to try to unravel the mysteries of matter. Researchers at the European Center for Nuclear Research (CERN) in Switzerland obtained evidence for the existence of a sixth quark. Quarks are believed to be the basic building blocks of atomic particles such as protons and neutrons. Until recently five quarks were known: up, down, strange, charm, and bottom. The discovery of the sixth—named "top"—confirmed the theory that, for reasons of symmetry, both top and bottom must exist.

The existence of an unusual form of matter—dense nuclear matter—was confirmed by German and American researchers at the Lawrence-Berkeley Laboratory at the University of California. The scientists produced the condensed nuclei by slamming a beam of niobium-93 nuclei against other niobium nuclei that were in a metal target. The discovery suggests that physicists may be able to construct a so-called nuclear phase diagram that spans a wide range of temperatures and densities. In addition, it may lead to the discovery of phase transitions to previously unknown states of nuclear matter, such as those that were present during the early moments of the universe.

Other research held the promise of more immediate application. Scientists at Sandia National Laboratories in Albuquerque, New Mexico, succeeded in focusing an intense beam of ions onto a spot only 0.13 centimeter (0.05 inch) across, demonstrating that ion beams could initiate the fusion of deuterium and tritium (two heavy forms of hydrogen). Such a critical process could produce large quantities of energy in a fusion reactor.

A laboratory accident led to the discovery that sufficiently powerful infrared laser light can melt diamond. A Cornell University graduate student, using a laser beam to heat a mixture of graphite and potassium bromide compressed between two pieces of diamond, accidentally melted a furrow across the surface of the diamond.

One finding in particular could have wide-ranging impact. Scientists discovered that low-level microwaves are absorbed by strands of uncoiled DNA (deoxyribonucleic acid—the basic hereditary material of cells that usually occurs as double-stranded coils in the cell's chromosomes). The finding could have significant health considerations for people exposed to this form of energy from microwave ovens, broadcast towers, radar, and high-voltage power lines. Unlike the way food absorbs microwave energy while it cooks in a microwave oven—thermally—the DNA absorbed energy through resonance, much like a vibrating violin string. A team of researchers led by Mays L. Swicord of the National Center for Devices and Radiological Health at the U.S. Food and Drug Administration (FDA) demonstrated this effect in the DNA of *Escherichia coli* bacteria. Such resonance might be able to knock off disease-causing molecules from the particular genes whose activities they are inhibiting. Scientists plan further studies to determine if coiled chromosomal DNA is as vulnerable to low-level microwaves as the uncoiled DNA.

Jane DiMenna

The recent finding that strands of uncoiled DNA absorb low-level microwaves has now prompted scientists to investigate whether coiled DNA—the type usually found in the cell's chromosomes—is also susceptible to this form of electromagnetic energy.

The substance in this vial is a sample of a new plastic developed at Los Alamos National Laboratory that has the highest conductivity of any known polymer.

Los Alamos National Laboratory

CHEMISTRY

A new technique was developed that promises to facilitate the production of more effective drugs, pesticides, and other useful chemicals. The method is based on the synthesis of optically pure organic compounds from a mixture of otherwise identical compounds that are either "right-handed" or "left-handed," depending on how they rotate a beam of polarized light. Herbert C. Brown and Bakthan Singaram of Purdue University discovered the technique, which yields 100 percent optically pure substances called alkylboranes; the alkylboranes, in turn, can be further converted into a variety of useful compounds.

There was also new work on superconductors, substances that have virtually no resistance to the passage of electrons. Soviet and U.S. chemists developed a synthetic process that they used to produce the first sulfur-based organic compound that is superconducting at ambient temperatures. Researchers at the Institute of Chemical Physics in Moscow and at the Argonne National Laboratory in Illinois synthesized a triiodide salt of a compound called BEDT-TTF, thus producing the first in a new family of compounds. One of these compounds is superconducting at a temperature three times higher than any known organic compound that is a superconductor at ambient pressure. ■ In other work on superconductors, researchers at Los Alamos National Laboratory in New Mexico developed a new plastic that has the highest conductivity of any known polymer. An improved variety of a conducting polymer called polyacetylene, the new plastic is able to conduct electricity almost as efficiently as metal. The polymer, which becomes superconducting when treated with cesium electride, is lightweight, soluble, and easily molded into different forms.

An artificial membrane that conducts electrons in darkness was developed by H. Ti Tien of Michigan State University. The membrane consists of a double layer of lipid molecules and as such is similar to the membrane that encloses mitochondria and other structures within cells. The new membrane may help scientists study the role that electron transfer across membranes plays in how cells use and convert energy from one form to another.

Toxic chemicals and their effect on the environment were the subject of much study during the year. A National Research Council committee discovered that no toxicity data were available for about 70 percent of 65,725 substances, including industrial chemicals, pesticides, drugs and inert ingredients in drugs, food additives, and cosmetics. Enough data were available for a complete health assessment of over 2 percent of the substances and partial assessment of 12 percent. Adding to the disturbing news was the report that of 664 toxicity tests examined, only 27 met the committee's quality standards. The committee recommended a four-stage testing process for evaluation of chemicals by the National Toxicity Program. ■ Indiana University researchers confirmed the belief that some chemical contaminants may be carried in the atmosphere and deposited far from their sources. The scientists found traces of dioxins and furans in sediments taken from a lake on Isle Royale, Michigan, in northern Lake Superior. The chemicals were present in proportions similar to those found in air samples obtained from Washington, District of Columbia, and St. Louis, Missouri. Although the amounts found were small, the discovery demonstrated that dioxins are stable once they are deposited in the soil and sediment.

Some unpleasant chemicals may have practical uses. Atomergic Chemical Corporation of Plainview, New York, reported the synthesis of the bitterest substance known to date: a white crystalline powder called dinatonium saccharide. Bitter even when diluted to one part in 20 million, the substance may find use as a shark repellent or as an additive to poisonous household products to discourage children from ingesting them. ■ Meanwhile, chemists at the University of Minnesota in Minneapolis came up with an efficient method for making large quantities of allyl methyl trisulfide, the active ingredient in garlic. The substance inhibits blood clotting and may have other medical uses.

Marc Kusinitz

MEMORIES
THAT LOSE THEIR COLOR

by Ellen Ruppel Shell

It was bad enough when Theresa's turned blue and Carla's yellowed. But when Rhea's high-school-graduation picture faded to a murky shade of purple after only eight years, the girls' mother, Judy Corwith, marched it back to the photography studio and demanded retribution.

"In a small town like Reedsburg [Wisconsin] word gets around fast," says studio owner Robert Fehrenbach, who reprinted the Corwith photos and hundreds of others. "We lost a lot of customers."

Fading Phenomenon an Unpleasant Surprise

Fehrenbach figures thousands of photographs produced in his studio have suffered from fading or cracking. This came as a shock to him and his wife, Bernice, who have operated a successful business since 1963. But it is no surprise to Henry Wilhelm.

"Compared with most other types of artistic media, color photographs generally fade fairly rapidly when displayed," says Wilhelm, a color-image-preservation expert. "Since people tend to display their best or favorite photos, they actually single them out for destruction."

Unwitting consumers are not the only ones affected by this phenomenon. Professional photographers throughout the country have watched in horror as their best work fades into oblivion. Some museum curators who have seen acquisitions of a decade ago fade are refusing to purchase photographs printed on the most widely used paper. Others demand storage facilities costing $50,000 to $100,000 to protect what stock they have.

Print Deterioration Depends on Many Factors

"The changes in these photographs are erratic and unpredictable," says James Enyeart, director of the Center for Creative Photography at the University of Arizona, home of one of the world's largest and most distinguished 20th-century collections. "We have color prints dating back to 1956 that are in fine condition. But we have others that have changed so dramatically in 8 to 10 years that they bear absolutely no resemblance to the original."

If photographs maintained by professional archivists can suffer such a fate, what hope is there for that album of wedding or travel shots you've stored in the attic or shoved to the back of the bedroom closet? That depends on the kind of photographic paper used and the temperature, humidity, and light intensity in your closet. It also hinges on the type of paper or plastic sheets holding the photos in the album, on whether the prints were treated with lacquers or sprays after processing, and on whether you use a gas stove. Chances are, though, that unless you live in a frost-free igloo, that bridesmaid's dress or Hawaiian shirt will be much more vivid in memory than in a 10-year-old color print.

Photo Manufacturers Finally Face the Issue

Anyone who has ever washed a pair of madras shorts or replaced a set of faded curtains knows how unstable color dyes can be. But it was not until the 1980's that the major photographic manufacturers were willing to bear witness to that fact. With advertising slogans like Eastman Kodak Company's "take a moment out of time . . . and make it last forever," and "wedding candids to last a lifetime," the last thing the industry wanted consumers to think about was the longevity—or lack of it—of their products. But pressure from professional photographers, archivists, and filmmakers has dragged the issue of image stability out of the closet and into the limelight. It can be a very unflattering light indeed.

"The majority of color photographs are not suitable for display," says Klaus B. Hendriks, director of picture conservation at the Public Archives of Canada. "Unfortunately, industry didn't feel responsible for the fate of a photograph once it was finished. They couldn't make money telling people how to preserve their pictures."

Truth is, manufacturers haven't had to worry much about image stability until now because few consumers have made it an issue. After all, that picture of grandma on her wedding day that graces your mantle is still in great shape. That's because black-and-white photographs aren't really affected by light and heat. But black and white took a backseat to color in the early 1960's, and today at least 90 percent of the photographic market lies in color prints. More than 11 billion amateur color photographs are snapped every year in this country alone.

This black-and-white family portrait has lasted almost a century because it is not harmed by heat, light, or humidity.

Chromogenic Development Inherently Unstable

But not all color photographs are created equal. In the more stable color processes, dyes that form the final image are layered into the paper. These dyes respond proportionally to the amount of red, blue, or green light that strikes them. (Blue light creates yellow dye; green, magenta; and red, cyan). Your average, everyday print made from a negative, however, does not have image dyes already imbedded in the paper. Instead, the paper used in the popular process, called chromogenic development, contains dye precursors. These precursors can form dyes only after light converts silver halide crys-

tals in the paper to metallic silver, which then reacts with the developer. The products of this reaction then combine with the precursors to form the magenta, cyan, and yellow dyes. The density of the resulting dyes, and the concentration of each color in the photograph, is again proportional to the amount of light that hits the film when the picture is snapped and then the paper when it is developed.

The trouble with many of the dyes generated in this miniature color "factory" is that they are unstable. Light, especially ultraviolet and blue light, contains enough energy to cause chromogenic dyes to disintegrate into colorless fragments. Worse, the dyes can react with water vapor, oxygen, or contaminants in the air to wither even in the darkest recesses of the most carefully stored album.

Professional Prints No Better than Your Own

"Color photographs are the first colored materials known to fade in the dark," Hendriks says. "And this is especially true of chromogenic materials." Even the enhanced-stability paper that Kodak introduced in 1984 will only delay the inevitable.

That doesn't keep professional photographers who know this from using chromogenic products. Nor does it put a dent in the enormous amateur market. With the notable exception of instant films, virtually all products made for the snapshot set are chromogenic. This is what Kodak hoped for when it introduced Kodacolor, the first widely available chromogenic print system, in 1942. The idea was to create a color film suitable for use in box cameras that could be quickly mass-processed into prints for wall or wallet. The original Kodacolor was a stability disaster—just about every print made with the process before 1953 is now a faded orange blur. But it made color photography a reality for millons, and Kodak processing became so widespread that manufacturers were forced to come out with products compatible with it or go out of business.

"For all practical purposes," says Donald Hotchkiss, a 3M physicist, "the differences in stability among brands of chromogenic papers are trivial." That means the most expensive family portrait taken by studio photographers is printed on essentially the same material as the cheapest dime-store rendition. And the costly print will fade just as quickly as any 88-cent special.

Industry has long been aware of this irony. While saying stability is "not really a problem" and that they "get virtually no complaints" from consumers about it, Polaroid Corporation and Kodak maintain extensive color-stability laboratories, as do the Japanese companies of Fuji and Konishroku, Germany's Agfa-Gevaert, and Ciba-Geigy of Switzerland. But the companies kept test results pretty quiet until 1979, when a group of very vocal still- and motion-picture professionals and museum curators formed an international committee to look into the stability question. "It's a very difficult issue," Hotchkiss says, "because it's so hard to determine the point at which a color photo is no longer acceptable."

Real Colors Not as We Perceive or Want Them

Not surprisingly, Kodak led the way in research into color perception and the degree and types of fading that the human eye can and cannot ignore. It turns out that human memory is highly selective and usually inaccurate when it comes to colors. In fact, many precisely reproduced hues are actually offensive to the eye. Most people recall the sky as bluer, the grass as greener, and fire engines as redder than they really are. Film manufacturers actually build their products around these prejudices, with bluer-than-blue blues, lush greens, and sizzling reds.

According to Charleton Bard, supervisor of image stability at Kodak's Photo Technology division, inherent limitations in the three-dye system make it impossible to duplicate in a photograph all real-world colors simultaneously. "From a practical standpoint, though, this is not a problem," he says. "Our job is to make colors that people like, and what people like is significantly different from actual color."

Complicating things still further is the fact that different cultures demand different deceptions. Westerners, for instance, tend to dislike sallow skin tones, so prints made here give people a ruddy, outdoor look. The Japanese prefer their skin tones slightly whiter, while in India the preference is for skin with a slightly green tint, so pictures processed there make people appear a bit sickly by American standards. Even within the United States, the color laboratories respond to different cultural preferences: people's skin tones in the western United States, for example, should be just a bit rosier than in the East.

Kodak Simulates Photographic Aging

While color "quality" is a very subjective notion, color concentration—the amount of dye in a given photograph—is an absolute. A 30 percent fading of any one of the three dyes or a 15 percent loss of two is generally regarded to be unacceptable by photographic film and paper manufacturers. Since balance is actually more critical to human perception than is concentration, however, a 15 percent loss of two dyes may not be nearly as offensive as a 30 percent loss of one.

And, of course, anything is preferable to an actual color shift. "People are very sensitive to color changes," says Kodak's Thomas Hutteman, explaining that most consumers will put up with a faded red rose but never a green one. Most companies make a stab at better defining the delicate distinctions between a "good" and "bad" print with accelerated aging tests that compress the effects of years of storage or exposure into a few days or months.

Kodak's color-stability laboratories, housed in a drab glass building in the company's Rochester, New York, headquarters, are a series of what appear to be tanning salons and test kitchens. The former, some so bright visitors must don sunglasses to enter them, contain either lamps rigged with special filters to mimic high noon in Rochester on the longest day of the year, or the high-intensity fluorescent lights found in brightly lit office interiors. Color photographs taken with various films and printed on different papers line the walls, where they are systematically bleached by the rays.

High-energy ultraviolet radiation like that emitted by sunlight and fluorescent bulbs fades color photographs fairly quickly, despite the ultraviolet filters manufacturers build into the coating of photographic papers. Kodak reports that prints subjected day and night to 500 foot-candles of fluorescent light (about five times the amount found in the normal inner office, but only about one-tenth of the intensity of direct sunlight) show a noticeable decrease in dye density in 40 days and a dramatic loss of dye in about four months. How that translates into real-life exposure is unclear, but Henry Wilhelm, who maintains his own stability laboratory, says a chromogenic print hung on the wall will fade noticeably in a few years, significantly in 25. "These are not things you can pass on for generations," he says.

Cold Storage One Way to Preserve Pictures

To test fading in the dark, Kodak uses small ovens set at temperatures ranging from 24° C to 93° C (75° F to 199° F) and humidities that run from a desert-dry 2 percent to a tropically drenched 100 percent. Wilhelm reports just noticeable decreases or changes in color density at a projected 10 years of a photograph's life in an album, dramatic changes in fewer than 30 years. Since stability doubles with every 10-degree [Fahrenheit] decrease in temperature, fading in the dark can be significantly slowed by cold storage—or sped up by a trip to the tropics, where high heat, humidity, and film emulsion—eating fungi can consume chromogenically produced images in months.

Fading is also hastened by exposure to a number of air pollutants, such as sulfur dioxide emitted by gas stoves or automobiles, or by contact with certain plastics, such as glassine and cellulose nitrate, the very stuff of which some photo albums are made. Almost any post-processing treatment, particularly lacquer sprays made with commonly used solvents, will shorten a color photo's life. And the so-called magnetic photo albums, the kind with slightly tacky leaves, sometimes stain the pictures or stick to the prints long after you want them to. But putting photos in a frost-free refrigerator will increase their stability by at least a factor of 10, and photos frozen in a low-humidity freezer appear to last indefinitely.

While freezing your favorite prints and negatives may seem a bit compulsive, it is one way to make sure that your great-grandchildren will know what you looked like on graduation day. The U.S. Library of Congress, the John F. Kennedy Presidential Library, the Art Institute of Chicago (in Illinois), Harvard University's Peabody Museum, and Time Incorporated all have hefty cold-storage vaults for color-photo and motion-picture collections. But most photographers, professional or otherwise, do not. And some archivists complain that keeping photos in a deep freeze defeats their purpose. "I do not see it as appropriate to have a meat locker here because this particular institution is devoted to having works of art available for immediate access by our patrons," says Center for Creative Photography's James Enyeart. Several hours are required to warm a box of photos taken from cold storage to room temperature without cracking them, and this, Enyeart says, makes for very cumbersome viewing.

More Options: Instant Prints and Dye Transfer

Probably the best-known alternative to the deep freeze are the instant-color systems, such as Polaroid's SX-70 and 600 and Kodak's PR 10 and Trimprint. These products are made with dyes that are significantly more stable in the dark than chromogenic dyes. Unfortunately, chemicals in the lower layer of instant prints often migrate into the visible image, causing the picture to yellow in the dark. This problem is mitigated in the case of Trimprint, which allows users to peel off the back layer containing the undeveloped chemicals. But all instant prints are so unstable in light that Ronald Cieciuch, a chemist at Polaroid, suggests they not be displayed at all. Since instant photography produces no negatives, he recommends framing a chromogenic copy of an instant print and keeping the original in a cool, dry place.

While on display for only seven years, this wedding photo faded severely. The area that was covered by an oval mat also lost color to the light, but much less so than the rest of the portrait.

Max Brown/Preservation Publishing Co.

Another alternative is the dye-transfer process, which produces prints with projected lifetimes of 300 years in the dark. Such prints are so vivid and sharp that many advertising agencies and some professional photographers swear by them. In the dye-transfer process, separate relief images are made out of hardened gelatin for each color, then soaked with the appropriate dye and pressed into the photographic paper. The process requires at least three days of a highly skilled technician's attention and costs about $300 per 8-by-10-inch original print, more than most people pay for their cameras.

Cibachrome Prints Best Way to Go

The best bet for that special graduation-day picture is probably to print it on Cibachrome paper, which is made and marketed by Ilford Incorpo-rated. Unlike chromogenic papers, in which dyes are formed during processing, Cibachrome stock has fully formed dyes built into it. Unwanted portions of the dyes are washed away during processing, leaving a glossy, high-contrast image. Henry Wilhelm's research shows that Cibachrome prints made on glossy paper are the most stable color print on the market. But Cibachrome papers and chemicals cost about twice as much as chromogenic materials, though at about $20 for an 8-by-10-inch custom print, Cibachrome is far cheaper than dye transfer. There is one small catch: Cibachrome prints can be made only from slides. And shooting slides requires far more exacting camera settings than do prints made from negatives, which can be adjusted during development for under- or overexposure.

It's little wonder, then, that Kodak, a company committed to reaching the broadest of mass markets, chose not to introduce a Cibachrome-like product called Azochrome it had patented in 1941. A small selection of the few prints made with Azochrome before it was abandoned can be seen at the George Eastman House in Rochester. They are in excellent condition. But, according to Kodak spokesman Henry Kaska, "no one was really interested in Azochrome, and no one asks about it now."

Demand Grows for Enhanced-Stability Products

Still, Kodak scientists say they are always investigating alternatives to chromogenic materials. Wilhelm suggests that one of these may be an Azochrome-type process that can print off color negatives. Meanwhile, Fuji has hinted it may have a similar product out within the next few years.

This flurry of activity in color stability is a response to increasing demand for photographs that live up to company claims. Consumers complain to studio owners and professional photographers; they in turn complain to Kodak. Manufacturers have long had the means to produce products with enhanced stability but say their customers are unwilling to pay for a feature that might take years to show itself.

"Our industry depends on people accepting what's not exactly on target," says Peter Krause, retired president of Ilford Incorporated. "Most people don't even notice when a photo is faded unless it's severely deteriorated." Kodak's Bard agrees. To illustrate he reaches into a box and pulls out a completely faded print taken in 1953. "A woman sent me this and told me we should use it in our promotional material," he says. "People aren't even aware of color stability. All they care about is having a pretty picture now." Of course, this hasn't kept studio owners like Robert Fehrenbach from having to replace faded prints. "When you pay $1,500 for a set of wedding photographs," he says, "you sure as heck care if they last" □

An obsolete product called Azochrome was used to make this 1940's print, which still maintains its color stability.

International Museum of Photography at George Eastman House

ORNL

BEAM "MAGIC"

by John Free

D odging cabinets glowing with red instrument lights and other gear cluttering the laboratory, Bill Appleton strode toward a junction of high-vacuum ion-accelerator tubes that crisscrossed at knee level. (Ions are atoms that carry either positive or negative electrical charges, depending on whether they have lost or gained electrons.)

The physicist seemed at ease amidst the high-technology plumbing. He first began probing matter with ion beams as a doctoral student in the mid-1960's. Now, heading the particle-solid-interactions section of the Solid-State Division of Oak Ridge National Laboratory (ORNL) in Tennessee, he witnesses remarkable transformations of materials.

Above: Bill Appleton (left) and Jim Williams insert a metal alloy into an ion-implantation device.

Beam Technologies Amazingly Alter Materials

Appleton's mustached face appeared above several gleaming tubes. "A sample goes in here," he said, tapping the vertical junctions, "and we alter its properties by implanting it with ions." Virtually any element can be implanted in any solid with a stream of ions, often dramatically changing the solid's physical, chemical, electrical, or optical properties.

"For example, we can extend the life of a metal alloy for artificial hip joints up to 1,000 times," said Appleton. [An alloy is a substance made of a combination of metals or of a metal and a nonmetal.] "But because a hip joint already lasts 10 years," he added, "a tenfold improvement is more than adequate."

Nearby, a closet-size ion generator, the source of the metal-toughening "magic," hummed in its blue cabinet. The generator poured an invisible stream of ions down a tube into a metal test sample. A small window at the sample junction lets scientists alter materials with another form of energy: extremely brief but powerful bursts of laser light. Both laser and ion beams used alone or together can produce new properties in materials that "fool Mother Nature," says Appleton.

Among its remarkable abilities, beam magic can: toughen metals and ceramics to reduce wear and corrosion, modify solids without changing their dimensions, conserve dwindling strategic materials, eliminate toxic wastes from some metal treatments, and avoid energy-consuming heat treatments that warp metal components.

Ion Implantation Moves into Industry

Until recently, these powers have been of mostly academic interest, restricted to laboratory experiments. But now beam technologies that enhance the mechanical properties of materials are gradually being adopted by industry. In years to come, widespread ion implantation may lead to everything from longer-lasting razor blades to car-engine parts that outlast their owners. Beam technology could put a dent in the estimated $90 billion expense caused by wear and corrosion every year in the United States. And a variety of new metal alloys developed through ion and laser technology, such as

superconductors (substances that lose their resistance to electrical current at very low temperatures) and so-called amorphous (uncrystallized) metals, may lead to a variety of energy-saving improvements.

At least one beam technique has already found a comfortable niche. Some 2,000 ion implanters are in use—often around the clock—in the United States. The semiconductor (solids such as silicon that can act as both electrical insulators and conductors) industry uses them to implant ions in silicon wafers. These wafers are then sliced into tiny chips for electronic circuits. Ion machines for semiconductors, however, demand exceptional precision and purity to avoid ruining microcircuits.

But hardware for another promising use—toughening metal—doesn't need such precision. Pioneering work on this type of ion implantation began in the 1970's at Harwell, England, the British equivalent of ORNL. Britain's atomic-energy laboratory now licenses ion hardware and modifies metal as a business.

Zymet, Incorporated, a small firm in Danvers, Massachusetts, introduced the first ion machines used to strengthen metals in the U.S. (As of early 1985, Zymet no longer actively marketed ion machines.) Zymet's Z-100 implantation system had a relatively small vacuum

After positively- or negatively-charged atoms are produced from nitrogen gas in an ion-source chamber, the nitrogen ions are implanted in metalworking punches on a workpiece holder. The process greatly enhances the metal's durability.

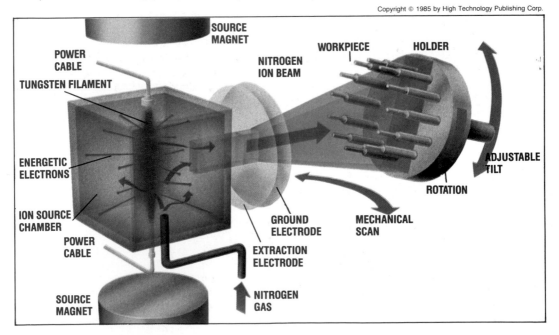

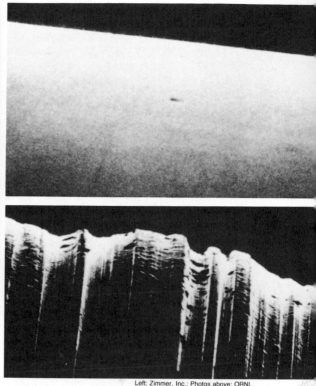

Ion implantation can improve corrosion resistance in artificial hip joints (above). Micrographs show a dramatic difference between implanted (top right) and nonimplanted (bottom) alloy samples after wear tests.

chamber—only 0.3 meter by 0.46 meter (1 foot by 1.5 foot). That space limitation, plus a half-hour cycling period for each load, severely limited ion-beam processing. "You need to treat high-value real estate," said Jim Hirvonen, Zymet's former research director. A few examples of his metaphor include precision tungsten-carbide tooling—punch sets that cost tens of thousands of dollars—bearings, and metal bone-replacement implants.

Steel Strengthened; Metal-Hip Joints Improved

Zymet's $150,000 implanter used nitrogen ions to toughen metals, although other ions also work. Accelerated by high voltage, nitrogen ions penetrate the surface region of an object. The ions "stitch" together atomic-level defects in metals and strengthen the surface in other ways.

Scientists are still mystified about some interactions that occur during and after implantation. But results—even spraying nitrogen ions into a microinch (one millionth of an inch) -thin surface layer of ordinary steel—amazed Hirvonen several years ago when he worked at the Naval Research Laboratory in Washington, District of Columbia.

Hirvonen recalled an experiment he and co-workers had conducted: Cylinders of low-carbon steel, shaped like finger-size hour-glasses, were implanted with nitrogen ions. Then the cylinders were put on a fatigue-test jig; weights compressed and stretched the samples as they spun at high speed. As expected, untreated cylinders snapped after 1 million test cycles. But before the ping of broken metal was heard from several ion-implanted samples, the treated cylinders had lasted substantially longer—100 million cycles.

Nitrogen ions can transform the surface of metals in another way. By enhancing corrosion resistance, ions are playing an important role in improving medical technology. Metal corrosion, curiously, is becoming a growing health problem. For example, a 58-year-old man visited his doctor complaining of soreness and swelling around his hips. Walking was difficult. Eight years earlier, suffering from a degenerative bone disease, he had been surgically implanted with ball-and-socket artificial-hip joints. (More than 75,000 such operations take place each year.)

The man's problem was that his body fluids were corroding the titanium-alloy balls cemented into his upper legs. Bits of metal were flaking off the pitted alloy and seeping into his blood. These particles were also abrading his plastic hip sockets. The cure involved a second major operation to replace the corroded implants with new ones.

"Physicians often tell us these balls look black when they're removed from patients," said Appleton. The discoloration, scientists suspect, is from oxidized titanium and polyethylene material. In a collaborative research effort with R. A. Buchanan of the University of Alabama at Birmingham, ORNL researchers discovered that ion implantation of nitrogen reduced corrosive-wear rates of the alloy by up to 1,000 times. In Buchanan's tests, cylinders of the titanium alloy were rotated between loaded polyethylene pads while immersed in fluids designed to simulate body fluids. "We've had strong encouragement from the Department of Energy to get this development into the hands of medical people," Appleton told me.

Beam Method Tested for Fighting Car Corrosion

Fighting corrosion is also a major element in the effort to prolong automobile life. Robert Chance, Monte Walker, and others at General Motors' (GM's) research laboratories in Warren, Michigan, have been studying ways of protecting the steel used on vehicles so as to minimize the need for critical metals such as chromium. One experiment sought other elements that might be effective ion-implanted corrosion fighters. Chance and Walker decided to implant arsenic, phosphorus, and antimony ions into dime-size disks punched from sheets of low-carbon steel. Different exposure times altered the ion concentrations; 60,000- and 190,000-volt potentials varied the ion-penetration depth.

To test for corrosion, they immersed the disks in acids and applied gradually increasing voltages to them. When a given voltage is reached—the breakdown potential—the metal breaks down and permits a sudden surge of current. Higher breakdown potentials mean better resistance to corrosion.

Phosphorus provided remarkable results. With the phosphorus-implanted steel, the researchers watched their instruments climb dramatically. Ordinary steel broke down at only 0.05 volt. But phosphorus-implanted disks held up until the voltmeters registered almost 1 volt.

"We're not trying to prove any particular element is the 'right' one for implantation," stresses Walker. "However, phosphorus clearly demonstrates the beneficial effect of surface-treating metals." Chance and Walker believe a wide range of vehicle applications is possible, and that the technology will reach automobile plants.

"Ion implantation may never replace conventional methods of corrosion protection," cautions Chance, "but it would offer a new dimension. If ion implantation ever did replace such methods," he says, "the initial applications would be highly specialized—mainly small components where high standards of performance are essential for safety or other purposes."

Ion Techniques Allow Many Alloy Combinations

The search for candidate elements for ion implantation continues. Both automobile manufacturers and petroleum companies such as Exxon have investigated the metal-toughening properties of numerous oddball elements. Experiments revealed, for example, that yttrium ions beamed into diesel-engine fuel-injection pumps boosted wear resistance 100 times as compared with chromium plating.

The unusual talents of ions in these techniques stem from some metallurgical facts of life (metallurgy is the science and technology of extracting metals from their ores and preparing them for practical and commercial use). First, blasting ions into a solid is a so-called nonequilibrium process: in ordinary equilibrium metallurgy, alloy elements are melted together and cool slowly. Metallic crystals grow in predictable structures as atoms settle into equilibrium. But many alloy combinations—silver and copper, for example—aren't possible. That's because the alloy components aren't soluble (won't dissolve completely) in each other.

That's irrelevant in nonequilibrium processes. "With ion implantation you can implant any atom in any substance to any concentration you like—whether Mother Nature likes it or not. You can just force it in," Appleton pointed out.

Furthermore, a companion technology called ion-beam mixing makes a staggering number of alloy combinations feasible. With this technique, a thin coating of material is deposited on a substrate. The coating is applied with conventional techniques: evaporation,

Ion Beam Mixing

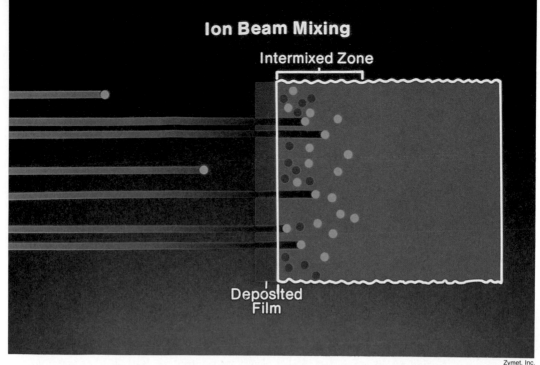

With ion-beam mixing, a thin film of material is driven into a substrate by an ion beam to produce an alloy.

chemical-vapor deposition, or sputtering—using ions to knock atoms from one material onto another. An ion beam then drives the coating into the substrate surface. "The beam adds a lot of energy to the surface—it stirs everything up," says Zymet's Hirvonen.

"Stitching" Ceramics into Engines

Both Hirvonen and Appleton anticipate important ion-mixing applications. "GM and other car manufacturers would like to make a car engine that can run at high temperatures without lubrication," Appleton said. "But the only materials that will stand up to that kind of thing are high-temperature ceramics. And the trouble with all ceramics is that, like glass, they break," he said.

Appleton paused before some graphs pasted to cardboard sheets in one of ORNL's surface-modification laboratories. The graphs, labeled with ceramics formulas plus experimental ion-implant elements—tungsten, indium, gallium, copper, and titanium—recorded the latest progress in toughening ceramics.

"To change the surface properties of high-temperature ceramics, we're trying to find the right elements, how much to use, and where to put them," Appleton said. ORNL's goal is to make better bearing and wear materials for adiabatic (no heat gain or loss) engines.

"The hardest thing with any coating is getting it to stick," Appleton said. He described how chemical-vapor deposition might coat piston-cylinder walls with ceramic material, then be "stitched" into place with an ion beam so it wouldn't break off. ORNL researchers have already doubled the surface hardness of ceramics with ions and boosted their fracture strength up to 30 percent.

Pulsed-Laser Processing Shows Promise

Laser beams at ORNL also produce amazing changes in materials: "That's a short-pulse ultraviolet gas laser," Appleton said, showing me a coffinlike white case atop a bench. Researchers use ultraviolet- and visible-light ruby lasers to melt the surfaces of samples with brief, powerful bursts of energy.

The pulsed-laser processing, which involves rapid heating and cooling of surfaces, is still largely experimental. Like ion implantation, it's a nonequilibrium process: cooling occurs so rapidly that atoms don't have time to settle into their normal equilibrium states. The technique can be used in combination with ion implantation and shows promises of making highly efficient solar cells. Laser pulses can instantly "heal" the crystalline surface of semiconductor materials that have been damaged when ions crash into them. In normal processing, prolonged baking at temperatures that can warp silicon wafers is needed.

Appleton believes that by 1989 laser and ion beams could also replace the technique now used to make glassy, or amorphous, metals. These metals, which promise significant energy savings by boosting the efficiency of electrical-power transformers, have a noncrystalline, glasslike structure. Glassy metals are now made by splat quenching: pouring pre-alloyed molten steel onto a spinning drum that cools it quickly.

"Laser and ion beams give you much wider latitude," said Appleton. Because laser-pulsed metals cool 100 times faster, alloy combinations are possible that couldn't be achieved with splat quenching. Slower, conventional cooling causes some alloy elements to precipitate out of the molten metal. With beams, glassy metals could also be formed on any substrate instead of on the thin foils necessary with splat quenching.

Ion and laser beams have also been used to develop new superconducting materials. One application has been in making compact but extremely powerful motors or generators. The beams solve a problem inherent in superconducting materials: "If you find a combination of elements that makes a good superconductor, a wire made with it is often so brittle that you can't wind it into a motor," Appleton told me. Laser- and ion-beam techniques make it possible to form a thin superconducting layer on the surface of flexible copper wire for winding.

Analyzing Materials with Atomic Billiards

As ion implantation and lasers alter the atomic structure of materials, extraordinarily sensitive instruments are needed to measure the results. In one corner of a laboratory, I spotted such a measurement in progress. Appleton pointed to an ion-beam tube that emerged from a room housing a 2.5 million–volt accelerator. It poured a beam of lightweight helium ions into a silicon-crystal sample implanted with antimony.

"What we measure are the number of particles that scatter from the atoms in a solid and their scattered energy," Appleton said. He

ORNL

Two researchers at the Oak Ridge National Laboratory use pulsed-laser processing and ion scattering to alter the structures of single-crystal surfaces.

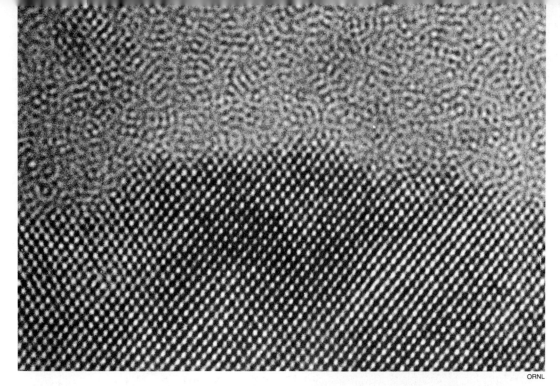

A micrograph of silicon shows the ion-implanted upper layer and the undisturbed crystal lattice below.

compared this ion-scattering analysis to bouncing marbles off billiard balls: the helium ions (marbles) scatter with different energies from silicon than from antimony (billiard balls), and detectors register this energy difference.

"These measurements allow you to find out exactly how much antimony there is, how far it is below the surface, and what the composition as a function of depth is," Appleton said. The results of these measurements appeared as a slowly developing graph on a computer-graphics terminal before us. "The beauty of this is that nothing happens to the sample," he said. "It's a nondestructive analysis."

Technical Obstacles Hamper Development

Is industry ready for such high-technology metallurgy treatments? At Carnegie-Mellon University in Pittsburgh, Pennsylvania, researchers reviewed surface-treatment technologies that might reduce U.S. vulnerability for strategic materials. They concluded that if technical barriers—current low-power machines, for example—could be overcome, ion implantation would help trim the demand for chromium and many other strategic materials.

Engineers, however, are slow to adopt new metallurgy technologies, although GM has used "conventional" electron- and laser-beam pro-

cessing in a few plants for years. These beams selectively heat and surface-harden portions of vehicle components, eliminating the need to heat—and often warp—the entire part. Still, these are really just high-technology versions of conventional metal-glazing treatments.

Before ion-implantation is adopted for large-scale metal toughening, larger vacuum chambers and more-powerful beam generators must be brought together. Such equipment exists already for other applications. Massive ion-beam generators have been built for experimental nuclear-fusion power sources and space weapons.

Despite the problems of running assembly lines through a vacuum chamber, Appleton and others are convinced that bringing beam magic into factories isn't prohibitively expensive. Said Appleton: "What we're talking about are technologies that will be standard practice [approximately] 10 to 15 years from now" □

SELECTED READINGS

"Ion implantation of surfaces" by S. Thomas Picraux and Paul S. Peercy. *Scientific American*, March 1985
"Ion-beam implantation" by Nicholas Basta. *High Technology*, February 1985.
"Materials research." *Oak Ridge National Laboratory Review*, Fall 1983.

THE PHYSICS OF FUN

by Carolyn Sumners

Rob Schuller may be the world's youngest physics teacher. Each weekend the Houston Museum of Natural Science in Texas pays this young teenager to play with toys. He shows visitors—especially the smaller variety—how to discover science while having fun. Rob's toys have mass, velocity, inertia (the resistance of matter to changes in its state of motion), momentum (the mass of a body multiplied by its velocity), and weight. His toys "feel" gravitational and centripetal forces. (Centripetal force is that which keeps an object moving in a circular path and that causes the object to constantly swerve toward the center of rotation.) They accelerate and decelerate. Through toys, Rob uses familiar experiences to draw children into the realm of physics.

Momentum Made Clear

Rob begins his show with the simplest of toys— the ball. He drops a light ball and a heavy ball from the same height at the same time, and they fall at the same rate. The result often surprises his audience, and Rob asks the children to "help" him explain what happened. He guides them along by asking if it is harder to pull a loaded cart or an empty one. Together, they determine that the heavy ball receives more gravitational pull, which it needs to fall at the same rate as the light ball. Rob then shows his expertise at tossing a ball straight up and catching it. He asks where the ball will fall if he repeats his toss while walking. Most of the younger visitors expect the ball to drop behind him. Another surprise: the ball shares Rob's momentum and returns to his hand.

Next, Rob rolls a piece of clay into a ball and drops it. Splat! But he says momentum can make the clay ball bounce 1.8 meters (6 feet) high. The trick is to stick the clay ball on top of a bigger, bouncier ball. He drops both balls, which his audience knows will fall at the same rate and arrive together. The big ball receives an upward push from the floor and starts to climb.

The clay ball on top captures the bigger ball's momentum and flies upward. Rob then drops the clay ball into a jar of water: it sinks with a splash. He asks for help in making the ball float. But curious observers must wait until the end of the program to see how dense clay can be made buoyant—with the aid of physics. The trick, of course, is to shape the clay into a boat.

The momentum story continues with Rob's favorite toy, the water rocket. He first fills the small rocket with air under pressure. When the air is released, its downward momentum shoots the rocket upward in a classic example of action and reaction. Rob then asks his rocket fans to predict what will happen when he adds water to the compressed air. Taking careful aim—remembering where the water will go—Rob fires the rocket. The water adds mass and therefore momentum to the escaping air, and the rocket soars even higher.

The World as Laboratory

Rob's Science in Toyland demonstration grew out of the museum's Informal Science Study, funded through the University of Houston by the National Science Foundation. My colleagues and I at the museum are developing educational materials and classroom programs that draw on children's familiar and enjoyable experiences to teach the language and concepts of physics. Inductive physics—that learned from memories of toys, amusement parks, sports, and playgrounds—makes sense to kids.

A sixth-grade girl inspired the study. I was trying to explain to her the "location" of the floor of a hypothetical space colony and why she wouldn't fall inward. But all my efforts, including swinging a bucket of water over my head, only caused more confusion. Finally, a sympathetic classmate told her to think about the rapidly spinning Barrel of Fun at the local amusement park. I will never forget the look of understanding on her face—she now had an experience to learn from. She could "feel" the centripetal force pushing inward from the sides of the barrel as its bottom dropped away, providing a structure upon which she could build abstract concepts.

Programs Prove to Be Successful

We aimed first at developing materials and curricula for the middle grades—roughly five through nine—since this is the period when kids too often decide to "tune out" science. For them, science must become so interesting and meaningful that it is worth remembering and pursuing. We found that even students who had never made a contribution in science class could describe the feeling of zero gravity while rushing down a roller-coaster hill.

A gravity-defying ride at an amusement park allows kids to experience the "feeling" of centripetal force.

We've since developed programs for students in all grades, including accelerated students. Older students not only tackle more difficult scientific concepts, they also get into matters of engineering. They can probe the mechanical details of how toys work, or they might analyze blueprints and accelerometer readouts from roller-coaster rides. We even challenge them to design their own toys and rides as an exercise in applying theoretical concepts.

We've now tested our programs on more than 5,000 students from around the country. In St. Louis, Missouri, for example, 12 ninth-grade classes spent a month working with our materials—experimenting with toys, studying amusement-park rides, and topping it off with a trip to the Six Flags Over Mid-America park. We tested the students before and after the program, measuring their knowledge in three areas: comprehension of mechanics concepts, recall of science experiences, and ability to apply mechanics concepts to new situations. Students of all academic abilities showed significant learning gains in each category, with slow learners recording the same percentage gains as accelerated students. Girls, who began with lower scores, reached or exceeded boys' scores. This came as something of a surprise; from sports to machines, most mechanics experiences have a definite "male" bias. But we found that the girls had ridden more amusement-park rides more often, a fact that gave them a relevant "knowledge base" for learning about physics.

The Yo-yo Meter

Now let's take a trip to an amusement park with Elizabeth Gregory. Elizabeth, age 11, became a "computer physicist" in a week-long course we ran at the museum. She began by running computer programs we've developed that simulate many thrill rides. Elizabeth designed loop coasters and watched riders stick tight even when upside down. She tilted curves so banking angles would hold riders squarely on their seats. She gave just enough spin to a gravity-defying barrel so passengers would cling to the walls. The girl made changes that could never be made in a real park, creating dangerous rides without risking a rider's life and limb. In all, Elizabeth began to see the physical principles behind these familiar rides.

Elizabeth then joined about 300 other computer physicists on a laboratory trip to Astroworld. They went equipped with scientific instruments and measuring devices picked up at a toy store. Elizabeth became an expert with the

Students in a museum course simulate a free-fall ride on a computer to better understand the physics involved.

A "toy scientist" on a laboratory trip to Astroworld in Texas watches a yo-yo meter while riding a roller coaster to "see" physical forces at work.

yo-yo meter, which she used to "watch" the forces she experienced on the rides. For example, on a suspended roller coaster called XLR-8, Elizabeth watched the yo-yo swing outward at each banked turn. The force of her body pushing against the seat confirmed the yo-yo's reading—the centripetal force produced by the banked curve exactly matched gravity's tug. The yo-yo proved that she would not fall off or fly away on this ride. On the scrambler, Elizabeth's yo-yo became a pendulum swinging back and forth. As she moved through the ride's complex spirograph pattern, her pendulum yo-yo faithfully maintained its swing, tracing each path in reverse as viewed by her moving eye.

But her most dramatic moment came on the loop coaster. Initially holding the yo-yo in her hand, with the string tied to her wrist for safety, Elizabeth released it when she was upside down at the top of the loop. The yo-yo seemed to fall "up" rather than dropping to the ground. As she had learned in class, she was traveling so fast that the yo-yo, sharing her momentum, kept going in a straight line. Elizabeth, however, was curving downward in the loop, so the yo-yo ended up in her lap.

Toys in the Classroom

For the past several years, I have presented workshops at teachers' conventions around the United States. The workshops emphasize how to bring student experiences into the class-room—from science show-and-tell activities in the lower grades to toy activities and amusement-park laboratories for older students. In Houston, I've watched toy laboratories grow in several elementary and middle schools, where children seem to thrive when studying the world in miniature.

Some toys mimic human behavior—flipping, swimming, hopping, rolling, jumping, waddling, and walking. Whether they wind up, roll down, rev up from being pushed, or use batteries, these toys all have a power source somewhere. Describing the energy flow in the mechanical devices offers a simple introduction to the principle of energy conservation.

Toys that roll are meant to be raced, of course. Proper laboratory equipment includes a long downhill ramp of plastic or plywood that slopes gently to a hard-floor straightaway. Some racers inevitably roll faster for very scientific reasons. Students discover that wheel friction is a killer, but several of the pint-size experts in this field testify that applying graphite works wonders. Crooked wheels waste too much of the precious gravitational energy. Wheel quality almost always takes precedence over wheel size. Aerodynamic styling can help if the race is close. Students who know that all objects fall at the same rate are often puzzled about what happens when mass is added to racers. Using clay and trial-and-error tactics, they soon learn that mass makes little difference

Left: These students receive a dramatic demonstration of the effects of momentum by ramming together a pair of roller skates affixed with dolls. Below: Slinkies are super for teaching certain concepts. In this gravity race, can you guess which slinky will hit the ground first? The stretched-out one will win since its center of mass was lower.

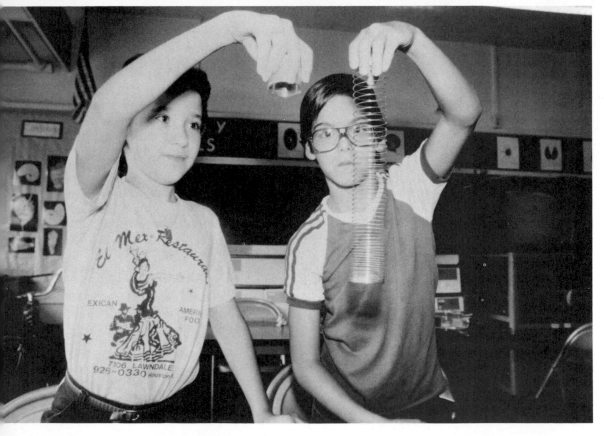

on the downhill roll, but the extra momentum carried onto the straightaway makes heavier racers better every time.

Braking Through the Sex Barrier

After one great race, a female contestant requested that we use dolls in a demonstration. But that pointed to something that had been bothering us: dolls—traditional "girls' toys"—don't lend themselves easily to science. Staring at a doll and wondering, "Where's the physics?" only leads to frustration. Dropping or throwing dolls in the name of science surely provides little encouragement for budding female scientists. Finally, we hit on the idea of safety.

Roller skates that clamp over shoes make excellent cars for carrying dolls. The students would crash the cars and study the results, adding safety features for the next crash. Doll-sized seat belts, shoulder harnesses, headrests, and padded dashboards grew from classroom supplies. Class interest ran high: the girls cheered when the dolls survived, and the boys rooted for the wreck.

Another class modified this idea, replacing the dolls with raw eggs. Each egg had a painted face that had to remain visible during its ride. A ramp running abruptly into a wall guaranteed equally forceful crashes for all participants. Losers cleaned up the mess. As an interesting safety note, the sole surviving egg was protected by an air-bag system made from a balloon.

Of Mice, Marbles, and Slinkies

Flipping toys also make fascinating physics. With a push from its long, curled tail, a toy cat can roll over. Tiny legs flip out and push toy cars and planes upside down and over. With a spring-loaded kick, a toy mouse flips high in the air and lands on its feet. A simple description of these forces and their directions is a lesson in Newtonian mechanics (the fundamental laws of mechanics developed by Sir Isaac Newton). Adding clay weights shows the delicate balance of each toy acrobat.

Marbles make excellent laboratory equipment. A ruler with a center trough along its length quantifies the marble player's art. Marbles of different sizes and speeds can be rolled along the trough into each other with great head-on accuracy. Students can see momentum passed from marble to marble in each collision. Students who do not "speak" algebra can still see that mass and velocity are both important in marble mechanics. A small marble must travel twice as fast as a marble with twice as much mass to stop it. And for observers, clear marbles make handy convex (curved or rounded like the outside of a circle) lenses that provide upside-down views of the world.

The slinky has long served teachers as a medium for demonstrating longitudinal (sound-like) waves and transverse (lightlike) waves. But we've also solved one of the greatest problems with slinkies: what to do when a slinky is stretched or bent. Damage usually strikes at the middle, rendering the toy useless. Such a slinky can be cut in half. The halves can then be dropped from the same height, with one half compressed and the other outstretched. In seeming defiance of the "all-fall-together" law, the stretched-out slinky hits the floor first. Students finally realize that it is the centers of mass that must be at the same height to make a gravity race fair.

From Model View to Real Ride

A car track with a ramp that hurls the car around a loop always proves a favorite. By adjusting the height of the ramp, students can change the car's speed in the loop. When the speed drops too low, gravity conquers inertia and the car comes tumbling off. Older toy scientists can calculate the exact height for the car's ramp in terms of the loop's diameter that gives the slowest acceptable ride. This demonstration gives students the opportunity to experiment with a model of an amusement-park ride before experiencing the real thing. From watching the car, students develop an idea of what it would feel like to be inside. Going on the ride lets the learner slip inside his or her experiment to get a different perspective on the forces involved.

Finding Physics in Every Toy

Every year when the holiday season approaches, toys are on many people's minds. Anyone venturing into a toy store will find physics on every shelf—even though only one aisle will likely be labeled "educational." These toys, such as chemistry sets or microscopes, take a science-inclined child into the world of adult scientists. But there is as much applied science and engineering in those other toys, the ones all kids want. Since many people automatically make a distinction between "fun" and "learning," the potential of these toys is often overlooked□

IN QUEST OF GRAVITY WAVES

by Marcia Bartusiak

S ome call it a telescope. But it's surely the oddest-looking telescope on Earth. No mirrors or lenses are aimed toward the heavens, ready to capture the light waves racing toward us from far-off galaxies. Instead, there is a hulking metal tank—a sophisticated thermos bottle, actually—that encloses a five-ton aluminum bar cooled with streams of liquid helium to a chilly −271° C (−456° F).

And this glacial mass of instrumentation doesn't sit on high mountains. It resides in the very heart of Stanford University's pastoral campus in California, in what looks like a deserted aircraft hangar, at the end of a narrow, winding concrete tunnel that was once part of the original Stanford Linear Accelerator Laboratory. Particle physicists used this cavernous end station to unlock the secrets of the atom. Today Stanford scientists are here with their

supercooled detector to snare a quarry that has ever eluded celestial observers: gravitational waves, a means of observing the universe's most baffling—and violent—goings-on.

Ripples in Space-Time

Albert Einstein first predicted the existence of these unusual waves about 70 years ago. It was a natural outcome of his famous theory of general relativity, which taught us to view gravity not as a mysterious force but rather as a curvature in space-time. Space, Einstein was telling us, is like a boundless rubber sheet, and large masses, such as our Sun, indent this flexible mat, causing any passing rocket, planet, or light beam to just follow the natural depression. Celestial bystanders perceive it as an attraction to the Sun and call it gravity.

Yet this century's most illustrious physicist

also realized that there would be peculiar side effects to this strange new geometric picture. Einstein's equations revealed that if a mass were suddenly accelerated or jostled to and fro, it would generate ripples in that sheet of space-time, similar to the way electrons moving along an antenna generate radio waves in the air. But while such electromagnetic waves travel through space, gravity waves actually disturb the fabric of space. This space-time rippling occurs every time you bang your fist on a table or jump rope, but only the most awesome cosmic events emit any appreciable waves. Particles and planets caught in the path of such a wave would experience space itself contracting and expanding.

Such a "spacequake" would provide astronomers with an entirely new form of information about the universe. "Visible and infrared light, radio waves, and X rays are emitted almost entirely by individual atoms, molecules, and high-energy particles," explains California Institute of Technology (Caltech) theoretical physicist Kip Thorne. "Gravitational waves, by contrast, are emitted by the bulk motions of huge amounts of matter, objects that are vibrating, collapsing, or exploding."

More important, these periodic distortions in the structure of space-time can blithely pass through interstellar dust, planets, and galaxies as if they weren't there. Nothing can absorb them. This penetrating power may allow astrophysicists to observe cosmic processes that, for now, can only be imagined on a computer-graphics terminal—from the last gasp in the life of a star to the titanic collision of two black holes.

The Birth of Gravitational-Wave Astronomy

The first attempt at snaring the ghostly ripples was made in the 1960's when Joseph Weber of the University of Maryland, the acknowledged father of gravitational-wave astronomy, built the first set of detectors. It was Weber who devised a nifty technological trick for trapping a wave: A gravitational wave, he surmised, would ever so slightly squeeze a solid cylinder in and out like an accordion. But then, like a bell, the bar would continue to "ring" long after the wave passed by. This ringing would be the gravity wave's calling card.

With massive aluminum bars operating on both the Maryland campus and at the Argonne National Laboratory near Chicago, Illinois, Weber announced in 1969 that he had registered some pulses. Based on the direction from which the strongest signals came, these bursts appeared to originate in the center of our galaxy. Spurred on by the announcement, several groups quickly constructed their own detectors. Excitement within the physics community, however, was short-lived. Though a few facilities have reported seeing pulses similar to Weber's, most have failed to detect the same kind

Joseph Weber's bar-type gravity-wave detector, the first such device ever built, is on display at the Einstein exhibit in the Smithsonian Museum of American History.

An open-end view of Stanford's gravity-wave device reveals the massive aluminum bar suspended inside.

In the course of the past several years, Stanford's most advanced gravitational-wave antenna to date has stood in stately isolation in its windowless cavern. The rumblings of passing cars and trucks are damped by suspending the 3-meter (10-foot)-long, 0.9-meter (3-foot)-wide metal bar with special springs. "You could actually gently hammer on the outside shield and not get a signal," says Fairbank proudly. And, as in Weber's original scheme, electronic devices positioned on the end of the bulky aluminum cylinder convert its minute movements into electrical signals that are recorded and scrutinized for a gravity wave's unique fingerprint.

Right now the Stanford bar can sense a shiver as tiny as 0.0000000000000003 centimeter (one thirty-millionth the size of a hydrogen atom), a world's record for the field. Further improvements are being made under the direction of senior research associates Michael McAshan and Peter Michelson. Their plans to install more advanced electronics and to cool the bar to within one-hundredth of a degree of absolute zero ($-273.15°$ C or $-459.67°$ F) are expected to increase the bar's sensitivity 100 times.

Since 1984 this futuristic telescope has registered a number of "events" that could not be explained away as laboratory jitter. Yet no one knows if they were gravitational waves. "With just one bar of this kind," says Fairbank, "the best you can say is, 'I saw some signals no bigger than a certain amount.'"

A Worldwide Effort

Scientists will be sure of what they are seeing only when additional, equally sensitive supercooled detectors come into use that can measure these disturbances simultaneously. Already the Stanford gravity-wave team is assembling a matching detector not far from their present instrument, and another twin is being built at Louisiana State University under the direction of Hamilton. The second Stanford detector will allow them to rule out internal-instrument error when a ripple is detected, and the Louisiana detector, similarly, will rule out local glitches.

It's truly a global pursuit. Other supercooled bars of varying designs and materials (niobium, sapphire, and silicon as well as aluminum) have either been assembled or are planned at the Universities of Maryland, where Weber continues his pioneering work; Roches-

of ringing. "What Weber was seeing remains interestingly unknown," says physicist William Fairbank, head of the Stanford gravity-wave project. But Weber's relentless effort resulted in a lush new field of experimental physics.

Stanford Leads the Way

Currently the Stanford group stands the best chance at capturing a bona fide wave. Even as Weber was constructing his first detector, Fairbank and colleague William Hamilton were designing a supercooled version. "We did this to eliminate the random noise in the bar," explains Fairbank, a world-renowned expert in low-temperature physics. "The normal motions of an atom at room temperature are 3,000 times greater than the energy put into the bar by that collapsing star at the center of our galaxy." The noise can never be eliminated entirely, but supercooling reduces these spurious signals, increasing the chances of picking up the fainter, gravity-induced movements.

ter, New York; Rome, Italy; Tokyo, Japan; and Western Australia; as well as in China and the Soviet Union. Like surveying instruments, an array of detectors will enable astronomers to more precisely pinpoint the source of an incoming wave.

Catching Ripples with Laser Beams

But watching bars of metal vibrate is not the only means of stalking these alleged ripples in space-time. More than a decade ago, researchers such as Robert L. Forward of Hughes Research Laboratories and Massachusetts Institute of Technology's (MIT's) Rainer Weiss recognized another way to catch a gravity wave: Attach mirrors to three heavy masses, suspend the masses in a vacuum some distance from one another, and monitor their relative motions with a laser beam to see if a passing gravitational wave has wiggled the weights.

Since a gravity wave acts by compressing space in one direction while expanding it in the other, a popular configuration for this setup is an L shape, with a mass at each end and one at the corner. "Envision a gravity wave coming straight down on the L," suggests physicist Ronald Drever, head of Caltech's gravitational-physics group. "Then the masses in one arm will draw closer together by a distance many times smaller than an atomic nucleus, while the other two get farther apart. A millisecond [one-thousandth of a second] later, as the wave passes by, the effect will reverse."

Test models of this setup have been built in Scotland, West Germany, and at MIT, and are under development in France and the Soviet Union. But Caltech now boasts the world's largest gravity-wave laser antenna. Each arm of their L configuration stretches out for 40 meters (131 feet).

Caltech Hopes for Telltale Blip

Operating the system is a more serious endeavor. First, a continuous beam of pure green light from an argon-ion laser enters the crook of the L and is split in two. Each half races down one of the evacuated arms and reflects off a mirror mounted on the end mass. This light bounces up and down the arm several thousand times, until eventually the two beams are directed back out of the arms and compared.

"We're looking for the slightest flicker of change in the beams," says Caltech gravity-wave physicist Robert Spero. Although the two beams are constantly in step with one another as they bounce within their respective arms, the optical system is such that they are made to be out of phase when they recombine. At this point they cancel each other out and produce a patch of darkness.

But a passing gravity wave would suddenly change the arm lengths. This in turn would

Researchers at the California Institute of Technology are testing the world's largest gravity-wave antenna.

Rene Sheret

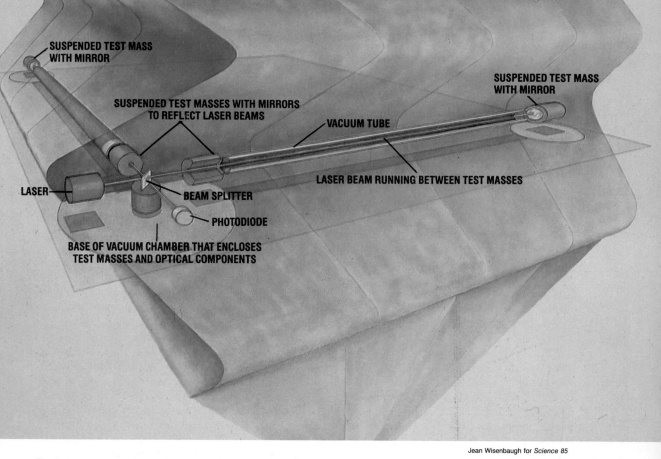

Jean Wisenbaugh for *Science 85*

The L-shaped detector depicted here works on the principle that a passing gravity wave (pink) will make the two masses of one arm move closer together and the masses of the other arm move farther apart.

change the phases of the beams that emerge from the arms. In greatly simplified terms, the two beams, once recombined at the center of the L, would constructively interfere and produce a tiny burst of light. "Ideally," says Spero, "we'll start out with a flat trace on a chart recorder, and a gravity wave would show up as a blip, a spike in the smooth trace."

Striving for Greater Goals

Though the Caltech scientists see their detector as still only a "test bed," they have conducted one serious search. For 12 days and nights in the winter of 1983, they hastily went on the air, as they like to put it, soon after radio astronomers discovered what they thought might be a strong gravity-wave emitter—a neutron star spinning a record 642 revolutions per second. Unfortunately, the cause of this high-speed rotation was not as predicted, making the star a dud as a gravity-wave source.

The Caltech gravity-wave astronomers will become worthy contenders if some $50 million in funding allows them to fulfill their ultimate goal: construction of two mammoth laser systems, each with arms stretching out some 5 kilometers (3 miles). They're collaborating on this ambitious proposal with Weiss's gravity-wave group at MIT. Each system will look more like an atom smasher than an astronomical instrument, only in this case, beams of light instead of beams of particles will be running down the giant tubes. "We'll need a quiet place," says Drever. "Perhaps a desert or even an underground mine." Separating the twin detectors by at least 1,610 kilometers (1,000 miles) will enable them to filter out local noises and so better check for real coincident pulses.

It won't stop there. Eventually gravity-wave astronomy is destined to take to space. Just as electromagnetic radiation comes in all sizes from radio waves to gamma rays, gravity waves will certainly vary in length, depending on the source. Collapsing stars, for example, are expected to send out ripples that stretch some 320 kilometers (200 miles) from peak to peak. But if a supermassive black hole residing in the core of an exploding galaxy gobbles up a star, it might send out waves hundreds of millions of kilometers in length. Because the bars, like a tuning fork, respond to limited frequencies, these very long wavelengths will be best detected by laser systems—especially space-borne systems, which have even longer arms.

Capturing a Real Event May Be No Small Feat

There are also plans to send an entire laser system out into space, but meanwhile scientists are still working hard to produce results from earthbound systems. At present an array of Stanford-type bar detectors could conceivably detect a supernova popping off in our Milky Way, and the gravitational pulse could be as revealing as a motion picture of the collapse itself. "There's just no other way for us to see this," says Caltech's Kip Thorne, "since the electromagnetic waves emanating from the core are completely absorbed by the outer layers of the star." Gravity waves, on the other hand, can travel freely from the stellar heart. The wave pattern might even reveal the core of the supernova bouncing for a brief moment—squishing down like a pancake and then stretching out like a football before settling down.

But there's a catch. Astronomers estimate that such stellar explosions, and the resulting collapse of the remnant cinders into ultradense neutron stars or black holes, occur in our galaxy only once every 30 years. Even improving the detectors to see out to the Virgo cluster would provide only a few events a year. That's small reward for such a complex enterprise. "But the universe always turns out to be more complicated than we originally think," Fairbank quickly counters. "People almost didn't want to look for X rays in space, believing they just weren't there."

Many Possible Emission Sources

Theorists are sure the same is true for gravitational waves. During the past decade, they've come to suspect that a whole circus of gravity-wave emitters lurk in the heavens:

• Binary neutron stars. Several years ago astronomers from the University of Massachusetts at Amherst discovered that our Milky Way harbors a most interesting stellar couple: two neutron stars orbiting one another about once every eight hours. And the fact that this orbital period is inexorably decreasing is indirect evidence that the binary system is emitting some energy in the form of gravitational radiation. "This type of system is our one, fairly sure bet," says Thorne. Current gravity-wave detectors are too crude to sense this continuous, weak emission. But when those 10-kilometer (6-mile)-wide balls of compact matter finally spiral into one another, they'll release a sizable burst. That isn't likely to happen in the Milky Way anytime soon; the next clash here may be 300 million years from now. "But in the 1990's the Caltech-MIT laser system might be able to see this type of event out to a billion light-years," says Thorne. "At that distance, it's reasonable to expect an event a week."

• Deformed neutron stars. If a city-sized neutron star develops a blemish on its surface— a 2.54-centimeter (1-inch)-high "mountain," for instance—it will continually transmit gravitational waves as that bump rapidly spins round with the star's rotation. "And sudden changes in the frequency of that signal," says Thorne, "would pinpoint 'starquakes,' enabling us, in collaboration with radio, optical, and X-ray astronomers, to study the inner dynamics of a neutron star. In a sense, the gravity-wave antenna would be used as a stellar seismometer."

• Colliding black holes. 'This is my favorite event in terms of the physics that could be learned," says Thorne. "If I had to lay bets on how we'll finally get 100-percent proof that black holes exist, it would be this." Black holes, of course, are those alleged celestial objects so dense that no bit of light or matter can escape their powerful gravitational grip. And if two of them should be orbiting one another, they will eventually spiral in, releasing a unique set of gravitational waves: first, an ever higher pitched whine during the final minute of the fateful twirl, then a cymbal-like crash as the holes coalesce, and finally a ring-down as the merged holes settle down. Gravity-wave antennas that are now on the drawing board have a good chance of seeing these momentous collisions out to the edge of the visible universe. With such a large vista, they could perhaps even see several a day.

"But if I bet money on the first event to be seen," says Thorne, "I'd say it's going to be something we haven't even thought of," just as quasars (highly energetic galaxies located at the edge of our visible universe) had not been imag-

In this artist's rendering, gravity waves travel through the universe moments after two black holes have merged.

ined by even the most farsighted of science-fiction writers before the birth of radio astronomy.

To Many, an Opportunity for Great Reward

Since spurious blips are being received by some detectors now, how will everyone agree that a gravity wave has actually traveled through our neck of the celestial woods? "It would be nice if, one day, four bar detectors and two big laser systems simultaneously detected a pulse, then three days later a supernova were observed in our galaxy," answers Caltech astrophysicist Stan Whitcomb. "That would be the 'Eureka' scenario."

But it's probably wishful thinking. "More likely," he says, "it will be a slow consensus."

It's a gentlemanly race, even though the contenders in this field are not unaware that a Nobel Prize may be their reward. Yet there are still some holdouts in the astronomical community, albeit just a few, who wonder if it's worth the intricate fuss right now, especially since the first gravity wave has yet to be clearly detected.

Fairbank has no such qualms. This courtly scholar, who has already dedicated more than a decade to this chancy endeavor, has a ready answer to these doubting Thomases: "Some of my colleagues remark, 'Why do you want to bother working on gravity waves? You don't know when you'll see a signal.' But I say it's not a gamble. Technology is allowing us to look into regions where we've never looked before. The real objective is not just the race to see who detects gravity waves first, although it's always fun and rewarding when you see something first. Actually, it's the chance to open this new window on the universe. This is the time of one of the greatest opportunities in physics" □

SELECTED READINGS

"Trying to rock with gravity's vibes" by Dietrick E. Thomsen. *Science News,* August 4, 1984.
"Gravitational waves from an orbiting pulsar" by Joel M. Weisberg and others. *Scientific American,* October 1981.

THE 1984 NOBEL PRIZES
Physics and Chemistry

by Elaine Pascoe

The 1984 Nobel Prize in Chemistry was awarded to Dr. R. Bruce Merrifield of Rockefeller University in New York for his work in developing a simplified method of manufacturing complex proteins. Although Americans claimed all of the science prizes in 1983, this award was the only 1984 Nobel to be given to a U.S. scientist.

The prize in physics was shared by two scientists at the European Center for Nuclear Research (CERN) near Geneva, Switzerland—Dr. Carlo Rubbia, an Italian physicist who is also a professor at Harvard University in Cambridge, Massachusetts, and Dr. Simon van der Meer, of the Netherlands. Both were involved in research that led to the discovery of three subatomic particles.

The Prize in Chemistry

Dr. Merrifield's technique, called solid-phase peptide synthesis, is a method of making proteins that involves linking amino acids into chains called peptides. These chains form the proteins that are the basis of life. Merrifield's technique is much faster than earlier methods of protein synthesis and results in higher yields of the end products. The process has made possible the production of important hormones and enzymes, and it is being used in genetic research.

Protein synthesis had been complicated by the fact that each amino acid has at least two reactive sites where it can link up with another amino acid—the amino end (N terminal) and the carboxyl end (C terminal). A scientist seeking to join two amino acids in a specific order would have to block the unwanted terminals (the amino group of one unit and the carboxyl group of the other) so that each amino acid would have only one terminal free. Then, to add a third amino acid, the scientist would have to remove just one of the blocks. Making a 10-unit chain through this method took months, and even with painstaking purification at each step,

as much as 65 percent of the starting materials were lost along the way. Making even longer chains by classical methods of synthesis was considered completely impractical.

Merrifield's idea was to anchor the initial amino acid to a solid support—a polystyrene matrix—and then begin building the chain from

Dr. R. Bruce Merrifield won the 1984 Nobel Prize in Chemistry for devising a new method of making proteins.

UPI/Bettmann Archive

the remaining free terminal. At each stage a simple washing technique is used to remove by-products and excess reagents (substances used for their biological or chemical activities). When the peptide is complete, it is separated from the polystyrene. The method cut manufacturing time from months to days and retained more of the starting materials, which made possible much greater yields of peptides and proteins of high purity.

Merrifield first used his technique in the early 1960's to make the hormone bradykinin, a nine-peptide molecule. He went on to produce more complicated chains, such as ribonuclease, which contains 124 amino acids. This important enzyme is used in research and in the treatment of certain cancers. Solid-phase peptide synthesis has since been used to create a wide range of proteins and peptides, including toxins, protein-growth factor, and various hormones and enzymes. Other researchers have adapted the method to study the synthesis of genetic material.

A key aspect of Merrifield's technique is that it is automated, so that the necessary reagents can be added at set intervals. This has allowed the method to be adapted for the commercial manufacture of important drugs such as high-blood-pressure medicines, and hormones, including insulin. Merrifield's assembly-line approach led the popular press to dub him the Henry Ford of protein synthesis.

R. Bruce Merrifield was born in Fort Worth, Texas, on July 15, 1921. He studied at the University of California at Los Angeles (UCLA), where he earned a bachelor's degree in chemistry in 1943 and a Ph.D. in biochemistry in 1949. While still in school, he worked as a chemist at the Philip R. Park Research Foundation, as a teaching assistant in chemistry at UCLA, and as a research assistant at the UCLA Medical School. In 1949 he joined the faculty of Rockefeller University, then known as the Rockefeller Institute for Medical Research, and in 1983 was named John D. Rockefeller Jr. Professor.

The Prize in Physics

Physicists have long sought evidence to support Albert Einstein's theory that all of nature's forces are unified in a single scheme. The four fundamental forces are gravity; the strong force, which binds nuclear particles together; electromagnetism; and the weak force, which controls radioactive decay. Current theory holds that right after the universe was born in an immense explosion (the Big Bang), electromagnetism and the weak force were identical. It is believed that they separated as the universe cooled and expanded.

The electromagnetic force is transmitted by photons—distinct particles, or quanta, of light energy. Scientists had reasoned that the weak force would be transmitted by similar, yet heavier, particles. The catch was to find the particles, which theoretically would be extremely short-lived and could be produced only by atomic collisions of immense, violent force.

For a long time scientists thought that existing atom-smashing machines would not be able to produce such collisions. But in 1976 Dr. Carlo Rubbia and other scientists thought of a way to modify the largest proton accelerator at CERN for this purpose.

The accelerator ring, which consists of a 6.4-kilometer (4-mile) circular underground tunnel, was originally designed to send protons crashing at high speeds into stationary targets. Rubbia's idea was to accelerate a stream of protons in one direction and send a stream of antiprotons (particles identical to protons but with an opposite electrical charge) racing around in the opposite direction. Collisions between protons and antiprotons would have much more force than any that had yet been produced—enough, it was hoped, to produce the weak-force particles in a manner that would allow them to be detected.

Rubbia campaigned successfully for the conversion of the machine, and led a team of physicists who designed a massive particle detector for the project. They expected that the particles would be extremely rare—perhaps 10 for every 1 billion collisions. Meanwhile, Dr. Simon van der Meer, also a member of the CERN staff, devised a method of keeping the typically turbulent antiprotons tightly bunched while shooting down the center of the tunnel until the moment of collision. Co-workers described Rubbia as the theoretician behind the project and Van der Meer as the technician who made it possible.

In late 1982 and early 1983, their work led to the detection of three subatomic particles—two W particles, one positively charged and one negatively charged, and a neutral Z particle—also known as intermediate vector bosons. The particles' brief existence (less than 1 million million millionth of a second) lent support to the Big-Bang theory of the origin of the universe,

Left: The 1984 Nobel Prize in Physics was shared by Dr. Simon van der Meer (left) and Dr. Carlo Rubbia (right). The men's work led to the discovery of three subatomic particles. Below: The physicists converted this Super Proton Synchrotron into a proton-antiproton collider to detect the particles.

Above: AP/Wide World; Below: CERN

and brought scientists one step closer to proving the unified-force theory.

Carlo Rubbia was born on March 31, 1934, and grew up in Gorizia, Italy. The son of an electrical engineer, he furthered an early interest in electronics with studies at the University of Pisa and then went on to do graduate work in high-energy physics at Columbia University in New York and the University of Rome. In 1960 he joined the staff of CERN, where he is a senior physicist.

Since the early 1970's Rubbia has also taught physics at Harvard University, making frequent trips between Geneva and Cambridge. Besides his work on the W and Z particles, he also headed a team of scientists that found evidence of another particle, the top quark, during 1984.

Simon van der Meer was born in The Hague, in the Netherlands, on November 24, 1924. He studied at the Higher Technical School in Delft and then worked in the physics laboratory of the Dutch Phillips Company doing electron microscopy. He later earned a degree in physical engineering from the Technical University in Delft, and then joined CERN in 1956, two years after its founding. His work there brought him an honorary doctorate from the University of Geneva in 1983 □

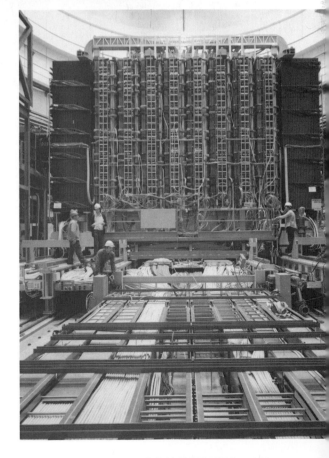

TECHNOLOGY

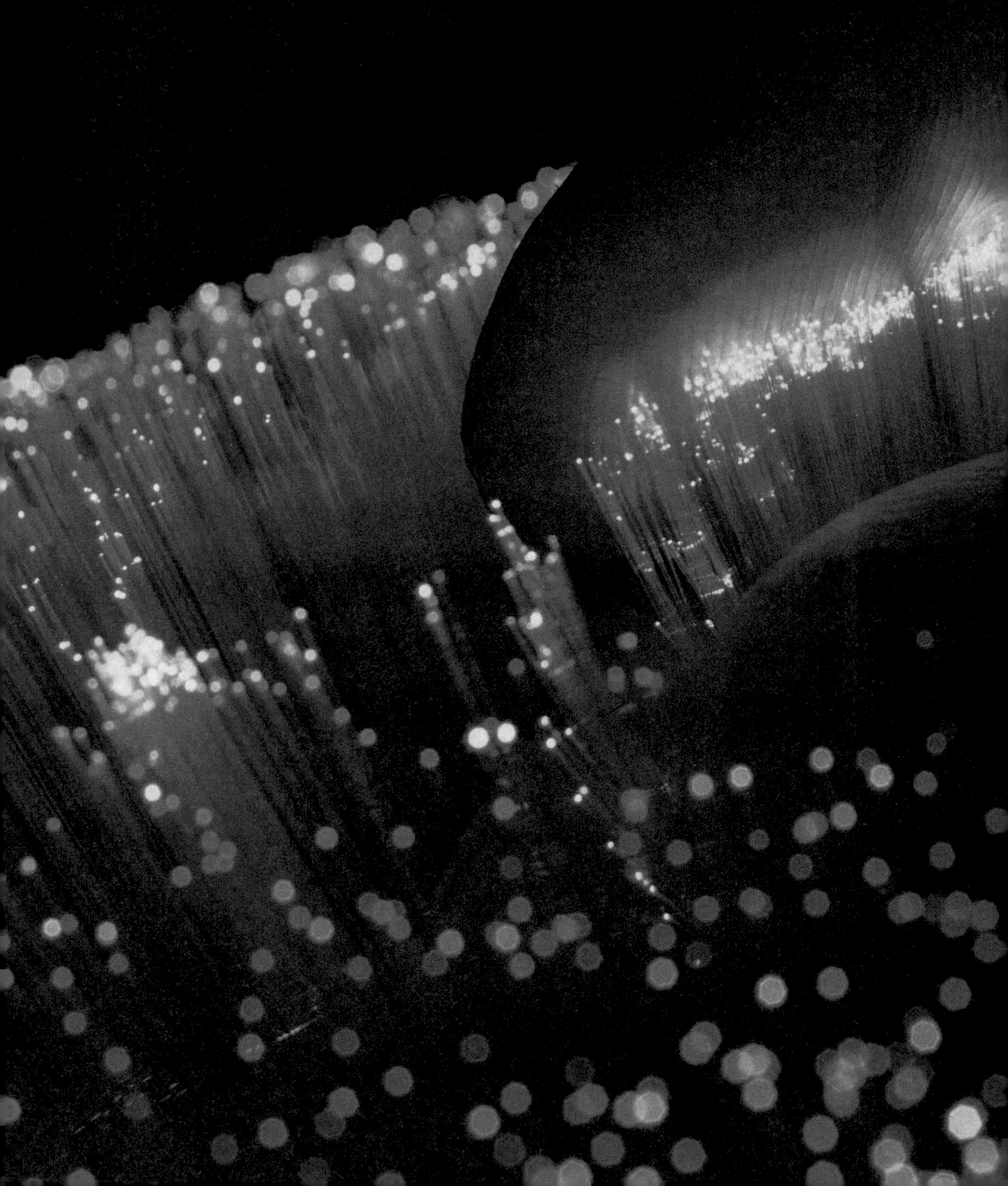

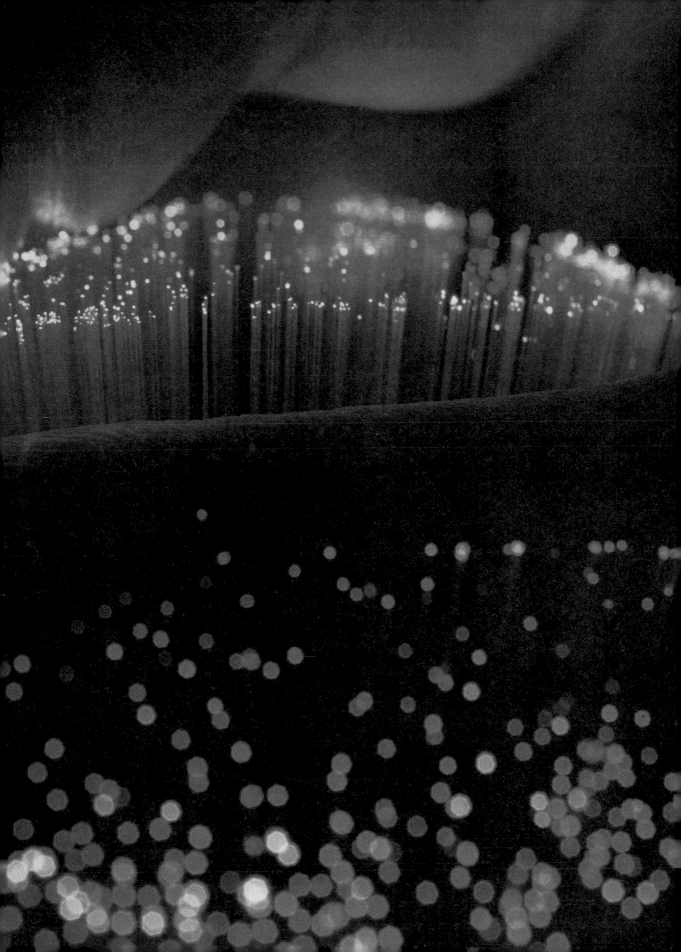

Mitsubishi Electric

Mitsubishi Electric Corporation designed and developed the world's first spiral escalator—a revolutionary departure in concept from the standard linear pattern. The new escalator is a major engineering achievement.

REVIEW OF THE YEAR

TECHNOLOGY

Television technology received much attention in 1984 with the introduction of stereophonic broadcasting, digital-signal processing, and a pocket-sized color receiver. Even black-and-white film took on color when it was transferred by a special process onto videotape. Computer-aided design helped to create new types of loudspeakers and escalators that wind around corners. The use of lasers as research instruments and in consumer applications also increased as researchers pushed lasers deeper into the infrared and X-ray regions of the electromagnetic spectrum (the entire range of wavelengths of electromagnetic radiation, including gamma rays, X rays, ultraviolet, visible light, infrared, to the longest radio waves), and manufacturers developed an inexpensive high-quality laser printer for use with personal computers.

TELEVISION'S CHANGING PICTURE AND SOUND

Television added a new sound in 1984 when about 10 television stations in the United States began stereophonic broadcasting. The Zenith Electronics Corporation developed a system in which three separate sound-carrying signals are transmitted in the space previously allotted for one. The main signal carries sound that can be received by any television set, while a component at a higher frequency carries the extra information needed to produce stereophonic sound. Another component can be used to transmit an entirely different audio signal, allowing stations, for example, to broadcast sound in an additional language.

The latest step in miniature television sets came from Japan's Hattori Seiko Company, which introduced the first flat-screen, liquid-crystal-display television capable of producing a color image. About the size of a small transistor, Seiko's "Elf" has a 5-centimeter (2-inch) diagonal screen. It uses a thin layer of rod-shaped, liquid-crystal molecules sandwiched between two polarizers. When an electric field is applied, the crystals reorient so that light is absorbed by the top polarizer to create a black spot, or "pixel." An array of tiny transistors made from a thin film of silicon deposited on a glass plate turns each of the 52,800 pixels in the display "on" and "off," creating an image. Microscopic red, blue, and green filters over the pixels provide color.

Digital-television sets began to appear in 1984. These sets promise crisper pictures and the elimination of "ghosts," the double images that sometimes ruin reception in cities and mountainous areas. In a digital television, tiny integrated-circuit chips handle the processing and storage of digital information. This technology allows viewers to split the screen for watching several channels at once, to freeze a particular picture, or to zoom in for close-ups. (See "New Technology for Television" on page 343.)

Digital artistry and computers also brought color to Cary Grant's eyes and Ginger Rogers' dresses in movies that were originally filmed in black and white. Two companies—Vidcolor Image in Toronto, Canada, and Color Systems Technology in Los Angeles, California—use similar processes to produce color videotapes from old films. An artist uses a computer-controlled graphics tablet and an electronic palette to hand-color three key frames at the beginning, middle, and end of each distinct scene in a videotaped film. The computer colors in the intervening frames by judging how much the luminosity has changed and how much movement has occurred from one frame to the next.

SWEETER SPEAKER SOUNDS

The production of true bass has required large speakers—until now. After a 14-year research effort, Bose Corporation has succeeded in packing a lot of bass into a little box. The company's new "acoustic wave" loudspeaker allows a portable high-fidelity (hi-fi) system to reproduce deep, full-bodied, low-frequency sounds although the enclosure consists merely of an 11.5-centimeter (4.5 inch) speaker mounted in a chamber smaller than a shoe box. Providing the key to the new design are two wave guides—essentially, long tubes—folded into a convoluted, computer-designed maze of passages. The chambers encourage the formation of standing waves that amplify the speaker cone's movements, thus reducing the large motions—and large enclosures—previously needed to produce true bass.

UP THE ROUND ESCALATOR

For more than 80 years, escalators have been going straight up and down. That changed in 1984 with the announcement of an innovative escalator that takes a longer, circular path to go from floor to floor. Since the angle between the top and bottom ends can be as great as 180 degrees, the new escalator can easily turn a corner or grandly sweep around a massive pillar. The design was a triumph for engineers at the Mitsubishi Electric Industrial Corporation in Japan, and required many computer calculations and numerically controlled tools to fashion the steps individually. Although the new escalators are at least three times more expensive than conventional ones, orders are coming in steadily.

BREAKTHROUGHS IN LASER TECHNOLOGY

Researchers have long hoped to construct a laser that emits X rays. In 1984 two groups—one at Princeton University in New Jersey and the other at Lawrence Livermore National Laboratory in California—brought lasers to the edge of the X-ray portion of the electromagnetic spectrum. In both sets of experiments, light from visible or infrared lasers is used to vaporize small samples of a solid material (such as carbon or the metal selenium) to create a plasma, or ionized gas. When one ion in the plasma loses its energy by emitting light of a certain wavelength, it triggers the same process in other ions, producing an avalanche of "soft" X rays—all with the same wavelength and in phase. Other materials, it is believed, could produce the kind of "hard" (shorter-wavelength) X rays used in medical devices. These would be useful for getting three-dimensional pictures of internal organs and of large molecules such as genes or proteins.

Lasers were also pushed into the far-infrared region during the year. Physicists at the University of California in Santa Barbara announced the development of the first powerful, tunable, free-electron laser to operate in the far-infrared region of the spectrum. By tuning the laser light to particular wavelengths, researchers can study the motions of atoms and molecules, particularly in solids and liquids.

Until recently, laser printers—powerful, fast, quiet machines—were too expensive for widespread use in the office or home. This began to change in 1984 when Canon of Japan brought out a much more affordable laser unit, which became part of new products such as Hewlett-Packard's Laserjet printer. Such printers work somewhat like photocopying machines. Flashing infrared-laser light plays across the surface of a positively charged rotating drum, neutralizing the charge wherever it hits. Positively charged "ink" sticks to these uncharged regions to form the letters and figures, and then is transferred onto paper. An entire page takes about seven seconds to print.

IVARS PETERSON

BUILDING THE ULTIMATE WEAPONS

by Janet Raloff

It is still a matter of wonder how the Martians are able to slay men so swiftly and so silently. Many think . . . they are able to generate an intense heat. . . . This intense heat they project in a parallel beam against any object they choose by means of a polished parabolic mirror of unknown composition. . . . Whatever is combustible flashes into flame at its touch, lead runs like water, it softens iron, cracks and melts glass, and when it falls upon water, incontinently that explodes into steam.
—H. G. Wells, *The War of the Worlds,* 1898

Science fiction has spellbound generations with fantastic tales of "death rays," like that prophetic 19th-century account by Wells. What the U.S. Department of Defense (DOD) would like to do is give life to that fantasy. But as scores of physicists have been learning for the past quarter of a century, fashioning a directed-energy weapon is easier said than done.

Technological Obstacles Abound

In fact, the term death ray is somewhat misleading, as these weapons are not being explored to stop troops dead in their tracks. In terms of their human lethality, beam weapons are just not as cost-effective as bullets. However, mere cannons and bullets are a weak defense against intercontinental salvos (simultaneously released bombs or projectiles) flying fast and heavy—and packing a punch that could knock out cities. Able to travel at the speed of light (light travels 300,000 kilometers, or 186,000 miles, per second), or close to it, beams of directed energy may be the only way of effectively routing such munitions semiautonomously at split-second speed, and from great distances.

However, progress toward this or any simpler beam-weapons application has meant hurdling one scientific obstacle after another. The problem has been to identify a technology able to deliver the destructive power a weapon would require in a package that is practical and affordable. Having already knocked planes and missiles from the sky with lasers, it might seem DOD was well on its way to achieving that. Not necessarily. In fact, it's unlikely a fully integrated weapons system could even be tested before the turn of the century. As new missions, new physics, and new candidate technologies

present themselves, researchers have to start all over, because in the beginning it's often hard to guess how well candidates will survive the practical constraints of making a reliable weapon.

Consider, for example, an early technology that suggested promise and yielded disenchantment: the carbon dioxide gas laser. In his book *Beam Weapons: The Next Arms Race,* laser-research analyst Jeff Hecht recalls the problem researchers had scaling it up from a laboratory curiosity. "To increase power, developers often resorted to the brute-force approach of enlarging the laser," he says. But that wasn't good enough here because the device reached "monstrous proportions" before it yielded beam power sufficient to be useful. Hecht observes, "This was the sort of laser that prompted someone whose name is lost to history to crack that 'a laser big enough to inflict militarily significant damage wouldn't even have to work—just *drop* it on the enemy.' "

Potentials of Directed-Energy Weapons Explored

Though DOD has studied particle-beam technologies even longer than it has funded laser work, the particle-beam program still has not established what the Pentagon terms "proof of concept." So this program doesn't focus on weapons, per se, but instead on demonstrating characteristics—such as firing rate, "bolt" velocity, and beam control—that would be needed in a weapon.

Spurring interest in these beams of accelerated atomic particles—usually electrons and hydrogen nuclei—is not only their potential for inflicting more damage than lasers, but also their ability to wreak the damage more quickly: They have been called "the ultimate weapon." Keith Taggart is assistant to the deputy associate director for strategic-defense research at Los Alamos National Laboratory in New Mexico, where work is under way exploring beams of uncharged particles for use in space. According to Taggart, particle beams today are at least on a par with lasers in terms of having suggested a weapons potential, and may in fact lead lasers in engineering. That such a statement would not have been accepted five years ago, let alone 10, points to the magnitude of reshuffling that has occurred among leading technology candidates in recent years.

In fact, the cast of available candidates is still evolving, the result of a continuing stream of new developments in the applicable physics.

Opposite: An artist's view of particle-beam weapons intercepting intercontinental ballistic missiles.

Similarly, new missions being considered for directed-energy weapons are changing the criteria—such as allowable size, weight, and "kill" reliability—by which the ultimate front-running candidates will be chosen.

For instance, since President Reagan, in a 1983 speech now remembered as the "Star Wars" speech, called for the development of technology to render Soviet intercontinental ballistic missiles (ICBMs) "impotent and obsolete," the beam-weapons program has focused increasingly on assessing its potential for strategic-defense missions. Chief among these new missions is one known as "boost-phase intercept." The most profitable time to kill an ICBM is in its boost phase, before its many warheads and decoys have been deployed. Though boost-phase intercept is today virtually impossible, beam weapons could change that.

In addition to particle beams, the technologies now appearing to offer the most promise for directed-energy weapons belong to three classes of lasers able to generate short-wavelength beams. As one Pentagon official put it "you want as short a wavelength as possible."

And that's why the hydrogen fluoride chemical laser is falling from favor. Still the best-developed laser technology of military interest, hydrogen fluoride's infrared wavelength is drawing too much heat from program critics for DOD to comfortably count on it as much more than an understudy to more immature, but promising, shorter-wavelength alternatives.

Short-Wavelength Beams Show Promise

Several factors are driving this push to smaller wavelengths. Among these is concern over beam spread. Since beam spread reduces the energy deposited per unit area on a target, it's important to limit it as much as possible by making the ratio of mirror size to beam wavelength very large. Taggart puts it another way: For any energy flux per unit area on a target that is chosen, the smaller the wavelength of light beamed, the smaller the mirror needed to direct that beam. "The effect is substantial," he notes. To deliver a 1.2-meter (4-foot) spot onto a target 1,000 kilometers (620 miles) away, he says, a laser with a 10-micron (10 millionths of a meter) wavelength [which would be in the infrared portion of the electromagnetic spectrum—the entire range of wavelengths of electromagnetic radiation including, in decreasing order, radio waves, microwaves, infrared, visible, ultraviolet, X rays, and gamma rays] would need a 10-meter (33-foot) mirror, while a laser with a 1-micron (1 millionth of a meter) wavelength [approaching the visible range of the electromagnetic spectrum] would need only a 1-meter (3.3-foot)-diameter mirror. "And there's a big difference between building a one-meter mirror and a 10-meter mirror," Taggart adds.

A second advantage to shorter wavelengths is that they tend to be absorbed better by the target. And a target can sustain damage only if the laser radiation incident upon it is absorbed.

This depiction shows a space-based laser satellite defense weapon hitting a target with an infrared beam.

DOD

The recently developed free-electron laser shown here proves power can be harnessed at short wavelengths.

Kosta Tsipis is director of the Program in Science and Technology for International Security at the Massachusetts Institute of Technology (MIT) in Cambridge. In his book *Arsenal: Understanding Weapons in the Nuclear Age,* he explains: "Only four percent of the light from an infrared laser illuminating a shiny aluminum target will be absorbed by it. The other 96 percent would be reflected and cause no damage to the target. On the other hand, ultraviolet radiation is largely absorbed by metallic surfaces [like those on a missile], so more than half of the energy of an ultraviolet laser that reached a target would cause damage."

There is a trade-off in moving to shorter wavelengths, though. The degree to which the atmosphere absorbs some of the beam's energy is also a function of wavelength. The shorter the wavelength, the more susceptible a high-energy beam is to experiencing jitter and defocusing, also known as "thermal blooming." Since lasers in the vacuum above Earth's atmosphere don't have to confront the problems of beam degradations caused by air, space has been called the laser's natural environment. And in fact, for the very-short-wavelength lasers, it is the only environment in which they have any value.

X-Ray Laser Most Exotic Short-Wavelength Device

Of these newer, short-wavelength alternatives, the excimer is most similar to chemical lasers in that its energy is also derived from the reaction between two types of atoms. A stream of electrons is used to create the "excited dimers," or excimers; these molecules can form only when their constituent atoms have been chemically excited and stripped of some electrons.

Two excimers, the xenon-fluoride and krypton-fluoride, have been identified as having weapons potential. However, the excimer molecule's short lifetimes means "the laser tends to produce only short pulses, which may not be useful for weaponry," according to Hecht. What's more, pulsed operation creates acoustic (sound) waves that can disrupt a laser's beam. Excimer lasers are particularly susceptible to that, Hecht points out, "because their short wavelength makes small aberrations more significant." Then there is the problem of scaling up to high power; the best excimer today has an average power less than one-tenth of 1 percent of what is possible with the best chemical lasers.

The free-electron laser could offer the best hope for harnessing high power at short wave-

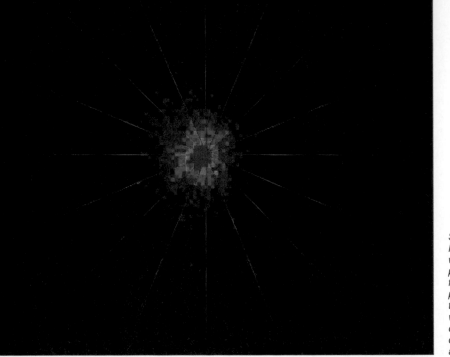

Scientists at Sandia National Laboratories, working to create a powerful X-ray laser, focused the beams of a particle accelerator on trapped argon gas, which released a burst of X rays as seen in this computer-enhanced image of the event.

Sandia National Laboratories

lengths. Conceived in 1971 and demonstrated for the first time five years later, this system uses a particle accelerator to bring a beam of electrons up to high velocity. The beam is then passed through an array of permanent magnets, known as a "wiggler" for the way its tailored variations in magnetic-field strength and direction deform the beam path. As electrons pass each of the wiggler's component magnets, their paths bend, a process that causes them to emit and absorb light. With the right magnetic-field design, the electrons will emit more light than they absorb. One only has to put mirrors at the right places to have a free-electron laser.

Though the initial free-electron experiment produced a beam having an infrared wavelength, in fact the laser is "tunable"—able to yield shorter wavelengths well into the ultraviolet—by changing magnet spacing and the electrons' input energy. Among its other advantages is a theoretical efficiency (percentage of energy entering the laser that is emitted in its beam) of between 30 and 50 percent—more than tenfold better than with chemical lasers. Its disadvantage, relative to excimers and chemical lasers, is the size and weight of its particle accelerator/wiggler package: hoisting them into orbit could prove not only difficult but also costly.

By far the most exotic and controversial of the short-wavelength lasers is the nuclear-powered X ray. Having a small nuclear explo-

sion as its energy source, its development and physics have, not surprisingly, been kept quite secret.

This laser concept, rejected in 1977 for having little apparent military value, is again under serious investigation by DOD's Advanced Research Projects Agency (DARPA). Much of DARPA's renewed interest is being credited to Edward Teller, a senior research fellow at the Hoover Institute on Stanford University's campus, and the physicist largely responsible for development of the hydrogen bomb. Teller has proposed that an X-ray laser could be packed aboard a missile and "popped up," or fired into space, at the first sighting of preparations for a Soviet ICBM launch. A single device would have up to 50 separate lasing rods—each able to independently target a separate missile or satellite.

Because its X-ray emissions are so efficiently absorbed by Earth's atmosphere, such a laser weapon has utility only in space. On the other hand, because its wavelength is so extremely short, any targets hit would absorb the beam's energy with devastating efficiency. The X-ray laser is also a one-shot device; the bomb that generates the energy to excite atoms in the device's lasing material will eventually vaporize the works. However, because X rays travel at the speed of light, they will get out before the device self-destructs.

Building a Battle Station

To develop a working X-ray laser battle station would be a truly awesome engineering marvel. The most detailed and accessible account of what would be involved appears in a chapter in Hecht's *Beam Weapons*. For instance, the typical battle station now being discussed would have 50 individual lasing rods, each one being a hairlike carbon fiber roughly 1 centimeter (0.4 inch) long and one ten-thousandth that in diameter. To identify targets and direct each laser's energy to them, each rod would need a separate pointing and tracking system. Not only could the alignment of each end of the hairlike rods be off no more than one-tenth of 1 percent, but this precise alignment would have to be able to withstand vibrations set up when the bomb detonates. They would be substantial vibrations, too; this fragile system could unleash trillions of watts of power during just one-trillionth of a second.

Such intense energy bursts could shatter a target. Lasers that deliver a continuous lower-power flux of energy could, if their beams were focused onto a small region of a target's surface, literally burn a hole through it and into the vulnerable electronic-guidance components and fuel. Lasers that deliver their energy in short, discrete pulses may be even more effective "killers" if they can heat the target enough to generate a plasma (ionized gas) in front of it. Laboratory tests have already demonstrated that subsequent heating of this plasma can produce shock waves destructive enough to rip open a target's skin.

Explains Herbert Flicker at Los Alamos: "The plasma has a higher absorption for the laser energy," so it absorbs more of the initial laser energy, and then reradiates it to the metal surface of the target using a shorter wavelength. "The net effect is a more efficient coupling [absorption of laser energy]," he says, "because you've destroyed the good reflectivity of the metal and replaced it with the reflectivity of the plasma, which is fairly low."

Propagating Beams in Space

When it comes to potent devastation, however, nothing can hold a candle to particle beams. DOD's research is focusing on two varieties: charged beams of energetic electrons and neutral beams of hydrogen atoms.

Charged particle beams are for travel through Earth's atmosphere. Though like-charged particles, such as electrons, normally repel each other, the large electric currents in a

An artist's drawing shows a satellite surveillance system detecting strategic aircraft with an infrared sensor.

DOD

beam moving through the atmosphere actually set up a strong magnetic field about the beam. This field effectively pinches the electrons into a tight, self-focusing beam.

This self-focusing works only within the atmosphere, however. In space, a charged beam would quickly disperse. Moreover, charged beams traveling long distances in space—something most space-based missions would require—would be bent by Earth's magnetic field in ways that would be almost impossible to predict. Finally, propagating charged beams in space would cause what's known as a "space charge" to build up on the particle accelerator itself, explains a DOD official: The result is that one would "need more and more energy to overcome that space charge that's not satisfied by a return current of ions and electrons created in the atmosphere."

This also explains why particles beamed in space must be electrically neutral. However, because particles must carry a charge to be accelerated to the high velocity and energy needed of a weapon, neutral beams are created by stripping electrons off an already accelerated beam of negatively charged particles. (Currently, DOD is planning tests of neutral beams made from accelerated negatively charged hy-

drogen atoms.) Not only are neutral beams in space immune to Earth's magnetic field, but they also keep their tight focus without magnetic pinching. That tight beam control would break down, of course, if the beam strayed into the atmosphere.

All this might suggest that propagating beams is easy, provided the right type of beam is used in the environment. Not so. Yet to be established in any environment is how to get a straight beam that travels distances "of military interest" without losing most of its energy, and one that can be "slewed" (swept from target to target like a flashlight's beam) with control.

At Lawrence Livermore National Laboratory (LLNL) in California, charged particle-beam studies using the new 50 million-electron-volt Advanced Test Accelerator (ATA) aim to acquire the first meaningful data on the possible range and stability of 10-kiloamp electron beams in air.

Previous tests of charged beams in full atmosphere have been conducted at low energies. And under those conditions, "the beam sort of falls apart," explains William Barletta, program leader for LLNL's beam research. The problem is that as the beam attempts to tunnel its way through air, some of its electrons collide

In tests of a laser system a gold-plated copper sphere is vaporized by converging carbon-dioxide laser beams.

In a neutral particle beam accelerator being tested at Los Alamos National Laboratory, a system of blades modulates an electric field that accelerates a hydrogen-ion beam.

Los Alamos National Laboratory

with air molecules and leave their energy behind as heat. Says Barletta: "Under normal conditions, the [beam] pulse will lose half of its energy after 300 meters [985 feet]"—hardly the range weapons planners envision. However, because the energy lost in heating causes the air to expand and become less dense, later electrons traveling down the beam path encounter fewer energy-robbing collisions. It's possible that propagation over long distances may be possible by shooting off each large "bolt" of high-energy particles as a string of tiny, discrete pulses, he says.

Destructive and Deadly

If these ATA tests prove successful, DOD may be on the road to developing a weapon with the ability to selectively strike and kill tens of targets a second. Charged-particle beams might be used in defending battleships from cruise missiles, in defending U.S. missile silos from incoming Soviet ICBMs, or in defending national command centers against bombers and air-launched short-range missiles.

Make no mistake: These would be potent weapons. Unlike laser beams, particles deposit their energy in a long, narrow cone throughout the target. High-energy electrons, for instance, can penetrate a few feet into solid aluminum. This penetrating ability makes the effective shielding of targets against them virtually impossible. A missile hit by a weapon beaming energetic electrons would undergo structural damage and experience nearly instantaneous detonation of any chemical explosives on board.

In addition to the destruction inflicted by the particles' transfer of kinetic energy (energy associated with motion) to any material attempting to slow them, there is the generation of potent secondary radiation. Army Major Charles Kinney described this phenomenon in the February 1983 *Military Electronics/Countermeasures:* "Surrounding the beam during its transit to the target is a cone of lethal gamma radiation . . . produced through the interaction of the relativistic electrons [those traveling at almost the speed of light] with molecules of air in the path of the beam. This radiation is extremely penetrating and could cause radiation sickness and death to crew members inside combat vehicles. Additionally, very strong electromagnetic pulses [high-intensity electromagnetic radiation] would be induced because of the electron-current passage through the atmosphere. . . ." And that electromagnetic-pulse

(EMP) radiation—which might even occur as electrons are knocked from atoms in the target's structural materials—is particularly lethal to electronic components.

Researchers working on the White Horse experiment at Los Alamos National Laboratory are focusing on propagation of a high-intensity neutral beam. Experimentally, all components of the system have been demonstrated to work. The goal of this project is therefore to verify that the integrated system performs; "You never know it works until you turn it on and try it out," Taggart explains. Moreover, he adds, it will test whether the hydrogen-ion source and particle-injector components—now "with a size that can be put into space"—perform as expected.

Asked whether there were any fundamental questions as to why this system might not work, Taggart answered: "None whatsoever. If it doesn't, it means we screwed something up" in the engineering. And it's because its success is dependent only on engineering, Taggart says, that "the particle beam is out in front of the pack." When it comes to what still needs to be demonstrated, he says, "We're talking about engineering, where the other directed-energy-weapons concepts [such as lasers] are still thinking about physics."

He points out, for example, that accelerator technology, already more than half a century old, is relatively mature. "Accelerators already operate at particle energies that are clearly useful for a weapon," he notes. What's more, there also exist high-current machines (current is a function of the particle density in the beam). What's needed to demonstrate the particle beam's weapons potential is high energy and high current in the same machine.

Not everyone shares Taggart's assessment, however. The Pentagon still describes DOD's particle-beam development as lagging considerably behind that of lasers (by 10 years or so, one usually hears). Moreover, one DOD official said that unlike lasers, particle beams have never "shot things down"; all of their targets have been immobile and in the laboratory. Nonetheless, it's Taggart's belief that "the Pentagon is slowly changing its mind" and coming to "acknowledge that particle beams are on the same developmental time scale as lasers."

Major Concerns Regarding "Star Wars" Policy

Even among those vocal critics of President Reagan's "Star Wars" policy, there is generally strong support for some level of continuing DOD investigation of directed-energy technologies. But criticism has exploded over the following:

• Spending on these and related "Star Wars" technologies. The Pentagon has proposed spending $22 billion through 1989 just to assess the technical feasibility of a ballistic-missile defense (BMD) that pivots about the availability of exotic directed-energy technologies. If a commitment to proceed with full-scale BMD were made, upward of $300 billion, perhaps $500 billion, might be necessary.

• Whether to develop such antisatellite- and antiballistic-missile weapons, the testing of which might violate existing arms-control treaties.

• Whether rendering Soviet ICBMs and satellites impotent would be more militarily destabilizing or less.

• Whether the Strategic Defense Initiative's (SDI's) vision of BMD is even technologically credible. Senator William Proxmire of Wisconsin summed up this argument in June 1984 in floor debate over SDI's proposed budget. "Even General James Abrahamson, the new chief of SDI, testified before the Senate . . . that the [Star Wars] defense system would be 'highly effective'—not perfect." Said Proxmire: Experts have testified that even if the "Star Wars" comprehensive defense "were 99 percent effective, enough Soviet warheads would get through to destroy every major city in the United States with a population over 500,000."

• And finally, whether by advocating development of a "Star Wars" defense the administration might risk raising false hopes and perpetuating the myth that the United States might be spared devastation in any nuclear exchange.

Jeff Hecht speaks for many when he says, "The best we can hope is not that beam weapons will end the arms race, but that they will buy us the time we need to end it" □

SELECTED READINGS

Beam Weapons: The Next Arms Race by Jeff Hecht. Plenum Press, 1984.

"Space-based ballistic-missile defense" by Hans A. Bethe et al. *Scientific American,* October 1984.

"Beam weapons: DOD's high-tech gamble" by Janet Raloff. *Science News,* July 14, 1984.

"Directed energy weapons—where are they headed" by Barbara G. Levi. *Physics Today,* August 1983.

John Stuart

The Great MACHINE COMPETITION

by Dr. Crypton

O n a brisk Saturday afternoon in November 1984, Harvard University was losing to Yale University in their annual football fest on the banks of the Charles River in Cambridge, Massachusetts. Just a ways downstream, at the Massachusetts Institute of Technology (MIT), 180 weary upperclassmen, wielding soldering irons and hot-melt-glue guns, were preparing for MIT's most frenetic sports event—The Harvest—a four-hour-long, remote-controlled battle of robotic Ping-Pong-ball reapers.

The Contest Objective

Come 7:00 P.M. Monday, 180 primitive machines—among them the "Deathmobile," the "Love Tractor," and "Die for Judy"—will compete one-on-one in a single-elimination tournament to see which machine can harvest Ping-Pong balls best. The stadium is room 26-100, the largest lecture hall on campus, and it will be packed with more than 1,000 cheering and jeering students, parents, professors, alumni, MIT administrators, and executives from the corporate world of engineering. The playing field is a 1.2-meter by 1.8-meter (4-foot by 6-foot) table with a slight, width-wide depression in the center that holds the "crop," a single layer of 300 Ping-Pong balls. (This is not as many balls as it sounds; in traversing the

Above: The "Deathmobile," assembled from hodge-podge parts, was the best ball reaper in a crazy competition at the Massachusetts Institute of Technology.

width of the table, they cover an area only 30.5 centimeters [12 inches] wide.)

The goal of each round, or "reap-off," which lasts a mere 30 seconds, is to harvest more of the crop than the opposing machine. Each harvester is remote-controlled by a button that supplies 5 volts (a volt is a standard unit of electrical potential difference) and a multidirectional joystick (hand-control device) that supplies a range of voltage. The machines start at opposite ends of the table, in front of a gutter into which the balls are collected. Each gutter is gently sloped so that the accumulating balls roll to one corner and drop into a transparent vertical cylinder. By comparing the balls' height in each cylinder, the spectators can tell at a glance which machine is winning.

Masterminding the Perfect Task

The man behind this madness is Woodie Flowers, associate professor of mechanical engineering. Each year for more than a decade, this gentle, bespectacled imp has organized a competition between student-built machines in course 2.70—"Introduction to Design," which mechanical-engineering majors have to take. What Flowers wants the machines to do changes from year to year. In 1976 he wanted them to play tug-of-war in a sandbox. In 1980, in the Skinny Dip competition, he wanted them to "swim" 1.5 meters (5 feet), jump up and grab a

suspended aluminum rod, and swim some more. In 1981, in the MIT Arms Race, he wanted them to put round pegs into square holes. But whatever he fancies the machines doing, the ground rules of the contest are always the same. Seven weeks before the competition, each student is given an identical kit of rudimentary materials and told to build a machine that will perform a specific silly task well.

Flowers and the nine other instructors who team-teach course 2.70 spend months coming up with a task. If they make it too difficult, few machines will be able to do it, let alone do it well. If they make it too easy, there will be little variation in the design and performance of the machines—and that, says Flowers, would be "no fun at all."

At an early point in planning The Harvest, Flowers changed the playing surface because he feared an obvious optimal strategy: a machine that would fire a huge net over the balls and then pull them back in one big sweep. "It would be a contest between nets—who could fire theirs the fastest," says Flowers, "and I think that would be rather boring." To prevent this possibility, he put up three 41-centimeter (16-inch) poles at 36-centimeter (14-inch) intervals across the center of the table. "If you're going to build a net now, you'll have to be really ingenious so that it doesn't get stuck on the poles. Still, a net might be a good idea. But, believe me, if someone

A fascinated crowd looks on as two students put their innovative machines to the test during the contest play-offs.

Ethan Hoffman/Archive

does build a net, someone else will build an antinet—two prongs sticking up to catch the net."

Kits Contain Imaginative Array of Parts

Having settled on Ping-Pong ball harvesting as the task, Flowers had to come up with the parts for 180 identical kits. "Each year," he says, "we try to build more and more real engineering experience into the contest. The first kits had rubber bands and razor blades and pieces of paper and tongue depressors and pipe cleaners. Now each kit is worth at least $100. Some of the parts are quite sophisticated, thanks to the generosity of corporate donors. This year there are two gutsy gear motors from TRW [Incorporated]. There's also a small solenoid [a coil of wire through which an electric current is sent to produce a magnetic field], a constant-force spring and a little camera motor donated by Polaroid [Corporation], from the 600 series, I think."

Flowers proudly displays the other items in the kit: three rubber bands; a Ping-Pong ball; cardboard tubes; plastic and aluminum tubing; sheets of plastic, Masonite, and aluminum; two cardboard boxes; a large plastic bag; a small mirror; two polarizing lenses; three steel shafts; six welding rods; a cloth band; cord; a string ladder; two hose clamps; rubber stoppers; rubber and plastic bushing (cylindrical lining); wire; seven gears; two rivets; two paper clips; a battery clip; a four-pin connector; a tongue depressor; a stick of hot-melt glue; a wooden slat; a small metal plate; two plastic gadgets with three vanes; two pen points encased in wood; and one-third of a cup of mixed widgets (tiny, high-precision parts). In spite of Flowers's contagious enthusiasm, it is hard to imagine building anything out of these parts, never mind a Ping-Pong-ball reaper that outperforms its compatriots.

The Countdown Begins

At 2:00 P.M. on Saturday, two days before the contest, many of the 2.70 students are constructing their harvesters in a huge, stuffy, subterranean machine shop. Some students have spent more time here during the past few weeks than anywhere else. A small room off the shop contains two tables for testing the machines.

2:20 P.M. Saturday. Megan Smith puts her machine on one of the test tables. The basis of her design is a one-way rake with hinged prongs. As the rake slides over the crop of balls,

the prongs swing back so that the balls can pass under it. The prongs then return to their original, vertical position so that as the rake is retracted, it pulls balls into the gutter. The rake is mounted on a two-wheeled cart powered by the TRW motors. One of the most constraining rules of the contest requires each harvester to initially occupy an area no larger than 36 by 36 by 36 centimeters (14 by 14 by 14 inches). To comply with this rule, Megan has divided her rake into two 33-centimeter (13-inch) pieces, mounted side by side to the front of the cart in an upright position. When the cart moves forward, the pieces swing down, one to each side, like flapping wings, to form one 26-inch-long horizontal rake. "I call it the 'Maltese Falcon,'" says Megan. "It collects zillions of balls by itself. But when it's up against an offensive machine, I don't know."

2:35 P.M. Saturday. Out in the shop, sophomore Eric Heatzig, a mechanical-engineering major ("until today," he says, joking), is building an offensive projectile for use against one-way rakes. The projectile consists of two nasty-looking metal sea urchins connected by string netting. Eric's machine catapults the projectile over the crop into the opponent's court, where, the harvest gods willing, it gets tangled in the opponent's rake. But it is not sufficient, the rules say, simply to disable the other machine. To win, you must also harvest at least one ball. For this, Eric has also built a rake, which, unlike Megan's, is launched and then reeled in by string. He'll have only one shot at harvesting the balls, but that's all it should take if the projectile does its job.

In practice, however, there's a little problem. The rake doesn't go far enough; it falls short of the balls. "It's too heavy," says Eric. "I'm thinking of putting wheels on it, so that after I fire it, it will roll into the balls before I pull it back. This is driving me crazy. I think I'll call the machine 'Disaster.'"

Across the shop Michael Hollins, a junior, is perfecting another kind of rake-jamming projectile. He plans to fire a large V-shaped piece of metal tubing at the center post. The arms of the V will fall in the opponent's court and presumably interfere with his harvesting. The ingenuity of the design is a trip mechanism by which the crotch of the V locks onto the post so that it cannot be pushed out of the way. "It works like a dream," says Michael.

"The real goal is to stop the other guy," says Jean Alpers, admiring Michael's machine.

"There's a Ping-Pong ball in the kit, you know. I thought, why not disguise the ball and tie a string around it? So when the other machine grabs it, you pull the machine over to your side and beat it up."

2:55 P.M. Saturday. Bruce Main, a junior, enters the test room and unfolds a net 1.2 meters (4 feet) long by 5 centimeters (2 inches) wide. His idea is to fire the net at the poles. When it hits them, it is supposed to drop down into the crop of balls on his side of the net. Then he'll reel it in. "I realize," says Bruce, "that I can get only half the balls, but half should be enough to win. I'm the only one with a net. Either it's an incredibly good idea, or else everyone considered it and rejected it for some reason I'm missing."

3:00 P.M. Saturday. Eric Chan, a senior majoring in biology, walks into the test room carrying a large cardboard box. A few students are testing carts that have snowplows and cowcatchers on the front that work by shoving the balls into the gutter. They have not yet seen Eric's machine, called "Simply 2," and they stop what they're doing and watch suspiciously as he takes it out of the box. "Simply 2" has a long expanding arm that flicks the balls backward into the gutter.

"I didn't want a vehicle," says Eric, "'cause they're not efficient. You have three motors, and one—the Polaroid—is worth nothing. If you use the two good motors to steer, you have no power left to gather balls. So I abandoned the cart idea. Instead, I tried to simulate how a human would gather balls. See, my arm even has a shoulder and an elbow."

"What's that?" a student asks, pointing to a large Day-Glo-orange silo at the base of Eric's machine. "Does it nuke the opponent?"

Eric laughs and takes the top off the silo. It is crammed full of the remaining parts in the kit. "I need all of this as a counterweight to keep my machine from slipping when the arm goes out." Eric has mastered the concept of center of mass.

6:14 P.M. Saturday. Bruce is disenchanted. He can't get his net to work. It needs to be weighted so that it can be catapulted and will slip down among the balls. Moreover, the net has to be scrunched up initially in order to meet the 36-centimeter (14-inch) rule. He has yet to get the net to expand in flight.

12:30 P.M. Sunday. Eric Heatzig's device depends on two springs, one to fire the rake-jamming projectile and one to fire his own rake.

But the rules of the contest permit only one preloaded spring. He has ingeniously rigged up a motor to pull back a second spring. He tests the rigging and it works, but he refrains from testing the machine as a whole. "I'm afraid to," he says. "What if it doesn't work? I want to get out of here. I hate this."

1:54 P.M. Sunday. Bruce is happy. The "Beast" is now successfully launching its net. But when the net is reeled in, it pulls the balls into the base of the machine rather than around the base into the gutter.

3:00 P.M. Sunday. Matt Phelps, a junior, arrives in the test room with his machine, "Die for Judy." On top of the machine is a small doll behind a tiny windshield. The doll wasn't in the kit, of course, but the rules allow decorations that are purely ornamental and serve no functional purpose. "We had a cockroach called Judy at the fraternity house," Matt explains. "We apprehended it and kept it in a jar. We overfed it with sugar water and it died. So to make up for this grave injustice to the insect world, my machine is called 'Die for Judy.'" Megan is completely crushed when the memorial "Die for Judy" beats the "Maltese Falcon" in a practice run.

6:30 P.M. Sunday. The elbow of "Simply 2" has become loose. "I forgot to put a washer on the screw," says Eric Chan, who has just learned one of Flowers' maxims the hard way: You can't fool Mother Nature, even for an instant.

5:00 A.M. Monday. "Simply 2" is uncharacteristically sluggish. It hardly bends at the elbow. Someone has tinkered with the voltage supplied by the joystick.

11:45 A.M. Monday. Eric Heatzig adds an accordionlike paper bumper to his rake. It will act as a shock absorber so that the rake won't rebound too much off the center pole.

3:01 P.M. Monday. Annabelle Kim unveils an innovative design on the test table. It's a two-wheeled cart with two small flippers, one on each side. Each wheel is powered by a separate motor. She drives the cart up to the crop and then, by making the wheels go in opposite directions, spins the cart in a circle. As it spins, the flippers flick balls all over the place. "I have to practice driving," she says, "or I'll give more balls to the other guy."

3:15 P.M. Monday. Eric Heatzig ventures outside into daylight for the first time in five days. "Everything's really bright," he says. "My eyes hurt like [mad]."

Above: Eric Chan's device, called "Simply 2," sweeps in Ping-Pong balls with an expandable arm faster than its tanklike opponent. Right: A student makes a few last-minute adjustments to his machine, "Die for Judy."

3:30 P.M. Monday. Eric puts skirting around his machine to keep balls from going under it and getting trapped. He is getting high from epoxy that's spilled all over the table. "I'd better get past the first round," he says. "I mean, some people can't even drive straight. Every year there's a lot of people who get so nervous they can't control their machines. This year there'll be people who slip into the gutter and then it's all over."

4:00 P.M. Monday. The test room is shut down so that the tables can be moved to the stage of the tournament hall. Some students continue to test their machines by taking them outside and harnessing a car battery as the power source.

6:01 P.M. Monday. While downing a tin of Danish butter cookies, Eric Heatzig notices that two of his rake prongs are too far apart; a ball might slip through. He welds another prong between them. Other students use this last hour to decorate their machines with slogans.

7:00 P.M. Monday. Before a crowd of more than 1,000, Flowers explains the rules of the contest. Tonight there'll be 90 rounds, in which half of the 180 harvesters will be eliminated. The contestants have 30 seconds to set up their machines and 30 seconds to gather balls.

In the first round, "Simply 2" is pitted against a weird, tanklike contraption. The arm

Photos: Ethan Hoffman/Archive

of "Simply 2" is slow coming out, but the tank is even slower. "Simply 2" is the winner. In some ways the contest seems anticlimactic. Everything happens so quickly.

Eric Heatzig's machine is up against a gigantic lazy-tong rake, but he easily wins when the rake fails to move.

The "Maltese Falcon," "Die for Judy," and Annabelle's spinning harvester also win. The "Beast" refuses to fire its net, and Bruce waits out the 30 seconds, tapping his fingers and grinning self-consciously. A harvester that relies on a jar of pennies for counterweight is disqualified for using parts not in the kit.

Michael is one of the last to compete. He is so nervous that he incorrectly hooks up the umbilical cord from the machine to the joystick. The V projectile never fires. The machine sputters and slips back into the gutter. In one humiliating moment, seven weeks of inspiration and perspiration have come to naught.

7:00 P.M. Tuesday. The 90 survivors of the preliminary bouts come together in the finals. The atmosphere is tense. Three television camera crews shove microphones in the students' faces as they rush to hook up their machines in 20 seconds. The president of MIT, the president of TRW, and six executives from Polaroid are sitting in the front.

In one of the opening rounds, Eric Heatzig's harvester is trounced by the "Love Tractor," a powerful rake that's extremely fast. Dave Cultice, driver of the "Love Tractor," is a master tactician. When he has gathered a few more balls than his opponent, he seizes the opposing machine with his rake and waits out the time.

A woman who is wearing orange Ping-Pong balls as earrings is eliminated by the "Deathmobile," a four-wheeled cart that simply drives over the balls and backs up, taking

Photos: Ethan Hoffman/Archive

Left: A woman wearing Ping-Pong-ball earrings pits her harvesting contraption against the invincible "Deathmobile." Below: Dave Cultice used a clever strategy to beat opponents with his "Love Tractor:" after a rake sweeps in lots of balls, it grabs its competitor and waits out the allotted time of the round.

The audience is tense during the final match as the ''Deathmobile'' breaks away from the ''Love Tractor's'' grip.

the balls with it. Many carts with only two wheels fail because they slip into the gutter—or are shoved there—and can't get out. The ''Deathmobile'' has front-wheel drive. When it slips into the gutter, it can climb out because its front wheels are still on the table. With ''Brain Dead'' painted on its side, the ''Deathmobile'' is cleverly equipped with skirting that prevents balls from getting stuck in its wheels—something that brings many lesser machines to a grinding halt. The driver of the ''Deathmobile'' is Brad Waller, dressed in black and wearing, over his normal glasses, a mean pair of sunglasses made from the polarizing lenses in the kit.

After a few rounds, it is clear that the best machines are the ''Love Tractor,'' the ''Deathmobile,'' and Annabelle's spinner. But only Annabelle's is a crowd pleaser. The audience shouts her name whenever her whirling machine spits back balls.

In the quarterfinals Annabelle is up against the ''Love Tractor.'' Dave repeats his time-tested strategy: He quickly rakes in a few balls and grabs her spinner. The crowd doesn't like it and protests loudly. Annabelle finally slips free and the crowd roars, but it's too late. As time runs out, the ''Love Tractor'' sweeps up a zillion balls.

The finals pit the 'Love Tractor'' against the ''Deathmobile.'' One of the judges removes a defective ball with a pock in it. The president of MIT comes onto the stage and throws the switch to start the round—but nothing happens. Something is wrong with the wiring. The crowd hisses, and the contestants move their machines to a backup table. The president tries again, and this time the machines race forward.

The ''Love Tractor'' rakes in the first few balls and, as usual, grabs its opponent. The ''Deathmobile,'' however, is strong enough to free itself immediately. Photographers and reporters swarm around the table. The president's view is blocked, so he climbs on the power source just in time to see the ''Deathmobile'' pull in an avalanche of balls. The 30-second limit runs out, and the ''Deathmobile'' is declared the winner, 87 balls to 75.

Before Brad's fraternity brothers can storm the stage, the president hands him a trophy: a cornucopia of Ping-Pong balls. Everyone is standing now, shoving their fists into the air, shouting, ''Deathmobile! Deathmobile!'' Brad looks out at the crowd and sighs, ''If I can get this far in the real world, I'll be happy.'' His fraternity brothers hoist him onto their shoulders and carry him off the stage, up the aisle, and out the door □

Electron Microscopy in Living Detail

by Alison B. Bass

Deep within the body, one micron (one-millionth of a meter) wide, live capillaries with gnarled, treelike branches. Kidney cells grow in delicate, coral-like formation, and bizarre-looking scavenger cells glide across the surface of the lungs in search of foreign prey. Long invisible under microscope, this teeming subcellular universe can now be seen alive and in three dimensions (3-D) with techniques developed by Professor Alan Nelson and his colleagues at Massachusetts Institute of Technology's (M.I.T.'s) Whitaker College of Health Sciences, Technology, and Management.

Two Technologies Used Together

The new technology combines the power of computer analysis with an electron microscope specially built to magnify living tissue samples and display them in 3-D on a video screen. Originally developed to help biologists unravel the cellular structure of the human body, these techniques are also being used to determine the durability of ceramics and other materials and the quality of integrated circuits in a semiconductor chip.

"What makes this work important and unique is its combined approach," says Thomas Hayes, deputy director of the Donner Biomedical Laboratory at the University of California at Berkeley. "Each of these techniques gives us information we've never had before; used together, they are far more than the sum of their parts."

Microtomography Yields High Resolutions

The electron-microscopy technique is similar to computerized axial tomography (CAT), a method of collecting data from multiple angles and using a computer to reconstruct those data into an image on a screen. But the new process, which Nelson has dubbed microtomography, differs in some important aspects. A medical CAT scan rotates an X-ray beam around a patient, producing a detailed picture of tissue inside the body. But in microtomography, the "scan" stays stationary and the sample is rotat-

New techniques in microscopy now allow researchers to view living objects in three dimensions, such as this cell.

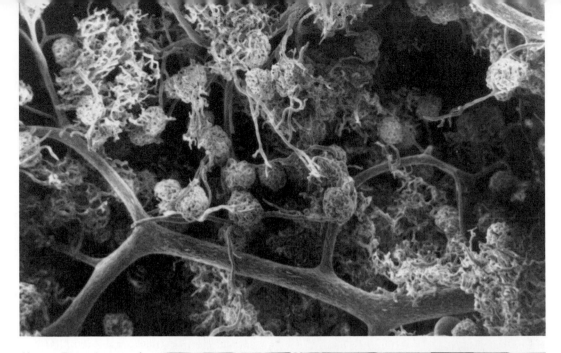

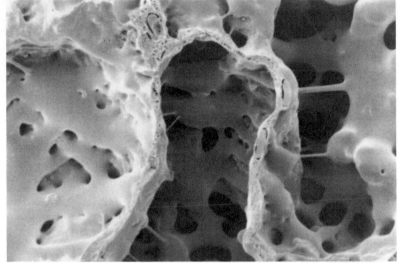

Above: Tiny clumps of blood capillaries are clearly visible in the outer layer of a human kidney. Right: This micrograph of lung tissue shows a single air sac, or alveoli, split open to reveal a capillary.

ed. Furthermore, the device uses electrons, not X-rays, to probe the varying densities of the target sample.

"Electron optics allow us to make our beam source incredibly small. If we tried to make the source of the X rays that small, we'd melt the X-ray tube," explains Nelson, who is director of Whitaker's Electron Microscopy Laboratory. "When the size of the radiation source becomes as small as your target, you can get very high resolution."

At the laboratory, researchers can collect data using either a transmission electron microscope (TEM), in which an electron beam passes through a thinly sliced sample, or a scanning electron microscope (SEM), in which a tiny beam is directed rapidly over the sample's surface. Both techniques yield resolutions better than one-millionth of a meter; that is, viewers can perceive the difference between two points that are only that far apart. With this kind of resolution and magnifications that exceed 50,000 times, microscopy has finally reached the subcellular level of the human body.

Special Chamber Protects Living Cells

Living cells, however, cannot be viewed under conventional electron microscopy. Since biological materials are poor conductors (transmitters) of electricity, they usually retain an electric

Corkscrew-shaped blood vessels surround a tumor cell in a cancerous rat. Normal vessels are usually smooth.

charge when struck with an electron beam and end up repelling it. This distorts the data. To overcome the problem, the sample must be coated with thin metal films to make it conductive—a fatal procedure for living cells.

Nelson and his colleagues have designed a chamber that preserves the cells in a normal environment yet allows the electrons to "peek through." The electron beam is maintained in an incredibly strong vacuum by a complex network of pumps that keeps out air and any other molecules that might absorb the electrons before they strike the sample.

"Basically, we squirt the electron beam through pinholes into the environmental chamber, and these pinholes are small enough to reduce the number of air molecules that escape," Nelson says. He has also devised a way to remove the surface charge that inevitably collects on a biological sample; however, the details of how that works are a trade secret. When the electrons hit the sample, they give off signals that are picked up by a detector and fed into the computer.

3-D Technology Provides Unique Views

The Whitaker researchers use these signals to create a continuous 3-D image. This effect, which can be seen without the polarized glasses used for viewing movies in 3-D, is achieved in much the same way a moving picture is produced from film sequences. Images of the sample—one tiny slice at a time—are reflected through a vibrating mirror onto the display screen in a sequence so rapid that the eye sees them as continuous. This 3-D technology was developed by Bolt, Beranek and Newman in Cambridge, Massachusetts, and Genisco Computer Corporation in Costa Mesa, California.

Harnessing the "third dimension" to an electron microscope permits researchers to view the actual structure of microscopic matter—be it a living cell, a ceramic particle, or a silicon chip—for the first time. Scientists at M.I.T.'s Ceramics Processing Research Laboratory have already used the device to determine the size and distribution of particles in submicron ceramic powders. "We can see how uniform the particles are," explains Paul White, one of the researchers. The more uniform the particles are, the stronger the ultimate ceramic product will be.

The first commercial application of this technology may come from its ability to examine the three-dimensional structure of rocks extracted from the Earth. "When you're drilling for oil, it's nice to know the stability of the rock through which you're drilling," says Nelson. "With this technique, you'd be able to study a sample of the rock to see if it can structurally support a bore hole."

An Intricate Look Inside the Body

In biology, the 3-D technique will open a new window on the structure of cells. Sheldon Penman, professor of biology at M.I.T., is planning to use the device to study the intricate architecture of kidney cells. His laboratory has developed a special casting preparation that reveals the internal scaffolding of these cells, and he is eager to examine it in 3-D. "The DNA [deoxyribonucleic acid] inside every cell is organized on this scaffolding," Penman notes. "But since nobody could see the underlying structure before, we have no idea what its function is."

Nelson and his colleagues have also devised a new technique for casting biological tissue, principally blood vessels, in plastic. They inject the vessels with tiny polymer molecules, which form a cast that provides an unusually fine view of the vessels' structure. Using this technique, the researchers have discovered that blood vessels surrounding a tumor grow in distorted, leaky shapes. This may explain how a tumor gains access to the bloodstream and spreads through the body.

What Nelson would most like to do is open his facility—with all its special features—to leading researchers nationwide. "In a sense, this technology is research-driven," Nelson says. "I'm always looking for new problems to solve" □

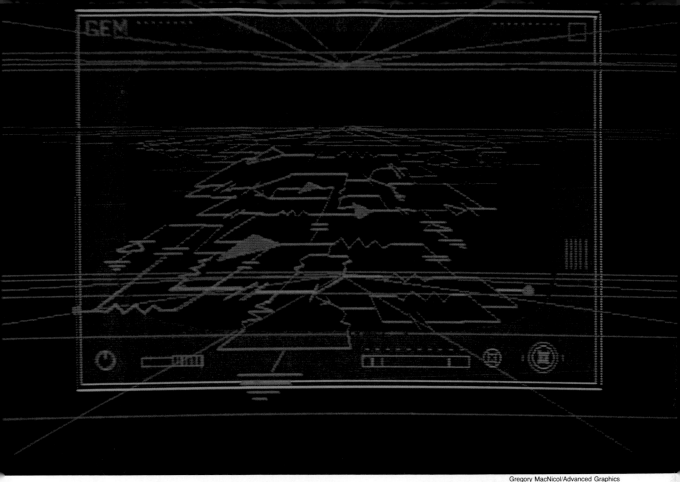

NEW TECHNOLOGY
FOR TELEVISION

by Gene Bylinsky

That hardy holdover of low-level electronics, the television set, is in the throes of a high-technology transformation. With the recent advent of digital-television (TV) sets on the market in the United States, a first step was taken toward making the ''boob tube'' as brainy as a microcomputer and perhaps eventually indistinguishable from one. The new sets let the viewer do tricks with broadcast images—such as zooming in on professional golfer Jack Nicklaus' putting grip—and in a few years digital technology will make television-picture quality as good as that of movie film. As for sound quality, the Federal Communications Commission (FCC) has already approved the broadcasting of stereo-television signals. And in various electronics-research laboratories, the decades-old search for the large, flat, color-television screen is finally producing some bright flickerings.

Revolutionary Changes in the Making

Except for the arrival of color and some changes in styling, the TV set hasn't changed much in some 35 years. But with the shifting away from traditional components to digital chips, the set will gradually become a member of the computer family, speaking the same digital language. The coincidental arrival of stereo will help to make existing TV sets in the United States—estimated to number about 172 million—seem old-fashioned. This suggests that U.S. sales of TV sets could be poised for a great leap forward. Gerald M. McCarthy, senior vice president of marketing at Zenith Corporation (a major manufacturer of television sets), sees stereo TV growing into "an enormously large business." Robert B. Hansen, Zenith's executive vice president, notes that digital chips will enable manufacturers to offer features that haven't been dreamed of yet. As he puts it, "Digital technology will give us 25 years of feature additions."

The prime catalyst for the move to digital, somewhat surprisingly, is International Telephone & Telegraph (ITT). Because ITT doesn't make sets in the U.S., few Americans connect the company with the industry, even though ITT subsidiaries sell millions of sets in Europe every year. The company's research on digital TV grew out of its work on developing digital telephone-switching systems to replace analog systems. In 1984 ITT put on the market a package of seven remarkable digital chips that can replace as many as 400 analog components in a television set.

Digital Systems Far Superior to Analog

Analog electronics predates the computer age; it works by trying to imitate events in the real world. Accordingly, in a television-analog system, a camera registers the sights to be broadcast as optical waves while microphones take in the sounds as acoustical waves. The cameras and the microphones translate both kinds of waves into analogous—hence the term analog—electrical waves and send them along through the air or over cable. Because these signals resemble those in the world around them, analog transmission can easily be contaminated by lightning or other electromagnetic "noise" generated in nature, or by synthetic electrical signals such as those from a washing-machine motor. To do their job, analog components must handle many variables, such as voltage, current, and the amplitude of the waves. Measuring and reconstructing the tiny waves after they reach the set is a difficult task carried out in small increments by myriad parts: capacitors, resistors, coils, and transistors. A single television set can have as many as 2,000 analog components.

A digital-receiving system—there are no digital-television transmissions—handles broadcast signals with much greater precision. It

Erich Hartmann/Magnum

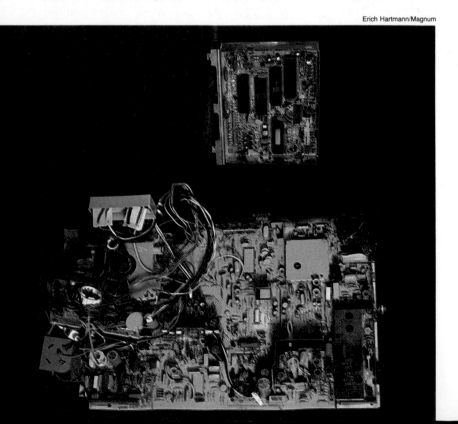

Small assemblages of digital chips (top) can replace hundreds of analog components (bottom) in a standard television set, which saves production time and boosts reliability.

takes a signal wave, breaks it up into a number of vertical slices, and translates what it finds into computerese. To each fragment, from the valley to the peak of the wave, it assigns a numerical value expressed as a string of ones and zeros—hence the term digital. To a computer chip, these come as "on" or "off" pulses, a language it understands. The result is greater fidelity in signal processing, partly because the digital system is more precise and partly because it can strain out random electrical signals like those from a washing machine. The precision is maintained even though the signals have to be reconverted to analog for display on the screen. And because digital transistors basically switch electrical pulses—a much simpler task than analog components' job of measuring and reconstructing those wavelets—the transistors are able to operate at lower voltage than their analog counterparts. Accordingly, digital transistors can be more easily microminiaturized and integrated into densely packed chips than their analog cousins. Some analog components cannot be microminiaturized.

ITT Paves the Way

ITT's pioneering in digital TV was born of necessity. In the late 1970's, the company's European TV-set business was "in really desperate straits," says Robert H. Allen, an ITT vice president. The company was being clobbered by more efficient producers. "In wrestling terms," says Allen, "the giants had us on their hip—with their big volumes and lower production costs." He adds: "We needed a winner."

The assemblage of digital chips that ITT came up with is indeed a winner, the result of a five-year effort by engineers at ITT's West German subsidiary, Intermetall. The goal was not so much to develop gee-whiz features—though ITT and others are doing that now—but to simplify the set, making it easier and cheaper to assemble. The seven chips, by replacing all those analog components, reduce the manufacturer's parts inventory, speed up assembly, and boost reliability. On the production line, a digital-TV set can be calibrated by plugging it into a small computer, and the desired settings made using a keyboard. In an analog set, the settings are often adjusted by hand with a screwdriver. ITT estimates that assembling a digital-TV set should be 20 percent faster than turning out its analog counterpart. And there's more good news. ITT's Intermetall now sells the chip assembly for about the cost of the analog parts it replaces. In time, the price will drop.

A long debate raged at ITT over whether to market the chips to other television manufacturers. Some ITT executives wanted the company to keep its secrets and use them to get into television production in the U.S. In the end, ITT decided against U.S. production and in favor of selling the chips to other set makers, figuring that it had a long enough lead to stay ahead of a number of U.S. and Japanese manufacturers that are rushing to develop their own digital chips. ITT expects the TV-chip market to expand to $500 million by 1988, and it plans to be the dominant player. Whether the company made the right decision isn't yet clear. But the world's leading television makers—such as Sony Corporation, Matsushita Electrical Industrial Company, RCA Corporation, Zenith, and General Electric (GE) Company—lined up at ITT's door to buy the chips.

Vast Capabilities, Long-lasting Quality

In 1984 ITT already had some of its own sets on the market in Europe, and recently Zenith, RCA, GE, and Matsushita began selling digital sets in the U.S. Most of the U.S. marketers are adding their own digital chips to the ITT package, giving each manufacturer some extra features to plug. This means consumers can expect some dazzling stuff. Simultaneous viewing of two or more stations without channel hopping, known as "picture-in picture," is one of the hottest new features available. Not only will sports zealots be able to watch two football games at once, they may also be able to zoom in on their heroes for close-up views or they may freeze a frame, to savor an interception. Other chips can eliminate "ghosts," those pesky double images that bounce off tall buildings and plague television reception in cities.

With fewer components to fail, a digital set should also last longer and grow old more gracefully. In an analog set, picture quality fades a bit as the set ages. The digital set, now turned into a kind of computer, has a built-in feedback system that adjusts the picture controls if they deviate from the original setting. "We tell the customer," says Ludwig Orth, vice president for ITT Europe, "that, until the last day, picture quality will be as good as on the first day because of the built-in computer system." And if the set needs servicing, the repairman can sit in front of it and adjust the picture with a small computer instead of craning back and forth between the back of the set and the screen.

One of the special techno-logical capabilities that digital television offers is viewing one program within another.

Toshiba

Better Broadcasts Now Possible

To engineers, the most spectacular contribution of digital-television technology, still a couple of years away but clearly visible on the horizon, will be vast improvement in picture quality. Dramatic progress has been elusive, despite the best efforts of set makers and broadcasters. Practically everyone has agreed that one solution would be to broadcast images with higher definition, which usually means somehow doubling the number of lines that can be transmitted over the air to the screen. In Japan, where the standard is 525 lines, the national broadcasting system (NHK) has experimentally demonstrated 1,125-line over-the-air transmission of excellent quality. The big problem is that the 1,125-line signal takes up too much room on the crowded broadcast spectrum, about five times as much bandwidth as an ordinary TV signal. Furthermore, such a system would make obsolete not only existing broadcast equipment but also all the existing TV sets.

Some engineers favor digital broadcasts, which would produce high-quality pictures but which couldn't be picked up by existing sets either. Digital transmission would also take up more bandwidth—three to four times as much as analog transmission. In time, progress with something called digital-data compression is expected to solve this problem—if satellite transmission, which has the potential to offer much broader bandwidths, doesn't solve it first.

The beauty of digital chips is that they can do wonders even with the existing broadcast signal. Researchers at RCA and North American Philips Corporation first demonstrated in the laboratory that digital chips can improve picture quality 100 percent, making it virtually as good as movies. ITT and others rushed the development of the appropriate chips, and they sold prototypes to set makers in 1984. The first chips, known as "line store" chips, are programmed to slip an extra line between each of the 525 lines now broadcast in the U.S.

With this capability suddenly in hand, such authorities as William C. Hittinger, executive vice president for research and engineering at RCA, see no need for a transition to higher-definition broadcasts anytime soon. "Clearly," says Hittinger, "we can double the number of lines, triple, or quadruple them simply by using enough memory to store the lines and display them in whatever sequence we want."

Stereophonic Sound Another Benefit

Digital electronics also enables set makers to provide higher-quality TV stereo. Stereo-TV broadcasting was slow in coming to the United States—the Japanese have had it since 1978—and not just because the FCC, which parcels out the nation's airwaves and decides what kinds of signals can be carried, was slow to act. U.S. broadcasters and television-set manufacturers couldn't agree until recently on a uniform stan-

A comparison between images on a conventional television screen (top) and a digital screen (bottom) shows how much sharper and brighter a picture can be with digital technology.

dard for beaming stereo signals. Not long after they did, the FCC gave them a green light.

For several years some manufacturers have been putting stereo speakers into their top-of-the-line TVs. Those sets can create a pseudo-stereo sound by splitting the monaural (single-transmission path)-broadcast signal into high and low frequencies. Owners of such sets—there are about 1 million in use—have also been exposed to full-fledged stereo by video movies and other prerecorded programs made in stereo.

As a result, says GE vice president Jacques A. Robinson, many consumers have elevated video-sound quality to a clear second after picture quality in their list of priorities. Television-marketing executives drool at the thought of stereo-TV broadcasting. Jack K. Sauter, a group vice president at RCA, says, "If the networks went to full stereo scheduling, stereo could easily become 50 percent of our console business." Consoles are disproportionately profitable for being only 20 percent of the industry's sales.

Owners of existing sets with stereo speakers will have to shell out about $100 for an adapter to pick up the stereo-broadcast signal. Digital-television sets will not need adapters, because the stereo signal will be handled inside the set by a special chip.

Broadcasters have an additional incentive to shift, because the stereo system has three audio channels instead of two. The third can be used in a variety of ways: to broadcast programs in a second language, to offer two levels of narration in educational programs (one for neophytes and the other for more knowledgeable viewers), or to broadcast descriptions for the blind. ''That channel,'' says James C. McKinney, chief of the FCC's mass media bureau, ''could create a separate communications business altogether. Television stations may sell it as a new radio channel. They could broadcast stock market reports, weather forecasts, or music all day.'' Since both stereo channels and the third audio channel are broadcast within the existing TV band, television stations can pick up something for nothing, at the expense of radio broadcasters.

Making Screens Larger, Wider, and Flatter

With higher-definition pictures and stereophonic sound, what more do you need to turn the living room into a movie theater? A bigger screen, for one thing. Many technologists are striving to widen the screen by altering the so-called aspect ratio, the relationship between the horizontal and vertical proportions of the TV screen. Today's 4:3-aspect ratio—the screen is only one-third wider than it is tall—may eventually be changed to 5:3. But such a change, besides requiring a new broadcast standard, would make it awkward to show old movies and TV shows that were filmed in the 4:3 ratio.

As for big-screen TV, it is already here. Henry E. Kloss, president of Kloss Video Corporation of Cambridge, Massachusetts, who pioneered projection television, is pushing projection screens as large as 1.8 meters by 2.4 meters (6 feet by 8 feet), with sharp TV images emitted from a ceiling-mounted or floor-based projector. The big TV manufacturers don't see wall-projection taking off, because the sets are expensive and require a lot of space. Instead, set makers have been emphasizing rear-projection TVs, which are just as high-priced but more compact. In these sets the projection is achieved inside the television cabinet, on screens as big as 114 centimeters (45 inches) on the diagonal. Even three-dimensional (3-D) TV may be on its way, if anyone really wants it. Researchers at North American Philips Corporation are experimenting with a way to shoehorn a 3-D signal into the current TV bandwidth.

And the technologists' old dream, to replace the bulky, pear-shaped, cathode-ray tube (CRT) with a flat screen for color TV, still lives. Such a screen could be hung on the wall, or

Researchers at Siemens AG are developing the most advanced flat screen for color television ever made.

Dirk Reinartz/Visum

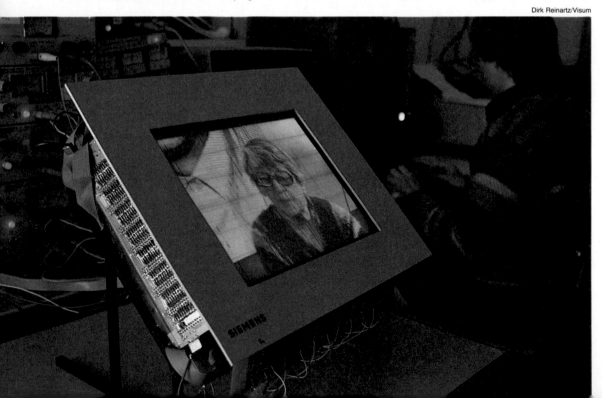

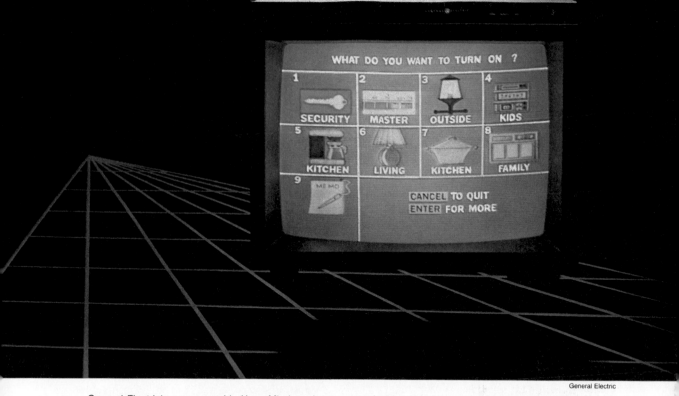

General Electric

General Electric's programmable HomeMinder unit turns any television set into a control center for the home.

fitted easily into a bookshelf, and the set would be lighter and easier to carry. Large, flat black-and-white screens are finding their way into computer terminals, but so far not flat-color screens. Perhaps the most advanced non-CRT color display is a 36-centimeter (14-inch) screen being developed by Siemens AG in Munich, Germany, in a joint project with ITT. This novel screen is only 8 centimeters (3 inches) thick, and it is ready-made for the age of digital-signal processing: the panel elements can be digitally addressed, eliminating the need to convert to analog for display. ITT hopes that the screen will be perfected as a display for a portable color TV. But many technical problems remain unsolved.

Television Takes on New Roles in the Home

Flat or fat, there is no question that tomorrow's TV set will be smart. With its digital brain ''transplant,'' it may be on its way to becoming the command and control center of the home. GE has already introduced a set that enables the viewer, while watching his favorite program, to turn down his thermostat or flick on his micro-

wave oven through a small remote-control panel. Those appliances would be connected to the set by electrical wires. When away from home, the GE-set owner can even telephone instructions to the appliances via the TV set. The set can also take phone messages when it is called, and alert the household to the message's existence with a flashing red light.

With a little imagination, it's easy to envision TV taking over the role of the telephone and the computer—or losing its identity and becoming just a part of a smart digital system that would envelop all three. In the meantime, your TV set is going to be a lot more fun to watch □

SELECTED READINGS

''Digital signal processing'' by Michael Riggs. *High Technology,* April 1985.

''Third-generation television: hi-fi for your eyes and ears'' by David Lander. *Popular Mechanics,* February 1985.

''New digital receivers deliver ultimate TV'' by David Lachenbruch. *Popular Science,* June 1984.

''Smart TV [digital television]'' by Len Hilts. *Omni,* April 1984.

WILDLIFE

REVIEW
OF THE
YEAR

WILDLIFE

An article of faith among wildlife researchers is "Habitat is wildlife." To that tried-and-true precept can now be added "Intervention works." Wildlife experts have long known that the only way a wildlife species can survive in the wild is to have sufficient living space in which to find food, water, and cover. However, some recent, specific programs to benefit wildlife have clearly been successful. Some focus on one species and some on a particular habitat.

SPECIAL PROGRAMS DO WORK

The peregrine falcon provides an example of how a specific program aimed at benefiting wildlife works. This spectacular bird of prey almost disappeared from the eastern United States because residues of the insecticide DDT thinned its eggshells—so much so that the eggs broke during incubation. Since the banning of the use of DDT in 1972, residues have decreased, eggshells have thickened, and peregrine reproductive success has risen markedly. The Peregrine Fund has released 1,266 captive-bred birds over the past 10 years, and hundreds of these are believed to have survived to adulthood. The key: banning the use of DDT.

Other bird species were also favorably affected by the DDT ban—most notably the bald eagle, probably the biggest and most well known wildlife success story of all. After suffering a large population decline in the lower 48 states due to DDT-caused eggshell thinning, the eagle population turned around following the DDT ban. From about 9,800 bald eagles in the lower 48 states in 1972, there are now about 11,800.

Researchers have built up a second flock of wild whooping cranes, thanks to eggs taken from wild nests and from captive birds. There are still only about 100 whoopers in the wild, up from 15 in 1941, but a second wild flock greatly reduces the chance of all wild whoopers being killed by a single natural disaster. The key to this success: risking the taking of second eggs from wild nests (typically, only one of two hatches and survives anyway).

Another example—the Tennessee Valley Authority transplanted ospreys, golden eagles, bald eagles, and peregrine falcons into areas

Wendell Metzen/Bruce Coleman

Recently added to the U.S. endangered-species list, the wood stork is losing its prime habitat to development.

where the birds had disappeared, and they thrived. This favorable outcome was due to protecting the birds from unrestricted shooting that had wiped them out in those areas in the first place.

OTHER GOOD NEWS

The bounce-back ability of many wildlife species after natural disasters is amazing. After the 1980 eruption of Mount St. Helens in Washington, hot ash seemed to have killed off all life forms in the area around the mountain. Now, however, mice and gophers that live underground and plants buried by the ash are resurfacing. Even trout survived in some of the lakes in the blast zone.

Black-footed ferrets, thought to be extinct in 1978, seem to be increasing; during the summer of 1984, 128 were found in Wyoming. ■ The population of the American crocodile, estimated at 500, is holding steady in the Florida Everglades. ■ And the snail darter, an 8-centimeter (3-inch)-long fish whose precarious existence in the Little Tennessee River held up a multimillion-dollar dam project, has been discovered in four other rivers. However, wildlife biologists point out that the population was killed off in the Little Tennessee when the controversial dam was completed.

Populations of some other species also seem to be showing favorable trends. The U.S. Fish and Wildlife Service completed a study that showed that healthy populations of trout, bass, bluegills, and pike can be found in almost three-fourths of the 1,300 rivers studied, and that the downward trend in water quality that began in the 1950's has ended. Even so, water quality was found to affect the fish population in more than half the rivers and streams studied, mainly limiting population levels rather than causing large die-offs.

BUT STILL SOME BAD NEWS

Some species are still in serious trouble. The Florida panther, dozens of which live in the Florida Everglades, is under heavy pressure from extension of an interstate highway cutting into its habitat. ■ The wood stork, the only stork that breeds in the United States, has lost three-fourths of its population in the past 50 years and has been added to the endangered-species list because of destruction of its favored habitat: cypress and mangrove swamps in the Southeast. ■ Also newly added to the endangered list is the woodland caribou, which numbers only 30 in the northwestern states. ■ And five species—three fish, a bird, and a mussel—are thought to have become extinct in the past three years: the Tecopa pupfish in California, the lawjaw Cisco

fish in the Great Lakes, the blue pike of Lake Erie and Lake Ontario, the Santa Barbara song sparrow in California, and Sampson's pearly mussel of Illinois and Indiana.

HABITAT ALWAYS THE MAIN KEY

The main key is always habitat. Without suitable habitat, wildlife can't survive—not even with special programs. During 1984 substantial new lands were added to the National Wildlife Preservation System and to the National Wildlife Refuge System. However, the wildlife habitat battle will be won or lost on private lands, where the great majority of U.S. wildlife lives. And, to date, the losses are serious. More than 120,000 hectares (300,000 acres) of freshwater wetlands are drained and filled for cropland and building projects each year. Nationwide, about 400,000 hectares (1 million acres) of all types of wildlife habitat are lost due to development each year. This loss of fencerows, wetlands, prairies, and forests continues to be the big wildlife story year after year.

An additional habitat problem is looming larger each year—habitat poisoned by lead pellets from spent shotgun shells. Many scientists believe that some 2 million ducks and geese die from lead poisoning each year and that many other species are affected. Most conservation groups are calling for increased restrictions on the use of lead shotgun pellets.

WHAT ABOUT "LOWER LIFE-FORMS?"

A continuing controversy among scientists, legislators, and bureaucrats concerns the degree of public support for special protection for "lower life-forms." It's clear that large segments of the public support special measures to protect grizzly bears, bald eagles, whooping cranes, and whales. But what about plants, mollusks, crustaceans, and insects? This question was partially answered in 1984, when the Fish and Wildlife Service revealed that more than 800 invertebrates were under review for possible listing as "endangered" or "threatened" (51 are already on the list). Although no one expects quick action in listing any of these species, the review suggests that the government agencies involved recognize that the public has become increasingly aware of the value of invertebrates—for recycling nutrients, pollinating plants, controlling pests, serving as sources of drugs and other products, and lending stability to the worldwide food chain. In fact, the most significant effect of the ecology boom of the 1970's may be a widespread understanding that the welfare of people cannot be separated from the well-being of the entire web of life.

BOB STROHM

Three Ways to be a BOOBY

by Tui De Roy

Famous for its diverse finches and dragon-like iguanas, the Galápagos Islands are also home to three kinds of funny-looking birds called boobies: one with blue feet, one with red feet, and the third with feet the color of oily canvas. All three belong to the genus *Sula,* a group of large seabirds. They all share features such as straight, daggerlike beaks and the large webs that unite all four toes on each foot (unlike the three toes of gulls or ducks). They capture the fish on which they feed by plummeting from the air dartlike into the sea and pursuing their prey underwater; and finally, all three live and breed in the Galápagos archipelago (a group of islands) in the tropical eastern Pacific. But how can three species, sharing so many common traits, coexist without acute competition?

Feeding Habits Differ

Upon closer examination one quickly finds that the similarities between these boobies have their

entering the water like an arrow. It may pursue the fish underwater for several more meters and usually swallows its prey before surfacing.

While this method dictates some inevitable similarities in the feeding habits of the three species of Galápagos boobies, each reserves a distinctive feeding environment, which it rarely shares with either of the other two. The masked booby is an interisland feeder, pursuing schooling fish that frequent the offshore waters within the archipelago. There it cruises over the ocean with steady wingbeats, its gleaming white plumage visible at great distances. It usually dives from an impressive height—30 meters (100 feet) or more—hitting the blue surface of the sea like a bullet. Flocks of masked boobies often follow feeding pods of bottle-nosed dolphins, the splashing of the diving birds mingling with the marine mammals surfacing for air, as these unlikely partners attack the fish from all sides.

The red-footed booby, on the other hand, is far more pelagic (oceanic) in its feeding habits, and it is indeed exceptional to see an adult of this species dive within sight of land. They

Left: A flock of blue-footed boobies gathers on a lava ridge in the Galápagos Islands. Below: The red-footed booby fishes way offshore and nests year-round.

Photos: Gerald Corsi/Focus on Nature

limits. And while they must all face basically the same variables of climate and seasonal changes, each has devised its own means of overcoming such problems as food shortages and fish migration. In fact, it is extremely rare to see all three species fishing the same tract of ocean. While blue-footed, red-footed, and masked boobies may in some places nest within a few hundred meters of each other, no two have developed the same solutions for raising their young successfully against the odds of fluctuating food supplies.

The fishing method of all the different species of boobies the world over has been much celebrated: the bird locates a fish from its usual cruising level of 9 to 30 meters (30 to 100 feet) above the sea, then swerves into a vertical plunge, beak pointing downward and wings flapping powerfully to increase its speed of descent, in what appears to be certain suicide. At the very last instant before hitting the surface, the booby folds its wings back along its body,

Blue-footed boobies have no set breeding cycle; they go about egg laying whenever food supplies are plentiful.

range far and wide over the open sea, where their primary prey appears to consist of flying fish.

Occupying the opposite extreme is the blue-footed booby, which not only remains close to land but does virtually all its fishing within a stone's throw of the rugged lava shoreline. Here it excels in the most daring of dives, plummeting with full force in less than 1 meter (3 feet) of water, and using its tail to maneuver around boulders in pursuit of its prey. When schools of spawning fish gather by the millions in mangrove-surrounded shallows, the blue-foots are quick to follow. In huge flocks they rain from the sky like a thunderstorm pockmarking the surface of the sea, so massive is their attack upon the small fish. Immediately after surfacing they take off again, replacing the descending birds in a steady stream. At any moment one expects to see booby impaling booby, but instead the water becomes progressively loaded with tiny, silvery fish scales, until the assaulted school disperses and the boobies, replete, move to the nearest shore to perch and digest. In a few hours the fish will have regrouped and the birds will return for yet another feeding frenzy.

If the prey is swimming too fast to allow such a direct approach from above, the blue-footed booby will skim the surface, dipping down slightly for a horizontal dive. Amazingly, the bird maintains enough speed underwater to continue flying when it emerges one or two meters farther on.

Nesting Behavior Also Varies

Feeding habits are only one aspect in which the boobies have diverged, while maintaining essentially the same techniques. Analysis of their breeding cycles shows even more strikingly how three similar birds have selected different approaches to consistent problems. As in many equatorial regions, seasons in the Galápagos are not well marked, which means that there is no particular time of year that guarantees adequate food supply for successful nesting. Already the response to this basic problem differs in each species of booby: the red-footed booby nests throughout the year, the masked booby follows yearly cycles with each small colony on a separate timetable, while the blue-footed booby is an opportunistic breeder that begins to nest whenever conditions are favorable.

The red-foot, ranging over wide distances, seems less affected by periodic changes in fish distribution than are the other boobies. Even so, food shortages can be reflected in chick starvation, and an occasional abundance may trigger the beginning of a concerted nesting period. While this ability to follow the food supply wherever it may be enables them to continue nesting through lean times, they must pay a price in the high energy expended traveling between the feeding and nesting grounds. As a result, the red-foots never lay more than one egg, and the single chick grows slowly, with the danger of starvation never far away. (Brian Nelson, a leading expert on boobies, even suggested that if it were at all possible, the red-foots would lay only half an egg, so tenuous are the conditions under which they breed.) In the Galápagos it takes four and one-half months for the red-foot chick to fledge, and it will continue to receive food from its parents for three more months thereafter before it becomes entirely independent.

The masked booby's nesting cycle, although highly mysterious in some respects, appears to reflect a life far less pressured by food shortages than the other two species. It has the most powerful dive, presumably reaching greater depths, and feeds on rather large pelagic fish. Although it is the largest of all boobies, and is considerably larger than the red-foot, its young reach independence almost two months sooner than the red-foot chicks. Yet a strange part of its breeding remains unsolved. While some masked boobies lay and incubate only one egg, most clutches consist of two eggs laid between five and seven days apart. Since both mates begin taking turns incubating as soon as the first egg is laid, the chicks hatch with as much as a week's age difference between them. Although they are feeble and uncoordinated for their first two weeks of life, the older chick soon begins to attack its sibling fiercely, jabbing at it persistently until it is driven out of the nest to die of starvation and exposure. But why should only one young booby survive in each nest, when food supply does not appear to present great problems? And if there is an advantage in raising a single chick, why does the female masked booby not lay a single egg as does the red-foot? These questions still remain puzzling.

Opportunistic Breeders

On the other hand, the story of the blue-footed booby is a beautiful example of a bird that has evolved to make the best out of unpredictable circumstances. Remaining close to shore and never traveling far from its nesting colonies, it is by far the most vulnerable to fluctuations in fish supplies. Thus, when the conditions are appropriate, the blue-foots begin their nesting activities in a sudden burst. A sense of urgency pervades the colony as the birds busily engage in their elaborate courtship dances, soon to be followed by egg laying. Although two is the normal clutch size, as many as four eggs may be laid at intervals of about five days, hatching with the the same time difference between them.

If food continues to be plentiful, all chicks will be amply fed, with both parents making

A masked booby parent guards its fuzzy, funny-looking youngster while its mate searches for food.

only short trips to sea, although the age difference between the siblings will continue to be reflected in their size throughout their growth. If, however, a food shortage takes place, the smaller chicks will at once become the losers·in the ensuing competition over the reduced amounts of fish brought in by the parents, and the size difference between the nest mates will gradually become greater. If the shortage persists, all younger chicks are certain to starve, while the older ones may continue to develop normally. This, of course, makes excellent sense in terms of selective pressures and overall population success, affording the blue-foot an extremely flexible system by which to raise the maximum number of young possible under the circumstances of each nesting period. Were all the chicks in a clutch hatched together, they would probably also all starve at the same time.

Even so, the survival of even just the oldest chick in each nest is not assured. If food becomes too difficult to obtain, parents may abandon their nests altogether, sometimes vacating an entire colony overnight and leaving behind eggs and chicks alike.

It is quite rare to see four large chicks together in one nest, for the demands of such a family must inevitably put a tremendous strain on the parents' ability to shuttle food back from the ocean, even in a time of plenty. I observed the results of this once on Isabela Island, where several hundreds of nests all contained large, healthy chicks, mostly in twos and threes, while an adjacent colony was in the midst of courtship and egg laying. In addition, many of the nests had both parents in attendance simultaneously, showing that they did not need to make prolonged trips to feed. Two weeks later I returned to the site, but I could scarcely believe where I was. A strange stillness prevailed, where so many whistles and raucous calls had filled the air; where plump chicks had stood, now were heaps of matted down covering mummified carcasses. Only a handful of juveniles, almost ready to fledge, still sat morosely in this doom. When at last one adult flew in from the sea, it was assaulted so fiercely by this desperate, starving band that it fled in panic without even feeding its own offspring. This, I realized, was a graphic example of the precarious breeding system of the blue-footed booby. Self-preservation had forced the adults to abandon their nesting effort in midstream. As soon as conditions improved, they would try again.

Blue-Foots' Courtship Most Elaborate

A booby colony, be it red-foot, blue-foot, or masked, has its own personality. On Tower Island tens of thousands of red-footed boobies nest throughout the island's dense, dry scrub, forming the largest breeding colony of this species in the world. In the late afternoon their slender silhouettes crisscross the sky as they return to their nests. At this time frigate birds may steal their catch, suspending the boobies in midair by a wing or tail feather to force them to relinquish the fish that they carry in their crops. (A crop is a pouched enlargement of the gullet, or throat, of many birds.) On the nests the harsh greeting calls of mates mingle to form a strange concert, while those that are beginning to breed employ themselves at collecting twigs and small branches.

The atmosphere around a masked-booby colony is a very different matter. It conveys none of the orderliness that prevails in a red-foot colony. Instead, aggressiveness is at the forefront and loud squabbles are frequent between neighbors and even between mates. To reduce this innate tendency and avoid serious confrontations, mating pairs are constantly appeasing one another. Much time is spent in mutual preening, both birds meticulously combing each other's head feathers, while ritualized jabbing between mating pairs is even built into the courtship displays.

Blue-footed boobies form close-knit colonies on open terrain near the shoreline. Their courtship is elaborate and enthralling to watch. The males, which are considerably smaller, display themselves ardently in an effort to draw the females' attention. Again and again a male will point his head and tail skyward while twisting his wings up and forward, simultaneously uttering a long, plaintive whistle. As soon as a female joins him, the true dance begins, every move gracefully emphasized with deliberate, slow motions. They touch bills, bow, nod, tuck bills, or point them up and away with an affected air. At times they will resume skypointing, taking turns in beautiful harmony, the male whistling, the female honking. Or they will arch their necks elegantly to the ground, picking up tiny twigs, pebbles, or feathers, which they present to each other or arrange ceremoniously into a semblance of a nest. Interspersed among these other activities, they also engage in bouts of true "dancing," rocking from one foot to the other and lifting their brilliant blue feet in a measured, rhythmical fashion.

Parental Duties Shared

The blue-foot pair shares full responsibility throughout the nesting, swapping places daily during the incubation period. Boobies lack brood patches, bare spots of skin on the breast used by most birds for incubation; instead they put their large, flexible webs to good use by wrapping them around the eggs to keep them warm. When the tiny chicks hatch—naked, blind, and helpless—they must be shaded from the sun during the day and protected from predators and cold weather at night. Again, the parents take turns at this duty, until the chicks have grown a protective coat of white down and can be left unattended on the nest.

During these early weeks of chick feeding, fathers take on the bulk of the work, while mothers contribute their part mostly during the latter part of the offsprings' development. Brian Nelson, who spent four months studying blue-foots on Hood Island in the Galápagos, concludes that since the male weighs only about two-thirds as much as his mate, he is more adept at performing skillful dives in shallow water near the nesting grounds, and would naturally be best suited to provide for the chicks when they need little food but must be fed frequently. On the other hand, the larger female, ranging farther offshore, is best equipped for bringing in heavy loads when the growing chicks may need only one or two feeds per day, while their overall requirements have become much greater.

"Boobies" in Name Only

At Punta Pitt on San Cristóbal Island, all three species of booby converge to nest. The red-foots build their platforms of twigs in low, salty bushes, the masked boobies select the cliff edges for their pebble-lined nesting scrapes, and blue-foots choose flat areas a little farther inland. Yet, as soon as these three birds—brought together by their common need for firm ground to nest upon—sail away into the damp sea breeze to fish, they will each take a separate course, both in space and habits. Their tameness and startling fishing methods have earned these birds a name tinged with scorn, but their ability to portion their environment's bounty to the benefit of all demonstrates that they are not such boobies after all □

SELECTED READINGS

"Dancing to a different beat" by Tui De Roy. *International Wildlife*, January–February 1983.
"Clowns of the Galápagos" by Thomas G. Bell. *Sea Frontiers*, March–April 1982.
"The guano ring" by Stephen Jay Gould. *Natural History*, January 1982.
The Sulidae: Gannets and Boobies by J. Brian Nelson. Oxford University Press, 1978.

After several successful dives for fish, a blue-foot clings to a jagged outcrop close to the shore.

Elliott Varner/Smith

SPECIES SURVIVAL:
A ZOO VIEW

by Julie Ann Miller

In an effort to maintain the genetic diversity of certain populations of captive animals, many zoos are now using special breeding techniques. Two species currently being managed this way are the Siberian tiger and the golden lion tamarin shown here.

M atchmaking at the zoo is rapidly shifting from an art to a science. In 1980 when curators at the National Zoo in Washington, District of Columbia, sat down to plan the next round of breeding for their captive population of golden lion tamarins (small South American monkeys), they had no protocols to guide them. So they decided to list all possible combinations of males and females and select the plan giving the least inbreeding—the fewest matings of closely related animals such as siblings, half siblings, and cousins. But the planners were immediately dismayed to discover that their breeding population of 13 males and 13 females could be paired up in 6 billion different ways.

New Age of Captive Breeding

"Things have changed a lot since then," says Jonathan Ballou, one of those matchmaking curators. Breeding decisions have become more objective and more scientific, he says. At a recent meeting at the National Zoo's breeding facility in Front Royal, Virginia, an international group of geneticists and zoo-animal breeders discussed new techniques for analyzing the genetics of captive-animal populations and described new breeding guidelines.

"These are sophisticated recommendations," says Ballou, an organizer of that meeting. "We are entering a new age of captive breeding."

The need for more sophisticated criteria in animal breeding grows out of the changing focus of many zoos. "Historically, zoo curators were concerned mainly with the welfare of individual animals," explains Katherine Ralls of the National Zoo. "They are now increasingly concerned with the welfare of entire captive populations, which has necessitated a change from the individual to the population way of thinking."

Concern with captive populations has arisen from the desire to develop self-sustaining groups. For many species, zoo curators can no longer count on periodically augmenting their collections with animals newly captured from the wild. And a small number of species, but a number expected to increase as habitat destruction continues around the world, exist only as zoo populations.

Problems with Small Mating Populations

The new age of captive breeding requires a major educational effort to train zoo curators in the application of population genetics to breeding programs, and it demands extensive coordination among breeders at the world's many zoos. Currently only a few species—including the Siberian tiger, golden lion tamarin, Przewalski's horse, and Speke's gazelle—are being intensively managed in this way. But about 30 species have been targeted for such programs.

The simplest method of breeding, and the one used most frequently in the past, is making matches among the small number of animals of a species residing at each zoo. And if a pair of animals reproduced successfully, it would be bred over and over again.

But this convenient procedure is unsuited to the zoos' new role. First, small populations, such as the animals of a given species at one zoo, tend to go extinct because of chance events. A series of births of animals of the same sex, for example, may end the population line, or a disease may wipe out the entire population at that zoo.

A second drawback of small mating populations is that they develop problems associated with inbreeding. These problems include low birth weights and high rates of infant death. Ralls and Ballou have examined breeding records of 44 species of mammals and found that in 93 percent of the species, mortality of inbred young is higher than that of noninbred young animals.

Finally, small breeding populations do not best preserve genetic diversity, one of the goals of modern breeding programs. Genetic diversity is expected to increase the likelihood of a species' future survival, both in captivity and in the wild, and to serve as a future resource for such human endeavors as medical research.

Specific Plans for Specific Goals

Currently there are a large number of potential breeding plans. The choice is dictated in part by the number, and family relationships, of the animals available. Participants in the conference stressed that the choice of breeding plan also should depend on the goals of the breeding program. Such objectives might be the adaptation of a newly collected species to captivity; long-term conservation of an endangered species; propagation of animals for release into the wild; or supply of domestic, laboratory, and game animals.

Of course, these plans are limited to animals that breed successfully in captivity. About one-sixth of all types of mammals and one-twelfth of all the world's species of birds have been bred in zoos in the past few years, according to the Species Survival Plan (SSP) guide produced by the American Association of Zoological Parks and Aquariums (AAZPA) in Wheeling, West Virginia. Recent successes with such new reproductive technologies as embryo transplants across species lines and frozen embryos are expected to extend successful captive-breeding plans to ever more species.

Genetics at Heart of Management Schemes

The participants at the meeting proposed two sample protocols for specific situations. "These are the extremes of a continuum," says Russell Lande, a theoretical biologist at the University of Chicago. In both cases the starting population should ideally be the offspring of at least 10 to 20 "founder" animals, and the group should have as much genetic diversity as possible. The total population in each case should eventually be divided into subunits, perhaps at different institutions or on different continents.

Take the case of animals being raised with the objective of eventually restocking a natural habitat—for example, the golden lion tamarins. The group recommends that these animals be bred to rapidly reach the "carrying capacity," the maximum population that can be contained in the zoo space available. Ideally this population should include at least 250 animals. Once the carrying capacity is reached, the breeders should try to maximize generation time, thus slowing the rate of subsequent genetic change.

The population should then be subdivided into groups of no more than 100 members. Between groups, a migration rate of one animal per generation should be maintained. Within each subgroup, breeding decisions should attempt both to equalize family sizes and to correct previous disparities in the number of descendants of each founder. The scientists should, through their breeding decisions, attempt to eliminate deleterious genetic changes, such as hernias in the golden lion tamarins. Whenever possible there should be continued introduction of wild animals into the breeding population.

In contrast, a different breeding plan is needed for adapting animals to captivity. This might be the goal of a program to create a zoo population of a nonendangered animal species, or it might be the first step in a long-term program to breed animals for eventual release.

In this case, the meeting participants recommend maintaining smaller subpopulations than in the previous example. The zoos should allow natural selection to occur, with no attempt to equalize the success of founders, to control family sizes, or to extend generation times. No wild animals should be introduced into the ongoing project, and animals should only infrequently be transferred between subgroups.

Computers Enhance Curators' Analyses

These recommendations and their implementation rest on a new alliance between zoo curators and geneticists who have long studied natural and laboratory populations. "We sought out the population geneticists, they didn't come to us," says Ralls.

One important effect of the alliance has been an emphasis on zoos' keeping accurate long-term records of their breeding programs. "Without continuously and scrupulously maintained records of each individual animal's lineage, fertility, sex, longevity, care, and medical history, populations cannot be managed to avoid inbreeding and other pathological patterns: Long-term preservation will not be possible," says the SSP.

"A few years ago only three or four places in North America kept such records," Ballou says. Today records from many zoos are maintained in the computerized International Species Inventory Systems (ISIS) at the Minnesota Zoo in Apple Valley.

Besides developing general breeding plans, one use of population genetics in the zoo is the analysis of medical problems. For example, computers can be used to determine whether a deleterious condition that appears among the animals has a genetic basis, and thus might be eliminated by manipulating the breeding program. Deborah Meyers of Johns Hopkins University Medical Center in Baltimore, Maryland, is a human geneticist who has analyzed pedigrees of golden lion tamarins. With computer programs designed to examine human pedigrees, she concludes that the hernia that occasionally appears in the tamarins is a genetic problem, probably due to a single recessive gene.

Although the computer programmer working with Meyers did not realize the data came from the zoo and assumed it was just a rather extreme example of human-inbred populations they had previously studied, zoo-animal pedigrees do raise special challenges. The major

Tom Mantzel, a participant in the Species Survival Program, feeds a rare black rhinoceros on his Texas ranch.

structural differences between human and zoo-animal populations are the prevalence of multiple matings and extremely close inbreeding, what one might call incest. "But these don't influence the computational approaches," says Elizabeth Thompson of Cambridge University in England.

Thompson has worked out detailed analytical methods to compute kinship relationships and the probability of a gene's becoming extinct. She has based her work on such human groups as an island population of 268, of whom 85 percent are descendants of 11 original founders, and a west Greenland Eskimo family in which 13 individuals—including three sister-brother pairs—comprised 11 marriages, none incestuous.

Gene Dropping

Another genetic technique, recently developed by Jean MacCluer of the Southwest Foundation in San Antonio, Texas, is simply called "gene dropping." MacCluer says, "It is quick to use. It is a tool easier than the more analytical methods."

MacCluer makes a computer model of a pedigree based on the records of a breeding population, and assigns each founder animal two hypothetical genes. Then she uses a random-number generator to determine which gene from each founder any member of subsequent generations receives. To analyze the genetics of a population, she repeats this operation 10,000 times. MacCluer's analysis, like others, does not take into account the forces of natural selection on individual genes.

This simple method gives guidance in devising breeding plans by computing the probability that a gene from one founder will be lost from the population or that a gene will become fixed as the sole variation. It can also tell whether animals with particular traits share genes from one founder.

One breeding program MacCluer has examined is that of the Przewalski's horse, also called the Mongolian or Asian wild horse, which is now extinct in the wild. All 409 living animals are descendants of 13 founders, of which one was a Mongolian domestic horse rather than a wild Przewalski's horse. MacCluer used the gene-drop method to determine which of the 13 founders has had the largest percentage of gene loss and which are at the highest risk of further gene loss. Breeders can now take these data into consideration to equalize the contributions of the founders to subsequent generations.

Replace or Make Room for More?

While most major zoos have accepted the new management goals for endangered species, there are still conflicts. For example, when successful breeding programs outstrip the available zoo space for a species—as in the case of the Siberian tiger—what happens to the excess animals? Although careful population management, sometimes including contraceptives, can minimize the number of excess animals, must zoos sometimes destroy individual members of an endangered species?

"Population analyses may reveal that existing aged animals should be replaced with younger animals of breeding age before the former die of natural causes. (Many zoo animals live much longer than they would in the wild due to good nutrition, protection from predators, and veterinary care)," states Ralls in the April 1984 issue of the British journal *Biologist.* "Although efforts can be made to place animals that are old or genetically redundant in zoo situations that are purely for exhibition purposes, this is often not possible, and euthanasia is at times the only practical method of making room for additions to the population."

The world is getting smaller to those who manage captive-breeding programs of endangered species. Because the new plans attempt to maximize the number of contributing animals, for many species the effective herd must include all animals of the species in zoos of the United States, or even of the world.

Although during the past few years individual zoos have successfully cooperated in matching unmated animals for breeding, some more far-reaching coordination is required to meet the new goals of establishing self-maintaining populations of endangered species. The ambitious Species Survival Plan attempts to provide a sound basis for the allocation of zoo space among vanishing animals; to minimize the problems of inbreeding, inadvertent selection, and genetic drift; and to coordinate scientific study of the problems facing long-term wild-animal husbandry.

The Arabian oryx is one of many species that have been chosen for inclusion in the Species Survival Plan.

Dick George/Tom Stack & Assoc.

The Siberian Tiger Survival Plan

The first specific program initiated by the SSP is for the propagation of the Siberian tiger, which is endangered in the wild. "Because of their requirements for vast reserves, and their direct competition and often conflict with man, the big cats will be the least preservable of species in the wild," say Thomas Foose, the AAZPA conservation officer, and Ulysses S. Seal of ISIS, both at the Minnesota Zoo.

Fifty North American zoos are participating in the Siberian tiger plan. These zoos have approximately 250 Siberian tigers, derived from fewer than 20 wild-born animals. The genetic legacy of the founders is quite disproportionate: Five of the founders have each contributed more than 10 percent of the genes in the current population, and eight founders have each contributed less than 1.5 percent.

A special challenge to the SSP program for Siberian tigers is the stabilization of the unfavorable age distribution of the population. The reason for the instability goes back to the early 1970's, when the captive Siberian tiger population in North America expanded rapidly until it abruptly saturated the zoo space available. The response by zoos was a drastic curtailment of

Zoological Society of San Diego

This herd of Przewalski's horses is now in an intensive-management program at the San Diego Zoo in California.

tiger reproduction. This soon resulted in more animals in older classes than in younger ones. Tiger births decreased in the 1970's, until there were only a few in 1978. They increased somewhat in 1980 and 1981, then declined again.

"If these trends continue for another 10 years, about 45 percent of females and 29 percent of the males would be past reproductive prime for this species," say Foose and Seal. "The population would be well on the way to demographic senescence."

Foose and Seal have advised zoos to resume reproduction of the tigers and to remove (and, if necessary, destroy) certain animals from the different age classes. Once founder representation is rectified, they suggest that every animal be permitted to participate in production of two litters several years apart, and that for each parent one offspring of each sex be recruited into the breeding population. They have also outlined procedures for incorporating new founder tigers, from the Soviet and Chinese populations, into the North American population.

Changing Viewpoint Creates Some Conflict

Survival plans for several other species, including the Przewalski's horse, gaur (a large wild ox

of India), golden lion tamarin, and snow leopard, are being worked out. But many practical difficulties remain.

"Changing from a management viewpoint based on the welfare of individual animals to one based on maintaining a healthy captive population over a long period of time is not easy," says Ralls. "It may be difficult to convince those in charge of zoo finances that it is necessary to purchase a new animal of a particular species when, apparently, several perfectly good ones are already on hand. . . . Furthermore, the best strategy from a population viewpoint often conflicts with maximizing the life spans of individual animals," she says.

"But failure to initiate sound genetic and demographic management of zoo populations," Ralls concludes, "will ultimately result in the extinction of many species in captivity" □

SELECTED READINGS

"Zoos forging new role in science" by Constance Holden. *Science*, July 13, 1984.
"Saving California's condors? [criticism of captive-breeding program by Friends of the Earth]" by Patti Barraclough. *Environment*, June 1983.
"Prison or ark?" by Jon Luoma. *Audubon*, November 1982.

Stephen J. Kraseman/DRK Photo

Lingering near Canada's Hudson Bay, a polar bear awaits colder days when it can hunt for seal on the ice.

WHITE LORDS OF THE ARCTIC

by William Mills

Around Cape Churchill in Canada on Hudson Bay's western shore in October or November, one could well have the good fortune to see 15 or 20 polar bears from a single vantage point. Already the observer would have seen more polar bears than most natives of the Far North see in a lifetime. As a matter of fact, many Inuit (Eskimo) have never seen a polar bear. Should a visitor be at Cape Churchill in February, he likely would not see a polar bear either, for normally the bears would be hunting on the pack ice and not grouped as they are in fall.

Polar bears were long assumed to be nomads (wanderers) that moved about over the entire northern circumpolar range. In the past few years, tagging methods have made it possi-

ble to determine that there are many subpopulations and that these groups are largely faithful to their respective areas. This certainly seems to be true of the subpopulation of western Hudson Bay. Tagging and recapture programs carried out by researchers such as Dr. Ian Stirling and Dr. Charles Jonkel indicate considerable population fidelity.

Winter Feasters, Summer Scavengers

The bears at Cape Churchill congregate and wait for Hudson Bay to freeze so that they can return to their primary food source, which is seal—and mostly ringed seal. These bears would have hunted the leads (channels of water through ice fields) in the bay all during the previous winter and would finally have gone ashore as the ice melted at the southern end of the bay. Once they are on land, the bears' hunting is largely over. During July, August, and September, they make their way slowly up the western shore, scavenging what they can.

If the bears are lucky, they run upon a dead whale or seal that has washed ashore. They may raid duck nests and have been seen to catch the adults before they can lift off the water or ground. To see a bear stalking a 57-gram (2-ounce) lemming is incongruous; to see it grazing on grasses and sedges is even more so, yet both occur.

Besides occasionally nibbling on sedge or grass, the bears can be observed eating kelp after the tide has gone out. As a matter of fact, they burrow out beds in the kelp for their napping. In the midst of the kelp beds is the familiar smell of "rotten eggs," or the results of anaerobic (without free oxygen) fermentation. Although the bears do not seem to mind it, the human observer is happy to move on.

Bear Behavior

During the fall waiting period, bears seem to be active in the morning. But at midday they gradually drift off to nap—either in these kelp beds or in the "daybeds" they dig out of snow. One can be startled to come upon a patch of snow and discover dark brown eyes peering from it; several bears may bed down together.

Mostly it is adult males and some infertile females one sees right at the coast. The occasional female with cubs that does come along does not linger if there are large adults around. Her concern for her cubs is constant. When a big male starts in the cubs' direction, they nearly always hide behind their mother. And she will defend them ferociously if they are threatened by a male. Even when the family is away from other bears, the mother continually sniffs the air for danger or, of course, for food.

Mock Fighting Prepares Bears for Real Battles

An exciting part of the bears' behavior during this part of the year is something known as "play fighting." This activity seems very serious the first time it is observed. But after a few days of bear watching, the differences between this behavior and real fighting become quite clear. In play fighting a bear may simply amble over and touch noses with, then perhaps lightly cuff, another bear that it knows well. The two begin to box and wrestle very strenuously. With both bears reared up in a standing position, they

Wayne Lankinen

With paws intertwined in a seemingly ferocious fight, these male bears are really wrestling playfully.

look for all the world like two giant sumo wrestlers waiting for the right time to get the first advantage. One bear may end up flat on its back still wrestling, or the other may wait until its partner gets back up. Watching this is like watching two giant white puppies at play. If a bear had been showing real aggression, it likely would have charged the other, perhaps roared or hissed; and if the other did not fall back, the bloody damage would soon be apparent.

Play fighting sometimes continues throughout the morning and afternoon. The exertion involved is certainly costing the bears a lot of calories at a time when their food supply is exceedingly limited. The reasons for the play are not precisely known, but such ritualized response obviously keeps two 450-kilogram (1,000-pound) animals from hurting or killing each other. Sheer physical exuberance may be a part of the motivation. This mock fighting also keeps them in shape for the real battles that will surely occur in the spring as the males compete for the females.

A mother bear keeps a constant lookout for danger as she takes her curious cubs on an early spring outing.

Preparing and Caring for Cubs

Denning areas for the females are inland and south of the Cape Churchill area. Separation of pregnant females seems to be characteristic of all known female denning areas of the circumpolar region. Although the bears have mated in May, the females undergo delayed implantation (the process of attachment of the embryo to the uterine wall). The egg usually lies dormant until September, when it implants itself in the wall of the uterus. The females dig their snow dens around November, and the cubs, normally two, are born from late December to January.

Investigators who have looked at the dens once the family leaves have remarked about their cleanliness. Soviet researchers have noted that females may leave the den very briefly to clean themselves. Little fecal matter is found in dens.

Most dens have ventilation holes. It is conjectured that the female alters the size of the hole in order to regulate the temperature inside. She may also regulate the level of snow above the den by scraping.

At birth the cubs weigh about a 0.7 kilogram (1.5 pounds). They have no fur, and they are blind. When the mother and cubs break out of the den between early February and early April, the cubs may weigh 9 kilograms (20 pounds). The family begins making its way to the sea, stopping several times a day for the mother to nurse. Temporary beds may be dug for resting. Once on the pack ice, the mother has the awesome job of not only feeding herself but of feeding her cubs, at least for the next year and a half. Cubs may stay with their mothers until they are two and a half years old.

An Unlikely Combination

Following the bears on the ice are the Arctic foxes. In summer the foxes feed on eggs, birds, and lemmings. They have undergone a significant transformation, changing from white to gray-brown for summer camouflage and must do so again when the snow comes. Frequently, the lemming (which does not hibernate in winter) is scarce, and during such years foxes are found more frequently with the bears. Although they are occasionally killed and eaten by the bears, this is a rarity. One only has to watch their nimbleness to see why. Since the bears are chiefly interested in seal blubber, there is abundant seal meat left for the fox, which must only compete with the ravens and gulls. Foxes will even dare to lick food from the giant paws of a bear.

Research Important in Protecting Populations

If polar-bear numbers were extrapolated from the concentrations at Cape Churchill, they would be very wide of the mark. Since the bear depends on the sea for its principal food, there are vast areas of the north where there are no bears. Although there are no firm population figures, biologist Dr. Ian Stirling says an educated guess would be about 20,000 worldwide. More than half of these are found in Canada. Current studies indicate that the Canadian population is maintaining itself despite its once having been thought to be endangered. Even though bears seem to be holding their numbers, there is no reason for complacency. As human incursion in polar-bear territory increases, so does the possibility of rapid repercussions on polar bears. The demand for oil has brought about extensive exploration in places where little human activity had previously occurred.

Under the auspices of the International Union for the Conservation of Nature (IUCN), representatives of the five "polar-bear countries" (Canada, Denmark, Norway, the United States, and the Soviet Union) meet every two years to discuss the current status of the polar bear and of bear research. One of the first points of agreement among these nations was the need to protect cubs and females. Subsequently, the emphasis has been on research for numerous reasons. Now that the overall population is known to be made of discrete subpopulations, it is important that these subpopulations be precisely delineated. Obviously, a polar bear's "home ground" will often not correspond to the boundaries of countries or their states or provinces. If protection is to be extended to a particular subpopulation, not only must its territory be known, but protocols between various jurisdictions must be worked out.

Minimizing Human Disturbances

A critical part of population description is the locations of denning areas. Soviet investigators have stated that females are readily frightened from their dens before parturition (giving birth). It is known that bears in zoos cannot have young unless they are shielded from noise and visual commotion. The same is likely in the wild. Obviously, seismic explosions could interfere with denning. Alaskan researchers Jack Lentfer and Richard Hensel of the U.S. Fish and Wildlife Service have suggested that there should be "one-time-only" seismic exploration and that the information be made available to anyone interested in drilling, thereby minimizing this

By tagging polar bears, researchers hope to learn more about their habitat needs to minimize human encroachment.

David Hiser/Aspen

kind of intrusion. They further recommend that such exploration be carried out in summer, when denning is not going on.

.What seems clear is that an overall ecosystem approach is needed. For example, the seal population, since it is the primary food source of the polar bear, must be studied, taking into account what the effects of a major oil spill would be. Often a critical factor is the time of year of such an occurrence.

Oil companies are, of course, interested in avoiding trouble with polar bears. Men have been lost around the work areas, especially at night. A number of methods have been used to discourage the bears from coming too close, many with only minimal success. Generally it is food that the bears are looking for, and people must learn to keep food secure and to incinerate garbage. Still, there are cooking smells that inevitably attract bears. One proposal of the Alaskan researchers is that support camps for oil and gas activity should be situated away from the coast, where the bears normally travel.

Polar-Bear Hunting Causes Controversy

Members of the IUCN's polar-bear nations do not agree about the hunting of polar bears. The Soviet Union has banned all hunting since 1957 and has urged other nations to do the same. Sports hunting is permitted in a limited fashion in Canada. Inuit may hunt polar bears in Alaska, Greenland, and Canada. One of the consequences of the Marine Mammal Protection Act of 1972 was that the management of polar bears was transferred from Alaska to the U.S. Department of the Interior, and restrictions on hunting polar bears were lifted for natives, providing waste does not occur. The result of this legislation is that females and cubs can't be taken.

Hunting or harvesting polar bears poses a knotty problem. The Soviets argue for a total ban. But others maintain that such a ban is not necessarily appropriate for them. Because the Soviet bear population was severely depleted by overhunting during and following World War II, a total ban is perhaps still needed in the U.S.S.R. But for Inuit and Indians, polar-bear hunting is an integral part of their culture. Currently in Canada, nearly all bears killed (under quota) are taken by Inuit in the Northwest Territories. The Canadian Wildlife Service argues that should bears be completely protected, the kill necessary for protecting human lives could be roughly the same as the current harvest. As human settlement grows, conflicts between bears and people are expected to increase. A Cree Indian was killed in the town of Churchill in the winter of 1983, and a wildlife photographer was severely bitten on the arm.

Avoiding the Grizzly's Grim Fate

There is little question that future research must be carried out if we are to act wisely concerning the polar bear. Many denning areas are still not known, and the delineation of subpopulations is still incomplete. Because of the remoteness of arctic regions, the polar bear has so far been spared the fate of the grizzly bear, which is now extinct in California, Texas, Oregon, North and South Dakota, Arizona, and Utah. With the support of a concerned public, it is hoped the polar bear can maintain its numbers □

SELECTED READINGS

"Masters of the Arctic ice" by Richard C. Davids. *Science Digest*, February 1985.

"How polar bears break the ice" by Fred Bruemmer. *Natural History*, December 1984.

"We've saved the ice bear" by Thor Larsen. *International Wildlife*, July–August 1984.

"Nanook bears watching" by Fred Bruemmer. *National Wildlife*, December 1982–January 1983.

Art Wolfe

Dense fur and a thick layer of insulating blubber help keep the polar bear warm while swimming in frigid arctic waters.

Jeff Foott

The Intriguing Ways of Nudibranchs

by Gary McDonald

Nudibranchs, or sea slugs as they're commonly called, may seem weak and vulnerable at first glance. They are small, slow moving, fleshy, frail, and in many cases conspicuously colorful. And they don't even have shells in which to hide.

But looks can be deceiving. Actually, these ocean inhabitants are ingeniously equipped to fend for themselves. By appropriating defenses from the animals they eat and live among, nudibranchs (rhymes with "tanks") thrive in a sea world populated by faster, larger, and better-armored creatures.

Graceful, Diverse Predators

Sea slugs are mollusks—related to clams, snails, and oysters. Like garden slugs, however, they are essentially shell-less snails—with one difference. Unlike their drab, terrestrial cousins, nudibranchs are generally graceful and striking in appearance, earning them the nickname "butterflies of the sea." Their real name, which means "naked gill," refers to an exposed, frondlike breathing apparatus.

All nudibranchs are predators, feeding on sponges, corals, jellyfish, and sometimes each other, and all are hermaphroditic—each individual possesses both male and female organs. An individual cannot fertilize itself, but can fertilize a mating partner while the partner fertilizes it. Both will produce egg masses that may contain hundreds of thousands of eggs.

Above: Lemon nudibranchs can transfer the pigment of their prey to their own skin as a means of camouflage.

Despite these similarities, nudibranchs are a widely varied lot. There are more than 2,500 species living in habitats as diverse as Antarctic seas and tropical mangrove swamps. In size, they vary from more than 0.3 meter (1 foot) long and 1.4 kilograms (3 pounds) in weight to creatures small enough to crawl between grains of sand on the beach. Some slugs are swimmers, and they set to sea as passengers on the jellyfish they eat. Most of them, though, are grazing carnivores that spend their lives crawling about on their chosen prey—sedentary colonies of corals, sea anemones, and sponges that are left alone by most other predators because they are dangerous or difficult to eat.

Diet Plays Major Role in Nudibranch Behavior

Choice of food is the determining influence on a nudibranch's life cycle. Most sea slugs are specific about what they eat, consuming only one kind of food; and that food, in turn, may strongly influence their behavior. Some nudibranchs apparently are able to change the way their eggs develop and hatch to accommodate times of feast or famine. When food is abundant, they lay eggs that hatch into miniature adults that crawl out onto the food and begin eating. When food is scarce, they lay eggs that hatch into tiny larvae (immature forms of an animal). The larvae float away on rafts of minute sea life called plankton (the term refers to both aquatic plant and animal life) and eventually settle on a new food source, where they grow into adults. This gives the settling young a better chance for survival and distributes the species to new areas.

Diet also affects the way the animal hides from its enemies. Since nudibranchs spend much of their time on a single food source, many have evolved to resemble it. To would-be predators, these sea slugs seem to merge with their environment.

Often the nudibranch obtains its camouflaging pigment from the prey itself. For example, the bright pink nudibranch *Hopkinsia rosacea* gets its color from a pink bryozoan, a kind of marine animal, that it eats. When deprived of this food for several days, it becomes pale pink. The lemon nudibranch is yellow when found on a yellow sponge and orange when found on an orange sponge; as it eats, it simply transfers the sponge's pigments to its own skin. Other slugs even approximate the texture of the sponges on which they are found. One diminutive species mimics the speckled color pattern of a bryozoan that it virtually never leaves.

Another nudibranch, *Fiona pinnata*, takes on characteristics of several different backgrounds. This sea slug lives out in the ocean on floating objects such as logs, drifting kelp, or the by-the-wind-sailor jellyfish, also known as Velella. When on Velella, which it eats, it turns bluish purple like its prey. When living on logs or drifting on kelp, it eats gooseneck barnacles attached to the objects. Then it becomes grayish white to pale cream.

A pair of colorful sea slugs cross-fertilize each other. Every nudibranch has both male and female organs.

Alex Kerstitch

A cannibalistic tiger nudibranch wraps its blue mouth around one of its own kind.

Alex Kerstitch

Slugs Use Many Tricks to Dissuade Attackers

Other sea slugs are bad tasting, or even dangerous, and they develop bright colors as warnings to predators. Members of one group, the chromodorids, take the pigment molecules of drab sponges that they have eaten and slightly modify the molecules to create bright shades of blue in themselves. Many such ornamented nudibranchs travel in the open without fear of predation because their bright colors and offbeat patterns advertise their bad reputations. A predator that has tasted one chromodorid is unlikely to go back for a second helping.

Slugs like these may draw chemicals from their diets to use as defenses. One widely distributed dorid nudibranch that feeds on acorn barnacles has been reported to secrete strong acid on its back. Several acanthodorid nudibranchs have a pungent odor that may discourage predators. One species gives off a strong smell similar to cedar or sandalwood, which becomes much more pungent if the animal is roughly handled or molested by a predator. Another species produces clouds of noxious ink that can dissuade oncoming attackers before they even make contact with the slug.

Still other nudibranchs are able to eat dangerous animals and then adopt their defensive mechanisms as the slugs' own. Most slugs belong to two of four basic groupings, or suborders, and those of the suborder Aeolidacea frequently eat sea anemones and hydroids—tiny cousins of the anemone. Anemones, hydroids, and jellyfish have stinging cells called nematocysts that they can use to capture food and ward off enemies. Usually the anemone's nematocysts explode immediately upon coming into contact with any foreign body. However, sea slugs are able to eat their prickly prey without discharging the stinging cells. How they do this is not entirely understood; scientists speculate that something in the slugs' mucus disarms or cushions the tiny, sensitive detonators. After these defensive mechanisms are ingested, they are stored in the tips of the nudibranch's finger-like appendages, where they can later be used for defense. Fish unlucky enough to attack one of these nudibranchs may be met with a barrage of exploding stinging cells that were originally part of a jellyfish or a sea anemone. Like other creatures that mistake nudibranchs for easy prey, they quickly discover that there's more to these intriguing slugs than meets the eye □

SELECTED READINGS

''Tender trapper'' by James Nybakken. *Sea Frontiers,* March–April 1984.

''When the sea slug strikes'' by Tracey B. Capen. *Oceans,* March 1983.

''Salute to sea slugs'' by Ron Russo. *Oceans,* July 1979.

Tom & Pat Leeson

MOUNTAIN GOAT MONOPOLY

by Charles Bergman

A big billy (male goat), white-bearded and suspicious, ambled onto the ridge below Mount Angeles. He paused at the edge of the 12-meter-by-12-meter (40-foot-by-40-foot) net suspended on poles like a tent for a religious revival. Barely 6 meters (20 feet) away, he looked at us, sniffed the misty air, and licked the nylon net with a thick black tongue.

"Now?"

"No. Wait till he gets to the center."

But he drifted out from under the net and into the subalpine fir forest. In a moment he made another pass under the edges of the net. Attracted to the buckets of salt in the center, he barely reached them on the third pass when a voice called out "Now!"

Two men jerked the pull ropes. The net collapsed. Before it hit the goat, he had already made three leaps toward the outer edges. In the same few seconds, the crew of biologists and park rangers sprang onto the bounding goat. He was one of the biggest they had ever caught, about 113 kilograms (250 pounds), and it took four men to wrestle him to the ground. One man slipped pieces of green garden hose over the goat's stiletto-sharp horns, another hobbled his hooves, and two more covered his bronze eyes with a blue-denim mask.

Goat Introduction Causes Major Problem

We caught the goat because he did not belong here. Mount Angeles is in the Olympic Mountains, one of the many peaks in the 3,600-square-kilometer (1,400-square-mile) wilderness of Washington's Olympic National Park. The problem is that mountain goats are not native to this area. Nearly 100,000 goats inhabit craggy cliffs and alpine meadows throughout the Northwest, from Washington, Idaho, and Montana northward into Alaska. But for interesting geological reasons, the Olympic Mountains, in the extreme northwestern corner of the contiguous United States, were one of the ranges without goats until a dozen were introduced about 60 years ago. Those few goats found the Olympics congenial, ideally suited to their needs, and their population exploded. Now there are more than 1,000 goats in the park.

Inspired by the peaks scarfed with snow, an early explorer named the highest peak Mount Olympus after the ancient Greek "Home of the Gods." But putting mountain goats here turned out to be like putting Rototillers in heaven. They are chewing up the plant life and digging up the meadows. Although the mountain goats seem to epitomize Olympic National Park, they are nevertheless "exotics," and they have upset the delicate ecological balance of the wilderness system.

In an attempt to solve the goat problem, park biologists have developed a four-year experimental management project that includes capturing wild goats under drop nets and transferring them, in boxes dangling by cables from a helicopter, out of the park. Even more remarkable and innovative, they are experimenting with two kinds of birth control: hormone implants for some nannies (female goats) to inhibit estrus, and in-the-field surgical sterilization for others.

Bruce Moorhead, wildlife-management biologist for Olympic National Park, was the early prophet of the problems caused by the goats. He calls the proliferation of exotic spe-

cies "one of the most significant wildlife dilemmas in the world." The problem is especially intense for the U.S. National Park Service. It is required by its charter to preserve its lands in their original and natural state as refuges for future generations of both people and native wildlife. The irony here is that our national parks, as well as other wild areas, are being increasingly violated not only by human activities but also by animals. "In Great Smoky Mountains National Park," said Moorhead, "they have the introduced Russian boar, and the Grand Canyon National Park had feral burros. We have goats."

Burro Fiasco Prompts Better Goat Program

One notable attempt to control a population explosion of introduced animals involved the Grand Canyon burros. Released by prospectors around the turn of the century, the burros adapted easily, trampling the canyon and competing with the native bighorn sheep for forage. Between 1924 and 1969, the park tried to eliminate the burros, shooting or removing nearly 3,000. The effort was never successful, and so controversial that it ended up in court. The problem was finally resolved when the burros were removed by an animal-rescue organization at a cost of $500,000.

"We just couldn't jump into an adverse program," said Don Jackson, assistant superintendent of Olympic National Park. "You have to understand, we don't exactly have a population problem. One goat in the Olympics would be an overpopulation. One of our options is to eliminate the goats completely, like shooting them. But we decided to develop more humane options. We were convinced something needed to be done to protect the whole park—and pronto!"

"The project began modestly in 1971," said Moorhead, "when the chief ranger told me, 'I think those mountain goats need looking into.' Very little was known about them because they live in such inaccessible areas. So we began studies."

Belligerent Beasts Thrive on Isolated Island

They observed that mountain goats are not exactly sociable animals—they keep their distance and are often aggressive, circling and hooking each other. Among themselves, goats are rough and use their horns like knife fighters. While dust bathing, feeding, or resting, the goats will often lower their heads and stab at each other.

The jabbing and head tossing are so common that mountain goats have developed a thickening of the skin, called a dermal shield, in the groin and rear, for protection from sharp horns. Most adults have scars. Nevertheless, they hang out on the ridges in small groups, or "nodes," of from three to 30 goats.

Although mountain goats seem to move effortlessly across the sheer cliffs and rocky ledges where they are so at home, heights have their dangers even for them. The goats are not always as surefooted as is commonly supposed, and they sometimes fall to their death. In the Olympics most injuries to adults probably happen in winter on the icy cliffs. No biologists have witnessed a fall, but they have found carcasses.

The goats are not native to these mountains because the Olympics are a biological island surrounded on three sides by a moat of salt water. Their isolation makes them unique for the wildlife that they do not have. Although the park is one of the best places to go in the Pacific Northwest to see bear or elk or deer, several species of animals that are common to other mountains nearby are conspicuously absent here. "We've never had grizzly bears or wolverines," Don Jackson said. The alpine areas evolved without herbivores (plant eaters) such as bighorn sheep or the pika, a rock rabbit. The

Below: Tom & Pat Leeson; Bottom: Art Wolfe

Left: Two billies (male goats) butt heads in a threatening posture over a mineral lick. Below: Goats in Olympic National Park are lured to people for their body salts. Here, a nanny and her kid harass a weary climber.

plants and animals that did make it to the peninsula evolved on their alpine island in distinctive ways. The Olympic marmot, for example, is a different species from the marmots found in the nearby Cascade Mountains. Among the delicate alpine plants, which cover the summer meadows in a brilliant brocade, 12 are endemic (native) to the Olympics.

Love of Salt Attracts Goats to People

The exotic goats now exist throughout the park, and their craving for salt has led to frequent encounters with people. "The goats get this 'Big Mac attack' for salt," said Moorhead, laughing, "and they have come to associate salt with humans." They get salt from human urine, which is for them a kind of Olympian nectar. "They'll come on the trot when people are urinating."

They also get salt from human sweat. On a hike in the Olympics on a warm sunny day, some friends and I worked up a drenching sweat climbing uphill through the forests of huge conifers. When we reached the tree line, we took off our shirts as we pitched camp. Several goats came and started licking and chewing our clothes, including my T-shirt, for the salt.

So far no one has been seriously hurt by the goats, yet they can be disconcerting and are potentially dangerous. When several of us went backpacking into Royal Basin, we decided to camp under the dry overhang of a large rock. I awoke in the middle of the night to heavy breathing and a muzzle in my face. Thinking "Bears!" and too terrified to utter a sound, I slowly realized I was nose-to-nose with a nanny. Twenty mountain goats had invaded our campsite. Yet they seemed so tame that we simply went back to sleep.

The next day all of us—goats and hikers—were still under the rock. For some reason, the goats particularly liked to stand in the fire pit. We couldn't shoo them away. We finally had to tap them on the horns with our ice axes to get them to move. According to Moorhead, "Some backpackers are hassled and scared when the goats hook with their horns like Spanish fighting bulls. They tilt their horns at you, but they're often only feinting. What they're after is your urine."

Extensive Plant Destruction

As they dig into the meadows with their hooves and snouts, the goats destroy alpine plants in the park, but there are many other ways they can do

Art Wolfe

A fence protects this meadow from goats so that researchers can study the animals' destructive impact.

damage. They tread with a heavy foot, trampling the delicate wildflower meadows and digging deep wallows in the dirt where they rest. During mating season in the fall, the billies paw rutting pits as part of their courtship ritual. Finally, slowly working their way along—what one biologist called "snuffling"—the goats graze the plants of the meadows and slopes. In goat habitat areas, some endemic plants have become harder to find.

When I accompanied a group of plant biologists, we ran into dramatic evidence of the goats' impact. Wallows ran down one slope like long gashes in the loose soil, one after another, some up to 9 meters (30 feet) long. "The meadows are very sensitive," Ed Schreiner, plant ecologist for the park told me. "They have only short summers for growing and the soil layer is thin. So they recover slowly. I trampled a small piece of meadow as part of an experiment to measure recovery rates. In this dry area, the phlox would take over two centuries to recover. This was also goat habitat."

Art Wolfe

Biologists prepare a tranquilized goat for transport to a new home outside of Olympic National Park.

Capture Operation Carefully Timed

The only hope for protecting the park is controlling the goat population. So far 155 goats have been caught and deported. The captures tend to take place in pulses during warm weather, but the sun can be a rare commodity in the Olympics, particularly in June when the capture operation begins. Blowing in from the Pacific Ocean, the clouds hit the 2,100-meter (7,000-foot) peaks that rise only 40 kilometers (25 miles) inland from the coastline. The result is up to 500 centimeters (200 inches) of rain on the west slope—the wettest place in the contiguous United States.

While Moorhead would rather run the capture during August, when the weather is usually better, he chose June because the goats' craving

for salt is greatest between the snow season and summer. "The transition from scruffy winter feed to the lush vegetation is hard for them and they lose sodium," he said. "They replace it directly with salt. They have a peak interest for a couple of weeks and we have to be there."

When the goat crew is in full swing, the capture net can be busy. For two to three weeks, Klahhane Ridge is crowded with plant and wildlife biologists, park rangers, university faculty, veterinarians, game-department officials, helicopter pilots, and volunteers—25 people on a given day is not uncommon. When several goats wandered under the drop net at once, the scene resembled a scrimmage, with the players tackling the goats. Once the goats were on the ground, the biologists began the "medical protocol."

Preventing Trauma During Handling

Under the stress of handling, the goats can develop what is called "capture myopathy." Two of the first goats captured in 1976 died of the syndrome, which results from emotional stress, extreme physical exertion, and increased body temperature. The trauma of handling causes such muscle exhaustion and lactic acid buildup that fatal muscle degeneration (myopathy) and paralysis occur. To reduce the trauma, biologists must minimize the time they spend handling the goats. Big capsules of sodium bicarbonate are forced down their throats to counter the lactic acid. Shots of Valium are given to relax muscles, and penicillin to counter infection and pneumonia. In addition to weighing, measuring, and collaring the animals, biologists also read goats' ages. Since their horns grow in summer and are dormant in winter, the animal wears its age etched in growth rings.

Once the goats are processed, they are kenneled in individual crates and flown off Klahhane Ridge suspended from a helicopter. Trucks and boats then carry them to a new area outside the park. The crate is carpeted with snow to keep the goat from overheating. Like other ruminants (cud-chewers with multichambered stomachs), goats have hitchhiking microorganisms in their stomachs to help them digest their tough forage. These microorganisms, however, create a sort of furnace in the goat's stomach, which is one of the ways the goat stays warm through an alpine winter and one of the reasons it rests on snow patches to cool off in the summer. But the heating also contributes to capture myopathy.

Birth-Control Techniques Show Promise

The goats that I helped capture were released from their crates near Lake Chelan, on the eastern side of the Cascade Mountains in Washington. In past years other goats wound up in Idaho, Nevada, and Utah. Olympic National Park tries to ship the goats to native habitats where they were once plentiful but have for various reasons declined. "We don't want to export our problems," explained Don Jackson.

There is so much concern about the goat population that Moorhead has also been experimenting with birth-control techniques. The head veterinarian in these surgical experiments is Dr. Jim Foster of Woodland Park Zoo in Seattle, Washington, who developed both the medical protocol and, along with Dr. Stephen Seager of the veterinary college at Texas A & M University, birth-control techniques for the wild goats. Said Foster: "The plan is to implant ten nannies with hormones and to sterilize by tubal ligation about three more. Then we'll follow them over the next two or three years with radio collars to assess their reproductivity. We also want to see if there are any side effects on their social behavior."

The small implant is slipped under the skin of the goat's neck. It is synthetic progesterone in a silicone base, which inhibits estrus and is time-released over three years. Nannies usually breed for about six years. "The implant cuts her fertility in half," said Foster.

So far only 10 females and one male have been sterilized. In 1983 for the first time, we caught a male, collected semen, and performed a vasectomy. Near the navel, Seager cut a small incision, through which he inserted a fiber-optic tube. Through a nearby second incision, Seager and Foster slipped the cauterizing instrument. The females have been given a tubal ligation through a similar operation.

Foster is optimistic about both the implants and the sterilization. "We found two of the three nannies with implants in 1982," he said, "and they did not have kids. Personally, I think these techniques are going to be quite feasible."

Final Management Plan Still Undecided

Moorhead is not sure which of their experimental programs will work on a large scale. Effective sterilization requires capture of a sufficient number of goats. Recent test captures in the remote interior of the park indicate that most of the goat population is not tamely drawn to salt.

David Fritts

Researchers are experimenting with birth-control techniques as a means of restricting the goat population.

Where goats can be obtained, the cost of capturing and transferring each one is about $1,500. According to Moorhead, "We don't want to be forced to destroy them, but we have to take more active measures. The public has always been behind us in supporting more humane methods and we will be having public hearings [soon]. We still don't know what our final recommendations will be, but time is running out." It is hoped that the sterilization and birth-control implant programs will work out. If not, then it may be time for these creatures to leave their Olympian range and thrive in a wilderness where they are native □

SELECTED READINGS

"Growing by leaps and bounds" by Douglas Chadwick. *National Wildlife,* August–September 1984.
"Olympic mountain goats" by Michael Hutchins and Victoria Stevens. *Natural History,* January 1981.
"Mountain goats: daring guardians of the heights" by Douglas Chadwick. *National Geographic,* August 1978.

IN MEMORIAM

ADAMS, JOHN BERTRAM (63), British physicist who was executive director general of the European Organization for Nuclear Research (CERN) in Geneva, Switzerland (1976–81), and head of CERN's particle-physics laboratory (1969–75). He was the driving force behind the design of the research group's giant particle accelerator in the early 1970's. Knighted in 1981; d. Geneva, March 3.

BARGHOORN, ELSO (68), U.S. naturalist whose studies of South African fossils, reported in 1977, showed that primitive plant life existed on Earth at least 3.4 billion years ago. He had been a member of the faculty at Harvard University since 1955; d. Carlisle, MA, Jan. 27.

COLE, KENNETH (83), U.S. biophysicist whose studies of electrical resistance in nerve cells led to rapid advances in neurophysiology in the 1930's and 1940's. He was with Columbia University (1937–46), the Naval Medicine Research Center (1949–54), and became head of the biophysics laboratory at the National Institute of Neurological Diseases and Blindness in 1954. He was awarded the National Medal of Science in 1967; d. La Jolla, CA, April 18.

COMROE, JULIUS H., JR. (73), U.S. author, educator, and expert on the human cardiovascular and respiratory systems. He taught for many years at the University of Pennsylvania and from 1957 to 1973 directed the Cardiovascular Research Institute at the University of California at San Francisco; d. Hillsborough, CA, July 31.

CORI, CARL F. (87), U.S. biochemist, born in Bohemia (now Czechoslovakia), who shared the 1947 Nobel Prize in Medicine with his wife, Gerty, for their research on metabolic chemistry. They isolated and synthesized phosphorylase, an enzyme that helps convert glycogen (an animal starch) into sugar in the body. Cori headed the department of biochemistry at the medical school of Washington University and, after 1960, was a visiting professor at the Massachusetts General Hospital and the Harvard University School of Medicine; d. Cambridge, MA, Oct. 20.

CROWLEY, RALPH MANNING (78), U.S. psychoanalyst noted for his approach to the treatment of schizophrenia. A graduate of the Northwestern University Medical School and the Washington-Baltimore Psychoanalytic Society, he later moved to New York City to join the staff of the William Alanson White Institute; d. New York, NY, Oct. 30.

CUTLER, MAX (85), Ukrainian-born physician who was a leading U.S. cancer expert. He specialized in radiation therapy as well as surgery and pathology and in 1938 founded the Chicago Tumor Institute. He served as its director until 1952, when he entered private practice in Beverly Hills, CA: d. Camarillo, CA, July 6.

DIACUMAKOS, ELAINE G. (53), U.S. cytobiologist who helped develop microsurgery techniques for genetic research. Head of the cytobiology laboratory at Rockefeller University in New York from 1976 until her death, she was involved in the first successful transfer of a working gene into the defective cell of a living mouse in 1979. Her work also involved studies of cancer cells and cellular resistance to drugs; d. New York, NY, June 11.

DIRAC, PAUL ADRIAN MAURICE (82), British physicist who shared the 1933 Nobel Prize in Physics with Erwin Schrödinger. The prize was awarded for his work in completing Schrödinger's quantum-wave theory, which was credited with reconciling the quantum theory with the theory of relativity. Dirac taught at Cambridge University in England until 1971, when he joined the faculty of Florida State University. He was a member of the Order of Merit of Great Britain and a Fellow of the Royal Society; d. Tallahassee, FL, Oct. 20.

DORF, ERLING (78), U.S. geologist known for his studies of fossilized plant life. He taught at Princeton University for 48 years and received several awards for his teaching and writing; d. Princeton, NJ, April 16.

DUNHAM, THEODORE, JR. (86), U.S. astronomer whose observations disproved the theory that Venus' atmosphere is similar to Earth's. The work was conducted in the 1930's, while he was on the staff of the Mount Wilson Observatory in California. He also discovered methods of determining the chemical makeup of cells. He held posts in medicine and surgery at Harvard University and the University of Rochester, and in astronomy at several Australian universities and the Harvard College Observatory; d. Chocorua, NH, April 3.

EHRICKE, KRAFFT A. (67), German-born rocket specialist who worked in the U.S. space program. A member of the German rocket-research team in World War II, he later joined the U.S. Army missile program and became a U.S. citizen in 1954. He was manager of the project that designed Centaur—the first liquid hydrogen–propellant rocket—and later worked as a space adviser in several capacities; d. La Jolla, CA, Dec. 11.

ENGSTROM, ELMER W. (83), U.S. engineer who helped develop color television. He directed television research for the Radio Corporation of America (RCA) and was president of the firm during the 1960's; d. Hightstown, NJ, Oct. 30.

FALK, ISIDORE S. (85), U.S. bacteriologist who promoted public-health care. He campaigned for the enactment of Social Security and headed research for the Social Security Administration in the 1940's and 1950's. Later he was professor of public health at Yale University and the recipient of numerous awards; d. New Haven, CT, Oct. 4.

FORBUSH, SCOTT E. (79), U.S. geophysicist who shed light on the relationship between cosmic rays and magnetism. During the 1930's, at the Carnegie Institute of Washington, he found that eruptions on the sun produced magnetic waves that shielded the Earth from cosmic radiation. He was elected to the National Academy of Sciences in 1962; d. Charlottesville, VA, April 4.

FRANKEL, GOTTFRIED S. (83), German-born U.S. entomologist who discovered the hormone that causes insect metamorphosis. Associated with the University of Illinois since 1948, he also did innovative studies in the coevolution of plants and insects. He was a member of the National Academy of Sciences; d. Urbana, IL, Oct. 26.

GESCHWIND, NORMAN (58), U.S. neurologist whose pioneering studies linked the structure of the brain to aspects of human behavior such as language and left-handedness. He taught at Harvard Medical School, the Massachusetts Institute of Technology, and was neurologist in chief at Beth Israel Hospital; d. Boston, MA, Nov. 4.

HALSTEAD, JAMES A. (78), U.S. physician known for his studies of nutrition. His research spanned such areas as nutritionally caused dwarfism, psychosomatic illness among soldiers, and the health of U.S. presidents. He held various positions in the Veterans Administration; d. Boston, MA, March 2.

HATHAWAY, STARKE R. (80), U.S. psychologist who, with J. C. McKinley, developed the Minnesota Multiphasic Personality Inventory test, a widely used measure of mental illness. He was on the faculty of the University of Minnesota from 1930 to his retirement in the 1970's and directed the division of clinical psychology there since 1951; d. Minneapolis, MN, July 4.

HOLDEN, WILLIAM H. (87), U.S. physician and explorer who studied the Tarumá and Waiwai Indians of the Amazon. In 1937–38 he led a major expedition through British Guiana and Brazil and discovered that the Waiwai were free of diseases such as cancer, high blood pressure, and heart disease, which he attributed to the lack of stress and conflicts in their lives. He was on the staff of the Museum of Natural History in New York City; d. New Albany, Nova Scotia, Aug. 13.

HOOBLER, ICIE MACY (91), U.S. biochemist who was an authority on nutrition and child development. She began her career work at the Merrill Palmer Institute in Michigan. A former president of the American Institute of Nutrition and the first woman to head a division of the American Chemical Society, she received the Francis P. Garvan Medal in 1946; d. Gallatin, MO, Jan. 6.

HUNSACKER, JEROME C. (98), U.S. aeronautical engineer who designed the first aircraft to fly the Atlantic Ocean (the flying boat *NC-4,* in 1919). Associated with the Massachusetts Institute of Technology since 1912, he taught that school's first courses in aeronautical engineering; directed naval-aircraft design in World War I; and designed the *Shenandoah,* the first U.S. dirigible. He received the Navy Cross, the Presidential Medal for Merit, and numerous other awards; d. Boston, MA, Sept. 10.

KAPITSA, PYOTR L. (89), Soviet physicist who was awarded the Nobel Prize in Physics in 1978 for his life's work. He began his career in Britain but in 1934 was detained in the U.S.S.R.; since then he directed the Institute of Physical Problems and became a leading Soviet scientist. His pioneering work focused on solid-state and low-temperature physics, and he invented advanced refrigeration methods. Dismissed from his post from 1946 to 1955 after declining to take part in the development of nuclear weapons, he was twice named a Hero of Socialist Labor (1945 and 1978), the highest civilian award in the U.S.S.R.; d. Moscow, April 8.

KAPLAN, HENRY S. (65), U.S. radiologist who coinvented (with Edward Ginzton) the first medical linear accelerator in the United States (1955). Such machines are used today to treat cancer with radiation and have greatly increased survival rates for Hodgkin's disease and other cancers. Associated with Stanford University, he was the first radiologist elected to the National Academy of Scientists (1972) and received the Atoms for Peace Prize (1969) and the Charles F. Kettering Prize (1979); d. Palo Alto, CA, Feb. 4.

KASTLER, ALFRED (81), French physicist whose studies of light waves laid the foundation for the development of the laser. He received a Nobel Prize in 1966 for developing the double-resonance method of studying atoms, in which both light and radio waves are used to examine atomic structure. His discovery that light of a certain wavelength causes atoms to emit light waves of a uniform wavelength helped lead to the invention of the laser; d. Bandol, France, Jan. 7.

KIDDER, ALFRED, II (72), U.S. anthropologist who was an expert in Andean archaeology and pre-Columbian art. For many years he was moderator of the archaeology television program "What in the World." He taught at Harvard University and the University of Pennsylvania and was associated with museums at both schools; d. Bedford, MA, Feb. 2.

KRAMER-LASSER, EDNA E. (82), U.S. mathematician and educator who was the author of many acclaimed books in her field. She was professor at the Polytechnic Institute of New York from 1948 to 1965; d. New York, NY, July 9.

LEVINE, SAUL (61), U.S. nuclear engineer who was a noted authority on the safety of nuclear-power plants. He served 17 years with the Navy and a similar amount of time with the Atomic Energy Commission and the Nuclear Regulatory Commission, from which he retired in 1980. He also directed the AEC's Reactor Safety Study of 1974; d. Evanston, IL, Oct. 18.

LILIENFELD, ABRAHAM M. (63), U.S. physician whose work helped broaden the field of epidemiology to include chronic as well as infectious diseases. He taught at the University of Buffalo and at Johns Hopkins University, and he was the author of 12 books and the recipient of many awards in the field of public health; d. Baltimore, MD, Aug. 6.

LOW, GEORGE M. (58), Austrian-born U.S. engineer who headed the Apollo space project and later was president of Rensselaer Polytechnic Institute. He took over the Apollo program in 1967, after a launch-pad fire killed three astronauts; later, as acting administrator of the National Aeronautics and Space Administration, he helped negotiate agreements that led to the joint U.S.-Soviet space mission in 1975. He was awarded the Presidential Medal of Freedom posthumously; d. Troy, NY, July 17.

MCLEAN, NOEL B. (77), U.S. underwater- and aerospace-electronics expert who headed the Woods Hole Oceanographic Institution from 1961 to 1973 and worked for a number of private firms. He received the Distinguished Public Service Award for his work in sonar development and other marine-electronics technologies; d. Doylestown, PA, Sept. 17.

MERRILL, JOHN PUTNAM (67), U.S. surgeon who headed the team that performed the first successful kidney transplant (1954, at Peter Brent Brigham Hospital, in Boston). He is also credited with perfecting the artificial-kidney machine and with major work in tissue compatibility. During World War II, he was the Air Force surgeon aboard the flight that dropped the first atomic bomb over Hiroshima, Japan; d. Boston, MA, April 4.

MILGRAM, STANLEY (51), U.S. psychologist noted for his studies of obedience to authority. In experiments conducted at Yale University in the 1960's, he found that people would follow the instructions of authority figures even when by doing so they were instructed to inflict pain on others. The findings were published in his famous book *Obedience to Authority* (1974). He taught at Yale University, Harvard University, and the City University of New York; d. New York, NY, Dec. 20.

MUETTERTIES, EARL L. (56), U.S. chemist widely known for his research and writing in many areas of inorganic chemistry. As associate research director for Du Pont (1965–73), he helped develop a new boron-hydrogen compound that was the basis for many new substances. Later he taught at Cornell University (1973–78) and the University of California at Berkeley (1978–84); d. Oakland, CA, Jan. 12.

NEWCOMB, THEODORE M. (81), U.S. psychologist who founded the department of social psychology at the University of Michigan and wrote several widely used textbooks on that subject. He was elected to the National Academy of Sciences in 1974; d. Ann Arbor, MI, Dec. 28.

ODISHAW, HUGH (67), Canadian-born director of U.S. participation in the International Geophysical Year of 1957–58. Interpreting data from that research effort occupied him until 1972, when he became dean of the College of Earth Sciences at the University of Arizona in Tucson. He had previously held posts in government and industry, and he headed the physical-sciences division of the National Academy of Sciences (1966–72); d. Tucson, AZ, March 4.

PHILIPS, FREDERICK S. (67), U.S. biologist who was among the first to develop chemotherapy treatments for cancer. He taught at Cornell University and was associate director of its Sloan-Kettering division; d. New York, NY, March 24.

POTTER, DAVID M., III (79), U.S. engineer who invented a meter to measure the flow of liquids. The flowmeter, for which he was awarded the Franklin Institute's Longstreth Medal in 1959, has since been used in everything from rocket engines to oil wells. He was also an explorer, taking part in Arctic expeditions in the 1920's; d. Phillipsburg, NJ, Sept. 29.

ROBITZEK, EDWARD H. (71), U.S. physician who helped test and develop the tuberculosis drug isoniazid in the 1950's. With others, he received an Albert and Mary Lasker Foundation Award for the work. He was affiliated with Sea View Hospital and Home in New York City for most of his career; d. Salisbury, MD, Feb. 20.

ROCK, JOHN (94), U.S. physician who helped develop the birth-control pill in the 1950's. He was the first to fertilize a human egg in a test tube (1944) and among the first to successfully freeze human sperm. He taught at Harvard Medical School, founded and directed the Fertility and Endocrine Clinic at the Free Hospital for Women in Brookline, MA (1926–56), and later directed the Rock Reproductive Clinic in Brookline; d. Peterborough, NH, Dec. 4.

RYLE, MARTIN (66), British astronomer whose development of new techniques in radio astronomy brought him a Nobel Prize in Physics in 1974 (shared with Antony Hewish). Working at Cambridge University, he devised the technique of aperture synthesis, which uses many small antennas rather than a single large one to enable astronomers to make detailed maps of distant celestial objects. He was knighted in 1966 and was Britain's Astronomer Royal (1972–82); d. Cambridge, England, Oct. 14.

SACHER, EDWARD J. (50), U.S. psychiatrist known for his work on the roles of hormones in mental illness. A specialist in depression, he taught at the Albert Einstein College of Medicine (1966–75) and Columbia University (1976–81) and received several awards for his research; d. New York, NY, March 25.

SCHOPF, THOMAS J. M. (44), U.S. paleobiologist who was a specialist in marine fossils. He taught at the University of Chicago, founded and edited the journal *Paleobiology,* and received the Paleontological Society's Schuchert Award in 1976; d. Texas, March 18.

SIMPSON, GEORGE GAYLORD (82), U.S. paleontologist who was world-renowned for his research in vertebrate evolution. He was a curator at the American Museum of Natural History (1924–59); taught at Columbia, Harvard, and other universities; and led many expeditions in search of fossils; d. Tucson, AZ, Oct. 6.

SPEDDING, FRANK (82), Canadian-born U.S. chemist who helped develop the atomic bomb. He was credited with devising a method of producing metallic uranium on a large scale. He taught at Iowa State University (1937–68) and founded and headed its Institute for Atomic Research (now known as the Ames Laboratory); d. Ames, IA, Dec. 15.

TIETZE, CHRISTOPHER (75), Austrian-born U.S. physician who became widely known as an expert on pregnancy and birth control and was among the first to point out the hazards of oral contraceptives. He worked with a number of national and international groups, including the Population Council, and was the recipient of numerous awards; d. New York, NY, April 4.

ULAM, STANISLAW M. (75), Polish-born U.S. mathematician who played a major role in the development of the hydrogen bomb and who discovered the Monte Carlo method of studying probabilities to predict the outcomes of complicated situations such as atomic chain reactions. He was associated with the Los Alamos National Laboratory and taught at several major universities; d. Santa Fe, NM, May 13.

WEISSBERGER, ARNOLD (85), German-born U.S. chemist who made important contributions to the development of color photography. He worked for Eastman Kodak Company; d. Rochester, NY, Sept. 2.

YOUNG, CHARLES J. (84), U.S. inventor who helped develop methods of transmitting images by radio and also held patents for copying machines, weapons-detection systems, and other devices. He worked for the Radio Corporation of America (RCA) since 1930 until his retirement in 1965; d. Princeton, NJ, Oct. 2.

ZELSON, CARL (69), U.S. physician who studied drug-withdrawal effects in newborn infants born to heroin-addicted or methadone-taking mothers. He practiced pediatrics in New York and taught at New York Medical College; d. New Haven, CT, Dec. 23.

ZIMMERMAN, MARTIN (57), Swiss-born U.S. expert in plant physiology who conducted wide-ranging studies of the ways in which plants transport nutrients and moisture from the ground to their leaves. He taught at Harvard University; d. Cambridge, MA, March 7.

INDEX